INTRODUCING
QUALITATIVE
RESEARCH

INTRODUCING QUALITATIVE RESEARCH

A Student's Guide to the Craft of Doing Qualitative Research

Rosaline S. Barbour

SAGE Publications
Los Angeles · London · New Delhi · Singapore

First published 2008

SAGE Publications Ltd
1 Oliver's Yard
55 City Road
London EC1Y 1SP

SAGE Publications Inc.
2455 Teller Road
Thousand Oaks, California 91320

SAGE Publications India Pvt Ltd
B 1/I 1 Mohan Cooperative Industrial Area
Mathura Road, Post Bag 7
New Delhi 110 044

SAGE Publications Asia-Pacific Pte Ltd
33 Pekin Street #02-01
Far East Square
Singapore 048763

Library of Congress Control Number 2007922946

British Library Cataloguing in Publication data

A catalogue record for this book is available from the British Library

ISBN 978-1-4129-1266-2
ISBN 978-1-4129-3460-2 (pbk)

Typeset by C&M Digitals (P) Ltd., Chennai, India
Printed on paper from sustainable resources
Printed in Great Britain by TJ International Ltd, Padstow, Cornwall

For Mike and Alasdair

CONTENTS

OVERVIEW

As recently as thirty years ago qualitative research was the preserve of a relatively small group of 'consenting academics' usually working within sociology or anthropology. Much of this work was unfunded – or funded by individual institutions as part of the career development of a specific researcher – and its focus was on addressing disciplinary concerns. To the casual observer located outside these particular academic settings, such work would probably have appeared somewhat esoteric or exotic, given, for example, the predominance of anthropological fieldwork carried out with communities or populations who were distant both geographically and in terms of their 'otherness'.

There has, however, been a sea change over the past fifteen years or so, as qualitative research has rapidly established itself as an acceptable approach within a broad range of disciplines. Psychology, in particular, has moved from its previous reliance on experimental research design to engage with qualitative methods and has assembled its own 'toolkit' – and terminology, including interpretative phenomenological analysis (IPA) (discussed in more detail in Chapter 10). Educational and social work research have also adopted qualitative methods, which is perhaps not surprising, given their reliance on interaction as a key component of professional practice. The extent of the enthusiasm for qualitative methods is apparent in the appearance of new journals, including *Qualitative Social Work,* launched in 2002. Notwithstanding the relatively new emphasis on evidence-based medicine, even the bastion of medical research has embraced qualitative methods and has sought to develop its own way of capitalizing on the insights afforded. Qualitative research, certainly, does not appeal to everyone within these newly-recruited disciplines, but it will be interesting, in particular, to see if the radical changes to medical curricula – with the introduction of problem-based learning and a focus on partnerships with patients – give rise to more doctors who are well-disposed towards doing qualitative research.

When I embarked on my postgraduate studies in the late 1970s there was not the huge number of textbooks which have since proliferated. Although Glaser and Strauss had published *The Discovery of Grounded Theory* in 1967, this had not yet attained the 'cult status' it now enjoys and was presented as a set of ideas which might be helpful, but which need not be slavishly followed. With the exception of the Glaser and Strauss text, I resorted, as a graduate student, to seeking out the few methodological commentaries provided in the anthropological literature and those produced by members of the Chicago School, as methodological texts *per se* were yet to be embraced as a viable genre.

Recent years have seen a seemingly endless supply of qualitative methods texts. Indeed, the irony of making such a comment while adding to this list of titles has not escaped me. While textbooks are a valuable resource, today's novice qualitative researcher is certainly spoilt for choice. New researchers are frequently daunted by the sheer volume and diversity of texts, each making a convincing, even compelling, case for following a particular set of techniques, although not always successfully demonstrating the distinctiveness of the favoured approach. Students from disciplines such as nursing or social work (the relative newcomers to academic research in general and qualitative research in particular) are those most likely to be afflicted by this sort of crisis of confidence, which often leads to them scouring the methodological literature for the 'right' approach on which to hang their study – whether this be 'hermeneutics', 'phenomenology', 'ethnomethodology' or 'discourse analysis' (to name but a few of the terms I have heard students invoke as they wrestle with developing their own studies). Although reading widely can be a good thing, it can also immobilize students, who frequently find themselves torn between equally persuasive texts. Reflecting on my own experience of being thrown in at the deep end, there is a lot to be said for learning throughout the process of doing research. Delaying entry to the field until one is 'ready' and 'adequately prepared' carries the risk of the researcher becoming suspended indefinitely in indecision, forever falling short of that unattainable goal.

My justification for producing yet another qualitative methods textbook is that it aims to bridge that gap by providing a vicarious apprenticeship. Qualitative research is presented as a 'craft skill' (Seale, 1999) located midway between esoteric theorizing and mechanistic application of method. Based on a tried-and-tested workshop format, this book should provide a resource to illuminate the 'black box' of how individuals actually go about doing research. By means of multiple examples and exercises, the reader will be able to access and engage with a wide range of practical and conceptual processes at different stages of research projects. I have drawn heavily on my own research experience and there is more to this than the usual academic vanity. It is only with regard to one's own work that one is qualified to speak of the gap between the everyday experience of doing research and the polished accounts that are eventually published – the knowledge of the reasoning behind the choices made, recall of fieldwork dilemmas, piecing together how arguments were built up (either by painstaking interrogation of the data, serendipitous insights or a combination of the two) and the things that are left out along the way. Some of the exercises presented in this book involve extensive commentaries (or text-based conversations with the reader) which seek to illuminate how qualitative research designs and analyses are developed through an iterative process.

BOOK OUTLINE

Although qualitative research is characterized by an iterative rather than linear model, the book addresses the various stages involved in the qualitative research process: formulating a research question, constructing a research design, developing schedules/topic guides, interpreting data, creating a coding framework, and writing up. It views these stages within the broader context, locating qualitative research in terms of epistemology and discussing the relative merits and skills required by different methods – ethnography, interviewing, focus groups and action research.

The Introduction to the book (Chapters 1–3) addresses, firstly, The Scope and Contribution of Qualitative Research, which considers the place of qualitative research in relation to philosophical traditions and covers what qualitative research can and can't provide. It also provides a short history of qualitative research across several social science disciplines, reflecting also on the growing popularity of qualitative research in medicine and social work. Research Design (Chapter 2) looks at the choices the researcher must make and pays particular attention to sampling; and Chapter 3, on Ethics, focuses on the implications for research design and planning projects, in the context of securing ethical approval. However, this chapter emphasizes the need to consider ethical issues throughout the entire duration of a research project, including the important issue of the impact on the researcher as well as those being researched.

The section on Generating Data is split into three chapters which reflect on the principles of generating qualitative data, utilizing Jennifer Mason's (1996) distinction between 'collecting' and 'generating' data, and emphasizing the active role of the researcher. The introduction to this section also covers the implications for eliciting data of the epistemological underpinnings of qualitative research, as discussed in Chapter 1, and discusses the role of the researcher's persona, background and disciplinary leanings. The three chapters on generating qualitative data focus, respectively, on Ethnography (Chapter 4), Interviewing (Chapter 5), and Focus Groups (Chapter 6). These chapters discuss the strengths and weaknesses of these different methods, development and use of 'research tools', and the challenges of generating data. In particular, the exercises demonstrate the impact that methods can have on the interaction between researcher and respondents and the form and content of the data generated.

The third section of the book concerns Complex Research Designs in Practice, and includes a chapter on Mixing Methods (Chapter 7). This chapter takes a critical look at the rationale for employing mixed methods, considers the challenges and provides some advice as to how to address the many issues thrown up. This discussion again relates back to the material presented in Chapter 1. Although the main focus of the textbook is on generating and analyzing qualitative data, there is some discussion of the issues raised by mixed method approaches, including those which seek to combine quantitative and qualitative approaches. Using examples from projects in which the author has personally been involved, and drawing on the work of others, particular attention will be accorded to questions of research design, sampling, and the more difficult challenges presented by attempts at 'triangulation'. Challenges are also encountered in working in multidisciplinary research teams and some suggestions are made with regard to how these can be utilized as a resource in analysis. (This point is further developed in Chapter 10.) A separate chapter is devoted to Action Research (Chapter 8), which can be especially demanding, seeking to combine research and practice (often clinical practice). Action research, moreover, is frequently interdisciplinary and nearly always involves mixed methods. The dilemmas raised in carrying out action research in a variety of fields will be discussed.

Section 4 addresses Analysis, with Chapter 9 (Analysis Groundwork – Storing, Coding and Retrieving Data) covering the practicalities involved in the early stages of the process. Chapter 10 has the title Interrogating Your Data – Identifying Patterns and is concerned with moving beyond allocating coding categories to trying to furnish an explanation for the patterns that are identified. This is further developed in Chapter 11, which deals with Theorizing and Qualitative Data Analysis. Each of these chapters draws extensively on materials developed for use in workshops, echoing the conviction of this volume that the best way to learn about doing qualitative research is to actively engage with the practical – and particularly conceptual – challenges raised. Also in keeping with the view of qualitative analysis as an iterative process, Presenting and Writing-up Qualitative Research (the topic of Chapter 12) is viewed as another stage of analysis.

The Conclusion consists of one final Chapter 13, which explores New Challenges and Perennial Dilemmas. The topics addressed here include the possibilities afforded by the internet, the potential and challenges of secondary analysis and the broader issues regarding the role and remit of the researcher and the political mandate to research.

SUGGESTIONS ABOUT HOW TO USE THIS BOOK

This book is intended as a resource for qualitative researchers at various stages in their careers. Although it aims to talk the novice researcher through the entire process and the underpinnings of qualitative methods, it also raises more thoughtful questions along the way, and is thus also intended as a spur to more thoughtful and critical engagement on the part of more experienced researchers, including those who may be engaging with new approaches. This textbook provides commentaries and exercises that can be engaged in by the isolated researcher or used as a basis for a qualitative methods course, since it includes materials that can be employed in a small group setting. It seeks, therefore, to de-mystify the process of teaching qualitative methods and provides helpful hints for the teacher or workshop facilitator as well.

Readers are invited to work through the various processes outlined in the book, drawing on the resources provided. The book aims to provide 'fly on the wall' access to discussions where much of the conceptual work surrounding qualitative research is carried out. Drawing on the author's own experience, the book uses informative examples and even some excerpts from team meetings, supervision and consultancy sessions to illustrate many of the processes involved in qualitative research, which are otherwise hard to capture. This is put in context by locating the ensuing debates within the wider extensive methodological literature.

The material presented includes sections of 'worked' and 'unworked' transcripts (i.e. coded and uncoded) and a provisional coding frame. It will also allow the reader, through exercises, to work on developing more comprehensive coding frames, reflecting the iterative process of qualitative data analysis. Exercises include a step-wise reworking of the process of analysis using pre-coded excerpts and demographic details from a condensed 'real' dataset from an interview study. This dataset also provides excerpts for use in an exercise involving theorizing using qualitative data. The exercise requires the reading of several related papers (or summaries) across a range of research topics, which are then used in conjunction with data excerpts in order to interrogate and develop theoretical frameworks.

The exercises allow for the development of critical and analytical skills through reading selected papers and engaging in a range of focused tasks. However, the reader is also invited to dip back and forth between sections, using this as a postmodern text – relying on the detailed index to guide her/him to specific passages which may be useful. The exercises do not force all readers to work their way sequentially through each of these methods, providing for a greater degree of choice and, importantly, the potential to engage with exercises as part of group sessions, allowing readers to benefit from the additional insights to be gained from comparing notes with fellow novice researchers, whether in relation to jointly- or independently-generated data. For example, this book can give a reader who is predominantly interested in learning how to conduct one-to-one interviews, the opportunity to gain experience in developing interview schedules, formulating and using prompts, generating data through interviews, developing and refining a provisional coding frame and formulating an explanation for the patterns identified in the data. Group exercises also provide valuable first-hand insights into both the potential and challenges of doing qualitative research in multidisciplinary teams. If the book is used on a course where students are concentrating on different methods, each can gain from the insights afforded by being able to compare their own experiences with those pursuing a learning route that emphasizes other methods. This means that they can gain direct experience of viewing these methods in context, which will equip them to make informed research design decisions for future projects. Thus, the book is also intended as a resource for those teaching qualitative methods courses.

THE RESEARCH TOPICS

The process of doing qualitative research will be illustrated by reference to examples, data excerpts, and datasets derived from a wide range of research projects. The author has been involved in many of these, either in the capacity of main researcher, collaborator, supervisor, consultant or adviser. The data excerpts presented have been generated on a range of studies, including observational fieldwork for my own doctoral thesis on professional socialization for social work and fieldnotes from a study of midwives' roles and responsibilities. They are also drawn from two series of focus group workshops, one of which engaged with the topic of fathers' attendance at deliveries and the other on perspectives on parenting. A pre-coded condensed dataset from interviews with couples about their experiences of sub-fertility and service use is also used as the basis for specific exercises. Further excerpts from this same dataset are presented to be used as a resource in interrogating theoretical frameworks using the example of 'biographical disruption' and related reading materials. Drawing on the work of others, however, will allow for exploration of the processes and dilemmas involved in carrying out research in a number of disciplines, including anthropology, criminology, education, nursing, psychology and social work, and the broader discipline of sociology. Many projects now involve interdisciplinary research groupings and the issues arising in this context will be discussed, particularly the ways in which differences can be used to advantage both in relation to making decisions about research design and reflexively analyzing data.

CONCLUSION

This book explores the challenges of doing hands-on qualitative research and attends to the important issues of funding and the political contexts which shape our engagement. It also highlights the unique potential of qualitative methods, provided that these are applied thoughtfully, rigorously and reflexively. The exercises are designed to illuminate the processes involved and to encourage high-quality qualitative research which can contribute effectively to policy, practice and the development of theory.

SECTION 1
INTRODUCTION

This section of the book sets the scene by locating qualitative research vis-à-vis the debates that have surrounded its development. Chapter 1 takes a critical look at the scope and contribution of qualitative research, considering individual researchers' dispositions as well as political and funding imperatives. It outlines the contribution that qualitative research can make, the sort of questions it is best-equipped to answer and highlights what is distinctive about the qualitative research endeavour. A short outline of the major qualitative traditions is provided, tracing the development of symbolic interactionism, ethnomethodology, phenomenology, conversation analysis and discourse analysis, showing advantages and disadvantages of each; the features they have in common; and their points of divergence. The major methods of generating qualitative data are also presented. In particular, this section guides the reader through the vocabulary of qualitative research and introduces her/him to what can be described as 'the qualitative mindset'. This involves questioning some of the key assumptions associated with quantitative research and means that what might be considered as shortcomings can, with a shift in perspective (and sufficient attention to rigour) be seen, instead, as resources. The remainder of the book shows how to use qualitative research to full advantage.

In Chapter 2 research design is presented as the key to ensuring that researchers make the most of qualitative approaches. The reader is given guidance on how to formulate a question amenable to using qualitative methods and attention is paid to matching research questions and appropriate methods. This chapter also stresses the importance of sampling, since this is what ensures that comparative analysis can be carried out. The rationale behind qualitative sampling is outlined, together with examples of sampling grids, which allow the purposive selection of individuals or groups in anticipating some of the patterns which will be interrogated through the process of analysis. Case study research is also discussed under the general heading of sampling. Also covered here is advice with respect to developing and writing a research proposal.

Chapter 3 provides a short history of ethical issues, locating the current situation within the broader historical and political context. This chapter also gives some guidance with regard to applying for ethical permission. Rather than focus on the mechanics of this process, however, the reader is encouraged to anticipate ethical issues as these may arise throughout the duration of the project – including dissemination of findings. Also emphasized here is the importance of considering the impact on the researcher and the need to ensure her or his safety.

1

THE SCOPE AND CONTRIBUTION OF QUALITATIVE RESEARCH

AIMS

- This chapter illustrates the range of questions that qualitative research can answer.
- It sensitizes the reader to the debates that have characterized the development of qualitative research and equips her/him to appreciate the benefits of this approach through emphasizing the underlying assumptions about the nature of knowledge and how we can study the social world.
- It outlines the advantages and disadvantages of the range of methods used by qualitative researchers and enables the reader to judge the appropriateness of matching particular methods with specific research questions.
- It introduces the vocabulary and concepts appealed to by qualitative researchers and summarizes both distinct features and commonalities of the major qualitative traditions.
- It provides a set of questions to facilitate critical evaluation of qualitative papers, which also encourage thoughtful research practice.

INTRODUCTION

Qualitative research is not for the faint-hearted, but it can be exhilarating and can provide unique and valuable insights. If you've read even this far the chances are that you are attracted to doing this sort of research. There has been some debate within qualitative research as to whether such researchers are 'born' or 'made', but I suspect that, for most of us, the answer lies somewhere in the middle.

This chapter begins by examining the role of different dispositions, or types of curiosity, in driving the focus and design of qualitative research studies. It will then go on to consider what is distinctive about qualitative research, illustrating the unique contribution it can make to knowledge. The next section presents the range of methods that can be employed in order to generate qualitative data. Following this, the chapter turns to qualitative traditions and the philosophical ideas about the nature of knowledge and how to generate it, together with ideas about the social world and how this works. The following section presents the iterative research process that characterizes qualitative research and which, through its flexibility, affords both analytic potential and ample challenges. The importance of reflexivity is stressed, including the need to be reflexive about some of our own assumptions, deriving from our previous research experience, disciplinary background, or pre-dispositions. Some of the perceived limitations, or difficulties encountered in designing and conducting qualitative research are examined. Some of these are shown not to be relevant, since these overlook some of the distinctive principles underlying the qualitative research endeavour. If expectations and assumptions are reviewed, however, and these ideas about shortcomings are recast, it is argued that they can, instead, be viewed as strengths. This raises the issue of how we evaluate qualitative research and it is argued that we need to use a different set of questions from those routinely asked of quantitative research, and that we also should be wary of checklists for reviewing qualitative work, which may still harbour some of the inappropriate assumptions highlighted earlier. The accompanying exercise suggests asking a set of questions designed to address the rigour of the research, while acknowledging that this represents an ideal. It may be unrealistic to hope for positive answers to all such questions and we need to think carefully about the reasons for reading the paper in the first place.

DISPOSITIONS

Tricia Greenhalgh (1998), who trained as an anthropologist prior to studying medicine, consequently has a unique insight into research endeavours situated at the conjunction between the two sets of disciplinary concerns. She points out that qualitative research taps into a different sort of curiosity. Recalling a story told to her by Cecil Helman, she uses the analogy of two children observing leaves falling from trees in autumn to characterize two different 'research mindsets': one which is drawn to counting and calculating the rate of leaf-fall and predicting when trees will become totally bare and the other which involves pondering the broader context where only some trees lose their leaves and the diversity of sizes, shapes and colours of leaves involved. To paraphrase Greenhalgh (and Helman), the 'calculators' are prone to becoming quantitative researchers, while the 'ponderers' are much more attuned to qualitative research approaches.

Although this obviously involves some over-simplification, it is certainly the case that we have tended to overlook the importance of the match between researcher and research methods. Trow (1957: 33) observed: 'Every cobbler thinks leather is the only thing – most [researchers] have their favourite research methods with which they are familiar and have some skill in using. ... We mostly choose to investigate problems that seem amenable to attack through these methods.' While this does not preclude researchers with a quantitative 'mindset' undertaking qualitative projects – or, indeed vice versa – this notion of deeply rooted dispositions helps to explain both why certain broad research questions, or properties of the data produced, 'grab' some individuals more than do others. This selectivity can be seen at work in the many examples provided throughout this book.

WHAT IS DISTINCTIVE ABOUT QUALITATIVE RESEARCH?

Qualitative research answers very different questions from those addressed by quantitative research, and some criticisms directed against qualitative research have, at times, failed to take this into account. Qualitative methods cannot answer questions such as 'How many?', 'What are the causes?', 'What is the strength of the relationship between variables?' It can, however, provide an understanding of how official figures are created through social processes. Research, such as that done by Lindsay Prior (2003) on suicide statistics and documentation used in psychiatric hospitals and Mick Bloor (1991) on death certification, has examined how the categories are interpreted and employed by those doing the recording. Studies of this sort have also sought to explain how this has come about – due to policy emphases and working practices. Even a seemingly straightforward issue, such as how hospital waiting lists are managed, has been shown to be subject to fascinating variation, which has as much to do with social processes as it has to do with clinical factors (Pope, 1991).

Qualitative research can make visible and unpick the mechanisms which link particular variables, by looking at the explanations, or accounts, provided by those involved. Quantitative research excels at identifying statistically significant relationships between variables, such as social class and health status, and frequently produces diagrams which show the distribution and strength of this association for people located at different points on the social class spectrum. Quantitative analyses can, of course, further explain such associations by determining the relative influence of individual variables for sub-samples of the population under study, or by looking at the effect of clusters of related variables. What eludes such approaches, however, is the capacity to explain *how* the 'macro' (i.e. social class position, gender, locality) is translated into the 'micro' (i.e. everyday practices, understandings and interactions) to guide individual behaviour. This is where qualitative research can provide a fuller picture.

Although qualitative and quantitative research answers very different questions, researchers often have common interests in seeking to understand a particular phenomenon and the two approaches can be complementary. An interview study sought to find out what demands HIV/AIDS made on professionals and how they dealt with these challenges (Barbour, 1993, 1995). Semi-structured interviews were used to elicit the perceptions of workers in four Scottish cities, which were characterized by different epidemic patterns and varying histories of service development. By leaving it up to the interviewees to identify which aspects of their work they experienced as most demanding, interviews established that organizational aspects of their work and new professional challenges loomed as large for staff as did the more predictable problems posed by caring for young people (many of whom were already stigmatized by virtue of their drug use or sexuality) who were dying. Although there had been a number of quantitative studies which had sought to measure levels of burnout among AIDS-related workers, these had concentrated mostly on the issues raised by the interface with patients. Had this study been followed by a survey employing a structured questionnaire to try to quantify the impact of AIDS-related work on satisfaction or burnout, it would certainly have been useful to have augmented these pre-validated scales. Additional questions could have been incorporated which investigated the way in which work was organized, since the interviews had shown that the demands of working in multidisciplinary teams, and responding to particular management styles, allocation of resources and the implications for career development were of particular importance to professionals (Barbour, 1993). Rather than pre-defining the variable likely to be important to those we study, qualitative approaches allow respondents to identify those issues which are salient for them and to explain how these impact on their daily lives and, in the case above, how these affect how they go about their work and how these affect their job satisfaction. It is for this reason that qualitative methods are often utilized in order to inform the development of structured research instruments, such as surveys, and mixed methods research is discussed more fully in Chapter 7.

By employing qualitative methods it is possible to study *how* people understand concepts; what sort of 'trade-offs' they might make to themselves in weighing up, for example, health promotion messages and deciding whether or not to take these on board. An early and influential publication in the field of medical sociology explains how individuals process information and make decisions:

> A person is unlikely simply to return from the doctor's surgery and take the treatment that he has been prescribed. It is more likely that the doctor's action and the treatment will be discussed and evaluated. Medication decisions will be made in the light of these discussions, in the light of the person's experiences with the treatment, and in the light of past experiences with the doctor and other illnesses and treatments. ... People live their problems and illnesses socially; they cannot be viewed as isolated individuals responding automatically to the instructions of their doctors. (Stimson and Webb, 1978: 152)

Qualitative methods can allow us to access these 'embedded' processes by focusing on the context of people's everyday lives, where such decisions are made and enacted, rather than simply looking at patient characteristics or the content of consultations. It is not only members of the public, the 'lay population', however, who weigh up information in what might be seen as idiosyncratic ways. A study by Fairhurst and Huby (1998) examined how general practitioners (GPs) evaluated the results of randomized control trials (RCTs) in a specific area of medical practice (the management of hypocholesterolaemia). Drawing on cognitive theories of education, they showed that knowledge trickled down to GPs. Very few had actually read the papers in question, but relied on sources of evidence rather than the evidence *per se*. That is, they were more likely to accept the findings if these were passed on to them by someone they trusted – whether this was a highly regarded journal summarizing the findings or a respected colleague. Reinforcement was required from several sources before GPs were persuaded of the need to alter their own clinical practice. Thus, although the evidence in question was located at the hard (quantitative) end of the methods spectrum, it was evaluated qualitatively by GPs and qualitative methods were required in order to study the process involved.

Qualitative methods can help us to understand apparently illogical behaviours. One of the best-known studies in this category was Hilary Graham's (1993) work on economically disadvantaged lone mothers and their smoking behaviour. Given the cost of cigarettes, both financially and in health terms, smoking by women in this situation could be regarded as being at variance with health advice and their own best interests. However, Graham's research highlighted the positive functions of smoking for the women in terms of allowing them to manage the exigencies of their circumstances and responsibilities. Smoking allowed the women to affirm their adult status in the face of insistent and pervasive child-rearing demands, without necessitating either lengthy engagement in this alternative pursuit or requiring them to leave the home or children in their care. It was also a sociable activity in which they could participate with friends in the domestic setting. Compared with other activities which might have conferred these same benefits, smoking was also relatively inexpensive and nicotine, moreover, is a powerful appetite suppressant, enabling the women to limit their own food intake while providing the optimum amount of food for children.

Even where individuals accept advice or templates advocating particular ways of behaving (whether these relate to individual health-related behaviours or models of professional intervention) there can be 'many a slip betwixt cup and lip'. In other words, these are unlikely to translate seamlessly into changed practices. Qualitative research is particularly well suited to studying context. It also excels at illuminating *process*, whether this is organizational change or individual decision-making, since it allows us to examine how changes affect daily procedures and interactions. This may lead to us uncovering unintended as well as intended consequences of new arrangements.

PROVIDING INSIGHTS INTO UNINTENDED AS WELL AS INTENDED CONSEQUENCES OF ORGANIZATIONAL CHANGE

In the course of carrying out research into smoking policies in the workplace in the late 1980s we selected several case studies of organizations at varying stages in the process of developing and implementing such policies. Discussions with a range of staff in one workplace alerted us to the unwitting potential for more egalitarian relationships, as we learnt that, since the introduction of the smoking policy, one of the junior typists now habitually took a cigarette break with one of the managing directors. These chance meetings had provided the senior manager with insights into the illogicalities and impracticalities in the way the typing pool was run and led to work being organized in a different way thereafter. Needless to say, this is not a line of questioning that would have occurred to the researchers, but in further case studies we did invite participants to reflect more widely on the broader consequences of the new smoking policy in terms of lines of communication and organizational hierarchies.

Recently my colleague (Julie Taylor) kindly provided me with a parallel anecdote, relating to the unintended outcomes of the recent smoking ban in Irish pubs. Apparently, the opportunity of engaging with members of the opposite (or, indeed, same) sex, afforded by the practice of huddling outside to 'have a fag', has led to non-smokers feeling left out and to the coining of a new word – 'smirting' (a hybrid of 'smoking' and 'flirting') – to celebrate the dual possibilities involved.

Qualitative methods can explain apparent discrepancies, such as the low rate of formal reporting of racist incidents in one area of Scotland, which was at variance with police officers' experience 'on the beat' and their knowledge of the localities involved. Colleagues at Glasgow University (with myself acting as consultant to the project) carried out a questionnaire study, one-to-one interviews and focus groups with a range of people living and working in the communities concerned. We were interested in unpicking how incidents came to be defined as 'racist', and what people considered were the likely consequences of lodging a formal report. Qualitative methods, in particular, allowed us to 'problematize' both the concept of racism and the process of reporting, moving back several steps both from our own understandings and those of the police and looking at how people made sense of these ideas on a daily basis. Focus groups, in particular, showed that 'racism' is a very complex issue and that the definition of incidents as racist is far from straightforward, since this is embedded in multiple considerations and attributions, including perceptions of police and legal processes, and the degree to which responses are premeditated or intended to cause offence (Barbour, 2007).

Qualitative research can 'de-mystify' by providing detailed accounts of experience and there is an extensive catalogue of such research in relation to patients' experience of chronic illness. Ethnographers, in particular, often see their work as providing 'thick description' (Geertz, 1973: 5). Some commentators, for example, Crombie with Davies (1996), have characterized qualitative research as being 'descriptive', using this to distinguish it from quantitative research, which is seen as furnishing explanations.

Qualitative research, however, can and does provide explanations – albeit of a different type and focus than quantitative studies.

Perhaps this misconception has been fuelled by the limitations of some variants of qualitative research. While some such researchers seek to develop analytic explanations, and to interrogate and generate theory, there is also a body of qualitative research that seeks solely to 'bear witness' rather than bringing theoretical or disciplinary concerns to bear on understanding the data generated. Some such work purports to illuminate 'lived experience', which is a term that particularly exercises one of my colleagues, who points out that this involves a tautology. Such a description may also serve to elevate to the academic arena work more akin to that of the stable of 'confessional journalism'. While the intent of such work may be admirable, this represents the very least of what qualitative research can achieve. Even if researchers identify with the more limited aspiration to elucidate experience, they might still benefit from questioning their methods and developing a more robust approach to data analysis. If such studies paid more attention to sampling, identifying and explaining patterning in the data, they could say much more about the mechanisms involved and would, therefore, be much better placed, not only in relation to advancing disciplinary theoretical debates, but also with regard to making recommendations relevant to policy or practice. This is, after all, more likely than are empathic accounts *per se* to ameliorate conditions for those whose cause such studies seek to champion. (These issues are also highly pertinent to Action Research, which is the subject of Chapter 8.)

THE RANGE OF QUALITATIVE METHODS AND TRADITIONS

Before moving on to enumerate the principal ways of generating data in qualitative research and their attendant philosophical underpinnings, is it necessary to make a distinction between 'methods' – the specific practical measures and tools employed to access or create data through different forms of interaction with those we are studying – and 'methodology' – the more general discussion about the assumptions underpinning different methods and the implications, challenges and limitations of choices for the process of conducting research and its ultimate products.

Documentary and visual sources

Although this book concentrates on the active generation of data through interaction with research 'respondents' or 'participants', there is a substantial amount of qualitative research that relies on pre-existing materials as sources of data. Biographers and social historians have routinely drawn on diaries, letters and archival material in their work, capitalizing on the properties of such material to be used to explore issues which might not have been current at the time of their production. This can increase the capacity of such materials to shed light on events and how these were perceived by individuals at a particular point in time, without the attendant concern about the representational intent that might arise when considering items produced more recently or for research purposes – although writing for posterity is, in itself, a powerful motive and there is no guarantee that such documents do not wilfully distort.

Prior (2004: 375) has recently bemoaned the de-emphasis on written documents in scholarship and methods text, and the attendant privileging of oral data generated through talk and interaction. However, there are some examples of researchers who have utilized both past and contemporary documents to provide data for their analyses. David Armstrong (1983) turned his attention to medical textbooks and analyzed the ways in which these have defined the patient and the body. Seale analyzed English language newspaper stories relating to representation of people with cancer appearing during one selected week. His analyses centred on the use of militaristic language and sporting metaphors (Seale, 2001a) and religious themes (Seale, 2001b) and provided valuable insights into how people with cancer are continuously and often unthinkingly constructed. Independently produced texts are also highly relevant with regard to understanding how societies and individuals make sense of important and challenging issues such as death and disaster. Bridget Fowler (2005) has recently studied obituaries as texts, and Mike Brennan (2006) has focused on analyzing the recent phenomenon of condolence books. In all of these cases the focus of the analyses transcends the original intent of the materials and provides an alternative frame of reference, highlighting the complex functions and significance of texts as these are produced and consumed (Prior, 2004). As Prior (2004: 388) comments: 'Documents are never inert'.

The embeddedness of texts is crucial to our understanding of how these work, and Prior's advice to the novice researcher suggests that employing document analysis alongside other qualitative methods may be particularly fruitful. He urges them to 'look at the documentation, not merely for its content but more at how it is produced, how it functions in episodes of daily interaction, and how, exactly, it circulates' (Prior, 2004: 388).

Document analysis is sometimes included in mixed methods approaches, particularly in the field of action research, where documents may help to place interventions within the broader policy context. An ongoing PhD student's project, for example, is currently looking at stakeholder involvement in the development of diabetes services, and has drawn on both national and local policy documents, looking at how lay involvement, in particular, is constructed and how it can be built into the new structure of 'Managed Clinical Networks'.

This list is forever expanding as new technologies arrive and possibilities expand. For example, qualitative researchers have also been turning their attention to the potential afforded by visual methods. This has involved a range of approaches, whereby visual images have been treated as a source of data for analysis, as well as a way of eliciting data, and representing findings. Photographs and videos, in particular, afford a novel way of researching topics or issues that may be elusive or hard to capture in terms of the capacity of the spoken word. Because of their ready accessibility, such methods afford great potential for use in more participative approaches, including action research. Like other qualitative methods, such materials can and, indeed, should be employed collaboratively and reflexively (Pink, 2004). Given the development of on-line publishing there are a wealth of possibilities in terms of photo-essays, video-essays and hypermedia links, resulting in qualitative methods practice that is constantly in a state of flux. (For further discussion of visual methods, see also Banks (2007). A more recent source of ready-made data is the internet and a growing number of researchers have harvested material from online chat-rooms and discussion groups, using this as a basis for their qualitative analysis of the 'text' thus produced. (Some of the implications for developing qualitative research to draw on this resource are further explored in Chapter 13.)

Observational fieldwork

This method was widely used by anthropologists studying other cultures, but has also been popular within sociology, where it has allowed researchers to see how work or social practices are enacted on a daily basis. It affords an opportunity to view behaviour in a naturalistic setting, akin to the 'fly on the wall' format so beloved of television documentaries, where the influence of the researcher is minimal and can uncover inconsistencies between how people perceive and present their own involvement and what they actually do in practice. Thus, it can illuminate the discrepancies between intent and outcome. This method is the mainstay of ethnography (see Chapter 4), which does sometimes employ other methods alongside observational fieldwork, including analysis of documents and interviews or focus group discussions.

Interviews

One-to-one interviews are perhaps the most commonly used method in the qualitative 'toolbox'. Indeed, quantitative studies sometimes also refer to the use of interviews, but, here, are usually referring to more tightly structured schedules. The hallmark of interviewing in qualitative research is the use of open questions, which allow respondents to focus on the issues of greatest importance to them, rather than the agenda being determined entirely by the researcher's interests. Most qualitative researchers favour the use of semi-structured interviews, which allow for the ordering of questions to be employed flexibly to take account of the priority accorded each topic by the interviewee. Chapter 5 is devoted to interviews and also discusses in detail the role and contribution of narrative interviews.

Focus groups

Focus groups have become much more popular in the social sciences over the past ten years or so. Since focus groups are of somewhat mixed parentage, drawing on the marketing research tradition, organizational research and community development, this has given rise to some confusion regarding terminology. Some researchers refer to group interviews, which I would see as veering towards the more structured end of the spectrum, with the researcher putting each question to each of the participants in turn, whereas focus group discussions focus on the interaction *between* participants, with the researcher taking a less active role in directing talk. As is argued in Chapter 6, focus group research is inherently flexible and can be employed in the exploratory phase of projects to inform the development of more structured 'tools' such as questionnaires, or even for developing consensus guidelines for clinical management. They are also, however, a useful – and in some respects unrivalled – stand-alone method whose value lies in their capacity to illuminate group processes and the way in which meanings and even action plans are developed and refined through interaction.

Diaries

Although frequently used as part and parcel of survey research, diaries are less frequently employed in qualitative research. They can, however, provide useful insights with regard to what is happening in respondents' lives between interviews carried out at various points in the course of a longitudinal study and can be used prospectively (Elliott, 1997). Diaries can be as structured or unstructured as the researcher wishes, and can be valuable in identifying issues for exploration in interviews, which might not otherwise have come to the researcher's attention. Although, in common with the personal diary, which is a popular source for biographers, they tend to focus on individuals' experiences, these need not be confined to the purely 'confessional'. Diaries can provide otherwise elusive contextual details and thought processes involved in making choices and decisions and can also be used to record intentions. They provide scope for articulating issues that might not be picked up in interviews and for accessing what would otherwise remain 'hidden' or 'muted' accounts (Elliott, 1997).

Diaries can also be used to good effect in the context of participatory research. If, for example, participants are invited to reflect on the focus and conduct of the research project – a respondent version of the 'fieldwork diary' (as traditionally kept by anthropologists, but a useful reflective tool for all qualitative researchers) – this can provide a mechanism for ensuring that the concerns of those taking part in research are incorporated into the design and analysis.

Diaries are unlikely to be used as a 'stand-alone' method, but can be used to advantage in mixed methods studies, which may seek to combine different qualitative methods or use a mixture of quantitative and qualitative methods of collecting data. Mixed methods approaches, and their potential and challenges, are explored in Chapter 7.

Enhanced case records

This is an approach which is helpful in studying professional or clinical practice, but which, again, is unlikely to be used in isolation. 'Enhanced case records' (McKeganey and Boddy, 1988), designed by researchers and guided by their interests, provide an opportunity to bridge the gap between the details contained in pre-existing records, which (even if researchers had permission to access these) are unlikely to yield the information required by researchers since these have been compiled with a different goal in mind. For an example of the use of enhanced case records see Chapter 2.

Case study research

Although this is frequently presented as a distinctive approach to qualitative – and, indeed, quantitative – research, I have chosen in this book to discuss case studies under the general heading of sampling (see Chapter 2 on research design). This is where the case study approach pays true dividends, since it allows the researcher, through careful selection of 'cases' (whether these are research settings or individuals), to make instructive comparisons. Even where research involves a single case study, the reasons for choosing this setting and due consideration of its 'typicality' (or by virtue of particular unusual features) allow the researcher to speculate as to the 'transferability' or 'theoretical generalizability' (see the discussion later in this chapter on evaluating qualitative research) of the study's findings.

Critical incident technique

This is another approach which is sometimes referred to as a distinctive qualitative method. It has its origins in the aeronautical industry where it was developed to study 'near misses' of aircraft and, by focusing on what (almost) went wrong, was able to identify the more elusive factors that give rise to unproblematic outcomes the rest of the time. Again I have chosen to discuss this under the heading of sampling (see Chapter 2) as it involves a deliberate attempt to seek out 'negative' or 'deviant' cases and to use these as a resource in theorizing about more common patterns. Although it is most often invoked in relation to considerations of research design and sampling, the 'critical incident technique' embodies an idea very similar to that informing the notion of 'analytic induction', which refers to the important role played by exceptions in the process of analysis and the refining of our explanatory frameworks. This will be revisited in Chapters 10 and 11, which are concerned with analyzing qualitative data. (For a detailed history of the critical incident technique and its use within qualitative research see Butterfield et al., 2005.)

Action research

Some research aims explicitly at changing professional practice or improving the circumstances of disadvantaged or disenfranchised groups. Such projects frequently rely on mixed methods designs and emphasize the cyclical nature of the research endeavour, moving continuously between the phases of identification of the problem, planning of the intervention, implementation and evaluation of the change. This type of research is the subject of Chapter 8.

THE RANGE OF QUALITATIVE TRADITIONS

Commenting on the challenges of teaching qualitative methods, Martyn Hammersley asks the question that exercises all who are involved in this endeavour: how best to 'prepare students for participation in a research community that is riven by methodological, philosophical and even political disputes?' (Hammersley, 2004: 556).

Before attempting to outline the main positions and approaches to doing qualitative research it is necessary to introduce the related, but separate, concepts of 'epistemology' and 'ontology'. 'Epistemology' refers to theories of knowledge, how we come to know the world, and our ideas about the nature of evidence and knowledge. This concerns 'the principles and rules by which you decide whether and how social phenomena can be known, and how knowledge can be demonstrated' (Mason, 1996: 13). 'Ontology' refers to our views as to what constitutes the social world and how we can go about studying it.

It is also necessary to issue here a disclaimer, since I believe that any attempt to categorize qualitative traditions in terms of their distinctiveness is doomed from the outset. Undoubtedly, the novice qualitative researcher is likely to be assailed with a confusing variety of recommended approaches. The problem of providing a clear and comprehensive run-down of the principal traditions is exacerbated by the existence of several variants of virtually any approach, as these are espoused both by different disciplines and individual researchers, who have each been exposed to a unique and sometimes idiosyncratic constellation of specific techniques, methodological and philosophical approaches. This chapter has already highlighted the ways in which individual motivations and different sorts of curiosity can influence the research questions we ask and how we go about addressing these. Individual researchers are also likely to employ specific methods (such as interviews or focus groups) and methodological approaches (such as conversation analysis or discourse analysis) in a way that is congruent with their own preferred position and disciplinary legacy, choosing to emphasize some aspects or properties of the approach or method and de-emphasize others. The particular 'spin' put on methods and approaches as each discipline and individual researcher adopts and adapts it, renders problematic any attempt to produce a definitive typology. It is a fallacy to assume that a method or even a broad approach produces similar data, interpretations and analyses, irrespective of the researcher employing it (Barbour, 1998a).

I have sought, therefore, to provide a brief description of the main qualitative traditions, including their origins, usage, and their epistemological and ontological underpinnings. However, in addition to examining claims as to the distinctiveness of these orientations or sets of techniques, I have explored the overlaps and similarities. Along with Seale (1999), I would argue that it is important to read around the various methodological 'offerings' available, with a view to weighing up the relevance of each – or, indeed, hybrids of two or more – for the particular research topic in hand. This, of course, will be anathema to researchers intent on making a case for a particular favoured approach. I would suggest, however, that we could all benefit from taking, at the very least, a critical look at our own preferred methods and assumptions in the light of other approaches and variants of these proposed by other researchers. Seale (1999: ix) advocates using the methodological literature as 'time out in the brain gymnasium' and it is in this spirit that I offer the following summary.

Symbolic interactionism, ethnomethodology and phenomenology

The symbolic interactionist research tradition is associated particularly with the work of members of the second wave of the Chicago School of sociology, who were active in the period following the Second World War and who tended to concentrate on studying the social and interactional processes as enacted by members of specific 'cultures', such as particular occupational groups (Hughes, 1958) or 'underworlds', for example those of gambling, prostitution or fraud. Several researchers – including myself – have also used a symbolic interactionist framework in order to study the process of professional socialization (e.g. Becker et al. (1961) on medical students; Dingwall (1977) on health visitors; and Barbour (1983, 1984, 1985) on social work students. This body of research has studied how new recruits' engagement in collective interactional activity both makes sense of and effects shifts in self-concepts and ways of looking at the world.

Blumer (1969: 184) outlines the assumptions that underpin the application of symbolic interactionism as being:

> … that human society is made up of individuals who have selves (that is, make indications to themselves); that individual action is a construction and not a release, being built up by the individual through noting and interpreting features of the situation in which he acts; that group or collective action consists of the aligning of individual actions, brought about by the individuals' interpreting or taking into account each other's actions.

Although the Chicago School and, indeed, most proponents of symbolic interactionism have relied on ethnographic fieldwork to generate data, interview or focus group transcripts are equally amenable to analysis informed by this perspective and sympathetic theoretical approaches (such as those provided by Goffman's (1974) 'frame analysis' which I used as the main theoretical framework for my own PhD). In contrast to many of the methodological approaches developed more recently, symbolic interactionism did not purport – even at the height of its popularity – to offer detailed guidance on how to 'do' such work. This may partly explain why symbolic interactionism has latterly become unfashionable, rather than falling out of favour for its perceived limitations.

In terms of staying the course, 'phenomenology' and 'ethnomethodology' have fared a little better than has symbolic interaction, but fashions constantly change and may suddenly throw previously neglected approaches into the spotlight. In scanning the current methodological literature or methods sections of published papers, you are much more likely to come across discussion of 'phenomenology', which shares many of the assumptions underpinning symbolic interaction, since both concentrate on the process of interaction and active construction of meaning. A central figure in the development of the phenomenological approach is Schutz (1972), who sought to extrapolate individuals' and groups' taken-for-granted or common-sense categories, focusing on the notion of 'accounts'. Phenomenology has been espoused by both sociologists and psychologists, although the former are perhaps more likely to have employed ethnographic methods. Ethnomethodology's pedigree situates it as developing around the same time as phenomenology and bears many of the hallmarks of the influence of the work of Schutz. It is exemplified by the work of Garfinkel (1967), who was concerned with how individuals build a stable social order both in specific interactional encounters and in society more generally. Literally meaning 'folk' methods, ethnomethodology again focused on common-sense practices in routine and everyday interaction, with an interest in what happens when this is disrupted and expectations are breached. This last aspect perhaps explains its links with conversation analysis (discussed below), which focuses, among other things, on how 'repairs' are enacted and facilitated during the process of interactional exchanges. It aims to study the 'local rationality' of members' practices:

> Why it makes sense, for participants, locally, in their practice context, to do things as they are done, even if this is at odds with how these practices are planned, evaluated or accounted for 'elsewhere', 'in theory', or at higher hierarchical levels in an organization. (ten Have, 2004: 162)

Conversation analysis and discourse analysis

I have left until last discussion of these two more recent approaches to qualitative research, as they both marry philosophical rationales with the elaboration of specific methods. Originating in the work of Harvey Sacks (1972; who, incidentally, had worked with Garfinkel), the focus on psychiatric and psychodynamic theorizing still informs conversation analysis (CA). This approach has been employed across a wide range of disciplines, including 'anthropology, sociology, communication, linguistics, sociolinguistics and pragmatics, as well as psychology' (Drew, 2003: 132). It focuses on talk not merely as a medium through which views are communicated, but emphasizes what talk allows interactants to *accomplish*. Puchta and Potter (2004: 9) explain:

> Conversation analysts in particular have argued that ordinary talk, mundane talk, the kind of everyday chat we have with one another is fundamental to understanding all kinds of more specialized interaction. ... Talk is ... something we use to perform an enormous variety of the practical tasks of living.

Conversation analysis focuses on detailed analysis of talk in various types of social interaction, elucidating the everyday and routine aspects such as turn-taking and pauses. It is concerned with the systematic patterns and normative frameworks that comprise talk, and this can provide insights that it is not possible to produce using other methods, since it elaborates:

> how interactants signal to others that they are ending their turn at talk or that they wish to talk, select and change the topics of discussion, and display to others that they are properly attentive to, and involved in, the interaction. Analyzing these issues involves paying close attention to features of social interaction that are often missed or glossed over by even the most careful observers of institutional settings who have only one opportunity to observe each social interaction. (Miller, 1997b: 87)

Peräkylä (2004: 166) emphasizes that, although it is theoretically informed, conversation analysis 'has developed through empirical studies that have focused on specific observable phenomena'. This underlines the emphasis on naturally occurring interactions, rather than researcher-convened encounters. Although concerned first and foremost with the text produced, CA studies do also, in some contexts, examine the consequences for the encounter, including the outcome and how this is achieved. Not surprisingly, since it can allow the researcher to study how 'micro' relationships (including professional–client encounters) are enacted, this approach has been utilized frequently to examine medical consultations (see, for example, many of the papers in the journal *Communication and Medicine*). It has also been employed in other professional settings, for example to provide an understanding of how social workers manage exchanges with clients through persuasion (Suoninen and Jokinen, 2005).

Both conversation analysis and discourse analysis rely on a set of conventions for transcribing, which allow for the minutiae of interaction to be captured, including timing of pauses, overlaps in talk, and details such as rising and falling inflections, and even a laugh inserted mid-word. (For a comprehensive guide to this method, known as Jeffersonian transcription, see Silverman (1993) or the appendix provided by Puchta and Potter (2004). Given its focus on the mechanics of talk, it has been presented as having a 'restricted notion of culture and [paying] scant attention to that which is beyond text' (Stokoe and Smithson, 2001: 228).

Discourse analysis (DA) is described by Willig (2003: 164) as having emerged from ethnomethodology and conversation analysis. It also has its origins in the discipline of linguistics or sociolinguistics (Hepburn and Potter, 2004). It has, however, 'emerged in different disciplinary environments': 'Often these traditions are structured by, and against, the basic issues of the [various] parent discipline(s): how sentences cohere linguistically into discourse; how social organization is made up; how cognition is respecified in interaction.' (Hepburn and Potter, 2004: 180).

This description reflects the related, but somewhat different focus of linguistics, sociology and psychology. Willig (2003) distinguishes between two variants of discourse analysis – 'discursive psychology' and what she terms 'Foucauldian discourse analysis', presenting these as addressing different sorts of research questions. She views the first approach as allowing for the study of how participants use discursive resources and with what effects – what she refers to as 'the action orientation of talk' (2003: 163). Although not developed by Foucault himself, 'Foucauldian discourse analysis' is based on his concept of the 'discursive regime' and is concerned 'with language and its role in the constitution of social and psychological life' (2003: 171). Citing Parker (1992), Willig elaborates: 'From a Foucauldian point of view, discourses facilitate and limit, enable and constrain what can be said, by who, where and when' (2003: 171). Some other commentators, however, argue that such distinctions are not helpful (e.g. Miller, 1997c).

Writers such as Willig emphasize the importance of psychological theory, arguing that both approaches to discourse analysis involve the use of concepts such as memory, attribution and identity. While this certainly renders discourse analysis amenable to the study of psychological phenomena, it can, however, provide an extremely fruitful approach for researchers with different disciplinary concerns, such as sociologists, for example, many of whom are also interested in studying identity and the active presentation of self through talk and performance. Sociologists are also very interested in what Willig describes as the main thrust of what she calls 'Foucauldian discourse analysis': namely 'the role of discourse in wider social processes of legitimation and power' (Willig, 2003: 171).

LIMITATIONS AND POSSIBILITIES

If you have found somewhat confusing this brief foray through several decades and traditions, then you are by no means alone. Having posed the question as to how best to prepare students for an academic setting characterized by disagreement and competing paradigms, Hammersley (2004: 557) concludes that 'we should encourage students to become neither ostriches nor fighting cocks'. This presents quite a challenge, especially in a publishing context that can be seen as privileging the new and innovative at the expense of the pragmatic.

There are considerable overlaps, however, between approaches that, in some quarters, are hailed as being distinctive – even unique. It is only by engaging with this methodological literature, interrogating the boundaries between approaches and cultivating an open-mindedness about how to go about generating and analyzing our own data that we can ensure that we develop the full potential of qualitative research and its richness. There is nothing shameful about developing hybrid approaches. Indeed, Norman Denzin (1989) is cited by Melia (1997) as having made what she terms 'a heroic attempt to pull a good deal together under the term *interpretive interactionism*', which:

> signifies an attempt to join traditional symbolic interactionist thought with participant observation and ethnography; semiotics and fieldwork; postmodern ethnographic research; naturalistic studies; creative interviewing; the case-study method; hermeneutic phenomenology; cultural studies and feminist critiques of positivism. (Melia, 1997: 28)

As Melia concludes, this may be 'an impossible task'. She points out, however, that 'it puts interactionist thought centre stage while allowing space for current methods debates' (Melia, 1997: 28).

Virtually all of the qualitative approaches outlined here have been subjected to criticism on the grounds that they focus on the 'micro' to the exclusion of the 'macro' and ignore the relationship between the two. Such a separation, however, is not inevitable: although they certainly concentrated on the form and content of interactional episodes, the sociologists of the Chicago School had all been trained in the classical sociological tradition and remained mindful of the importance of social structural issues, including class and status, and I would argue that these can be seen to inform the accounts produced, even while these focus on the 'micro'. The theoretical insights provided by such studies can offer an explanation as to how these processes impact on society at a higher level than that of the small group. However, this is possibly a property of the theoretical and disciplinary grounding of the researchers involved, rather than an inherent capacity of the approach.

Referring to a particular body of sociological work, including that of Crow (2002), Mason (2006: 14) points out:

> There is, for example, a long qualitative tradition that sees everyday or interpersonal interactions, life experiences, narratives, histories, and so on, as informing us not only about personal or 'micro' experience, but crucially also about the changing social and economic conditions, cultures and institutional frameworks through

which ordinary lives are lived. In this sense, the macro is known through the lens of the micro – social change is charted in how it is lived and experienced in the everyday.

Some promising signs are also evident in what might be a somewhat unexpected quarter – the 'softest' end of the qualitative spectrum, represented by the 'micro' approaches of CA, DA and ethnography. The distinctions that various commentators have sought to make between these orientations and methods may not be an altogether helpful one and there are some signs that these approaches may be converging. Some DA researchers, moreover, have adopted semi-structured interviews, moving away from reliance on naturally-occurring interaction and, as Miller (1997c: 155) points out, ethnographers can, in any case, produce 'near transcripts'. Other writers, such as Myers and Macnaghten (1999), have argued that focus group data can be analyzed as text. Some versions of discourse analysis are closer to CA, while others pay greater attention to context and some commentators view discourse as ideological language that produces culture through 'an explicit repertoire of justifications and explanations, and an implicit, embedded theory about why people act the way they do' (Merry, 1990: 110, cited by Miller, 1997c: 163). This emphasis on context also affords the possibility for *comparison* and, thus, for interrogation and elaboration of theoretical frameworks, rather than merely illuminating 'micro' processes.

Miller (1997c) makes a plea for an interesting synthesis of ethnomethodologically-informed ethnography and conversation analytic techniques in order to study institutional discourses. She explains that approaches to discourse analysis that focus on concrete procedures also

> involve strategies and techniques for analyzing how competing discourses are articulated in settings, and how interactants' use of institutional categories and vocabularies is related to the interactional contingencies associated with the interaction order and social settings, including their social positions in the settings. (Miller, 1997c: 164–165)

This also hints at the potential for such an approach to begin to redress the imbalance between the 'micro' and the 'macro'. Miller (1997c: 168) argues: 'Ethnographic and conversation analytic research strategies and techniques involve especially useful procedures for seeing and analyzing occasions when dominant discourses are displaced by alternative discourses'. While Miller may well be referring here to alternative discourses as created and contested in one-to-one or small-group interaction, this also holds promise in terms of allowing qualitative researchers to address wider social, cultural and political change. To date, however, most qualitative research has not claimed to provide explanations for wider social developments. Seale (1999: 39) comments:

> For the most part, the qualitative alternative has been presented as a vehicle for answering questions about *what* is happening in a particular setting or *how*

realities of everyday life are accomplished. The issue of *why* things happen in the way they do is more rarely addressed as an explicit project, though a place for this in qualitative research is increasingly argued as the threatening shadow of determinism [or the search for underlying causes and rules] appears to have receded.

Encouraged by no less an example than that provided by Norman Denzin in his attempt to produce a 'composite' approach to qualitative research, I find myself repeatedly advising current PhD students to adopt a broadly social constructionist approach (Berger and Luckman, 1966). This, I would argue, is the most promising potential solution in terms of bridging this important gap in the capacity and aspirations of qualitative research that has been identified by Seale. Depending on how it is employed – and I would advocate a broad and permissive or inclusive definition – social constructionism can effectively marry the 'micro' attention to interaction (advocated by symbolic interactionism, phenomenology and ethnomethodology – and even CA and DA) and more 'macro' elements (taking into account the social, economic, political and policy context) in which data is being generated and with regard to which it should be analyzed. Structural features can be accessed and interrogated through careful, theoretically informed sampling, and even the 'micro' can thus be subjected to comparative analysis (this argument is presented throughout the chapters that follow). This approach is also in line with the view of social constructionism espoused by Gergen (1973), who highlighted that phenomena are specific to a particular time, place and culture, arguing for what he called a 'historical social psychology'.

DIFFICULTIES OR RESOURCES?

The idea of predispositions, as outlined earlier, also goes some way towards understanding some of the problems that may be encountered by researchers engaging in qualitative studies. Many researchers, particularly those who have been trained in the quantitative tradition, may eagerly embrace qualitative methods while continuing to subscribe to some lingering assumptions which are no longer appropriate and which lead them to perceive or, indeed, manufacture problems where these do not really exist – at least not if one shifts one's perspective to conceive of these not as challenges but as resources.

'Truth' is relative

One of the most persistent questions raised in relation to reporting qualitative research findings relates to their veracity – 'How do you know that people were telling you the truth?' The answer is, of course, that none of us can ever know this for certain. While it is common practice in survey research to include cross-checking questions that are designed to catch respondents out in terms of providing information that seeks to mislead, qualitative research deals with contradiction in a very different way, that recasts inconsistency as a resource or intriguing analytic puzzle rather than a problem of disconfirmation.

Qualitative researchers generally subscribe to the adage that 'if people believe things to be real, then they are real in their consequences (Thomas and Thomas, 1928). In the course of carrying out my PhD research into professional socialization for social work, I was alerted to the popularity of the belief, among students, that social workers were deserting the profession after short periods of employment due to burnout or disillusionment. An examination of the scanty figures available established that attrition was no greater than for other comparable professions, such as teaching or nursing, both of which also involved a predominantly female workforce with the attendant likelihood of career breaks. However, this belief in the face of less than compelling evidence led me to question why the idea seemed to hold such appeal for the social work students I was studying. The belief may have been unfounded, but the consequences for retention in the social work profession could, indeed, be far-reaching, if most new social workers held similar views. Misconceptions may have their own internal validity and public or lay perspectives can be very sophisticated. This is something which the advertising industry have recognized and their use of qualitative methods – especially focus groups – has involved probing for sometimes illogical associations made by consumers with respect to products or potential advertising campaigns which may impact on their purchasing decisions and brand loyalties.

Multiple realities

Sometimes apparent contradictions surface not in the context of an individual's account but in relation to two competing accounts of the same event. Of course people put a certain 'spin' on a story, telling it to make a particular point, and a health care professional's or policeman's version of events is likely to differ markedly from the account provided by a patient or someone who has been arrested. Two workshop sessions unexpectedly provided an example of two conflicting versions of the same event – in this case an admission to hospital. While a patient in one workshop told her story to illustrate the incompetence of medical professionals, a health care professional (who had apparently witnessed this same incident) did not have the emotional investment that the patient had, and chose instead to present this as a routine call-out dealt with in a fittingly professional manner. Clearly the two versions were being produced from very different standpoints and illustrate how two people can process things according to varying sets of criteria, reflecting the nature of their involvement.

The role of qualitative research is not to determine which account is the more accurate or 'truthful', but is rather to use these accounts as a resource in order to understand how 'situated accounts' are told in a way that allow speakers to achieve a different purpose through emphasizing some aspects of their stories and de-emphasizing others. We all give a slightly different account of ourselves and our actions to a group of friends 'down the pub' than we would present, for example, at a job interview. Focus group participants – and our dinner party acquaintances – often engage in telling 'horror stories' which tend to be amusing and make for compelling listening. Indeed, most of us will have been involved in embellishing such tales to dramatic effect.

Views are not static

Novice qualitative researchers often complain that it is extremely hard to assign their respondents into the categories they are employing to try to make sense of their views and perceptions. A colleague who had held a series of focus group discussions with health care professionals was attempting to place their views in terms of whether they were supportive or dismissive of the importance of breast feeding. She exclaimed, 'Just when I think I can safely put someone in one box they go and say the opposite!' While her frustration is understandable, this is a difficulty that she had imposed upon herself through conceptualizing views as being dichotomous and fixed. Incidentally, this notion often surfaces in relation to trying to utilize interview or focus group data as 'back door' surveys. This is problematic – but misguided – for two reasons: first, qualitative research excels at unpicking views, uncovering the subtleties and gradua- tions involved rather than applying crude measures; and, secondly, since qualitative research sampling does not aspire to representativeness (see Chapter 2) measuring views will not produce statistically generalizable results. It is those self-same recalci- trant comments – those that defy categorization – that comprise the most valuable pieces of qualitative data. They are the fascinating grey areas that force the researcher to question straightforward models or typologies and go on ultimately to develop more sophisticated explanations. Qualitative methods, by virtue of their immediacy and capacity to encourage respondents to question their ideas, may elicit contradic- tory remarks – even within the space of one interview or focus group discussion.

This is only a problem if one conceives qualitative methods as providing a 'back door' route to measuring attitudes, which is really the preserve of quantitative meth- ods. Provided that researchers pay attention to such contradictions and explore these thoroughly in their analyses, qualitative methods can afford unique insights into the process of change, unpicking the limitations people place around their views, the circumstances or situations that may cause them to shift perspectives and the contexts or settings in which they are likely to espouse different attitudes.

EVALUATING QUALITATIVE RESEARCH AND ITS CONTRIBUTION

Some critics of qualitative research in the past have railed against what might look from the outside as an approach that relies on 'making things up as you go along'.

While quantitative research relies on a roughly linear model in terms of research design – necessitated by the scale and financial resources required – flexibility is the hallmark of qualitative research. Even the focus of the research can alter as data is generated and preliminary analysis suggests a new or slightly shifted emphasis. With respect to sampling decisions (discussed fully in Chapter 2), it is not essential to stipulate detailed inclusion and exclusion criteria at the outset of a project, together with detailed sampling strategies, as these can be augmented as the project unfolds and potential new groups (or rationales for bringing a different range of individuals together in a group if doing focus group research) are identified. (This does, however, raise important challenges in terms of requirements of ethics committees, as discussed in Chapter 3.) Since qualitative research does not seek to recruit representative samples, but to encompass diversity, expanding sampling in this iterative fashion does not pose a problem in terms of generalizability, since statistical generalizability is not a goal in the first place. This does not mean, however, that qualitative researchers can shirk the responsibility of ensuring rigour. It is important to be transparent about the process of analysis, in particular how coding categories were developed and used. Reassurance is also required that the researcher has interrogated the data thoroughly, drawing on the whole dataset, and that s/he has avoided simply picking out the sections (or individual articulate respondents) that support favoured theories or explanations while 'sweeping under the carpet' any potentially contradictory examples. Some consideration should also be given to placing study findings in context, by demonstrating when and where they might be transferable to other situations or settings and to how they add to the knowledge already produced by previous studies.

The growing acceptability of qualitative methods and the willingness of powerful institutions, such as medicine, to seek to incorporate such research knowledge into the 'evidence base', has led to several attempts at developing checklists for evaluating qualitative research papers (e.g. Popay et al., 1998). While this development has shone a much needed spotlight on qualitative research practice and has involved a long overdue acknowledgment that there is such a thing as bad qualitative research, there is a danger in that these checklists can be used prescriptively, despite the original intentions of their initiators. I have argued elsewhere (Barbour, 2001) that slavish adherence to checklists can be invidious in that it can lead to researchers adopting 'technical fixes' in writing up and in designing and conducting qualitative studies. I have described this situation as 'the tail' (i.e. the awareness of and desire to comply with a set of criteria) 'wagging the dog' (i.e. the qualitative research endeavour).

This does not mean, however, that we can abandon all attempts to evaluate qualitative studies. Instead, I would argue that we should read such accounts critically, asking a range of questions. The important difference in such an approach is that it is not necessary to tick a 'yes' in response to each and every question, but rather to place the studies in context, taking account of the constraints under which they were carried out and judging their relevance for the task in hand. We are generally unlikely to be reading qualitative research with an eye to grading it or deciding whether or not to include it in our literature review. There is little point in taking an 'all or nothing' attitude – a study that may be found wanting in some respects may well provide useful hints on methodology or focus on questions in developing our own 'tools'.

In seeking to appraise qualitative research papers critically using a scoring system modified from a quantitative template, we are in danger of missing the point. It is essential that we don't slip into the tempting but ultimately unproductive activity of *criticizing an orange for not being more like an apple*. The exercise that accompanies this opening chapter, therefore, presents a set of questions that you can use to evaluate qualitative papers. It emphasizes the need to locate qualitative research in its rightful context – as a distinct approach with its own internal consistency and means of ensuring rigour. Qualitative research is underpinned by a set of assumptions that are at variance with many of the tenets of quantitative research. Although there is an inevitable risk of over-simplification, these can usefully be summarized as follows:

HINTS ON USING QUALITATIVE RESEARCH METHODS

- Qualitative research asks different sorts of question – not those relating to outcomes or strengths of association, but questions about process, understandings and beliefs.
- It excels at illuminating context and process as a route for explaining actions and events.
- Under the broad banner of qualitative research, here is a wide range of competing approaches, underpinned by differing philosophical assumptions and favouring a variety of methods.
- Certain methods and methodological approaches appeal more to some individuals than to others.
- Don't be afraid of using a hybrid approach – the main thing is to be able to justify your rationale.
- Qualitative methods can be used in conjunction with quantitative methods – or other qualitative methods – in order to illuminate different issues or contexts.
- Individual researchers are likely to put their own 'stamp' on methods and methodological approaches as they conduct qualitative research, as are individual disciplines.
- Qualitative research involves an iterative process, whereby the research design, 'tools' and even the research question can evolve as the project unfolds. This allows for the testing of emergent 'hypotheses' or explanations.
- In reviewing qualitative papers we need to ask different questions from those used to review quantitative studies.

FURTHER READING

Barbour, R.S. (2000) 'The role of qualitative research in broadening the "evidence base" for clinical practice', *Journal of Evaluation in Clinical Practice*, 6(2): 155–163.

Barbour, R.S. (2001) 'Checklists for improving the rigour of qualitative research: A case of the tail wagging the dog?', *British Medical Journal*, 322: 1115–1117.

Malterud, K. (1993) 'Shared understanding of the qualitative research process: Guidelines for the medical researcher', *Family Practice*, 19(2): 201–206.

Pope, C. and Mays, N. (eds) (1995) *Qualitative Research in Health* Care (2nd edition), London: BMJ Books.

Riessman, C.K. (ed.) (1994) *Qualitative Studies in Social Work Research*, London: Sage.

Smith, J.A. (ed.) (2003) *Qualitative Psychology: A Practical Guide to Research Methods*, London: Sage.

EXERCISE

I have provided a set of questions which may or may not be relevant for you, depending on why you are reading a paper in the first place. You may be reading it because it relates to the same substantive topic as does your own potential study; you may be reading it because it provides details about using a method you are considering; or you may be reading it because the theoretical framework it espouses may be helpful with regard to analyzing your own data. It is, therefore, with these disclaimers that I offer the questions listed below.

It is likely that you already have your own store of potential papers to use in this exercise. If not, you should find many examples in a journal relevant to your discipline or field. There is a wide range to choose from here, including those most frequently cited throughout this book: *British Medical Journal, British Journal of General Practice, Communication and Medicine, Discourse and Society, Health, Health and Social Care in the Community, Journal of Advanced Nursing, Qualitative Health Research, Journal of Interprofessional Care, Qualitative Social Work, Social Science and Medicine, Sociology of Health and Illness, Sociology, Sociological Research Online* (available free for private individuals and subject to subscription for institutions at: <http://www.socresonline.org.uk>), and *Sociological Review*. This, however, is not intended as an exhaustive list, as many other journals are increasingly publishing qualitative work.

In order to get you started on this exercise, however, you might like to look at one or two 'sample' articles from the list below. I have selected these papers because they cover a range of methodological approaches, use a variety of methods to generate data, have been published in very different journals, and represent a number of disciplines (sometimes even within the research teams involved). Some articles in the list are available online free of charge to private individuals, meaning that you should be able to carry out this exercise even if you do not have access to an academic library. Each of these papers raises issues with which we all grapple as qualitative researchers trying to work within the word limits, remits and focus of journals with audiences that may be wider than our own disciplinary or practice-based constituency. What we don't know, of course, is how many versions were written before the one that finally appeared in print. Sometimes other details are missing that might help us in making sense of papers reporting on qualitative findings. Think also about other things you might like to know about the background to the studies involved. Some of these papers also make a reappearance in discussions and exercises in later chapters. The suggested articles are:

Belam, J., Harris, G., Kernick, D., Kline, F., Lindley, K., Mcwatt, J., Mitchell, A. and Reinhold, D. (2005) 'A qualitative study of migraine involving patient researchers', *British Journal of General Practice*, 55: 87–93.

Black, E. and Smith, P. (1999) 'Princess Diana's meanings for women: Results of a focus group study', *Journal of Sociology*, 35(3): 263–278.

Clark, A.M., Whelan, H.K., Barbour, R.S. and Macintyre, P.D. (2005) 'A realist study of the mechanisms of cardiac rehabilitation', *Journal of Advanced Nursing*, 52(4): 362–371.

Evans, J. and Chandler, J. (2006) 'To buy or not to buy: Family dynamics and children's consumption', *Sociological Research Online*, 11(3), <http://www.socresonline,org.uk/11/3/evans.html>

Exley, C. and Letherby, G. (2001) 'Managing a disrupted lifecourse: Issues of identity and emotion work', *Health*, 5(1): 112–132.

Hussey, S., Hoddinott, P., Dowell, J., Wilson, P. and Barbour, R.S. (2004) 'The sickness certification system in the UK: A qualitative study of the views of general practitioners in Scotland', *British Medical Journal*, 328: 88–92.

MacGregor, T.E., Rodger, S., Cumming, A.L. and Leschied, A.W. (2006) 'The needs of foster parents: A qualitative study of motivation, support, and retention', *Qualitative Social Work*, 5(3): 351–368.

Saunders, T. (2004) 'Controllable laughter: Managing sex work through humour', *Sociology*, 38(2): 273–291.

Virdee, S., Kyriakides, C. and Modood, T. (2006) 'Codes of cultural belonging: Racialized national identities in a multi-ethnic Scottish neighbourhood', *Sociological Research Online*, 11(4), <http://www.socresonline,org.uk/11/4/virdee.html>

Potential questions to ask

1 Is the topic/research question shown to be important? Is it contextualized with reference to current/relevant clinical/theoretical debates?
2 Is a qualitative approach appropriate?
3 Is the method/combination of methods appropriate?
4 Is enough detail supplied about: (a) the research team; (b) the research setting?
5 How systematic was data 'collection'?
6 How appropriate is the chosen sampling strategy and how adequately is this approach justified?
7 How successful has the sampling strategy been in producing the desired range/diversity of respondents/groups/settings?
8 Is the process of analysis adequately described?
9 What reassurances are provided that data have not been selectively analyzed/presented?

   (a) Have identifiers been used (to show that the whole dataset has been used)?
   (b) Has attention been paid to contradictions/'deviant' cases?
   (c) Has some form of counting been employed (in order to identify patterns)?
   (d) Have opportunities for comparison been fully utilized?
   (e) Is attention paid to potentially competing explanations?

10 Do quotations/extracts work in terms of illustrating the points made?
11 Are findings from any other studies discussed and any points of divergence explained?
12 What qualifications does the author place around findings and their generalizability/transferability?
13 Are the conclusions justified?
14 Are the conclusions useful? In terms of policy, practice, generating further research questions, or developing theoretical frameworks?
15 To what extent are the shortcomings of the paper due to requirements (or perceived requirements) of specific journals?

2
RESEARCH DESIGN

AIMS

- This chapter equips the reader to develop an appropriate research design.
- It shows how to make a case for a specific piece of research and examines the rationale for selecting research team members.
- Hints are provided on formulating and firming up research questions and on matching these with appropriate methods or combinations of methods.
- It emphasizes the importance of sequencing of methods and timetabling and presents examples.
- It explains the principles of qualitative sampling and shows how to use purposive sampling to advantage in order to facilitate comparisons.
- Finally, this chapter demonstrates the importance of placing qualitative research in context and equips the reader to examine critically the limitations of her/his own studies.

INTRODUCTION

This chapter guides the reader through some of the choices which have to be made in the course of putting together a research proposal and embarking on a piece of qualitative research. Many research methods texts urge the novice researcher to start with their research question and to plan their research design accordingly. However, this rather glosses over the potentially fraught issue of how to go about formulating a research question in the first place, and the first section of this chapter will attempt to provide some advice with regard to this challenging and sometimes elusive task.

One of the most important decisions to be made concerns the methods selected and some guidelines are provided to help the reader in choosing between the wide range of alternatives on offer. The important distinctions between ethnographic fieldwork, one-to-one interviews, focus group discussions, and action research approaches will be explored, paying attention to the purposes of the research, the nature of the research relationship, the potential for engagement and the anticipated content of data. This relates back to the different methods for generating qualitative data and the epistemological debates outlined in Chapter 1. The potential and challenges of mixed methods approaches is discussed in Chapter 7 on mixing methods.

Particular attention will be paid to the principles of qualitative sampling, which is often misunderstood and leads to irrelevant criticism of qualitative methods as failing to provide representative findings. The purpose of qualitative sampling – usually called 'purposive' or 'theoretical' sampling – is to reflect the diversity within the group of people or the phenomena under study rather than to select typical cases. Sampling holds the key to the comparisons which can be made using the dataset generated, and hence determines the analytic potential of the data. Thus, qualitative researchers are anticipating the process of analysis even as they recruit respondents or select research settings. The rationale and mechanics of qualitative sampling will be addressed, with special consideration to the subtle differences impacting on this process, depending on which method is being employed. It will be emphasized that practical, ethical and political issues are interrelated.

FORMULATING THE RESEARCH QUESTION

In my own experience of working with graduate students, formulating a research question is often a fairly drawn-out process. It is undoubtedly important to give some thought to couching the research question, since this may have profound implications for the ultimate success and rigour of the research project. It is not uncommon for students to arrive with a stated interest in a fairly broad topic. Writing in 1977 about their experience with graduate students, Cohen and Taylor remark:

> 'Could you give me some ideas for my research project?' is the standard opening question from students of the sociology of deviance. 'What are you interested in?' is the immediate reply, and somehow or other a list of possible subjects emerges: the gay liberation movement, prisons, drugs. But what can realistically be 'done' about these research topics? After putting the student off yet another review of the literature, or a demonstration that labelling theory neglects power, structure and history, we find ourselves supporting any project which sounds vaguely like getting the student out of the library and into contact with people in the world out there. Arming him with romantic Chicago School injunctions about capturing reality in his notebook, with all the west coast methods texts that tell him that soft qualitative research is as valid as anything else, and with a commitment to naturalism, appreciation and being on the side of the deviant, we send him into the world to 'tell it how it is'. This is all to be achieved with the aid of that most simple of research technologies: talk. (Cohen and Taylor, 1977: 67)

We like to think that nowadays, with the many research methods texts at our disposal and, hopefully, a more sophisticated understanding of a range of approaches, choices and their implications, we have moved on from such vague injunctions. However, while we may have considerably more resources at our disposal and have the potential to delay our students even further by arming them with a huge array of texts, the challenge remains essentially the same for student and supervisor. Reading published reports, while instructive, can belie the uncertainties and difficulties that lie behind the apparently effortless choices involved in honing the research question and formulating an appropriate research design. Marshall and Rossman (1995) describe the process as involving funnelling down your research question, making sure that it is 'do-able'. This means identifying exactly what it is about a particular setting, field of study, or experience that interests you. Then you will need to think about who you should talk to in order to generate data, thinking all the time about whether these individuals or groups are likely to be the most instructive exemplar of the processes and issues you want to study. Later in this chapter I have drawn on some recent examples involving supervision of PhD students in order to provide practical advice. The first question is usually 'Why do you want to do this study?'

Motivation

There is often a considerable personal slant which influences the topics selected for study, with a researcher's own experiences leading her/him to develop an interest in studying an issue. This is not always mentioned, perhaps because of the spectre of 'objective inquiry', which still has some influence and leads us to be coy about our real motivations, lest we be accused of not being 'proper (social) scientists'. However, some textbooks do acknowledge this important conjunction (for example Marshall and Rossman, 1995). Indeed, Vickers (2003) claims that 'it is rare to find a productive scholar whose work is unconnected to his or her personal history' (Vickers, 2003: 619). Although such confessions rarely find their way into articles appearing in mainstream journals (such as the *British Medical Journal*), clues are often provided in the authors' details, which give the reader information about professional affiliations and qualifications and can lead to us interpreting the content of the paper somewhat differently. The details supplied on the authors of the article by Belam et al. (2005) is a case in point, as it is only here that we learn that one of the patient participants held a PhD and I do wonder whether at least one of the doctors involved was also a migraine sufferer. What is interesting, however, is that these issues are not tackled within the text of the paper.

Within sociology, there is a stronger tradition of making personal interests explicit and researchers such as Shulamit Reinharz (1979) discuss how they have drawn on aspects of their non-academic selves – in her case as a dance therapist – to identify potential research areas. Another example is provided by Lee Monaghan's (1999, 2001) research into body building, which capitalized on his familiarity with gym and exercise culture. Paul Atkinson (2004) more recently has put his love and knowledge of opera to good use in carrying out ethnographic research on this topic. It is probably fair to say, however, that such conjunctions between personal interests and biographies are most likely to occur either at the outset of research careers or once academics are firmly established. Carolyn Ellis (1995) published an account of her experiences relating to the death of her husband, but was already an established ethnographer. The influence of personal experience is particularly likely with postdoctoral research since such undertakings are not so dependent on funding streams, relying mainly on departmental resources or self-funding. However, many departments are now seeking to organize postgraduate research in order to fit with thematic programmes, so the luxury to pursue personal concerns through research may soon become less apparent.

My own first forays into qualitative research were driven by my curiosity regarding intriguing transformations of friends and acquaintances. This led me to carry out research in the same two settings – that of a religious sect (the Divine Light Mission) and a social work training course. My motivations echoed those of Roy Wallis who also studied a religious sect:

> There was a further reason for my interest in Scientology. Reflecting upon my motivations, and aware that sociologists rarely interest themselves deeply in phenomena to which they are personally or politically indifferent, I conclude that Scientology partly interested me because as a species of social democrat I was fascinated and repelled by the apparent authoritarianism and even occasional totalitarianism of this movement. I wanted to understand how it came to exercise such extensive control over, and to mobilize such enduring commitment from, so many of its followers. (1977: 151)

FIRMING UP YOUR RESEARCH PLAN

Application procedures have tightened up considerably in the last few years and I am by no means sure that my own PhD proposal would pass muster in this new world. I recall that in this document, now lost to posterity, I relied on a rather vaguely stated intention to understand the process of professional socialization for social work 'through students' eyes', invoking, by way of an explanation as to the methodological approach to be followed, several published accounts of the process of medical and nursing training. Although it may have many benefits for the student, the requirements of submitting a detailed research proposal has undoubtedly increased demands on the supervisor, who must guide choices in a much more explicit way than before. Some funding schemes (such as the Health Services Research PhD Programme operated by the Scottish Chief Scientist's Office, from which I have myself benefited as a grant-holding supervisor) require the supervisors to produce a detailed proposal using a form very similar to that used for regular research projects. Studentship proposals outline the rationale and broad focus of the research, while leaving some room for the student, who is appointed, to fine-tune the proposal to match her/his own interests. I would argue, however, that, although latter day PhD proposals may look rather different on paper from those produced some thirty years ago, the personal journey of the individual student remains similar, beset with uncertainties and doubts – sometimes exacerbated rather than reduced by the existence of research plans and commitment to specific approaches which later come to be questioned.

It could be argued that writing a qualitative research proposal is more demanding than producing a quantitative proposal, where it is likely that existing templates can usefully be brought into service. Because of the inherent flexibility of qualitative research and the extent to which the focus of the analysis and findings depend on the content of the data generated, there are limits to what a qualitative proposal can provide by way of a description of what will actually take place. Morse (2004: 494) emphasizes:

> …a researcher cannot prepare a proposal that will definitively outline the steps and strategies of the research process, so that the results of the project will be promised or predicted. At best, the qualitative researcher can prepare a proposal that states:
>
> *This is an interesting topic worthy of investigation; this is what we know and don't know about this question; this is how I will go about looking at this area; and, it is important to know about this area because of this and so, and the results of my study will enable us to move forward in this way or that way.* (original emphasis)

Morse also describes very well the crisis of confidence and indecision that frequently affects novice researchers. Morse's advice is to read around their preferred topic and to keep a note of which papers enthuse them most and how this influences their own ideas. This is likely to provide an indication of the disciplinary focus and methodological approach that fits best with the researcher, but of course it is important to bear in mind the proposed topic, as this will also impose certain limits.

EXAMPLES OF SUPERVISORY ADVICE

I have recently been involved (with colleagues) in providing guidance to two new PhD students with respect to the topic areas of cancer survivorship and recovery following stroke. Both have arrived at these provisional topics by virtue of their role as expert nurses in these areas of practice and the first student (Student A) also has personal experience of cancer survivorship of a close family member. In both cases the

(Continued)

students have been directed towards a range of recommended papers (some of which they had already read), chosen to cover both quantitative and qualitative studies, with a sociological and psychological focus, both within and outside their substantive areas of interest.

Understandably, it is often hard to persuade researchers assailed by a huge literature of the value of this latter tack. One of the best pieces of advice, I think, is to stress the importance of re-reading papers from the new vantage point afforded by having reconsidered the topic. This is key to 'worrying away at' and refining the research question. If it is done in a supportive environment, then it should be possible to capitalize on the insights afforded rather than simply plunging the student into greater uncertainty. Regular meetings with advisers are crucial in providing support and progressing the 'armchair walk through' advocated by Morse (2004).

Whereas the 'cancer student' (Student A) had retained an open mind with regard to the type and stage of cancer that she wished to study, the 'stroke student' (Student B) had already decided that she wished to focus on the period 3–4 months after the stroke when quantitative research has demonstrated that there is often a peak with regard to re-hospitalizations and the breakdown of 'accommodation' to life post-stroke. The challenges provided illustrate two extremes of the spectrum: one student needing to focus her research question and design and the other risking being overly specific at too early a stage in the process.

In working with the two students and other supervisors, I have been involved in posing a series of questions, which may help you to clarify your own research ideas. Not all of these questions need to be answered before embarking on the study, but all should have at least been considered. They cover the same areas as Marshall and Rossman's (1995) headings of 'should-do ability', 'do-ability' and 'want-to-do-ability', highlighting the need to consider the links between motivation, practicalities and the existing knowledge base. These questions include the following.

'What' questions

What is it about this topic that potentially interests you?
What experiences do you want to understand?
What events do you want to explain?
What gaps does the study fill?

Student A had attended a workshop I had presented on theorizing (see Chapter 11) which used papers relating to 'biographical disruption' (in relation to a number of substantive topic areas). After reading these and other papers, she began to phrase her research question around this issue. Although this confirmed my suspicions that she was attracted to a broadly sociological and constructionist perspective, there were, I considered, dangers in stipulating this as the focus of her research. What if 'biographical disruption' did not feature prominently in the accounts she generated? Much sociological research has illuminated the journey from 'person to patient', but we have been much less focused on the equally important experience of moving back from patient to person (as eloquently argued by Hilary Thomas, 2004). It was likely to be this latter phase that this student's research would illuminate, and taking 'biographical disruption' as a starting point rather than including it as one of a range of potentially helpful theoretical frameworks was likely to prove a hostage to fortune.

With regard to Student B's 'stroke' project, I am not convinced that a purely qualitative approach is what is required. If, for example, previous research suggested that re-hospitalization is associated with severity of the original stroke, then this would not provide the sort of intriguing puzzle that qualitative research is so well placed to investigate. At the very least, a further reading of the quantitative literature may yet yield ideas as to which aspects of this identified period are likely to be important and thus help to firm up the research question.

'Why' questions

This relates to the justification for the study. Why do we need to do this study?

In both cases there is a large qualitative literature covering patient experience and so it will be important to identify a new slant for the proposed research. Much of the cancer literature focuses on the experience of diagnosis, treatment and the immediate recovery period rather than focusing on longer-term implications. By comparison, the topic of recovery, which is only beginning to be addressed in medical sociology, affords the opportunity to contribute to an exciting new area – but only if Student A finds this equally interesting.

With regard to Student B's potential study, the justification for carrying this out is implicitly much more closely related to nursing practice. It may be more helpful to turn the question on its head and ask 'Why do some people make a steady recovery while others are beset with adverse events that lead to re-admission to hospital?'

'Who' questions

Who, ideally, are you interested in talking to? Whose views or experiences do you want to capture?

The cancer research literature is often cancer-site-specific. There could be potential in comparing the experiences of people across a range of cancer types. This would also enhance the 'transferability' of findings. Men and women may also have differing experiences and this may be something she wishes to pursue. If, for example, Student A was particularly interested in issues concerned with reproductive decision-making, then she might wish to focus on younger cancer patients, including those who had experienced cancer during childhood. This would not necessarily limit her sample to those who had experienced cancers likely to affect reproductive capacity – an interesting comparison might be made between those in this position and those who have experienced other types of cancer, which would allow her to interrogate, among other things, the concept of 'biographical disruption' and its relationship with impaired fertility.

If Student B continues to focus on individuals at the 3–4-month post-stroke watershed, I think it will be important that she looks at those who do *not* require re-hospitalization as well as those who do. It will also be important to investigate the experiences of those with different patterns of re-hospitalization. It may, however, emerge from a re-reading of published papers that home circumstances play a significant role in determining or mediating experiences of stroke recovery, including re-admission to hospital. In this case, it would be important to try to recruit a sample that encompasses considerable variety in terms of whether people live alone, with a partner, with or without dependent children, in a lively community or in relative isolation, including those in urban and rural environments, which may pose different challenges and afford varying levels and types of support.

'Which methods' questions

Which methods of eliciting data are going to generate the sort of data you're interested in?

The experience of cancer survivors could arguably be accessed either through one-off interviews, a series of interviews (to capture change over time) or via focus group discussions. The choice depends to some

(*Continued*)

extent on the nature of data that the researcher wishes to elicit and the practicalities or logistics that would be involved. If Student A is interested in collecting individual accounts, then one-to-one interviews will be preferable, as these encourage narrative reconstructions and 'biographical work'. She might, however, decide that she is interested in how cancer support group members collectively construct ideas about survivorship, in which case she would be well advised to think about holding focus group discussions with these pre-existing groups.

I'm not convinced that Student B's study question is one that is amenable to being answered using an entirely qualitative approach and it may be that re-reading of the quantitative literature or even some limited survey work or case-note review would be helpful in firming up the research question. However, if her focus were to shift to that of experiences on hospital wards, then it might be profitable to allow for a period of observational fieldwork – either as a stand-alone method or alongside other methods, such as interviews. Again, if she became interested in how stroke survivors access and interpret information, this might lead her to consider support groups as a potential site for focus group discussions.

Hopefully, what is apparent from the above discussion, is the interrelatedness of the research question and the viability of methods.

'Where' questions

Where will you go to try to recruit your sample?
Where are you most likely to be able to access the experiences and events that interest you?

With regard to Student A's project, teaching hospitals should be able to furnish a comprehensive sampling pool, as all patients will have passed through such centres at some point during their illness 'career'. This may, however, be unnecessarily cumbersome, as she will not be wishing to recruit a large sample.

If Student B continues to focus on re-hospitalizations, then hospital would seem to be a sensible place to recruit her sample. However, she will, by definition, then be missing out on those patients who are not re-admitted. This would severely limit her capacity to answer the question she appears to want to pose. Stroke survivors' groups might afford a more workable means of recruiting those who make a steadier recovery.

'When' questions

When do you want to recruit and talk to people?

The notion of cancer survivorship is, by definition, an indeterminate one, covering the entire period between cessation of treatment or disappearance of either initial or secondary symptoms to death (by whatever cause). This can cover decades and it is, obviously, impractical to attempt to design a longitudinal study that could chart this entire period. This does not, however, mean that it is impossible to obtain insights into this lengthy time period, as it is possible to recruit individuals at various points along this trajectory and follow them all for a requisite length of time, providing, if not individually then at least collectively, an insight into long-term survivorship. Another PhD student has been studying the experiences of partners of people with heart disease and has recruited partners of individuals occupying different disease classifications (in terms of severity). She has interviewed partners on two occasions with a 6-month interval. Some of the first interviews have taken place shortly after diagnosis and a couple of the second interviews have taken place after the death of the individual with heart disease, thus affording a glimpse of experiences at a wider variety of points along the route from diagnosis to bereavement than a cursory glance at the study design might suggest.

I still think that it might be helpful to examine stroke patients' experiences at a wider variety of time points – even if the student still wants to extrapolate on what happens during this crucial 2-month time slot. It may well turn out that, although some individuals appear to sail through the 3–4-month watershed with no adverse events, there is a minority of patients who experience this 'trough' later on. While qualitative research excels at uncovering in-depth experiences, it is difficult to make sense of data that relate to a very narrow set of circumstances without the benefit of being able to contextualize this. At the risk of overstating the problem, Student B may end up being in the situation of 'knowing everything about nothing'. While quantitative research focuses on 'representativeness' (i.e. on studying those who fall in the middle of a statistical distribution), qualitative research illuminates by taking 'outliers' into account (i.e. those who offer extremes or exceptions to general principles). A qualitative research project could certainly enhance the understanding provided by quantitative studies which have shown the 3–4-month peak in re-admissions, not only through explaining what happens to patients at this crucial period, but also by studying those who do *not* succumb at this point. It is even possible that those who do not experience problems at this point in time have even greater problems later on, when services may not be so 'geared up' to providing a response (in terms of counselling and support rather than clinical care *per se*).

Again, some sleight of hand – or hidden knowledge on the part of the supervisor that is not made explicit – is in evidence, in that many of these questions relate to or anticipate aspects of research design (that are discussed more fully later in this chapter). In particular, many hinge on the comparative potential of the proposed study, which is the single most important factor in determining its analytic potential. Comparative potential is dependent on being able to contextualize the piece of research, through careful selection of the research setting and continuous reflection as to its unique or shared aspects, and also the comparisons that the sampling strategy affords (again these are discussed in more detail later in this chapter). The material presented above encompasses many complex issues and reflects discussions with students over several supervision sessions as they work to develop their proposals.

RATIONALE FOR CHOOSING A QUALITATIVE APPROACH

David Silverman (1993) has suggested that some researchers choose a qualitative approach not for what it will allow them to accomplish but on account of what they fondly imagine it will allow them to avoid; namely engagement in demanding statistical analysis. One of my colleagues likes to question prospective PhD students on this very issue and it is certainly important to disabuse anyone who does hold this default view of qualitative research. At least in the early days of the new-found enthusiasm for qualitative methods, the idea circulated that *anyone* could do qualitative research, since it merely involves talking to people – a skill that many professionals already feel that they possess. To an extent this may be the case, but not anyone can do *good* qualitative research. Extensive though professionals' interactional skills may be, it is important to recognize that these have been honed in a slightly different context and have been exercised in pursuit of another goal. Shelley Day Sclater ruefully recounts her initial forays into interviewing research respondents about their experiences of different forms of divorce dispute resolution, reflecting that 'good lawyers don't necessarily make good researchers'. She goes on to explain that she had a 'tendency to ask too many questions, interrupt, guide the direction of talk, take sides, and so on' (Andrews et al., 2004: 113). (Chapter 5 discusses in detail the art of asking questions in interviews and offers some hints as to how to ensure that you elicit the sort of data that you require.)

Many qualitative research proposals and written reports are unfortunately weakened by taking a defensive approach to justifying the choice of qualitative methods. Introducing concepts such as 'bias', 'objectivity' or 'triangulation' can have the effect of raising concerns that might not otherwise surface for reviewers or readers. Particularly when moving from working within the quantitative tradition, these are likely to be issues with which the individual researcher may have to wrestle, but that does not necessarily mean that s/he needs to reproduce this in written accounts of the project. This risks being repetitive and may well weary the more experienced reader – or, indeed, examiner! A far better tactic is to emphasize the strengths of qualitative methods, and the following chapters will, hopefully, convince you that there are many.

WRITING A RESEARCH PROPOSAL

Drawing up plans for a PhD affords the student the relative luxury of time, but you are likely in some instances to find yourself writing research proposals within a much tighter timescale. Some researchers carry out PhDs in conjunction with funded projects and may have to make decisions quite quickly with regard to identifying the focus for their PhD, deciding whether or not it is going to be necessary to generate parallel data, for example, or simply to add items to an already planned interview schedule. Funding bodies operate with deadlines and may issue a call for proposals in relation to a specific topic. This cuts down on some of the agonizing involved in making decisions about PhD study, as at least some of the focusing work will already have been done. It can be tempting, however, to write a proposal around what you, the researcher, want to do rather than what the funding body is explicitly asking for. Sometimes, however, serendipity delivers, when one has an idea for a research project that eventually meshes with requirements put out in a call for proposals.

The same advice as provided to PhD students applies to the process of firming up ideas for a proposal to a grant-awarding body. I will discuss this under the following headings:

- Making a case for the research
- The research team
- Choice of methods
- Sampling strategy and data analysis
- Timetabling considerations
- Outputs and dissemination.

Making a case for the research

This involves familiarizing yourself with the relevant literature (which may well be quantitative as well as qualitative), identifying the gaps in the knowledge or understanding already provided by this existing body of work, and showing how your proposed study can fill this gap. You may find, on reading the literature, that although there have been several surveys carried out which have identified interesting associations between particular variables, there has been no qualitative work that has investigated the mechanisms through which these are linked. Our current proposal for a focus group study on Attention Deficit Disorder (ADHD) – sparked by an audit of prescribing practice which showed marked differences from region to region – is an example in identifying such a gap, and will, if funded, allow us to establish the processes through which guidelines and treatment decisions are interpreted and put into practice. The longitudinal study of sub-fertile couples attending a fertility clinic (which has furnished the data excerpts provided in the exercises included in Chapters 10 and 11) represented an attempt to move beyond the somewhat crude 'success rates' of fertility clinics, as measured by successful conceptions and live births. It used a series of interviews to document couples' decision-making processes as they weighed up options *en route* to personal outcomes (either in the form of a pregnancy or alternative resolution through adoption or reconciling themselves to remaining childless). Most fertility clinics triumphantly display photographs of successful happy couples with healthy babies, but do not generally portray other 'end points' to fertility treatment. Another study in which I was involved (Clark et al., 2004) outlined the evidence in relation to the benefits for patients of cardiac rehabilitation, but highlighted that while research had recorded low attendance rates, there had been little research into the ways in which personal and structural factors may combine to support or discourage attendance.

Funding bodies differ with respect to how sympathetically they are likely to view a request for resources to pursue research on a topic that fascinates you but which has, for example, little obvious relevance for clinical practice. In relation to government funding, in particular, it helps enormously if your interests coincide with a stated priority area, or recent policy initiative, and it is well worth spending time reading the research brief (if you are writing a proposal in response to a call) and looking at projects previously funded by that body. Sometimes proposals might be funded as small grants (to provide 'seed money' to allow the researcher to work up a more extensive later study), as fellowships, or as development projects (particularly where money has been set aside to build research capacity and capability among identified groups of practitioners). A study of general practitioners' (GPs') views and experiences of sickness certification (Hussey et al., 2004) was funded in the latter capacity, and allowed the team to explore an area of interest fuelled by anecdotal experience, but which had not received research attention – at least in the UK context.

Funding councils, on the other hand, are likely to look for proposals that display an in-depth knowledge of relevant theoretical frameworks and which hold promise in terms of furthering disciplinary knowledge. It is, of course, possible to work up proposals for either type of funder (and, indeed, to write up papers that address both practice and theoretical issues – often for separate journals and audiences) but getting the right emphasis is important. Matching research ideas to potential funders is, in itself, quite a skill and research units that invest in routinely providing such information as part of their infrastructure arrangements appear to have higher levels of success in securing funding.

As Janice Morse (2004) advises, in preparing a proposal for funding, it is crucial that you familiarize yourself with the relevant guidelines. It is useful to look at proposals that the particular funding body has approved, since this will give you an indication of the preferred format, style and concerns of the awarding body. Costing is also key to success here and limits on available monies may have an impact on the scale of the study planned.

The research team

Specialist – even clinical – expertise may be important in ensuring that appropriate questions are posed (both in terms of the research aims and objectives and in relation to developing relevant topic guides or interview schedules). Involvement of key representatives of the groups to be studied (whether these are professional or lay groups) may also facilitate recruitment and help inform realistic sampling strategies. Likewise a research team should ideally include an experienced qualitative researcher, who can provide reassurance to the funding body that the work – particularly data analysis – will be adequately supervised and that the project will ultimately deliver what it has promised. It is important to start such discussions with potential co-grantholders at an early stage in the process, in order to avoid 'tokenism', which can lead to later problems. This also ensures that the research question and design can take account of this specialist knowledge, so that 'ownership' and commitment is shared. It can also pay to capitalize on existing job remits, which can have the dual advantage of keeping costs down, while providing reassurance that the project will have a direct impact on practice (should this be of importance to potential funders).

A project on the introduction of methadone prescribing, for which I secured funding, along with three colleagues, was designed to elicit the views of both GPs, who had assumed this new role, and methadone users, who were on the receiving end. The background to this study is also instructive, as it illustrates the sort of environment in which health services research projects are frequently conceived and carried out. It was funded via the UK Department of Health's Mental Health Stream and was a response to a call which they put out. Although it appeared a 'bit of a long shot', we decided to pursue funding from this source as drug dependency was mentioned – albeit quite far down – on their list of potential topic areas. One of the collaborators on this project had a dual role as a university researcher and Health Authority General Practice Lead. This provided us with the opportunity of collaborating closely with the GPs involved in the study to identify specific training and support needs, with the added assurance that the Health Authority had a commitment to putting these in place. As my Health Authority co-investigator was already in post, this afforded us the possibility of carrying out relevant pilot work prior to the start of the research project *per se* (which was, in effect, an offshoot of his existing remit, which required him to consult regularly with the GPs and monitor progress) and was also instrumental in keeping costs down which may have been a factor which contributed to our bid being successful.

Making decisions about methods

Apart from the leeway still afforded in PhD studies, observational fieldwork (certainly as a stand-alone method) has latterly become less common. As Dingwall (1997: 55) reflects, 'Observational methods have suffered from the absence of powerful external sponsors'. Ethical committee requirements have exacerbated access problems through the frequent insistence that everyone involved be asked to sign a consent form (see Chapter 3). This is generally unworkable in practice and ethical considerations have also served to curtail the previously popular period of pilot fieldwork often carried out in order to firm up research questions and focus. In the current climate, I suspect that research proposals will have to provide a particularly robust defence of the decision to employ observational methods. Some aspects of professional practice or particular leisure activities, however, may only be accessible through observation and it is here that justifications of this approach are likely to be more sympathetically met. Action research projects, in particular, often offer a bit more leeway in terms of making a case for an observational component. Even if this is not explicitly stated, the nature of access involved is likely to afford similar opportunities to contextualize the data generated through other methods.

More commonly the choice will be between interviews and focus group discussions and this is a decision that exercises many qualitative researchers. Interviews are generally preferable when one is interested in eliciting individuals' narratives (i.e. when you want to locate events chronologically in their lives or treatment histories). Although many people will happily share experiences in a group setting, it can be extremely difficult to tease out individual accounts in the probably somewhat disjointed and jumbled accounts that are likely to arise in focus group discussions. Sometimes, however, focus groups are chosen not for their inherent properties, but as a perceived short-cut to what is essentially interview data, with groups being utilized in order to save time. (As outlined in Chapter 6, however, this may be a somewhat short-sighted strategy.) Some studies opt to give respondents a choice as to whether they wish to participate in one-to-one interviews or focus groups and sometimes individual interviews have to be carried out with some people due to logistical difficulties that prevent them from attending focus group sessions.

A good source in terms of helping you make the decision as to whether to use interviews or focus groups is Crabtree et al. (1993). Some researchers assume that one-to-one interviews are more appropriate for discussing 'sensitive' topics, but focus groups can provide 'safety in numbers' and, importantly, permission to talk about difficult topics in a supportive environment. It is particularly important to consider the ethical implications of bringing people together in focus groups and what the implications might be for people of acquiring what may be unwelcome or disturbing insights into the experiences of individuals in a situation that prefigures their own future (especially with regard to disease progression) or the possible impact on future relationships if the research utilizes pre-existing groups. (These considerations are all discussed in Chapter 6.) Focus groups can provide a timely means of generating data from groups who are about to be involved in an intervention study, and are valuable in accessing a particular moment in time (as did the focus groups carried out by Black and Smith (1999) – one of the papers listed in the Chapter 1 exercise – in the immediate aftermath of Princess Diana's death). You might also give some thought to employing some of the other methods outlined in Chapter 1. For example, if you are trying to access people who are spread throughout a wide geographical area, you may profitably consider utilizing telephone interviews or using teleconference facilities in order to run focus groups. (For extra considerations regarding such methods, see Chapters 5 and 6.) Whatever your decision about methods, you should explain *why* this is the most appropriate one for your study. If you decide to employ a mixed methods design, it is especially important that you explain your rationale and expand a little on how the methods will complement each other. Will they illuminate different aspects of the phenomenon under study? How will you analyze the different datasets; for example, is there potential to develop a shared coding frame? (For more detailed advice on designing mixed methods studies see Chapter 7.)

Sampling strategy and data analysis

While qualitative proposals should avoid talking about 'response rates' and thereby inviting unwelcome questions about 'representativeness' and 'bias', it is important that you show you have given some thought as to potential difficulties involved in recruitment.

For example, if you want to include people who may be out of touch with services, you should give some consideration to strategies such as 'snowball sampling' (using respondents' own networks) or perhaps placing adverts in local newspapers. Detailed advice on sampling is provided later in this chapter and data analysis is the subject of Chapters 9, 10 and 11, which also provide several exercises). However, in line with the advice above on emphasizing the strengths rather than potential weaknesses of qualitative research, you should indicate in your research proposal how your sampling strategy will enhance the comparative potential of your dataset. The 'technical fixes' often borrowed from the various checklists discussed in Chapter 1 should be referenced only with extreme caution. If you are going to say that you intend to recruit a 'purposive' or 'theoretical' sample (discussed below, but essentially referring to selecting participants on the basis of characteristics or attributes likely to be relevant and give rise to differing accounts) you need to provide some more information. You should give some indication of the characteristics and diversity you wish to cover and how you intend to use this *purposefully* (Barbour, 2001) to make comparisons and identify patterns in your data. Likewise, you would be well advised to refrain from saying that your data 'will be analyzed by computer', or even that you will 'use the constant comparative method', unless you give some examples of the sorts of comparison you might make. You should also provide some reassurance that rigour will be applied to developing an appropriate coding frame (including how you propose to go about revising this) and that you will systematically and thoroughly interrogate your data. (See, in particular the exercise at the end of Chapter 10 with regard to this issue.)

Timetabling considerations

Most grant proposal forms ask applicants to provide a timetable, which should show that the project is achievable within the time period involved. Even if you are not asked to provide this, drafting a timetable provides an object lesson in matching aspirations with resources – both in terms of researchers' capabilities, expertise and time commitments and the amount of funding available. (I have not discussed the costing of research proposals under a separate heading, but it is important to bear this in mind, costing adequately for transcription, for example, and for travel to research team meetings as well as journeys involved in generating data.) With qualitative research a key factor is allowing sufficient time for transcription (if required) and analysis. You will need to decide whether it is most important to produce timely findings or to develop sophisticated theoretical explanations. Although the two are not necessarily mutually exclusive aims, many researchers find themselves writing up their more theoretical papers months and sometimes years after the official funding period has come to an end. This is especially true for contract researchers, whose situation is vividly described by Goode (2006). Nowadays, dissemination is often included on proposal forms and it is important to fit this around the pressing deadline for the final report.

The project on the introduction of methadone prescribing was a very short one and it was funded for only six months out of the total nine months allocated to the work. This is quite different from standard academic research projects, and sticking to time was only possible through employing standardized pro-formas and enhanced case records, with analysis of interview transcripts (16 with GPs, 25 with methadone users) relying on a combination of full transcription (for sections of specific interest) and systematic notes (for others). The grant-holders were all involved in this process, together with the dedicated research assistant (who carried out interviews with the methadone users) but time was still very tight. The funding body's application form invited us to specify 'Key milestones in the duration of the research' under the headings of 'month', 'activity', and 'criteria for measuring success'. In other words, a timetable with objectives and continuous evaluation of progress. The table which we included in the grant application is shown in Table 2.1.

Outputs and dissemination

When writing health services research proposals I have to confess that this is the section when I am most in need of input from my clinical colleagues. Of course, the anticipated output will vary depending on the funding body and its agenda. Some research, particularly that done by practitioners, is likely to make detailed recommendations for improving practice and many projects have implications for the content of training provision. Depending on the focus of the study, recommendations can, of course, also relate to providing support for patients or clients, and their relatives or carers. Outputs can be a template or model for practice, a plan for a later intervention study, a structured measuring scale, or a questionnaire for use in a later study. Not all studies, however, are required to furnish 'recommendations' for practice and may, instead, concentrate on demonstrating the transferability (or 'theoretical generalizability' (see Chapter 11)) of the findings. In some cases refinement or revision of a theoretical framework might be seen as ample justification for the period of funding. Although it is tempting to promise the earth in order to secure funding, it is important not to provide 'hostages to fortune' here too. It is certainly worth revisiting the funding brief (if there is one) or looking at the recommendations made in previously published papers. As with all pieces of writing, don't forget to read and re-read your own proposal, as it is important not to 'miss a trick' in terms of preparing the ground for your 'outputs' in the earlier part of your proposal.

Many funding applications now ask for details of proposed dissemination, but, even where they do not, it is worth considering this issue as it will help you in formulating your 'outputs'. Some funding bodies are also keen for applicants to show how they plan to involve participants in the design of the study – and sometimes in analysis of data – in which case dissemination is likely to be an ongoing process throughout the

Table 2.1   Key milestones in the duration of the research

Month	Activity	Criteria for measuring success
	Pilot work	
1	Discussions with GPs	Achieving co-operation
	Production of consultation	Obtaining GP input into this activity
	monitoring pro-formas	Involving GPs in this activity and securing their
	Development of enhanced case records	co-operation in completing these
2–3	Initial interviews with GPs	Gaining access to carry out interviews
	Preliminary analysis of GP interviews	Continued return of pro-formas by GPs
	Continuation of monitoring exercise	
3	Initial feedback on findings on service	Analysis of pro-formas and production of an
	uptake	interim report
	Introduction of enhanced case records	Continued engagement of GPs
	Development of interview schedule for	Recruitment of Research Assistant
	use with methadone users	
	Funded project	
4–7	Interviews with methadone users	Appointment and training of RA
	Development of interview schedule for	Gaining access to users via GP surgeries
	follow-up interviews with GPs	Obtaining users' consent to carry out
		interviews
		Identification of common themes and emergent
		issues
4–5	Feedback on findings on service	
	uptake	
4–8	Ongoing monitoring of service uptake	Cumulative analysis of pro-formas and
	Continuation of enhanced case records	continued return of pro-formas by GPs
	exercise	Continued return of enhanced case records
		by GPs
5–6	Preliminary analysis of interviews with	Transcription of tapes/identification of key
	methadone users	themes
		Maintaining access and engagement of GPs
6–7	Follow-up interviews with GPs	
7–8	Further feedback on service uptake	
	Cumulative analysis of monitoring	
	pro-formas	
7–8	Further analysis of GP and methadone	Production of final report
	user interviews	
9	Dissemination sessions	Attendance of GPs at dissemination sessions

duration of the research. It is still important, however, to consider how to share your findings with a wider community, including that accessed via academic conferences and publications. Not all funding bodies, however, allow for inclusion of travel and expenses in order to allow conference attendance, so it is important to consider these under costings.

SAMPLING: WHO TO STUDY AND IN WHICH CONTEXT?

Much early qualitative research focused on selecting a setting that afforded potential for exploring the issue central to research interests and relied on convenience sampling. My own study of social work training focused on the experiences of one cohort of students on one accredited social work course, selected due to its location in the university where I was registered as a PhD student. However, there was little to suggest that this course, or the students involved, were atypical (see further discussion below). Many other qualitative studies have relied on chance (for example recruiting consecutive clinic patients) in order to provide a range of interviewees or observational opportunities. For some hard-to-reach populations, researchers have employed 'snowball sampling', which capitalizes on the networks of a few key interviewees or focus group participants in order to recruit others who share some of their characteristics.

Latterly, qualitative researchers have become a little more strategic in their sampling, with many studies using 'purposive' or 'theoretical' sampling. Although some researchers distinguish between the two, I do not find this particularly helpful and am in accord with Mason (1996), who discusses these under the same heading. Essentially this approach to sampling relies on selecting interviewees or focus group participants by virtue of characteristics thought by the researcher to be likely to have some bearing on their perceptions and experiences – for example, that women may provide accounts that focus on issues not of salience to men, or that older people may be concerned about different aspects of treatment, communication, safety (or whatever topic the research involves). This involves the researcher in 'theorizing' – albeit at a very basic level – since at this stage it involves little more than surmise (unless, of course, quantitative studies have already identified significant variables which might also be profitable for investigation using other methods). For those researchers who do opt to differentiate between 'purposive' and 'theoretical' sampling, the sorts of decisions described so far would probably be labelled as 'purposive', with the description of 'theoretical' sampling being reserved for further sampling carried out once the research is under way and fieldwork suggests that other attributes of individuals or groups might be relevant. An example might be where a project begins to untangle differences in orientation (for example religious affiliations or attitudes towards risk) that appear to give rise to varying perspectives. This might lead to renewed efforts to recruit members of particular religious communities or, perhaps, people who engage in extreme sports.

Attempts to differentiate between 'purposive' and 'theoretical' sampling, however, serve only to emphasize the extent to which the distinction is inevitably blurred: some of this 'second-stage' sampling relies heavily on demographic characteristics, while other strategies adopted 'on the hoof' reflect more substantive theoretical concerns, and some initial sampling categories reflect fairly sophisticated theoretical concepts. Glaser and Strauss (1967), writing in the context of more generous funding in terms of the time available for research projects, recommended returning to the field as part and parcel of such secondary sampling strategies designed to encourage 'saturation'. It is not just time constraints that make this difficult in today's research climate; it may also be impossible to extend sampling to cover groups not originally identified in applications for ethical approval (see Chapter 3). However (as I have argued at greater length in Chapter 6), focus groups can provide valuable opportunities for effective and illuminating second-stage sampling, not through recruiting people who would otherwise have been left out of the study, but by configuring group membership in new ways. In our study of GPs' views and experiences of sickness certification (Hussey et al., 2004) we convened a second set of focus groups with three separate grades of GPs (GP registrars; GP principals and GP locums) in order to interrogate our hunch (from the first five focus groups involving a mixture of grades) that additional issues arose for doctors occupying these roles with slightly different remits and responsibilities.

The goal of qualitative sampling is not to produce a representative sample, but is rather to reflect diversity (Kuzel, 1992; Mays and Pope, 1995) and to provide as much potential for comparison as possible. A former PhD student (Brown, 2003) wanted to interview men who had recently experienced a heart attack. She used a short questionnaire, distributed via general practices, in order to furnish a sampling pool of potential respondents for the qualitative component of her study. Among the demographic details collected via this form, she had asked for details of the men's age and this identified two men under the age of 40 years and one man who was 85 years of age. Had she been concerned with recruiting a representative sample she would have excluded these three individuals, since they fell outside the 'normal distribution'. However, since this was a qualitative study seeking to maximize diversity, she opted to invite all three men to take part in interviews. The interviews were illuminating, in that they identified concerns and issues that exercised all three of these 'outliers' (underlining the commonalities of the sample as a whole) as well as highlighting specific concerns and issues (showing how their peculiar circumstances gave rise either to additional problems or placed these higher on their list of priorities).

As you draw up your research plan and even as you are involved in generating data, you should be asking 'Who might I be leaving out?', 'Might there be other types of people or other situations that are likely to give rise to differing experiences, perspectives or issues that are of relevance to my research question?' It is well worth considering how you could capitalize on the insights of those who are marginal to a situation, making more explicit the implicit use by anthropologists of 'key informants'. Depending on your research context, such individuals could be those who have left a religious sect (apostates) or those who have recently retired from a profession or work group. Like the 'outs' described by Dean et al. (1967) and cited by Hammersley and Atkinson (1995: 138), such individuals 'may have lost power, but are still "in the know"' and can provide potentially unique contextualized insights.

Many textbooks and published papers invoke the concept of 'saturation' mentioned in Glaser and Strauss' (1967) highly influential book – in relation to both sampling and developing coding categories. Essentially, this involves the assertion that the researcher or research team have sampled all the relevant characteristics or settings, providing reassurance that they have kept going until they have thought of all possible avenues to pursue. Ritchie et al. provide a more pragmatic version which suggests how the concept can be applied in the real world of qualitative sampling. They describe this stage as 'a point of diminishing return where increasing the sample size no longer contributes new evidence' (2003: 83). I have often thought that asserting that saturation has been reached is a somewhat bold claim and perhaps a bit of a 'hostage to fortune'. Melia (1997) refreshingly comments that some of the passages in *The Discovery of Grounded Theory* (Glaser and Strauss, 1967) have a somewhat mystical character to them.

Rather than taking refuge in the esoteric, a more structured approach can sometimes be helpful in drawing up sampling strategies for qualitative research. In order to sample effectively so that you maximize the possibilities for comparison, a detailed knowledge of the setting involved can pay enormous dividends. The sampling strategy for TOPAZ (Termination of Pregnancy Project), which is discussed in more detail in Chapter 3 in relation to Ethics, depended on the researcher acquiring a detailed knowledge of how the service operated, the sites involved, the process involved from assessment to TOP, and the clinical procedures available to women undergoing a termination of pregnancy. Two main options were involved, and were partly determined by the gestation: medical and surgical termination. Medical termination involved the insertion of a prostaglandin pessary, which caused the uterus to contract, with the foetus being expelled through the birth canal (as in a regular delivery). Surgical termination, on the other hand, involved evacuation of the uterus while the woman was under general anaesthetic. A chart detailing the stages and options involved in termination of pregnancy was a useful aid to sampling (see Figure 2.1).

Using this chart to guide sampling, we were able to achieve a sample which took into consideration the various stages (and therefore type of involvement of staff members) and allowed us to compare the effect that their own experiences had on their views (see box).

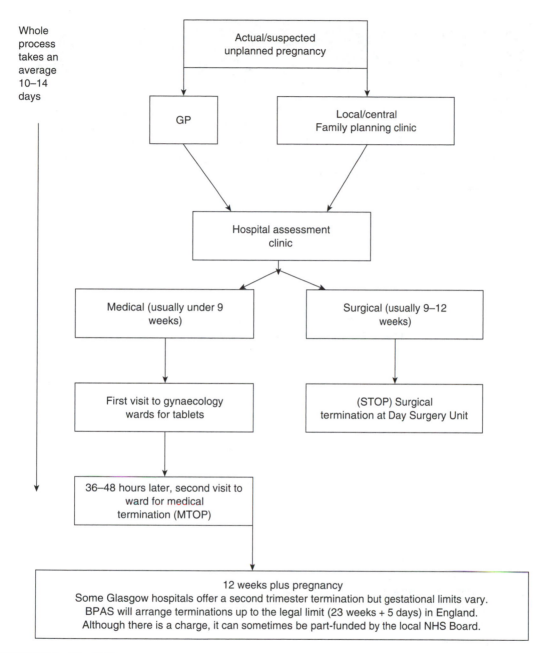

Whole process takes an average 10–14 days

Actual/suspected unplanned pregnancy

GP

Local/central Family planning clinic

Hospital assessment clinic

Medical (usually under 9 weeks)

Surgical (usually 9–12 weeks)

First visit to gynaecology wards for tablets

(STOP) Surgical termination at Day Surgery Unit

36–48 hours later, second visit to ward for medical termination (MTOP)

12 weeks plus pregnancy
Some Glasgow hospitals offer a second trimester termination but gestational limits vary.
BPAS will arrange terminations up to the legal limit (23 weeks + 5 days) in England.
Although there is a charge, it can sometimes be part-funded by the local NHS Board.

FIGURE 2.1   The TOP process

Reproduced by permission of the Family Planning Association (Kennedy, 2002).

NB: This diagram represents the organization of services in one locality at one specific point in time and should not be read as a more general template for the provision of termination of pregnancy services.

SAMPLING OUTCOMES FOR THE TOP STUDY

We managed to recruit 40 women (an average of seven per hospital site) with a variety of experiences (11 of whom had undergone previous terminations). Only nine women were interviewed after a significant time had elapsed since their termination, as follow-up proved difficult or impossible in most cases, particularly as the study had to be completed within a 12-month period (with interviews being carried out during months 3–10). However, those with experience of previous terminations were able to provide a retrospective account, in addition to reflecting on their experiences of care so far in relation to their current TOP. Our interview sample was as follows:

- 19 medical terminations of pregnancy (including two second trimester MTOPs)
- 20 surgical terminations of pregnancy (including two women who had to have surgical evacuations after failed MTOPs)
- 1 woman who attended the assessment clinic but then decided to continue with the pregnancy (with support from the hospital social worker)

Recruitment of professionals was also informed by the diagram of service provision. We collected the views of over 80 members of staff across the seven sites, using a mixture of focus groups, group interviews and individual interviews, as follows:

- 11 staff involved at the referral stage (in general practice or family planning)
- 21 staff involved in assessment clinics
- 26 working in Day Surgery (the STOP service)
- 19 working on gynaecology wards (the MTOP service)
- 9 with a post-TOP role (for example GPs, counsellors, social workers)

We had also to pay attention to the roles and levels of experience of staff we recruited in order to ensure a range in terms of our coverage. We spoke to:

- 19 gynaecology nurses
- 7 hospital consultants
- 8 family planning clinic staff
- 5 medical members of staff working at assessment clinics
- 4 hospital social work staff providing counselling to assessment clinics
- 4 counsellors (British Pregnancy Advisory Service and family planning)
- 4 other members of staff working at assessment clinics as nurses, auxiliaries or administrators
- 3 GPs (one in an affluent area and the other two in deprived areas)
- 2 senior house officers on gynaecology rotation
- 1 chaplain

NB: these numbers do not add up as several individuals had more than one role.

An added advantage deriving from our attention to the staged process and organization of termination services was the insights it provided with regard to making sense of staff options. Viewing the process as a complex set of procedures alerted us to the range of possible choices open to staff. Rather than simply options for or against involvement in terminations, there was a variety of responses and individuals weighed these up, sometimes coming to highly individualized compromises, whereby they could participate in procedures to a degree while maintaining their personal ethical standpoints. This illuminated for us the situation of the Specialist Registrar, who worked at an assessment clinic but opted not to carry out surgical terminations of pregnancy, and also the nurse, who was willing to insert a prostaglandin pessary to set the procedure in motion but who was not prepared to assist in surgical procedures.

It does not matter how well you have thought through your sampling strategies, successful recruitment is another matter and several commentators have highlighted how even individuals recruiting patients into randomized controlled trials can inadvertently or deliberately sabotage attempts at blinding (for example Schulz, 1995). We do often have to rely on gatekeepers to identify and sometimes to approach potential research participants on our behalf. These individuals may impose their own idiosyncratic sampling strategies – either intentionally or unintentionally – which may prevent us from accessing some people to whom we would like to speak. Even this need not be completely disastrous, however. Delamont (2004: 225) reminds us that failed access attempts are also data and this applies to attempts to influence our sampling procedures.

Collaborations with practitioners, however, can sometimes afford us the relative luxury of access to a sampling pool, as was the case with a study of patients' experiences of weight management in one general practice (Guthrie and Barbour, 2002). Working closely with the practice manager the two non-clinical researchers were provided with anonymized patient details. This information allowed us to select (from a potential pool of 240 people who had been on the receiving end of such interventions over the previous two years) individuals to be invited to take part in our study. Letters were sent by the practice manager and, by prior agreement, the GP co-grant-holder was not told which patients had been invited to participate. We wished to recruit a spread of patients (in relation to age, gender, socio-economic circumstances and the weight management intervention in which they had been involved) and the research team produced a 'sampling grid', which we updated in the light of replies from patients.

SAMPLING GRIDS

Where possible (i.e. where we had a choice between potential interviewees, as determined by their practice-held anonymized notes) we selected men and women of varying ages and socio-economic status (assigning people, as far as was possible, to the Registrar General's classifications of Social Class I or II, Social Class III, and Social

Class IV/V). We also sought to cover differing obesity profiles and were successful in recruiting individuals in each of the three categories of overweight, obese and morbidly obese (as measured when they embarked on the relevant weight management programme). As the majority of patients recruited to our study were obese, however, I have not shown their weight profiles on the grid reproduced here (Table 2.2).

Table 2.2   Sampling grid for weight management study

Age	Men			Women		
	SC I & II	**SC III**	**SC IV & V**	**SC I & II**	**SC III**	**SC IV & V**
Over 65 years	–	1	2	–	–	2
46–65 years	2	1	2	3	2	1
30–45 years	–	1	2	–	2	2
Under 30 years	–	–	–	–	–	–
Sub-total	2	3	6	3	4	5
Total	11 men			12 women		

The number of letters sent out exceeded the number of interviews we hoped to carry out, leaving us some room for manoeuvre in that we could, in theory, be selective should we receive more replies than required. Table 2.2 provides details of our final interview sample, but along the way we produced several interim grids which recorded our progress and identified gaps in recruitment.

Notably absent from our final grid are individuals under 30 years of age. We became aware of this omission (and that of people in their 50s, which is not shown on the grid) in the course of recruitment for the study. We were not too bothered by the lack of individuals in their 50s, partly because there were not a huge number in the sampling pool, but also because we were able to recruit people in their 40s and 60s. However, we were concerned about the non-response from people in the youngest age band and sought to augment our sample by targeting this age group with our invitation letters. This, however, produced no volunteers, so we concluded that we would simply have to be philosophical about this, acknowledge this shortcoming in our final report, and settle for retrospective accounts from older people about their experience of obesity and weight management when in their 30s or younger.

What, hopefully, the sampling grid illustrates is the number of 'balls' that the 'purposive qualitative sampler' has to keep in the air at any one time. However, it is important not to get too carried away by this process. We can all sit in our offices and draw up neat sampling diagrams, only to find that it is impossible to achieve our desired diversity of respondents, often due to factors beyond our control. It is certainly not necessary to fill (or, indeed, utilize in the analysis) all the cells in a sampling grid – a misconception that still sometimes exercises ethics committees – but it can still be worthwhile attempting to do so. It is important to realize that each individual fits into the grid in relation to a large number of variables. Neither is it necessary to have large numbers in any one cell, because, during the process of analysis, we will generally be making broader comparisons: comparing all men with all women; all obese people with all morbidly obese people and so on. At the very least, though, the process of compiling a sampling grid can provide further insights, as we come to realize that our carefully thought-out categories are not as straightforward as we had imagined when we compiled them at our desks in a spirit of idealized anticipation prior to confronting the 'real world' of our research setting.

One of our aims in carrying out this piece of research was to compare patients' experiences of different types of weight management intervention. Although we did ask patients about their experiences and views of the relative merits of a range of weight management programmes, interventions are not used in the sampling grid, because we soon discovered from practice records that many patients had participated in more than one. Our final sample of 23 patients, it transpired, had participated in a total of 48 interventions at some point in the past two years (see Table 2.3).

Table 2.3   Participation of patients in different types of weight management interventions

Type of intervention	No. of patients interviewed
Exercise referral	18
Sessions with dietician	12
Advice at specialist clinics	5
Men's group	4
Women's group	1
Commercial slimming programmes	8

Information about specialist clinics and commercial slimming programmes was not collected until the interviews were carried out, but interview schedules were flexible enough to allow us to generate data regarding patients' experiences and perceptions of these in addition to the interventions that we knew to have been provided within the general practice where the research was carried out.

A further sampling ambition of the researchers had been to recruit patients who had been successful in terms of losing weight, in order to compare their views and experiences with those of their unsuccessful counterparts. However, even a cursory look at practice records confirmed that this was an unrealistic aim, as it proved very difficult, in practice, to define what counted as 'success'. The final sample included seven patients who were still engaged in trying to lose weight; six who had lost weight over the past two years, but who had subsequently regained it; five who had lost and regained weight several times; and five who had lost weight and maintained this. Again, although we had the opportunity to make comparisons between patients, the picture was much more complex than we had at first envisaged. This, however, is data in its own right.

A sampling grid, then, should be seen as a potential tool to aid us in thinking through our sampling choices and decisions rather than being used as an immutable template.

CASE STUDIES

Although the case study approach has a long history in social science research (see Platt, 1992) many researchers have relied heavily on the guidance provided by Yin (1994). This has often resulted in a somewhat rigid application that fails to take account of the potential flexibility afforded by case studies. It is far more important to question the purpose of your research and whether a case study design might help you to interrogate your data than it is to pore over Yin's writings and agonize as to whether your study is or is not a 'real case study'. Sometimes this can unwittingly provide a diversionary activity that prevents researchers from getting on with generating their data. Rather than becoming immobilized by what may ultimately be an unfruitful debate, destined to reach no meaningful conclusion, I would urge you, instead, to think carefully about what using cases might help you to achieve in the context of your research project and, even more importantly, on what basis to select your 'cases'.

It is for this reason that I have chosen to discuss 'case studies' under the general heading of 'sampling'. This is, of course, at variance with how Yin himself sees the case study approach. He has stated that the case study. 'does not represent a sample, and in doing a case study, your goal will be to expand and generalize theories and not to enumerate frequencies' (Yin, 1994: 3). However, this reflects a somewhat limited view of qualitative sampling. While quantitative sampling has the goal of establishing frequencies and allowing us to examine the relationships between frequencies and different variables to identify statistically significant associations, qualitative sampling has an entirely different purpose. If we understand sampling as a means of ensuring comparative potential, and enhancing thereby analytic potential and the ability to interrogate and even build theory, then, I would argue, it is probably most helpful to consider case study designs under the general rubric of sampling. Locating 'case studies' within the context of sampling allows us to gain an understanding of their potential and how we might harness this most effectively.

Even selecting a setting in which to carry out a piece of qualitative research involves us in initial theorizing as to why this setting is of research interest: what are its properties and capacity to illuminate the phenomenon that we are interested in studying? Stake (1995) distinguishes between what he calls 'intrinsic' case studies, which focus on studying one instance in its own right, and 'instrumental' case studies, where specific cases are selected in order to allow us to study more general principles and phenomena. Although this may be helpful in characterizing different orientations at the outset of a research project, in practice, as the project unfolds and especially as analysis is carried out and an explanatory account is developed, I would argue that this distinction becomes blurred.

In most studies there is likely to be some attempt to place information derived in this one 'intrinsic' setting into the wider context. For example, throughout the period of my postdoctoral fieldwork I wrestled with concerns as to the 'typicality' of the social work course and students that I had opportunistically selected for study. I concluded:

There is, of course, no guarantee that my ready-made sample of students was representative of the social work student body as a whole. However, conversely, neither was there any reason to suppose that it was unique. Certainly members of staff informed the researcher constantly throughout the project that this particular cohort of students being studied was 'atypical'. I consider, however, that this comment was as much a product of fear about what the researcher might reveal as it was a product of concern for the rigour of my research methods. When I did distribute a questionnaire to the following intake of students, judged by staff to be more similar to their usual 'type of student', I found little difference between their ideas about social work on entering the course and those of the preceding year's students. They also gave similar reasons for their choice of career. (Barbour, 1983: 6)

I also interrogated this issue of 'typicality' by drawing on other empirical studies of social work training in particular, and professional training in general. I sought, too, to make implicit comparisons between social work and other occupations, using available literature on the sociology of the professions. Thus, 'intrinsic' and 'instrumental' case studies can, in effect, be used to similar ends. As Stake (1995: 16) explains: 'We want to appreciate the uniqueness and complexity of the case, its embeddedness and interaction with contexts. Hypotheses and goal statements sharpen the focus, minimizing the interest in the situation and circumstance.' By this, I suggest that he is talking about the value of the case not in its own right, but in terms of its capacity to illuminate. I'm not sure how helpful it is to become embroiled in discussions as to the differences between and the relative merits of 'intrinsic' and 'instrumental' case studies. Perhaps more important is the quality of the theoretical insights which they allow us, as researchers, to derive. I have similar reservations regarding the helpfulness of Yin's (1994) typology of case study designs, including 'single', 'multiple', 'holistic' and 'embedded' designs. Those aspects which make a single case study seem worthwhile – its capacity to illuminate the phenomenon we wish to study – can also be powerful incentives for selecting multiple cases.

There is no doubt that employing case studies can be extremely useful in terms of enhancing the comparative, and thus analytic, potential of our research. If we manage not to be daunted by the seemingly endless possibilities or coerced by potentially prescriptive advice, there is plenty of scope for innovation. In relation to quantitative research designs, Crombie with Davies (1996) discusses the potential of case control studies. This can profitably be translated into qualitative research designs. I recently talked to a colleague about her study of service provision for elderly patients with cancer. She had decided to employ a case study design and was involved in selecting specialist and generic settings to act as 'cases' for her research. She might also consider, however, using patients as cases, through identifying patients with similar characteristics and diagnoses but being treated in different ward settings. In some studies, of course, sampling can be serendipitously augmented, as when we discover an individual who has had experience of both settings we are interested in studying. We cannot, however, rely on luck, and thinking creatively about creating as well as identifying 'cases' can be useful in furnishing potential for comparison.

HINTS ON PLANNING YOUR RESEARCH DESIGN

In planning your research design ask yourself the following questions:

- Why do you want to do the study? *Personal interests? Desire to change practice? Desire to challenge policies? Theoretical interests?*
- What exactly is it that interests you? *Which people are you most interested in talking to? How would you access and approach them? How will you ensure the diversity and comparative potential of your sample?*
- Why is a qualitative approach appropriate?
- Who will be in your research team and how can you draw on this as a resource?
- What are the limitations and possibilities of the methods available? *Which method or combination of methods would be most appropriate? What challenges will this method or combination of methods pose?*
- How will you analyze your data?

FURTHER READING

Marshall, C. and Rossman, G.B. (1995) *Designing Qualitative Research* (2nd edition), London: Sage.

EXERCISE: FORMULATING AND REFINING RESEARCH QUESTIONS AND MAKING DECISIONS ABOUT APPROPRIATE METHODS

Select one (or more) of potential research questions listed below and think about how you would go about developing a research proposal around it. (Alternatively, you may already have your own research question in mind, and may wish to use this for this exercise.) Ask yourself:

- Which aspects of this broad question might you choose to investigate? (i.e. what interests you?)
- How might you revise/narrow down the research question?
- Who would you want to talk to and what would you ask them?
- How might you access such people/groups?
- What methods would you employ?

Potential research questions

1 **Do people view risk differently when they travel?**
2 **Are our notions shifting with regard to how long we think adolescence lasts?**
3 **What impact does media coverage of fertility treatment have on public perceptions of appropriate provision?**
4 **What do people think about fathers' attendance at deliveries?**
5 **What are the challenges of parenting?**

NB: You might want to delay reading the accompanying commentaries and consult these only when you have spent some time thinking about your potential response. Alternatively, you may wish to read one of the first commentaries to give you an idea of the sort of considerations that are involved and then engage with thinking about research design issues in relation to one of the other potential research questions.

Commentaries

Potential research question 1: Do people view risk differently when they travel?
Depending on your own disciplinary background and interests (whether this is travel medicine, tourism studies, sociology of risk, or economics) you may choose to approach this question very differently.

Your interests, for example, may be related to immunization and knowledge of specific health risks, in which case you could select a particular range of destinations. In this case, you might consider collaborating with travel medicine specialists in order to work up a proposal around this question.

Alternatively, you might be wishing to explore fears of terrorism post 9/11, in which case you might wish to compare American travellers with others (although in the wake of the London bombings you might also wish to look at English travellers, or at least those in the London area).

Among other possibilities you might think about contacting (via a travel agent) respondents who have booked package holidays (including perhaps adventure holidays). However, with so many people now booking travel independently via websites, you might consider other sampling strategies in order to access a wider range of travellers, such as independent travellers or gap-year students. You might also think about conducting interviews at an airport (thinking about capitalizing on seasonal variations in order to recruit different sorts of traveller, for example avoiding or utilizing school holiday periods, depending on which groups you are interested in).

Potential research question 2: Are our notions shifting with regard to how long we think adolescence lasts?

There are many ways in which you could approach this question. Again, depending on your own disciplinary focus, you might want to explore how this issue translates into specific contexts, such as the criminal justice system and sentencing, health or social care provision and the transition from child to adult services, or even educational models.

You might decide not to generate your own data, but to rely on media coverage, such as newspaper reports, television, or even problem pages. Alternatively, you could select observational fieldwork, interviews or focus groups in order to elicit people's perspectives. You might want to concentrate on the views of young people themselves, or you might want to talk to parents or other individuals, such as college or university lecturers, social workers, clinical psychologists or psychiatrists, who have professional contact with young adults.

Potential research question 3: What impact does media coverage of fertility treatment have on public perceptions of appropriate provision?

Your focus here might be on the social policy implications, funding decisions or, perhaps, the response to same-sex couples.

It is unlikely that merely looking at media coverage and analyzing its content would answer your question. However, you could still utilize pre-existing sources of data, by drawing on letters pages of newspapers or magazines, concentrating on the period immediately after a feature on this topic. Existing online discussion groups might also be a fruitful source of data, although these are likely to be run by groups with vested interests or particular 'axes to grind'.

You might choose to generate your own data, using interviews or focus groups, or you might even decide to set up your own online discussion group for research purposes (see the discussion in **Chapter 13** about uses of the internet).

Potential research question 4: What do people think about fathers' attendance at deliveries?

Rather than focusing on the general public you could decide to carry out observational fieldwork, particularly if you are interested in professional practice in maternity units. You could also use interviews or focus groups – perhaps to explore the intentions of couples expecting a first baby, as I did in an earlier interview study (Barbour, 1989, which also draws on observational fieldwork in labour wards, carried out as part of a bigger study of midwives' roles and responsibilities). If you are interested in discourses that are appealed to and created by different groups, you might want to carry out discourse analysis of naturally occurring discussions – perhaps at state-provided parentcraft classes or National Childbirth classes, which tend to attract couples of differing socio-economic backgrounds. (This is the topic involved in the exercise at the end of Chapter 6, which encourages you to generate your own data using focus groups.)

Potential research question 5: What are the challenges of parenting?
Although you might choose to focus on those about to become parents, I suspect that you are more likely to opt to study those who are actively engaged in parenting at the moment. You would have to decide which age groups you want to access – pre-school, 5–12 year olds, or perhaps adolescents? However, you might be interested in exploring the different perceptions of young (as compared to older) parents, or even grandparents who have assumed parenting responsibilities. The most likely sources for recruitment would probably be via schools or community groups. You might also want to think about including parents who educate their children at home or travellers whose children may attend particular schools only intermittently.

In the field, you are likely to discover that many people will have children of varying ages and that parenting even of young children is likely to involve anticipation of later stages. It would be a pity not to capitalize on this in-built comparative potential. One workshop focus group session yielded several participants who were grandparents and you might even think about including grandparents, particularly if you are interested in how ideas differ between the generations.

Your interest might be in parents dealing with particular health or behavioural problems affecting their children or themselves, and hence their capacity to parent. This might involve recruiting parents via clinics or specialist services.

3
ETHICS

AIMS

- This chapter provides detailed guidance on meeting the requirements of the ethical review process.
- It helps the researcher to understand the concerns that underpin ethical committees by providing a short history of the development of ethical review.
- It equips the reader to anticipate the ethical issues that are likely to arise in a range of projects using different approaches (including action research) and to take steps to minimize potential problems.
- Some hints are also provided with regard to responding to ethical dilemmas as these arise in the field, although it is emphasized that it is not possible to prepare in advance for all that is likely to arise as the research unfolds.
- It also encourages the researcher to consider carefully the likely impact on the researcher and to take steps to promote a safe and supportive environment.

INTRODUCTION

Recent developments surrounding 'research governance' have led to an even greater focus on the ethics of qualitative research, particularly in the field of health-related research. However, the whole research endeavour is characterized by a growing concern with accountability and the need to justify one's research design choices and the conduct of research to ever-widening audiences, including users, carers and research respondents. The implications for the future of research practice, and indeed the sorts of question which researchers will be allowed to address, will be discussed. Advice will be provided on how to tackle some of the questions which you are likely to be asked in relation to ethical issues.

Ethical considerations include paying attention to the way in which the research is presented to potential participants, the likely impact of taking part in research (both for individuals and pre-existing groups), the effect of sampling strategies, engaging with the researcher (and other participants) and dissemination sessions. Although this chapter is concerned primarily with the ethical issues which need to be taken into consideration in planning research, making initial decisions about research design and securing ethical approval, these should be considered throughout the research process. The role of gatekeepers will also be discussed, along with the perennial concerns surrounding 'informed' and 'process' consent. The chapter considers the ethical issues which require attention at the outset of a project, but it stresses the importance of engaging with further ethical issues that arise, including taking into account the possible impact on the researchers and ensuring safety during fieldwork encounters.

Mention ethics committees at any informal gathering of qualitative researchers and you are almost certain to generate impassioned accounts and even horror stories. It is easy to cast such bodies as the enemies of research informed by our own disciplinary concerns and to dismiss their knowledge of the qualitative research process. Indeed, I have my own store of horror stories, not least the difficulty that many ethics committees appear to have with regard to understanding the principles of purposive sampling and related misconceptions about 'representativeness'. While some responses are clearly based on a lack of understanding of the qualitative research endeavour, ethics committees do sometimes make valid points that cause us to rethink our research designs and help us to produce more robust plans.

Perhaps the tenet of many ethics committee members that 'badly designed research is unethical research' is the one that pushes the most 'buttons' for qualitative researchers. Having gone through what is usually a rigorous process of peer review as part of the procedures of grant-awarding bodies, this often seems another hurdle too many. Research design decisions are, however, inextricably bound up with ethical, and indeed political, issues, and on occasion an ethics committee might well highlight implications that have escaped the researcher, who is usually (in this age where grant income counts towards promotion prospects) only too relieved to have secured the funding. Funding bodies – often government agencies – are not immune from such pressures and may well fund studies with a strategic eye on how findings can be used as political gambits. While funding bodies may want a piece of research to be done very quickly in order to inform policy developments, ethics committees can sound a note of caution and force researchers to come up with research designs that are better thought-through and more likely to stand the test of time, which if not in the immediate interests of funding bodies certainly is likely to do more for our research careers.

A SHORT HISTORY OF QUALITATIVE RESEARCH AND ETHICAL APPROVAL PROCEDURES

'The bad old days'?

Until relatively recently qualitative research was not routinely scrutinized by ethics committees. When, as a matter of course, we submitted our proposal for our study of midwives' roles and responsibilities to the local ethics committee in 1983, the reply which arrived more or less said, 'I don't know why you've sent this to us. It doesn't involve any clinical interventions, so go ahead.' In other words, 'Don't call us, we'll call you!'

Following some well-publicized cases which led to public outcry and concerns about unethical practices, there can be little doubt that social science research needed to be subjected to some sort of scrutiny. The obedience experiments of Milgram (1963) have passed into the history books by virtue both of the issues raised by the deceit of participants and the uncomfortable findings that suggest that the division between a regular person following orders and a wicked torturer is not perhaps as clear as we would all like to think. Part of the concern about such studies, understandably, is the disrespect with which they appear to treat the people who have been recruited 'in good faith', only to be unmasked and criticized for something which they had not appreciated was part of the original research focus. Although here the research subjects *were* aware that they had entered into a contract, the nature of that contract was deliberately concealed from them, which gave rise to concerns about what exactly 'consent' to take part in a study implies.

Another frequently quoted piece of research which raises important ethical issues was the study carried out by Rosenhan (1973) with the title 'On being sane in insane places'. This study produced a fulsome critique of professional practice and could be viewed as part of that stable of research aiming to side with the 'underdog' (Becker, 1967) – on this occasion in the context of studying the patient experience of psychiatric care. While it undoubtedly produced findings that were useful in understanding how mental health diagnostic labels, including that of 'schizophrenia', were socially constructed, the study raised some ethical issues. This was mainly due to its reliance on covert observational research in US psychiatric hospitals. Fieldwork involved a team of researchers posing as patients, having reported fictitious symptoms (alongside otherwise genuine medical histories) to admission clinic staff, receiving a diagnostic label and being duly 'processed' as in-patients. The study also highlighted some of the shortcomings of staff interaction with patients and helped to explain how the process of depersonalization and institutionalization comes about as a *direct result* of psychiatric care, rather than as an accidental by-product. This contributed to the growing debate about psychiatric services, which ultimately led to significant shifts in policy and practice in relation to those with mental health problems – most notably, the move towards greater investment in care in the community.

Key to demonstrating the authenticity of Rosenhan's findings regarding the process of admission and treatment was the fact that the medical and nursing staff remained unaware of the researchers' true status. What was very interesting, however, were the reactions of some of the 'real' in-patients who, having come to the conclusion that they were not mentally ill and suspecting that they were undercover journalists, challenged researchers. Rosenhan defended his methods by arguing that it would have been impossible to have come by this data in any other way; alerting staff to the research function of the team would have denied insights into the very phenomena they wished to study.

None of the hospitals was identified in the subsequent report and it could be argued that the biggest risk involved was that taken by the 'sane' researchers, who underwent a singularly unpleasant experience (including taking unnecessary medication and being discharged with the label 'schizophrenic in remission') all in the name of (social) science. It is interesting, on reflection, that this appears as a single-authored study, especially given the sacrifice made by the other members of the research team. Perhaps revealing the names of the co-researchers, who presumably used their own names when being admitted to hospitals, would have led to hospital staff identifying themselves as 'victims' of what they were likely to view with the benefit of hindsight as a strategic attempt to discredit psychiatric practice?

Although such methods of gaining access are no longer considered acceptable for academic researchers, interestingly, undercover journalists still rely on similar techniques. A BBC documentary, *The Secret Policeman* (broadcast on 21 October 2003), involved a journalist posing as a police recruit at the Bruche National Police Training Centre in Warrington. The programme served as an exposé detailing the racist comments made by trainees. Notably absent – at least from the media coverage that I saw – was any discussion as to the extent to which Mark Daly (the journalist) himself might have been instrumental in creating the very behaviour he purported to have uncovered. In the ensuing coverage, the outrage was instead reserved for his 'findings' and their implications for the police force, who took the allegations very seriously. Interestingly, it was also a journalist, Laura Slater, who attempted to repeat Rosenhan's study (see *Guardian Weekend*, 31 January 2004 – 'Into the Cuckoo's Nest'). However, Slater's investigation concentrated on the diagnosis phase of the study and omitted the in-depth observational component, which, although perhaps less dramatic – or less attractive to journalists, at least – formed the most substantial part of the data on which Rosenhan's analysis was based. Although academic researchers have by and large steered clear of such controversial approaches to research, the use of the mystery shopper by market researchers is based on the same principle – a similarity also noted by Green and Thorogood (2004), who point out that quantitative research projects have occasionally drawn on this technique to study topics such as access to primary care. Another related development involves some recent 'reality' TV shows which have, among other things, temporarily convinced participants that they were boarding an alien spacecraft.

It would appear that researchers are being held to account to a greater degree than are their media counterparts. This may be fitting and proper, of course, but should perhaps give us pause for thought. Given the potential for blurring between the two endeavours, we might argue that ethical guidelines need to extend their focus to cover other professional groups.

The move to considering ethical standards

It is also easy to castigate previous researchers with the benefit of hindsight but the picture is not quite as straightforward as it might at first appear. Even though a particular study might not pass muster in today's ethical climate, the *absence* of standardized ethical guidelines could give rise to very thoughtful consideration of ethical issues and we can learn from some of these early examples of qualitative research, while still taking issue with some of the 'tactics' they employed:

LAUD HUMPHREYS' (1970) 'TEAROOM TRADE' STUDY

A well-known study within the sociology of deviance was Laud Humphreys'. 'Tearoom Trade' (Humphreys, 1970). Humphreys was interested in studying the behaviour of gay men, in particular their sexual activities in public toilets (restrooms in US parlance and 'tearooms' in the slang of the gay subculture). His book tells us that he had become interested in this topic while acting as a clergyman who was involved in counselling many homosexual parishioners. He had also subsequently completed clinical training in a psychiatric hospital and been employed as a campus chaplain. There are several references throughout the book to Humphreys' wife and children, but he does not explicitly discuss his own sexuality, except to emphasize that he had to find a way of collecting data that did not require him to take part in the sexual activities which he was studying.

It was relatively easy to gain access to observe the behaviour in which he was interested, as it took place in a public setting. Humphreys, however, chose not to reveal his research interests to most of his study participants, as he reasoned that he could only collect the data he wanted through 'passing as deviant' himself. Carrying out fieldwork in 'tearooms', he adopted the useful pre-existing role of lookout or 'watchqueen'. Humphreys was philosophical about paying the price for this covert observation, which resulted on one occasion in him being attacked by a group of youths, and on another being arrested and jailed.

Given the almost total lack of verbal communication during the sexual encounters that he observed and the difficulties inherent in initiating any 'interview-type' talk in this setting, Humphreys looked for another way of collecting more data on the men who engaged in these activities. Thinking laterally, he hit upon the idea of making a note of 134 car licence plates while the men visited the 'tearooms' that were the subject of his study. Having presented himself as a 'market researcher' he found 'friendly policemen' who were happy to provide access to registers where he was able to find the names and addresses of the men he had observed engaging in these sexual practices. He was then able to consult metropolitan area directories in order to obtain data on the men's marital and occupational status. Humphreys describes how he discreetly toured the areas where the men lived, observing details of localities, streets, houses and gardens, while he pondered how to approach the men without compromising them.

By coincidence, Humphreys was then asked to develop a questionnaire for a social health survey of men in the community. He took the opportunity to request permission to include his 100 potential interviewees as a sub-sample and this was granted. The same interview schedule was employed, and it resulted in Humphreys interviewing 50 of the 100 men whose licence plate details he had recorded. He details the efforts he made to ensure that the men would suspect nothing, altering his personal appearance by dressing very differently from the way he had when conducting fieldwork. Humphreys also explains that he kept under lock and key the original list of men recruited opportunistically to the study and did not share this information with anyone. The 50 men were later matched with an equal number of 'controls' and interviews were carried out with these additional respondents in order to ensure the generalizability of Humphreys' findings. He also explains that he went to considerable lengths to ensure that identifying details were not included in his published report. (In an extended edition of his book (Humphreys, 1975), he has since revisited this study and has reflected on how he might have used a different sampling strategy.)

It goes without saying that such a study would not nowadays get past 'first base', as university departments and supervisors are acutely aware of their responsibilities, both academic and legal. In some respects, however, Humphreys is to be commended for his efforts to preserve anonymity and cause as little disruption to the men as possible – exceeding the requirements that were in place at the time this research took place. While certainly not advocating Humphreys' approach, we should perhaps pause to question which is more invasive – including respondents unknowingly in a community sample or seeking to interview them because of their sexual predispositions? We have, thankfully, moved beyond the climate of paternalism in which Humphreys (and other researchers at that point in time) operated. However, openness may well, in some situations, protect the researcher at the expense of participants, who may not always appreciate us telling them *exactly* why we want to speak to them – because they are 'morbidly obese', for example.

THE CURRENT CLIMATE OF ETHICAL REVIEW

Concerns about ethics are long-standing, having been built on well-established principles, for example, the Declaration of Helsinki, (1975) (with five subsequent amendments) (McDonach et al., 2007). While professional codes of practice have a relatively long history (for example those of the World Medical Association, and the ethical codes developed by various social science disciplines, including psychology and sociology), ethical issues in research have of late come under increased surveillance. In the UK, health services researchers have been at the forefront in responding to new challenges raised by the introduction, from 2001, of ethical review and monitoring of research in the National Health Services (NHS) (known as 'research governance'). The previous system of Local Ethical Review had been shown to be inconsistent with regard to decision-making and to be subject to disparities in workload and resources (McDonach et al., submitted), leading to the setting up in 2000 of a Central Office for Research Ethics (COREC). A period of rapid transition has followed as this framework has been incrementally updated in an attempt to develop more accountable, integrated and standardized procedures for reviewing ethical issues. This situation has parallels in other countries, and several authors active in fields other than health research (for example Anthony, 2005; Milne, 2005) have recently commented on increased surveillance and problems with ethical review. Even where the practice of ethical review was already well established, the number of institutional ethics committees, for example, have increased in recent years (Tinker and Coomber, 2004).

With regard to ethical review of educational research, both Milne (2005) in the USA, and Anthony (2005) in Canada, highlight committee members' lack of knowledge of the classroom, collegial relationships and job remits as barriers to realistic appraisal of ethical applications from researchers working in this field. A number of studies have also identified as a problem the lack of methodological expertise of ethics committee members in relation to qualitative research (for example Dolan, 1999; Guillemin, 2006). Milne (2005) argues that federally mandated American Institutional

Review Boards are serving to limit the forms of research considered acceptable by policy bodies and ethics committees, due to their continued reliance on the biomedical research model. The prevalence of biomedical terms and inappropriate questions was certainly a feature of ethical review forms in the UK until relatively recently. (The heading relating to the purchase of animals – presumably for experimental laboratory research – used to always give me pause for thought.) However, considerable effort has gone into modifying the language used and re-vamping the forms so that applicants can now skip large sections (designed for clinical trials) that are irrelevant for qualitative projects. Nevertheless, a culture shift takes more than a change of language and there is still a vestige of inappropriate terms or implications that testify to earlier incarnations of the forms we currently use. Moreover, many local R&D monitoring forms, which you are likely to be required to complete as part of the process, have retained this focus.

Although many of the recent developments in ethical review in the UK and elsewhere have sought to streamline the process involved, for researchers in the frontline the last few years have been a period of considerable confusion and frustration, as the agencies and individuals involved have interpreted (sometimes in contradictory ways) the various pieces of legislation and changes to procedures and have made significant demands on our time as we attempt to comply with requests for information and ever-evolving ethical review forms. While some of the criticisms made with regard to inconsistent decision-making of committees relate to older systems (for example Tully et al., 2000), there have been a number of reports of recent experiences of glaring inconsistencies (Anthony, 2005, in Canada; Milne, 2005, in the USA). There has even been some systematic research into the phenomenon of ethical review (Angell, 2006, in the UK; Guillemin et al., 2006, in Australia) that indicates that there is still considerable room for improvement with regard to consistency.

Angell (2006) has recently suggested that there might be potential to develop the equivalent of case law in relation to ethical committee decision-making. The problem, however, may be that the goal of consistent decision-making is unachievable, or even undesirable, as this is likely to involve a somewhat rigid approach which may raise particular issues for the design of qualitative research, the hallmark of which is flexibility (as outlined in Chapter 2).

I doubt that any qualitative researcher would take issue with the need to take ethical concerns into consideration. Indeed, our methodological journals in particular are replete with papers discussing the ethical implications of doing research with vulnerable individuals and communities, and our responsibilities to those who take part in our projects. However, as Milne (2005) points out, ethical review of research relies on 'utilitarian ethics', with the committee deciding the overall harm or good a study might produce. This is likely to be a crude measure of what is a very complex process, and the implications of qualitative studies in their variety of guises and contexts are almost certain to raise more complex and varied challenges and issues than do standard drug trials, which are much more suited to regulation in this manner.

ETHICAL REVIEW APPLICATIONS

In seeking to provide some guidance on completing ethical applications I have chosen not to refer to a specific ethical review form since these vary and are subject to such rapid change. Instead I have concentrated on listing a number of general topics about which you are likely to be asked questions. Even if the form used by your particular ethics committee does not specifically ask questions relating to these issues, giving thoughtful consideration to such issues should help you to make a stronger case in relation to answering other questions. As in job interviews or PhD vivas, it is always possible to demonstrate your knowledge and grasp of the issues by weaving information through your other replies. The general topics I have selected are:

- Research design
- How to identify and approach potential participants
- What you're asking of participants
- Consent
- Reciprocity and remuneration
- Confidentiality and anonymity
- Impact on participants
- Engagement and participatory methods
- Impact on researchers.

Research design

This is the area where ethical review forms are possibly most likely to reveal their lingering attachment to the biomedical model of research. Even when modified to take account of a broader range of research designs, quantitative assumptions may still prevail. If these are not apparent in the actual language used, these may be reflected in the responses you are likely to receive in relation to your explanation of the rationale for your study. Ethics committees (and sometimes funding bodies) may not understand the principles of purposive sampling, asking, for example, how a researcher proposes to recruit a sample of only 24 interviewees who are selected with regard to a number of criteria, such as age, gender, employment status, length and severity of their problems, overlooking the fact that any one individual can be categorized to all five of these criteria, thus meaning that it should be possible to encompass all this diversity with as few as 24 people. Similarly, second-stage sampling (as advocated in Chapter 2) is likely to raise ethical committee eyebrows, particularly if it might involve contacting additional constituencies in order to recruit more participants. Ethics committees usually want to see the 'tools' that will be used in carrying out your research. The requirement that researchers provide a specimen interview schedule or focus group topic guide, however, sits uneasily alongside the enshrined qualitative practice of modifying such lists of questions in the light of insights derived from previous interviews or focus groups. There are, then, very real dangers that the ethical review process serves to discourage flexibility in qualitative research design, curtail strategies for enhancing the comparative potential of our studies and, thereby, lead to theoretically impoverished work.

However, instead of sighing and exchanging horror stories, we could perhaps apply ourselves more vigorously to trying to be more transparent about our rationale and intent. If we have a real grasp, for example, of what purposive sampling involves and what it allows us to do, then we are more likely to be able to convince others of its utility. I have taken, of late, to using a version of purposive sampling similar to the one outlined above. If second-stage sampling is unlikely to involve approaching new groups not included in the original list supplied (or might simply involve bringing the same individuals together to participate in groups where others share some important characteristic not used to convene first-stage focus groups), then it is important to spell this out. Leaving room for employing further sampling strategies need not be problematic if we give more thought at the outset to stipulating a wide range of people that we might approach, or allowing for a range of settings from which we might recruit participants. We can also do more to hone our skills in terms of writing interview schedules and focus group topic guides that provide information about the areas we wish to cover, while still leaving ourselves some room for manoeuvre.

Ethics committees may have rather fixed ideas about specific qualitative methods. Sometimes ethics committees assume *a priori*, and regardless of the sensitivity of the topic, that there are more ethical issues related to eliciting data in focus groups as opposed to interviews. Applications for ethical approval to carry out observational fieldwork are likely to fall foul of requirements concerning written consent (as mentioned in Chapter 1).

Providing the many samples of different information leaflets (see below) and variants of interview schedules or topic guides likely to be required by ethics committees can present a major headache for researchers, as can detailed enumeration of a study design involving several interlinked phases (with requisite numbers of participants for each phase). Although this can sometimes be viewed as an added obstacle, paying attention to detail at this stage can, nevertheless, be beneficial, provided that you do not offer too many hostages to fortune. When completing a recently successful ethics application for a multiple-phase study, we were not entirely sure of the parameters of our desired sample size, since we had no way of knowing, at the outset, how many individuals were likely to fall into the various categories of people we wanted to recruit. However, we opted to provide minimum and maximum numbers in each category, allowing a safe margin, and have managed, in the event, to achieve a sample that fits these somewhat generous boundaries. In retrospect, these calculations were actually very helpful in allowing us to cost conference calls and telephone interviews. The ethics review process also involved us in producing a more detailed timetable than we might otherwise have done, but again, this was useful in managing this complex project.

Although the ethical review process can potentially stifle some research ideas, there can also be benefits to thinking ahead in ways that may be relatively new to those of us who have been raised in a more permissive research environment that prizes flexibility and the iterative process of qualitative research over scheduling and timetabling. As well as the exhilarating theoretically-informed analyses, most experienced qualitative researchers can, if they are honest, also probably recall projects which have threatened to go 'pear-shaped' – sometimes for reasons beyond our control. But I would suggest that ethical review procedures could, in some instances, force us to cast a critical eye over our research plans and revise or even abandon these – perhaps with good reason.

How to identify and approach potential participants

Providing details about the sampling strategy, however, is not the same thing as considering exactly how and in what context you are likely to approach potential participants. Recruiting respondents outside the routine settings of clinic or educational establishment can call for creative approaches, such as using local radio stations or community events. However, a language and mindset that privileges notions such as 'population' and 'area characteristics', and which requires researchers to spell out in advance precise measures to be employed, can work against imaginative, resourceful, and opportunistic methods of recruitment. This could have the undesirable outcome of limiting research into certain topics or groups of respondents. Snowball sampling in particular, which is one of the few ways of gaining access to some hard-to-reach groups, is likely to be looked at askance by many ethics committees. Perhaps however, we could re-badge this as 'research contact-network sampling' or similar? Among other things, attention should be paid to the safety of the researcher (something generally not mentioned at all in ethics forms) and innovative approaches to contacting respondents may well raise challenges in this respect, since these are likely to remove the researchers from regular settings with their in-built safeguards. One important aspect of the increased documentation surrounding the ethical review process, but one that has received relatively little attention, is the need to spell out study titles, aims and objectives in ways that may turn out to be distasteful or to be perceived by potential respondents as insulting. When carrying out our study of obesity management in the general practice setting we had, mercifully, opted for the title 'Weight Management' for use in the letters we sent to patients inviting them to take part in interviews. This was fortuitous as interviews established that most of our respondents found the terms 'obese' and 'obesity' hurtful. In many cases we are interested in eliciting the views of people who have not taken up services on offer, such as immunization or cardiac rehabilitation programmes. This 'sampling by deficit' (MacDougall and Fudge, 2001) becomes especially problematic when combined with the provision of full information regarding the aims and objectives of the proposed study, since we risk 'putting people on the spot'.

Gatekeepers also play an important role in accessing potential research participants. Ethical committees' concerns are likely to centre around the potential of service providers in medical, educational and penal establishments to supply 'research fodder' to academics. We are often required to provide detailed information about the mechanisms for providing information sheets and how we propose to ensure that these are distributed consistently and routinely. However, as Wiles et al. (2006) point out, gatekeepers can also take it upon themselves to deny access to some participants who might otherwise be willing to take part, and thereby, in some instances, deny them the opportunity to benefit from research involvement.

What you're asking of participants

It is relatively easy to provide information with regard to how long a proposed interview or focus group session is likely to last and to show that you have given some thought as to how convenient the chosen setting will be for respondents or participants. However, it can be harder to spell out exactly what the focus of the research will be, particularly with regard to ethnographies or exploratory research projects. Even when we – and our respondents – know in advance what questions we are going to be asking, we do not necessarily anticipate what these answers will be. Respondents may carefully consider the implications for themselves, but both they – and we, as researchers – may not be able to anticipate the power of aggregate views or how their own experiences may appear when presented in contrast to those of others. It can also be hard to gauge the likely impact of talking about an issue, especially if this is the first time that the respondent has taken the opportunity to share her/his experiences. The researcher has no way of knowing at the outset whether an interviewee is a 'practised raconteur' (almost a professional respondent) or is embarking on an entirely new venture in agreeing to tell her/his story.

An example of research in a highly charged arena is provided by the Termination of Pregnancy (TOPAZ) study (Kennedy, 2002):

STUDYING TERMINATION OF PREGNANCY (THE TOPAZ PROJECT)

This study was concerned with the views about termination of pregnancy services of service users and service providers. The research was carried out in Glasgow, well known within the UK for its conflicting religious identities, which frequently culminate in acts of sectarianism (often associated with, but not exclusive to, football rivalries). Terminations of pregnancy are thus often carried out in a climate of secrecy and shame, due to a constellation of cultural and religious factors, which affect not only the women undergoing the procedure but also the professionals tasked with providing the service.

Perhaps because the study had been commissioned by Greater Glasgow Health Board, which already had an idea of the potential challenges, coupled with a commitment to finding out more about this difficult area of practice, we were afforded a sympathetic ethical review hearing and were given permission to adopt a flexible recruitment strategy with opportunistic elements. We had anticipated that it might prove difficult to recruit service users into the study and so decided upon a multi-pronged strategy. We distributed a leaflet (through a number of outlets, including Family Planning and hospital clinics) inviting women to complete the tear-off slip indicating that they were willing to be interviewed for the study and to provide their contact details. These contact details might simply be a telephone number and provision was made for women to contact the researcher should this be their preferred option. As the leaflet proved not to be very successful on its own, this strategy was augmented by the researcher attending clinics where she could provide further details for women potentially interested in being involved – after they had been identified by medical or nursing staff. Staff members had accurately predicted that women would often be amenable to taking part in the study when approached on the day they were having their termination.

We also had to be flexible in terms of where interviews with women were carried out: while it was possible to carry out some interviews in clinics, others took place in health centres, local cafés or in women's homes. In some cases, women who had been recruited at the clinic prior to their termination of pregnancy (TOP) were followed up by telephone.

The choice of the uninformative 'TOPAZ' as a title for the study acknowledged the potential for disclosure of terminations to family members and friends, with whom the woman concerned might not have shared her experience of termination. We designed a double-sided leaflet (which folded into three) using a discreet crystal graphic reflecting the study acronym and confined the more sensitive questions to the part of the leaflet that was not immediately visible.

Ethical review procedures have changed considerably since this study was carried out. It is doubtful whether, in today's climate of uncertainty, we would be allowed such flexibility in recruiting our sample. Most ethics committees now suggest that researchers use the participant information templates that they provide. This takes into account virtually all the issues that we wrestled with in designing our own leaflet and, on balance, I would argue that making such templates available represents a positive step, provided that there is still some leeway for the research team to customize the leaflets in order to make them relevant to the study in question and to attend to any additional issues that arise. It is also important to acknowledge, as did the researchers whose views were canvassed by Wiles et al. (2006), that it is possible to over-burden potential participants with information.

Consent

Informed consent principles are based on the premise that consent is 'knowledgeable, exercised in a non-coercive situation, and made by competent individuals' (Milne, 2005: para 26). As Milne (2005: para 33) further comments: 'Concepts such as informed consent, risk/benefit analysis, and confidentiality, are not inherent truths of ethics or categorical imperatives. They are constructs that have emerged from specific ethical philosophies.'

In contrast to the approach embedded in most formalized versions of the ethical review process, professional codes tend to acknowledge the possibility of conflicting interests between researcher and researched (see, for example, British Sociological Association, 2002) and do not portray this as an absolute or unproblematic ideal.

Since the focus of qualitative research may evolve as the study progresses, several writers (Munhall, 1988; Thorne, 1998) have recommended that we use the concept of 'process consent' instead of the blanket term of 'informed consent', which suggests (as do many of the features of ethical review) that this is a 'once-and-for-all' procedure to be attended to at the outset of a project and never thereafter revisited.

Additional issues may arise with respect to certain groups who may be perceived as particularly vulnerable. Ethics committee forms usually ask us to indicate whether we plan to include participants in such groups (often providing a list of those they consider to belong in this category). There are also legal frameworks to which we must be attentive, particularly in relation to research with children, for example (Masson, 2004). However, focusing on the legalities may divert attention and energies away from the equally important task of ensuring that appropriate methods and materials are used – for example, with children of different ages and cognitive abilities, or in order to develop genuinely participatory methods (see, for example, O'Kane, 2000). Other groups which merit special consideration are those with disabilities (Kroll et al., 2007, in press), learning difficulties (Tarleton et al., 2004), or mental health problems (Nelson, 2004; Owen, 2001), the elderly (Seymour et al., 2002) and those at the end of their lives or receiving palliative care (Cameron et al., 2004; Casarett and Karalawish, 2000). As well as acknowledging the special requirements of such groups, researchers who have commented on ethical implications are generally at pains to point out that these situations only serve to highlight more general ethical principles of which we should always be mindful. Written consent may be impractical and can cause considerable embarrassment if used unthinkingly with groups where there may be individuals with low levels of literacy. It is not always possible to anticipate when and where such problems may arise, since even quite comprehensive purposive sampling may not provide us with all the information about respondents' characteristics that we would need in order to assess accurately the likelihood of issues arising in relation to consent.

In some research contexts, where participants may be reluctant to talk to a researcher in the first place, we sometimes give them the added reassurance of allowing them to choose a pseudonym. Asking for a signature may sit uncomfortably alongside such measures and can compromise confidentiality and anonymity. Some groups of people, such as asylum seekers, who may be in the country illegally, are likely to feel threatened by such requests to identify themselves on paper. Coomber (2002) highlights the problems of pursuing recommended strategies for acquiring consent when researching criminal populations. As Ryen (2004) observes, written consent may be more acceptable in some cultures than in others, and it is always possible that requesting formal consent may only serve to heighten respondents' concerns. Asking for written consent, or providing repeated reminders that one is engaged in conducting research, may invite parallels with police cautioning and cause concerns to escalate to a level where it is the consent process rather than the research *per se* that creates ethical problems. Some researchers have insisted that covert or at least veiled approaches are needed if we are to study topics such as neo-Nazi groups or football hooligans (Scraton, 2004) and this has given rise to spirited debate. In such cases, however, it is perhaps the safety of the researcher that should exercise us.

In certain situations, obtaining written consent may simply be impractical. One PhD student had applied for ethical approval for a study which allowed her a period of observational work in the public area of a clinic in order to familiarize herself with the procedures involved by way of an introduction to her chosen topic of study. The ethics committee raised concerns about this proposed component of the study and made the unrealistic stipulation that she would have to obtain written consent from everyone who came through the door of the clinic. This she considered to be unworkable and, in the event, the research design was amended to exclude this pilot fieldwork. Wiles et al. (2006: 284) conclude: 'Formalized consent procedures do not provide an answer to the problem of ensuring potential study participants make truly informed choices. … Researchers need to be enabled to attend reflexively to the social context in which consent takes place.'

There are also special sensitivities and considerations involved when formalizing contracts in relation to service user-led research (Wright et al., 2004) or where members of communities are involved as co-researchers. Such projects generally demand a lot more of participants in terms of time and commitment. For example, in some contexts we may be asking them to develop and use new skills and the provision of adequate training and support should also be considered under the heading of ethical issues. Sharing data that is normally restricted to researchers can also compromise the standard guarantees of confidentiality conventionally given to research participants. For this reason, it is essential that the mechanisms for data sharing are discussed and that suitable measures are employed to minimize the potential harm or distress that could be caused. When we co-research with practitioners we are generally mindful of the need to insulate them from data generated from their own patients or clients (in order to protect both parties) and similar arrangements need to be formalized in relation to involving members of what can sometimes be fairly tightly-knit communities. These issues also arise with regard to sharing focus group transcripts in seeking to achieve 'respondent validation' (see further discussion in Chapter 13).

Reciprocity and remuneration

Small (1998) discusses some possible motivations for taking part in research, including the desire to 'give something back', to facilitate change, or, the much more complicated scenario whereby the making of a moral investment by participating in research is somehow seen as providing the individual with insurance against an unfortunate future. It is obviously important not to overstate the potential benefits of a particular research study. As Small (1998: 142) points out:

> … social research has few certainties. You don't know what research will have an impact before you do it: it's like adding to a pile, a heap of debris. Occasionally something is picked off this mound by wandering prospectors and at times something just seems to find its way onto the pinnacle.

Paying respondents is a rather vexed issue and sometimes what are essentially value judgements appear in the guise of ethical concerns. Ethical committees seem to query payments to the disadvantaged with rather greater regularity than they question 'locum' payments to provide cover for GPs, for example, in order to allow them to participate in our research. Milne (2005) reports that her proposal to pay a colleague for substantial time and work commitment to an educational action research project was turned down by her ethical committee because this was deemed to be 'coercive'.

The assertion that our interviewees might take part in our research only because of what are usually very small payments (in recognition of their inconvenience or travel expenses) seems to give rise to a disproportionate amount of concern. Certainly there are very important issues in relation to the often substantial amounts of money paid to healthy participants in clinical trials (with a recent high-profile case in the UK where one person died and others suffered irreparable damage to their health). However, the issues involved in qualitative research projects are not in any way comparable. As Dingwall (2006) remarked, in this case talking about medical sociologists involved in research, 'We don't give anyone nasty green stuff and we're never going to'. Does it really matter if the odd participant takes part in our research partly due to the attractiveness of a small financial reward? Both researchers – and latterly ethics committees – seem to spend a lot of time talking about empowering the disenfranchised and the impoverished through their involvement in our research, but ethics committees (and sometimes funding bodies) seem to baulk at giving them even a small amount of money.

Some researchers get around this problem by offering vouchers or participant packs, such as that provided by McKeganey et al. (1992) in their study of drug users. Another option is to avoid advertising payment or omitting to provide details of the amount involved. This was the advice provided by one of the researchers consulted by Wiles et al. (2006), who advocated giving participants money as a surprise at the end of interviews or focus group sessions. However, people may well glean such information through the 'grapevine' and this may lead to opportunistic participation. This is unlikely to pose a major problem for most qualitative studies, since we are often attempting to gain access to exactly these sorts of network in any case.

Confidentiality and anonymity

The need to preserve confidentiality and anonymity is an enshrined principle in the qualitative research endeavour and discussion of these issues is a feature of all grant applications and published papers. Ethics application forms all ask us to provide reassurances with respect to these separate, but related, issues. However, as with most of the other principles discussed here, we are likely, particularly as qualitative researchers, to find ourselves facing situations that are far from straightforward. Even having been known to have interviewed individuals in some settings can be tantamount to identifying them as individuals with specific characteristics or experiences (particularly if we have been zealous in providing information leaflets in all settings in which we do our recruitment, which is usually a separate requirement for ethical approval). Observing the confidentiality of one individual may compromise the well-being and safety of another, as Barnard (2005) discusses in relation to carrying out research with drug-using parents.

Checking with respondents before including excerpts from interviews or focus groups in published papers can seem like good ethical practice, but, like sharing whole transcripts, this can force them to revisit what was, for them, a painful discussion. In the case of focus group excerpts, an additional problem is that by identifying the participant in question through seeking consent, the researcher is thereby providing this future reader with information which will allow her/him to identify other speakers, regardless of the care exercised by the researcher to provide pseudonyms. Again researchers have to carefully weigh up the implications in each situation, rather than simply follow blanket guidelines.

There is considerably more to preserving anonymity than simply conferring pseudonyms and keeping original contact details separately under lock and key (as required by the Data Protection Act). Names are only one among many details that can lead to individuals being identified. It can be difficult to anticipate which aspects of descriptions might give rise to an individual or setting being recognized in subsequent reports or papers, and the researcher has to be constantly vigilant. For example, when providing quotes in written work, I have on occasion changed details, such as someone's gender or age (where this information is not relevant to the issue being discussed). Where we are engaging with our research participants in the role of co-researchers, however, we may wish to acknowledge their input, but this may involve listing them as co-authors. The terrain of reciprocities, emotions and the research relationship is a complex one (which is further discussed in Chapter 13) and cannot be adequately addressed merely by adhering to a set of guidelines.

Impact on participants

We are often involved in researching sensitive and potentially upsetting topics and, while it may be cathartic for individuals to talk to someone who is not emotionally involved, talking about upsetting topics is itself likely to be upsetting. Reviewing risks to researchers involved in talking to respondents about AIDS and sexual behaviour, Green et al. (1993) highlighted the 'culture of competency' and the related need to demonstrate good fieldwork relationships that might mitigate against researchers confessing to having experienced threats in the course of carrying out research. A similar conspiracy of silence may operate with regard to people becoming upset during interviews or focus group discussions. It is useful to remember that it is the distressing event about which they are talking that is upsetting respondents rather than the researcher in person, and we should perhaps be prepared to 'take the rough with the smooth' and sometimes we are required to respond not just as researchers but as concerned individuals. As Ryen (2004: 233) points out: 'Ethical challenges do not deprive actions of their symbolic value'.

Ethics committees sometimes focus on recruitment and the situation in which the data is generated rather than looking beyond this. It is certainly important not to simply 'take the data and run'. Kitzinger and Barbour (1999) have emphasized the importance, particularly for focus group research on potentially sensitive topics, of debriefing. This involves giving participants a chance to talk about their contribution immediately after the event and providing them with contact numbers should they wish to get in touch with the researcher at a later stage. It may also be helpful to have to hand relevant information leaflets and helpline numbers that you can distribute if it seems relevant. Again, discretion needs to be exercised as foisting these on an unwilling audience may have the opposite of the desired effect.

Requests to provide information about the intended outputs of our research overstate the degree of control that any of us have over the way in which our research findings are used. Given that we may not be entirely sure at the outset of a project of the direction of our interests (particularly theoretical ones), it may be difficult to provide precise details about the anticipated findings and their impact on our respondents. In so far as ethics committees concern themselves with the potential of our research to deliver relevant outputs, the criteria they use are likely to be similar to those employed by funding bodies (as discussed in Chapter 2). However, on some occasions researchers who have been funded to carry out theoretically-driven pieces of work can find themselves having to respond to questions which make much more sense within the biomedical or practice-based context.

Although those we research may sometimes forget that we are present in their midst, at other times this can place us in a difficult position, as was Goodwin when two anaesthetists involved in an ethnographic study chose to hold a 'confidential' discussion in her presence (Goodwin et al., 2003). Sometimes, however, we become party to information that relates to potential harm that could occur to our respondents and this can place researchers in an awkward dilemma. This is most likely to happen in the context of research carried out by researchers who are also practitioners and who would, in this other context, either refer the patient to another professional or agency or report the matter raised to other members of a health or social care team. While providing information leaflets or helpline numbers can partly address such issues, some researchers I have spoken to recount how they have sometimes stepped outside their role as interviewer in order to urge someone to seek medical advice and, on occasion, some have asked for permission to report the information provided in the interview context, since this has such important implications for the individual's health or well-being. It is all very well to engage in boundary work, seeking to be clear about where we draw the line between, for example, counselling and research interviewing, but, as Goode (1999) also points out, our respondents may also exert their own agency. This became apparent in the context of our study on couples' experiences of sub-fertility, where couples took the opportunity to engage in the sorts of exchange more characteristic of a marital therapy session than a research interview. That this did not arise with the younger researcher, but only surfaced in relation to my own interviewing, serves to remind us that respondents are actively involved in making attributions about our own predispositions and skills.

Sometimes it is our legal and moral obligations as citizens that are called into sharp focus as we go about conducting our research. Respondents, for example, may disclose their own and others' involvement in illegal practices and, apart from our personal reactions to such stories, we can be faced with very real dilemmas as to how we should use this information. It is hard to alert research participants to the legal obligations that come with the research role without lapsing into 'anything you say …' police caution mode. In some situations, the researcher would do well to take a leaf out of the book of the drugs workers I interviewed some years ago. When reflecting on the uncomfortable information that could come their way with regard to drugs shipments etc., several told me that they had become adept over the years at anticipating such unwelcome revelations and heading them off by stopping clients in their tracks before specifics were mentioned. It is not always that simple, however. Barnard (2005) talks about the challenges in carrying out research on drug-using parents and the potential to uncover practices that could endanger children's lives. In this case, she reflects that it is no easy matter to determine who the 'underdog' is and whose interests we should be protecting as part of the research contract.

Engagement and participatory methods

One important difference between action research and other forms of research endeavour is the way in which the researcher's role – and that of participants – is perceived. Rather than aspiring to be 'objective', action research avoids even getting caught up in this debate, favouring instead a view of the researcher as 'catalyst' (Hart and Bond, 1995: 22), with the express purpose of facilitating change through active involvement in the processes that are being studied. Action research also aims to avoid using the terminology of more conventional research, and thereby to forge different types of relationship in the field. Researchers working within the experimental paradigm refer to 'subjects', quantitative researchers (and some qualitative researchers) talk of 'respondents', while other qualitative researchers describe those involved in their research projects as 'participants'. Action researchers, however, prefer to view those with whom they engage in their projects as 'co-researchers'. Action research is frequently described as being research *with* people, not research *on* them (Reason, 1994). Lee (2001) takes the idea of co-researchers even further, and advocates making everyone involved in an action research project into 'practitioners-researchers-researched'. However, such rhetoric can serve to mask the impact of taking part in research, particularly issues that may arise for the researcher as s/he engages in fieldwork so close to work, if not home.

Researcher participants, even if they already know a researcher, may feel threatened by having a researcher in their midst. Many qualitative projects, and action research studies in particular, are likely to build into their research designs the potential for comparison. However, for those involved in projects, the fear may be that 'invidious' and unflattering comparisons will be made, which will show them in a bad light. The 'researcher-as-insider' can then be seen as betraying the trust of her/his peer group.

Impact on researchers

As qualitative researchers we prize our capacity to empathize with people who are located in contexts – or even societies – that may be very different from those we ourselves inhabit. While our marginal status can confer enormous benefits in terms of the analytic purchase that this inherently comparative stance affords, we may, from time to time, become acutely aware of the distance between us and our respondents. Sometimes this raises problems with regard to maintaining research access, but it can also raise more taxing emotional issues. Bourne (1998), for example, talks of the effect on the researcher of listening to heart-rending accounts of those who have lost family members to AIDS and highlights the cumulative effect of reading such transcripts and condensing their contents, and hence impact. If we are interviewing people who have had distressing experiences similar to those we have ourselves encountered, then this raises additional issues and this is something that we should be alert to as supervisors and employers. Borochowitz (2005), for example, talks of the implications for some of her students of using the topic of domestic violence for a qualitative methods class.

Our respondents are also active participants and may harness an interview situation for their own ends. For example, Grenz (2005) interviewed male clients of female sex workers and found that some of these men overtly sexualized parts of the research encounter. In some situations, the researcher may be engaging with respondents who themselves could pose a potential threat. Lee (1997) carried out some interviews with men who had been accused of sexual harassment against female co-workers and took considerable pains to dress in a way that she described as embodying 'prim scruffiness' (Lee, 1997: 559). While it may be relatively easy to manage our appearance, engaging with our research participants may raise even more challenging personal issues.

In encouraging frank discussion of views we may be subjected to attitudes that, as private individuals with specific affiliations and convictions, we may find abhorrent. As we listen to respondents expressing sexist or racist views, for example, we may experience extreme discomfort as we appear, to our respondents at least, to condone these views which we might in other context robustly challenge. Depending on the focus of our research and the depth of our immersion in these 'parallel universes', this can lead to painful soul-searching on the part of the researcher. In responding to these many challenges we engage in what Goode (2006) has described as 'repair work' to both our professional and personal selves.

Ethical review procedures, perhaps because of their origins in the context of highly controlled research environments, generally do not extend to minimizing the potential for harm to researchers as well as participants. As Scott (1984) has observed, young women are frequently employed as 'personable data collection tools' and may be subject to both physical and sexual danger in the field. The qualitative research culture, with its emphasis on developing 'rapport' with respondents, does not encourage such debates. Contract researchers in particular, who are forced by the job market to trade on their robustness and willingness to 'get out and do whatever it takes to get research done', may be particularly vulnerable but are unlikely to ask for support from institutions and senior colleagues.

A responsible approach to arrangements might include employing measures such as leaving a list of appointments with a colleague, carrying a mobile phone, and utilizing a 'phone-in system to report back once fieldwork visits have been completed. While guidelines are never a substitute for thoughtful practice, they can be useful in getting such issues as researcher safety on the agenda and may help in arguing the case for including the purchase of mobile phones in costing grant applications. There are encouraging signs that this issue is now being addressed. Recently, the Cardiff node of the UK Economic and Social Research Council's National Research Methods Centre has invited submissions to an enquiry into the well-being of researchers in qualitative research. For further details and an opportunity to contribute to online discussions, you can visit their website at www.cardiff.ac.uk/socsi/qualiti/commissioned_inq_2.html.

We may not all want to 'emote' with our line manager, but those of us who employ and manage research assistants should review provision within our own institutions and ensure that the researcher has access, wherever possible, to a network of other researchers or PhD students who can be an invaluable source of peer group support. Online discussion groups might also be a useful resource and have the added advantage that sensitive issues can be raised with individuals with whom the researcher does not have daily contact, which may be preferable in some cases.

IMPLICATIONS

The lesson to be learnt from all of this is that we need to give very careful thought to ethical issues, trying to anticipate the likely impact on research participants and our responsibilities to the wider academic community and society as a whole. However, the ethical review process – particularly where it retains attachment to criteria originally designed for the review of randomized control trials (RCTs) or quantitative studies, can work to inhibit flexible design and can thereby compromise comparability and theoretical sensitivity of qualitative studies.

Ethical review procedures cannot guarantee ethical research practice, although they can encourage researchers to give more consideration to the ethical implications of their studies. In order for this to happen, however, they need to ask relevant questions. Current systems of ethical review can result in the unintended but serious consequence of ethical issues being neglected once an application has been approved and the research is under way. Even when we rigorously follow ethical guidelines, and succeed in securing ethical approval, there is no room for complacency. Corrigan (2003) has argued that ethical review procedures may merely serve to encourage adherence to 'empty ethics'. While ethical guidelines may be helpful, they can never anticipate all of the issues that are likely to face the researcher. As Fine (1993: 267) has pointed out, irresolvable ethical dilemmas are 'endemic' to research. This does not, however, give us licence to simply shrug our shoulders – we may not find ready answers, but we certainly need to keep asking the questions (such as those outlined here). 'In the field ethical dilemmas have to be resolved situationally, and often spontaneously' (Ryen, 2004: 232). However, we can sometimes give this process a helping hand by spending some time thinking through the implications of our research design choices. There is, of course, always the danger that in highlighting some of the additional issues involved, we simply prompt ethics committees to attend to these by including even more prescriptive items in their already formidable forms, as evidenced by the way in which checklists for evaluating qualitative research have already been employed in some quarters.

The shortcomings of ethical review procedures impact on the wider society as well as the research community. In stark contrast to much of the rhetoric about involving research participants, and the inclusion of this as a heading in some ethics review forms, Dingwall (2006) has highlighted the implicit paternalism involved in the process of ethical review. In the context of the USA's federally mandated Institutional Review Boards, Milne (2005: para 4) cites Wax (writing as long ago as 1980), who pointed out that the activities of such agencies have served to deny populations 'the right to determine for themselves the type of relationship they might have with researchers'. Milne (2005) adds that this was still the case in the US context in 2004.

Some of the assumptions inherent in the process of ethical review reflect what has been called 'the illusion of manageability' (Anderson, 1992), which reifies managerial dominance within a consensus view of institutional functioning. This approach is associated with an emphasis on solving technical problems, while overlooking the vagaries and complexities that may be inherent to a system, and which may well defy control through the application of a set of procedures, however much work goes into refining these. Calls for case law (for example Angell, 2006) in order to address observed inconsistencies in the system reflect a similar set of unwarranted assumptions and thus probably do not afford a workable potential solution after all. Engaging in dialogue with ethics committees might seem a promising avenue for resolution of some of the aforementioned problems. However, details of membership of committees is not available in all contexts. Guillemin (2006), for example, notes that in Australia this information is not in the public domain unless individual committees choose to share this. Some ethics committees allow researchers to attend meetings where their proposals are being discussed, but this is by no means common practice, and some committees (for example the one experienced by Milne, 2005) do not allow this under any circumstances. Ethics committees are busy, and rather than burdening them with more work, we should perhaps be exploring the potential for delegating some of their responsibilities, particularly with respect to research that has no clinical component. Only when ethics committees include a critical mass of experienced qualitative researchers and move to acting in an advisory rather than a gatekeeping capacity are we likely to experience a system that actually encourages improvements in ethical practice. Sadly, it does not look as though this is about to happen. In the meantime, we could do worse than continue to debate constructively and creatively the important issues that are raised, rather than succumbing to focusing on our many frustrations.

HINTS ON ETHICAL CONSIDERATIONS

- Think carefully about the impact your research is likely to have on participants. This includes anticipating the effect of your sampling strategies and your identifying of individuals as coming within the compass of your study. Also important to consider here is the impact of engaging with other participants (if focus groups are used).
- Think through the implications of user-led or participatory research in relation to the impact on participants – particularly in relation to sharing of data.
- Give clear guidance to respondents and gate-keepers with regard to what will be involved in your research: how many people you want to talk to and for how long. Indicate what your broad topics will cover and make arrangements for securing written consent.
- Make sure that you provide assurances with respect to confidentiality and anonymity and think about how to ensure these in practice.
- Think about what you promise participants and do not raise their expectations unduly.
- Take steps to provide a secure and safe working environment for the researcher/s.
- Finally, if in doubt do contact the Chair of your ethics committee for advice and guidance.

FURTHER READING

Smyth, M. and Williamson, E. (eds) (2004) *Researchers and Their 'Subjects': Ethics, Power, Knowledge and Consent*, Bristol: Policy Press.

Wiles, R., Crow, G., Charles, V. and Health, S. (2006) 'Informed consent and the research process: Following rules or striking balances?', *Sociological Research Online*, 11(4), http://www.socresonline.org.uk/11/4/wiles.html

EXERCISE

Taking one (or more) of the suggested research questions from Chapter 2, or better still your own revised version (for which you have already developed a possible research design), jot down some notes in relation to each of the topics listed below. Then attempt to complete the relevant sections of the ethical review form used by your own ethics committee.

To recap on the research questions, these were:

1 **Do people view risk differently when they travel?**
2 **Are our notions shifting with regard to how long we think adolescence lasts?**
3 **What impact does media coverage of fertility treatment have on public perceptions of appropriate provision?**
4 **What do people think about fathers' attendance at deliveries?**
5 **What are the challenges of parenting?**

Topics to consider

- *Research design*
- *How to identify and approach potential participants*
- *What you're asking of participants*
- *Consent*
- *Reciprocity and remuneration*
- *Confidentiality and anonymity*
- *Impact on participants*
- *Other responsibilities*

SECTION 2
GENERATING DATA

This text follows Jennifer Mason (1996) in making a distinction between 'collecting' and 'generating' qualitative data. The idea of 'generating' data takes account of the active role played by the observer, interviewer or focus group moderator in producing data through interacting with respondents. The discussion will highlight the significance of reflexivity, that is the impact which the researcher has on the data elicited and the impact of the research process on the researcher.

The unfortunate tendency, in some quarters, to present qualitative research as the application of a set of techniques has taken de-mystification a step too far. This text will attempt to reassert the skill involved in negotiating the qualitative research encounter in order to elicit the sort of data which is required. For example, the ease with which experienced researchers ask questions belies the amount of work involved in developing and utilizing conversational gambits and the careful scripting of questions.

The book follows the conventional format of outlining the range of qualitative methods for generating data, discussing, in turn, the potential of ethnography, interviewing (semi-structured, one-to-one interviews and joint interviews, and their more focused use in narrative and life-story research as well as in eliciting experiences and perspectives), focus group discussions and action research, grounding the discussion in examples of work which has employed these various methods. Here, too, the skills required of the researcher will be emphasized. However, it is stressed that these techniques do not produce identical findings in the hands of different researchers and the reader will be directed to the relevant excerpts which illustrate the impact on data content of different researchers' personae and the roles attributed or conferred by respondents.

Even with well-designed research 'tools', it is likely that the researcher will encounter some problems, as 'one size fits all' approaches may have varying degrees of success with different individuals or groups. Some common difficulties are described and some suggestions will be made as to how these might be overcome, through the skilful use of prompts and implementation of flexible sampling strategies. Excerpts from fieldwork notes, interviews, focus group discussions and participatory consultations will be provided and the reader will be directed to the sections which demonstrate the use of specific interjections or invitations to further explore issues raised by respondents, or to encourage reluctant speakers.

The following chapters will seek to de-mystify the 'sleight of hand' which often appears to be involved in terms of formulating questions which elicit the sort of rich data required by qualitative researchers. This applies equally to the selection of fieldwork data and developing interview schedules, focus group topic guides and participatory research consultations. The book will draw on 'real' materials used in previous projects and in projects currently under development. This has the benefit of allowing for reflection on what makes for a successful schedule or topic guide and provides some advice on how to avoid some of the most common pitfalls. In particular, the role of pilot work will be stressed.

4
ETHNOGRAPHY

AIMS

- This chapter aims to provide a flavour of ethnographic research through a vicarious apprenticeship involving targeted exercises.
- It equips the reader to design ethnographic studies.
- It encourages the reader to think carefully about what counts as data and how to optimize opportunities for accessing significant activities, events and settings.
- It informs the reader of the considerations that need to be taken into account with regard to negotiating access.
- It provides hints on developing templates for observation and for recording fieldnotes.
- It alerts the reader to the analytic potential of reflexivity and paying attention to relationships in the field.

INTRODUCTION

This chapter will trace the development of ethnography and the influence of the various social science disciplines, current and past debates on the practice and the contribution of ethnographic research. The discussion will also draw on fieldwork data generated by the author in past projects (on socialization for social work and the negotiation of responsibility in the work of midwives), using data excerpts to illustrate the specific challenges and dilemmas raised by this approach to generating qualitative data. Other topics covered will include a discussion of the role of the ethnographer and the practicalities involved in the planning of observations. The last section will deal with generating and analyzing fieldnotes.

Although ethnography is often associated with the anthropological tradition, Delamont (2004) reminds us that it has been used in sociology for just as long a time. Indeed, ethnographic methods were a mainstay of the work of sociologists in the

Chicago School, which has proved to be extremely influential even to this day. Clearly, carrying out observational fieldwork in a previously unknown culture is likely to raise challenges somewhat different from those involved in carrying out ethnography closer to home, but the similarities are, perhaps, more surprising. More recently, ethnographic approaches have been embraced by proponents of what has been termed 'psychological anthropology', defined as 'the study of individuals and their socio-cultural communities' (Casey and Edgerton, 2005: 1). The person-centred ethnography' advocated by Casey and Edgerton is intended to address 'the tensions between individual agency and culturally hegemonic forms' (2007: 8), and thus affords a means of reconciling the micro and the macro (as discussed in Chapter 1). The contributions to the edited collection produced by Casey and Edgerton, it is argued,

> …demonstrate the vitality of integrative, psycho-cultural approaches – those that engage and synthesize multiple historical, theoretical genealogies of psychological anthropology, whether psychoanalytic/psychodynamic, phenomenological, linguistic, psychoadaptive, ecological, medical, cognitive, embodied, or informed by the neurosciences, psychology, cultural studies, and social history. (Casey and Edgerton, 2007: 3)

This extensive list gives an indication both of the potential scope of ethnographic work and the challenges of synthesizing insights and theoretical frameworks inspired by such a disparate and potentially contradictory range of disciplines and traditions.

Some researchers refer to their work as 'ethnographic interview' studies and this can lead to considerable confusion. Along with Mason (1996: 60–61), I would generally recommend reserving the term 'ethnographic' for approaches that use observational methods as 'a central plank'. On some occasions, however, this term might be useful to convey that interviews have been carried out in a setting to which the researcher has had extended access, which, although it might stop short of observational fieldwork, nevertheless can be shown to have informed the analysis.

AIMS OF ETHNOGRAPHY

The task of ethnography has been described as that of providing 'thick description' (Geertz, 1973: 5) through the active and frequently protracted engagement of the researcher in the setting under study. As Punch (1994) says, the ethnographer *is* the research instrument. Although it is tempting to confine our observations about the research endeavour and writing to work carried out by academics in further education institutions, much might be learned from casting the net a little wider to look at other genres of investigation and reportage. This last comment about the ethnographer her/himself being the most important of all research 'tools' appears also to be relevant for much travel writing, which Paul Theroux, for example, has described as a 'minor form of autobiography', whereby the text consists of much more than a list of 'sights' or provision of historical context, but revolves around the layering-on of the writer's personal reactions to images and events.

With anthropologists working in the classical tradition, travel writers also share responsibility for interpreting the exotic or foreign – the 'other'. Recently there has been some debate around the usefulness of constructing research participants – or respondents, depending on the type of research involved – as 'the other'. (This is discussed further in Chapter 13.) What we write is recorded for posterity and history can shape our written products in ways that are beyond both our understanding and control and ethnography can play a role in enacting power relations in addition to recording these (Clifford and Marcus, 1986). Nevertheless, the task for the ethnographer studying her/his own culture remains that of rendering the familiar strange, through questioning taken-for-granted assumptions and categories, some of which s/he may also have espoused in the recent past. While anthropologists and travel writers – traditionally immersed themselves in the field for periods that might span a couple of years, ethnographers working in their own cultures – and often with tighter timescales – tend to spend shorter periods of time carrying out observational work.

Ethnographic research can encompass both the sweeping and the very focused. This approach can be used whether the researcher wishes to understand the workings of an entire culture or how specific tasks are routinely accomplished in a particular setting. Although the classical anthropological tradition favoured the use of observational fieldwork as a stand-alone method, it has been utilized alongside a wide range of other methods – often in order to inform the development of interview schedules or focus group topic guides, or even to assist in the design of questionnaires. In the case of mixed methods studies, observational fieldwork often takes the form of pilot work and the data produced may or may not be subjected to detailed analysis. However, the variety of 'hanging about' frequently advocated in order to familiarize oneself with a new area of study is nowadays much harder to justify to ethics committees and funding bodies, but I do wonder whether research designs may, consequently, be impoverished. Of course, when a researcher is conducting interviews in the field s/he may well spend significant amounts of time sitting about in a ward, clinic, or office waiting for interviewees, and while consent to carry out observational work may not have been formally obtained, it is virtually impossible to spend time in such settings without obtaining valuable insights into everyday practices. This may result in the inclusion of further questions in an interview schedule and, at the very least, gives some indication of such things as the pace of work and the tenor of personal communication that characterizes a particular 'backdrop' to the more clearly defined phenomena that are of interest to the researcher. I can still recall the slightly frenetic air and jocularity of an AIDS unit where I waited (sometimes throughout entire shifts) to interview staff members. This 'accidental fieldwork' certainly provided valuable insights into the 'gallows humour' that enabled staff to deal with heart-wrenchingly difficult situations in caring for people of their own age who were dying. Interviewees sometimes referred to discussions that had taken place in the staffroom and shared their own interpretations with the researcher, thus helping to contextualize interview talk and assisting me in initial theorizing as I sought to make sense of my interview data. (Of course, it is important not to be seduced by respondents' interpretations, as Staller's (2003) research, discussed in Chapter 10, illustrates.)

NEGOTIATING ACCESS

Negotiating access, although essential at the outset of a project, is not confined to the initial stages, but is rather the subject of continuous renegotiation through the entire fieldwork period. To engage in ethnographic research is to expose oneself to the potential for both discomfort and uncertainty. Meeting a new colleague who was also involved in observational fieldwork, I was immensely relieved when he asked me if I, too, spent much of my time 'feeling like a lemon'. Hammersley and Atkinson (1995: 114–115) refer to the potential of the marginal reflexive ethnographer as providing an analytic space. In the field, however, it can be difficult to convey this to those we observe, who frequently challenge our claims to what they view as 'their' space. Even where some individuals may accept our presence unquestioningly and even indicate that we are welcome, it is likely that there will be a range of reactions to the researcher in their midst. The following excerpts from my fieldnotes on one project illustrate the continuous nature of access negotiations and the way in which concerns can surface at different points in the course of a project.

STUDY OF THE ROLE AND RESPONSIBILITIES OF THE MIDWIFE IN SCOTLAND

Observational period in a teaching hospital labour ward. Excerpts from fieldnotes over a five-week period.

9 November (Day 1 of my observational period)

I met with the Nursing Officer who explained that I'd probably find things easier next week when the labour ward Nursing Officer was back. She added that some sisters had been there for years and that I'd probably encounter some resistance. 'You'll see for yourself, but there are the younger ones, too, who are quite keen.' The Nursing Officer's PA then took me to the labour ward and introduced me to the sister on duty. ... I went and chatted to Sister O. and Sister N., who were with a patient about to have an epidural. Sister N. then left and a medical student arrived. Sister O. asked the medical student and myself to leave when the anaesthetist came. I then went and spoke to Sister M., who was with a patient and the patient's friend. Sister M. introduced me to the patient and handed me the patient's record, indicating the bit that said, 'Baby for adoption – does not want to see baby'. ... Her contractions were coming more frequently and Sister

M. enlisted an auxiliary to help move the woman to the delivery room. She asked me to go to Sister C. and ask her to send a student midwife to come with 'us' (indicating that I was to return as well, it appeared) for the delivery. … I found a medical student and we both went to the delivery room. Apparently the fetal heart was dropping (as low as 88 at one point, Sister commented). Sister M. instructed me as to how to 'phone for a paediatric nurse, as she thought this would be necessary. However, Dr K. then arrived as Sister was scrubbing and instructing the woman on how to push. After Sister M. had performed an episiotomy she asked Dr K. to 'phone', which she did. … Sister M. then instructed the student midwife with regard to delivering the placenta, also explaining to the researcher that she had decided on an episiotomy for fetal distress and that there were no maternal indications as the perineum was 'stretching fine'.

11 November

The ward was quieter today – just 4 patients, as opposed to 7 or 8 the previous 2 mornings. … Dr D. came to examine the 4th patient. Dr D. instructed the Staff Midwife to put the patient on syntocinon: 'Start at 10 – that's usual isn't it? Just put her on the usual regime.' Sister N. commented to the researcher, 'If you're looking at what we're doing, dear, we've a lot of work with machines, so put that down when you're deciding if we're worth the money'. Staff Nurse K. also asked if I was interested in the time factor in carrying out procedures. … I then sat with Sister B., who was feeling for a patient's contractions after Dr D. had given her a pessary. She asked about the aims of the study and I explained that the focus was on midwives' roles and responsibilities. Sister B. told me that, in this hospital, midwives were able to do a lot. 'For example, this morning I came on at eight and went straight away and delivered a patient. Then I came back and a woman had been waiting for some time so I repaired her episiotomy. We get to do suturing here, lots of VEs (vaginal examinations), topping up of epidurals. Although the doctors make the decisions, we know what that decision is going to be. Like yesterday, that lassie who'd been pushing for ages – I knew there was no way she wasn't going to have to be forcepped. But the doctors know better sometimes than the midwife who's been with her all the time. They didn't know what her contractions were like or see her pushing for a while.'

19 November

A fairly uneventful morning. I chatted at length to all 8 women in labour or about to be induced. However, no decisions appeared to be involved in their care – i.e. during the half hour or so I spent with each. Sister N. came and looked at the casenotes of one patient, who was being attended by a student midwife and an obstetric nurse. Also present were the woman's husband and – I think – a physiotherapy student or physiotherapist doing a course. Sister said, 'I'm sorry, but there are just too many of you here. You're only allowed two. The 'physio' and myself immediately volunteered to leave. Sister came with me and explained at some length that it was far too many people to have around when you're in labour. 'They tend not to consider the patient here.'

22 November

… I then went and talked to Sister N., who was attending a patient who'd had an epidural. I asked her who decided a patient should have an epidural. 'Sometimes the medical staff, sometimes the midwife – it just depends on the circumstances. The patient might request one too, although others prefer to do without.'
 … Another patient is sitting in the dayroom, attached to an ambulant monitor. I'd overheard Sister J. tell Sister G. that someone wanted to use the Leboyer (natural birth) Room, whereupon both sisters had pulled faces.

(Continued)

Sister G. commented, 'Well, it still smells of paint. I wouldn't fancy being in labour with the stink of paint all around.' Staff Midwife L. was with this patient and accompanied her to see the birthing chair. Sister J. whispered to Sister B. (overheard by the researcher, who was in earshot) 'She's off to see the chair – she's one of *these*.'

I've managed to be fairly unlucky this morning in that I seem to have got to each patient at a time when no decisions as to her treatment were being made. The doctors do not do rounds and see patients at intervals dictated by their condition and progress. I did notice, however, that three of the beds appeared to have their screens round at times other than when the doctor was visiting or other treatment was being carried out. As this is where Sister N. is working, I did wonder whether this had anything to do with my presence, although she was quite pleasant when I approached her and (as usual) explained my presence to her patient.

When I returned from lunch a quick scan of the ward revealed that one of the women in labour appeared to have been transferred to a delivery room. I approached Sister G., saying that I wondered if I could go through to the delivery rooms if any of the women I'd met with had been transferred. She says, 'Well, I don't know about that. You'd have to get permission.' I explain that I have already spoken with the women, who have all said that they would be happy for me to accompany them. Sister G. says that I would need permission from the Nursing Officer. I explain that I have the Nursing Officer's permission and have already attended some births where the women concerned had given permission. I add that this is part of the original research remit, as I'm interested in all aspects of the midwives' work. 'Well', says Sister G., 'I'd have to check on that.' (This surprises me as I would have expected the midwives to have mentioned among themselves that I had been attending deliveries.) I explain that the project has ethical clearance, as I assume that this may be what she's referring to. Sister G. then disappears and returns 10 minutes later, saying – to my surprise as she hadn't seemed at all keen – that she's asked this newly admitted patient and she's agreeable to me coming into the delivery room with her. I go through to the delivery room with her, saying to the student midwife and Sister B. (who are attending), 'I understand Sister G.'s asked if I can come in?' 'Yes', says Sister B. and smiles, 'Permission granted'. The patient smiles over between contractions. Sister B. tells the student midwife to go and scrub up. Sister O. comes and asks Sister B. if two obstetric students can come in, saying 'Can you ask the patient?' 'It'll be OK', says Sister B. 'If she doesn't object to anyone else coming in, she won't object to that.' The two students come in…

…I think there has been some talk among the midwives about the research project as there seems to be some resistance today from them as a whole. Sister L. said to me in the duty room, 'I don't know what you're researching us for, to be honest?' I decide to treat this as a request for information, as she smiles when she says it. I go on to say that, hopefully, the study will detail how the tasks and responsibilities vary from unit to unit. Midwives ought then to be able to place their own unit on a continuum with regard to the amount of responsibility they have. The study will also give a picture of what midwives, as a whole, think of the work. She nods and adds, 'I don't see how you can keep track of it all, though, unless you're actually doing the work yourself'. I take this to be a reference to the fact that I'm not a midwife, which she has already established by asking me directly (although I did explain when I first introduced myself to her last week that I was a sociologist – as is my usual practice). While waiting for the student midwife to scrub up (for the delivery discussed above) Sister B. had also asked me if I am a midwife and I have explained that I am not. She replied, 'Oh, so do you *need* to see the births then?' I explained that I do, as the study is concerned with all aspects of the midwife's work and I'm particularly interested in the decisions they have to make during deliveries. When I go back to the ward area there appear to be about 8 medical students present – some sitting at bedsides and others in the dayroom. There is also a party of antenatal patients being shown round. As Sister N. appears to be the only sister in the ward at present I decide not to push my luck by joining students at a bedside and so I leave for the day.

I have included a substantial amount of fieldnote extracts in order to illustrate the necessity of continually re-negotiating access throughout a fieldwork period and to give some idea of the differences between the ways in which individual 'informants' perceived and received an observer in their workplace. Re-reading these excerpts, more than twenty years later, I still cringe as I recall the acute discomfort involved for the researcher.

In any fieldwork situation the researcher will, by necessity, only have partial access. The excerpts presented here also reflect my frustration that, at times, it looks as though the interesting snippets are occurring elsewhere, or at other times (such as when I've gone for a coffee or a lunch break or have been back at my university base). In many fieldwork situations, the observer may be barred from participating in certain activities or attending particular events because of her/his gender or age. Such considerations are very important in anthropological fieldwork, as conventions and prohibitions vary from society to society. However, there are many subtleties involved and the acceptability of a researcher's presence may depend on the situation and the individuals involved. Researchers must respect such groundrules – whether these are articulated or merely implied – and ungranted requests for access are themselves data. For example, such exchanges between researcher and gatekeepers (who need not be powerful in institutional terms) can provide valuable insights into sensitivities, valued activities and power relationships.

The adage, 'It's all data' applies especially to fieldwork situations. I did not request permission to attend one-to-one tutorials when carrying out my fieldwork on a social work course, as I had already picked up that these were viewed as sacrosanct, possibly harking back to social (case)work's roots in psychotherapy. To have made such a request would, I think, have been regarded as unacceptably intrusive and would have damaged the researcher's (already questioned) academic credentials and knowledge of social work education.

THE ETHNOGRAPHER'S ROLE AND RESEARCH RELATIONSHIPS

One of the earliest texts I consulted when embarking on my PhD studies was Schwartz and Schwartz (1955), who outlined possibilities as involving a continuum stretching from the passive observer at one end to the active participant observer at the other end. However, it is unlikely that either extreme will be workable in practice: one cannot remain entirely passive when in close daily contact in the field and it is also likely to impede one's research function if the observer becomes completely active. Instead, it is more helpful to aspire to the middle ground suggested by Delamont, who argues that 'participant observation' does not mean that the researcher is involved in *doing* the same things as those s/he is studying, merely that s/he interacts with them while *they* do these things (Delamont, 2004).

However, the boundaries between the marginal observer and the 'observed' can prove to be permeable in practice, causing anthropologists to coin the term 'going native' to describe those situations where they consider (often in retrospect) that they have strayed from their non-involved researcher role. Reflecting on one of my most uncomfortable experiences while observing the cohort of social work students whose professional socialization was the subject of my PhD, I realize, in retrospect, that I had slipped into appealing to the 'moral rhetoric' of the course, which privileged the sharing of feelings and the pursuit of personal growth:

> During the second year of the course I had joined a class (as was my habit). On this occasion the topic was groupwork and a series of classes had been arranged that dealt with different types of groupwork by allowing students to experience each in turn. At the start of this class I was rather taken aback by the lecturer's comment. He said, 'I'd like to ask Rose why she's here. I'm a bit surprised at your presence?' Sue, one of the students added, 'Yes, I wondered about that. I thought perhaps you were sneaking in, hoping we wouldn't notice.' Angela added, 'Yes, I wondered about that', and Judith agreed, saying, 'Yes, so did I but I wasn't going to say …'. Sue then continued, saying, 'Yes – why have you come along today? You know, you write down who's sitting next to you and what everyone says. (I had briefly kept a note of seating preferences at the beginning of the course, but had long since abandoned this practice and had also been careful to confine my writing to situations where students were also taking notes.) The lecturer then said, 'Are you attending this class as a participant, just, or as a researcher? Because I think that my reaction would be to say "welcome" to you as a member of the group but not as a researcher.' I replied that I supposed that I'd come as both really, as usual, but that I did not envisage the content of the classes as being all that relevant for my research. I had not, I explained, given the matter much thought, but had just drifted along with the students as I did to all the classes.
>
> One way of responding would have been to have offered to leave at this point. However, I considered that this would lead research participants to think I had, indeed, been 'trying to sneak in' and involved an attempt to deceive them. This could have done irreparable damage to the research relationship, which was already strained at this point, so it was therefore necessary to produce an argument as to why I should stay. I replied that the classes sounded interesting and attractive and that I welcomed the chance to participate in a way that observing in class did not generally allow. However, this did not seem to be producing the desired result. I then hesitantly offered the following: 'Well … I suppose I was curious. … I wanted to see what happened at a groupwork class. I wanted to join in and … perhaps to find out something about myself. I suppose I didn't ask permission to come, because … well … I was afraid people might say, "No!".' I was then told by the lecturer that I could stay.

I later added the following commentary to my fieldnotes:

Although my presence at this class might have been viewed as problematic by my research contact due to the nature of its content, I consider that this challenge was partly a product of the strained relations between staff and students at this stage. Students had just returned from their six-month placements and staff were disappointed and a little annoyed by their non-attendance at classes. The last term prior to these placements had been characterized by some hostility towards the researcher, who, being in a marginal position, became the target when conflict between staff members arose (concerned with promotions, etc.) and when students were concerned about their impending placements. During this period I had been asked to leave a class whose overt content was the teaching of social work skills rather than the 'sharing of feelings'. On another occasion a member of staff had told me that staff were unclear about my intentions and would appreciate it if I made these clear. Likewise, the issue of my attendance at these groupwork classes cannot be viewed in isolation from the strained interaction between staff and students at this time and my own marginal position as a participant observer.

This excerpt also recalls quite vividly, nearly thirty years later, the acute discomfort involved. Constructing a role as a participant observer is not a one-sided process and, as Vidich (1955: 356) commented: 'In every case the fieldworker is fitted into a plausible role by the population he [sic.] is studying and within a context meaningful to them.'

The researcher, of course, has some control over the image s/he wishes to project. Dress plays an important part in how we are perceived. Reflecting on preparation for observational fieldwork with helpline workers for the National Society for the Prevention of Cruelty to Children, Hepburn and Potter (2004: 180) comment: 'We spent a bit of time that morning deciding what to wear – what gradation of "smart casual" sends quite the right "professional yet informal" message. It feels a little like being interviewed for a job.' Regardless of the amount of thought put by researchers into 'identity management' we are likely to overlook many important signifiers of our status and social class – for example, many of us unthinkingly wear our wedding rings (Kitzinger and Barbour, 1999). Burman et al. (2001) comment on the positive impact on research relationships with schoolgirls they studied of the fashionable clothes of one of the young research team members. Such options are more feasible for some researchers than others, either by virtue of age, gender, or perhaps even bodily shape and size. We do not, however, always know in advance which of these indicators, which we take for granted, may be of significance to our research participants and how acceptable all of these are in the research setting. Benford, who carried out an ethnography of the nuclear disarmament movement, talks about the researcher's 'potential to discredit or complement a group's everyday performances' (Hunt and Benford, 1997: 110).

Sometimes, of course, the researcher's gaucheness may serve as a welcome reminder to participants and others who may be observing the situation, of their competence. The prostitutes studied by Saunders (2004) took great delight in her discomfiture when one 'punter' tried to hire her services. Similarly, the midwives I observed on one labour ward were very amused by my terror on being given a newborn baby to hold while the obstetric team dealt with a haemorrhaging mother. They recounted this story many times to other members of staff and decided to 'take me in hand' by assigning me a pre-term baby to feed and change on those days when his parents were unable to visit.

In the course of carrying out observational research for my PhD thesis I listed no fewer than 16 roles which were assigned to me at various points throughout my two-year fieldwork period:

1. **Facilitator of student awareness.** The use of this role illustrates students' propensity to explain my role with reference to the 'moral rhetoric' (Kleinman and Fine, 1979) of the department under study, which emphasized the importance of practitioners being reflective. However, due to concerns about confidentiality and the potential to create a 'self-fulfilling prophecy' by highlighting developments as these arose, I could not always share to the degree required by this imperative. This led to me sometimes being viewed as…

2. **A withholder of valuable information.** This was really a no-win situation, as the only other available explanation for my reticence was that of…

3. **Incompetent researcher,** who was not able to make sense of the data being collected by summarizing important issues and progress. Understandably, this was a somewhat uncomfortable role.

4. **Student biographer.** This was a role also highlighted by Olesen and Whittaker (1968), who studied the process of professional socialization for nurses, and who referred to this as 'keeper of the student past'. Students were anxious that, in this capacity, I should attend and record meetings they called to discuss their course. They also felt that they had some claim on my data and from time to time asked whether their individual interview transcripts would be available for them to consult at a later date.

5. **Friend.** Since there were only 20 students on the course and I was in close daily contact with them, it would have been virtually impossible not to have become involved in the reciprocities of feeling and action that constitute friendship. Coupled with this was the similarity in age and social background between myself and the students and the degree to which our social circles overlapped in a relatively small and compact city.

6. **Fellow student.** Students frequently assigned me the role of fellow student, whose efforts went unacknowledged. A common joke centred around my almost perfect attendance at classes as compared with their own more sporadic engagement and the fact that I would not receive a certificate at the end of the

course. On one occasion a student introduced me to a friend – albeit with some hesitation – explaining that I was doing the course as well. Presumably this was due to the tortuousness of providing a more accurate description. However, it is significant that this was the shorter preferred option.

7. **Interviewer.** This gave rise to some concern on my part, as students tended to regard my research activities as being confined to my interview performances, despite my repeated emphasis on my interest in what happened in class as well.

8. **Conspirator.** This was an amalgamation of the roles of friend and interviewer. This was the role being assigned when, for example, a student might pull a face at me in class, alluding to a 'secret' shared in a one-to-one interview. This sometimes referred to comments from other students and this pulling of faces was something which they indulged in with each other – presumably referring to previous conversations.

9. **Validator of students' importance.** This role became apparent when I visited students on their placements, when they frequently took the opportunity to introduce me to as many people as possible, as someone who was 'doing research on their class'.

10. **Social catalyst.** This term was coined by Olesen and Whittaker (1967) and reflected the potential to act as 'go-between' afforded by my marginal position.

11. **Source of information.** Students indulged in a great deal of gossip with regard to relationships between staff members – particularly in the wake of the resignation of the professor. Likewise, lecturers assumed that I had more information about students and would sometimes ask me if I knew why they were not attending particular classes.

12. **Self-seeking academic.** This was another uncomfortable role, which arose as a result of the strong anti-academic bias among students who were not persuaded of the relevance of research to social work practice. Although direct challenges were rare, I did feel implicated in comments about researchers 'only wanting to secure publications' or 'to make a name for themselves'.

13. **Spy.** This potential role only became apparent when the issue of falling attendance at classes was raised by members of staff. However, it is possible that this was continuously present. A rumour circulated that I had been observed to take notes on where individuals were sitting in class and several students asked me whether I kept a record of who attended classes. I had taken such notes, but these were purely for research purposes and the information was never shared with members of staff.

14. **'Shrink'.** This view of me was apparent in comments relating to the attention that I appeared to pay to every utterance of students – and, indeed, staff members. Interestingly, this role attribution was confined to those who defined the social work role in psychoanalytic terms, and suggested that they were seeking to understand my behaviour within their own preferred frame of

reference or 'comfort zone'. Although this did cause me some discomfort, it was not an altogether unwelcome attributed role, as it did, at least, confer some idea of competence – albeit misplaced – on the part of the researcher.

15. **'Silly young woman'.** Although the assignment of this role could be irritating, it did, nevertheless, serve the useful function of encouraging participation as a generous act in the face of exasperation. The male student who said in a 'teasing' manner, 'Oh … you do ask a lot of deep questions, don't you?' did go on to give a considered response to the questions on my interview schedule to which he referred.

16. **Colleague with a research function.** This role became particularly apparent when the students were absent from the department on placements and via my continuous presence and participation at research seminars attended by staff members but not students.

Several ethnographers have written about their relationships with key informants and the conflict they have experienced in terms of writing up their research, pondering whether they can be viewed as having betrayed the trust of people with whom they have been in close personal contact for extended periods of time. As in any social situation, the ethnographer is likely to warm to some people more than others and participants may come to view the researcher as a friend. Later extracts (reproduced in Chapter 10 to show how I developed my coding categories for analyzing this data) highlight the suspicion with which social work students viewed the academic endeavour. Practitioners doing research with members of their own professional group, and with whom they share values and assumptions, may find especially difficult such challenges to their integrity, for example the charge that they are using the research (and hence the participants) to enhance their career prospects.

PLANNING OBSERVATION

One of the studies discussed earlier concentrated on the work of midwives as they provided care to women at antenatal clinics, on the labour ward, in postnatal wards and in the community. As the focus was on 'normal' pregnancies and deliveries, we omitted antenatal wards and special-care baby units from the observational part of the study (although these areas were covered in our subsequent postal questionnaire). In order to maximize coverage and the potential for comparison, we chose to study midwives working in a variety of organizational settings, including both large and small teaching hospitals, non-teaching hospitals, peripheral maternity units, general practitioner (GP) units (where medical back-up for deliveries was provided by GPs who had completed obstetric training), and health centres (where some of the community midwives were based).

Again, in order to ensure that we observed as wide a range of situations and interactions as possible, we employed several strategies to guide our fieldwork plans.

Sometimes we positioned ourselves in a particular place (for example an individual consulting room or the staffroom); sometimes we observed a particular event, such as a ward-round or shift hand-over; sometimes we spent a period of time with an individual midwife as she moved between labour rooms or visited different women at home; and on other occasions we moved between several different parts of the settings during an observational period (for example moving between consulting rooms or labour rooms and/or the staffroom).

In addition to carrying out observations during the normal 9–5 working day, we included night duty. As the boundaries between midwives' work and doctors' work was a particular focus of the study, this was important, since medical staff were not usually on hand during the night, giving rise to a different set of decisions and negotiations for the midwives who had to call out doctors, rather than seeking advice or input as they were passing. Observation was usually concentrated in 2–3 hour sessions, although night duty sessions covered whole shifts. (A knock-on consequence of doing night duty was that midwives viewed us rather differently thereafter, perhaps because this demonstrated our commitment to understanding what their work involved. There was something inescapably intimate about sitting through the night chatting during 'slow' periods when waiting for labouring women to arrive.)

A perennial question in relation to carrying out fieldwork is how to select what to record from the huge range of interactions and events that are likely to occur. The answer, as so often with regard to qualitative research, is that 'the salience hierarchy' (Wolfinger, 2002) depends on your research question. In some studies the research question is not refined until a preliminary period of fieldwork has been carried out but, particularly with funded studies, it is likely that there are some broad questions that suggest a focus for selecting significant snatches of interaction. Our study was concerned with examining the role and responsibilities of midwives in a range of settings. It concentrated on the intersection between their work and that of medical and support staff. We were therefore able to focus on the tasks and procedures carried out in each setting and fieldnotes were made in relation to a set of questions which provided a template. These are listed here:

- What procedures were routinely performed by (a) midwives, (b) medical staff, (c) support staff?
- In what circumstances were these routines not adhered to?
- To what extent, if at all, were tasks carried out by midwives then repeated by doctors, or vice versa?
- To what extent, if at all, was dissatisfaction expressed, or conflict evident in the carrying out of tasks or procedures?
- What were the major decision areas? Were decisions made with reference to policies/guidelines taken by midwives or taken by medical staff? Who had the final say?
- Whom, if anyone, did midwives and medical staff consult before carrying out any aspect of their work, and what was the nature of consultation between midwives, medical staff and support staff?

- Who deferred to whom, and on what issues, and were there any circumstances in which there was overt conflict between midwives and medical staff and between midwives and support staff? If so, how was it handled?
- Who was regarded as accountable by whom?
- Was there a difference between midwives' responsibility for the care of normal and abnormal cases, and, if so, how was the transition negotiated and made? (Askham and Barbour, 1996: 36)

This template allowed us to focus on the routine or mundane aspects of practice as these unfolded in daily clinical encounters. Wolfinger (2002) recommends comprehensive note-taking which recreates the order in which events happened and this can be particularly helpful in attempting, retrospectively, to tease out why specific situations and exchanges arose. No topic is too mundane for inclusion in fieldnotes, as simple activities such as the laying out of equipment has ritualistic and potentially directive consequences, as became apparent in relation to how midwives managed preparation for routine examinations and blood tests in antenatal clinics:

> In their work in antenatal clinics, senior midwives might again find themselves paired with relatively inexperienced medical staff; and midwives, in general, tended to be more familiar with the protocols of individual consultants than were their often more transitory medical counterparts. This could be used to the midwife's advantage, in that she could use an individual consultant's alleged preferences to justify making a particular decision or taking a particular course of action. More frequently, however, midwives simply encouraged junior medical staff to follow the guidelines set down by the consultant in charge. Midwives were skilled exponents of the delicate use of tact – or what Kitzinger, Green and Coupland (1990) have termed 'hierarchy maintenance work'. This involved a whole range of approaches from laying out specific forms or setting out syringes and containers in anticipation of blood samples being taken, to indicating verbally what a consultant's protocol specified. Midwives were thus able to influence the content and outcome of antenatal consultations while allowing junior members of the medical staff ample opportunity for 'face-saving'. (Askham and Barbour, 1996: 43)

These procedures were often managed via unspoken, tacit understandings and agreements, and in this case midwives frequently referred to their role in 'keeping an eye on the housemen'. Midwives also often acted as 'go-between', explaining doctors' advice to women in lay terms, providing counselling, or voicing concerns on the part of the women concerned:

> I had observed a midwife at an antenatal clinic talking at some length with a patient prior to the arrival of the consultant. A large part of this conversation had been devoted to discussing a vaginal discharge which the woman had been experiencing. When the consultant arrived he asked the woman, 'And how have you been?' to which she replied 'Oh, fine, thanks.' Here the midwife laughingly interrupted and said, 'Now, that's not what you've been telling me, is it?' The woman

then went on to raise the topic of her discharge with the doctor. (Fieldnotes, Teaching Hospital Antenatal Clinic)

Through recording the unremarkable and unproblematic, we can be alerted, in contrast, to those occasional instances where such 'rules of engagement' are breached.

GENERATING AND ANALYZING FIELDNOTES

A perennial problem experienced by ethnographers is managing the taking of detailed notes without drawing attention to this activity, which might potentially render participants self-conscious or even threaten access arrangements. Like many other ethnographers I have frequently resorted to taking notes in the toilet, but have also had to rely on noting down key issues or phrases to act as an *aide-mémoir* for writing up more detailed notes once I had returned to my university office. This sounds difficult but becomes easier with practice, and some snippets of interaction are so vivid that they stick in the mind for days, months, and sometimes even for years. Benford, who carried out participant observation in relation to the nuclear disarmament movement, describes how he sought to utilize any opportunities that involved writing in order to openly carry out this activity (Hunt and Benford, 1997). He explains that cultivating a reputation as 'a reliable stenographer' allowed him to take notes without being conspicuous while his other useful identity as a 'camera bug' gave him licence to unobtrusively photograph the movement's activities. He adds that he provided copies of photographs to other individuals and group representatives and established himself as the 'official historian'. Useful though such advice can be, these tactics can occasionally backfire. Being privileged to be invited to a meeting called by social work students, at which they were to raise some concerns about their course, I offered to take notes of their discussion, but established that someone else would report back to the lecturers involved. In the event, my handwriting proved to be illegible and I was landed with the uncomfortable task of relaying the key points that had arisen, placing me in the undesirable and unenviable position of acting as group spokeswoman.

Keeping detailed fieldnotes and searching these rigorously in order to identify patterns and exceptions is what allows us, as ethnographers, to elucidate the assumptions underpinning routine, everyday behaviour and the functions of rituals – both conscious and unconscious. This, however, raises difficult questions regarding the layering on of meaning and the capacity of our own cultural and disciplinary frameworks to furnish an explanation. We are not, however, alone in seeking to develop our understanding, and it is possible to draw on the insights of our research participants, either through asking questions relating to specific interactions or events observed and recorded (as we did in the 'Midwives' Study' through the interviews which followed close on the heels of our observational fieldwork) or by inviting commentaries from key informants.

In the course of our fieldwork we had noted the occasional instance of midwives openly questioning doctors' decisions. During one ward round a midwife disagreed with a registrar:

> Registrar: I think Mrs Brown can probably go home tomorrow.
>
> Sister: Well, we'll see how the feeding is going. It wasn't too good yesterday.
> (Fieldnotes, Teaching Hospital Postnatal Ward)

Here, as in many other areas of their work, midwives could appeal (as did the individual above) to the midwife's unique role as provider of care and support to both mother and baby. Although decisions regarding patients' discharge were one of the few regularly cited by midwives (both in interviews and the postal questionnaire which followed) as falling within the doctor's remit, some midwives acknowledged that they could influence such decisions. In response to a question about who made discharge decisions, one midwife was particularly forthright: 'Discharging patients? Well, in the end it comes down to us. We put words into the doctor's mouth and he puts pen to paper to sign' (interview with Teaching Hospital Postnatal Ward midwife).

It is doubtful whether such a response would have been elicited had not the interview been embedded in observational fieldwork. While this particular interviewee does not refer explicitly to situations observed on the ward, many other midwives did refer in the course of their interviews to specific instances that we had observed and which illustrated the points they were making. Having viewed the midwives repeatedly *in situ* as they dealt with the everyday exigencies of their work environment and the situations arising, we were more likely to be viewed as trustworthy recipients of such insights.

On occasion midwives were observed to resort to correcting junior doctors in the presence of patients:

> Houseman: (*To patient – 30 weeks gestation*) Have you heard your spina bifida test is OK?
>
> Midwife: No – we don't notify patients if it's all right – only if there's anything…
>
> Houseman: OK (*He then checks for oedema and palpates, commenting that the head seems to be 'well down'.*) Can we use the sonic aid? (*The midwife puts jelly on the woman's abdomen and uses the sonic aid.*)
>
> Midwife: (*To patient*) We'll have to check your blood today – are you taking your iron pills? (*The doctor takes a blood sample.*) We're now coming to the stage where the baby takes all its iron from you.
>
> Houseman: We'll see you in four weeks. See your own doctor in two weeks.
>
> Midwife: Dr D. (*Consultant*) only sees them at 30 and then 36 weeks.
>
> Houseman: That's less than the others – I'd like to see them oftener.
>
> Midwife: Well, it is less, but in this area their general health is better. Obviously if their blood pressure is high or that, you'd want to see them oftener.
>
> Houseman: Sure – in six weeks then.
> (Fieldnotes, General Hospital Antenatal Clinic)

There were a few instances where midwives not only questioned doctors' decisions, but took steps to actively resist these, or at least to limit the potential damage:

After the clinic ended, Sister R. came into the room and spoke to Dr L. (Registrar).

Sister: What's this – letting a woman out with a blood pressure of 150 over 110? Dr H. (*Consultant*) would have a fit! She shouldn't be out like that.

Registrar: No … no – she's OK. I told her to come back next week.

Sister: Next week?! She should be taken in (*admitted to the antenatal ward*) straight away!

Registrar: No – we'll leave her.

Sister: OK – but it goes in the casenotes.

             (*After this exchange I went with the midwives for coffee and I overheard Sister R. telling Sister C. about this case.*)

Sister: (*To Sister C.*) I'm not taking that nonsense from a Registrar – I always go straight to the Consultant. (*She then tried, without success, to 'phone the Consultant, and explained that, in the meantime, she would contact the community staff and get them to visit the woman at home the next day.*) She's a wee lassie, too, and her blood pressure was 80 last time. She's just the sort to go eclamptic on us – and she's 28 weeks. (*Staff Midwife D. had already explained in an aside to the researcher that with that blood pressure you would be expecting the woman to have a pre-eclamptic fit at any moment.*)

Sister: (*To researcher*) Dr H. (*Consultant*) would have a fit if he thought that the woman was walking about like that. I'll make sure that the record's kept straight, though – I've learnt that by experience.

             (Fieldnotes, General Hospital Antenatal Clinic)

That such disagreements were rare occurrences does not mean that midwives were excluded from the decision-making process – only that they did not have formal responsibility.

Although the researcher was not herself a midwife, the above excerpts show respondents providing me with the clinical information required in order to interpret situations. Indeed, the role of the naïve stranger – and the licence to ask questions – was at many times a useful one, even once I was pretty sure I could tell without asking why midwives were taking certain actions. However, some aspects of behaviour, particularly in settings very different from those in which we ourselves have been socialized, may well elude our perceptual and explanatory frameworks.

One of the most well-known discussions of the role of personal experience in understanding the emotions of members of another culture is provided by Rosaldo's (1983) account. While carrying out fieldwork with the Ilongot, a tribe of head-hunters, Rosaldo struggled to understand their attachment to this practice, which appeared to him senselessly barbaric. This all changed, however, following a tragic turn of events, when his young wife fell to her death while out walking during this period of fieldwork, whereupon Rosaldo found himself consumed by bereavement and the emotions surrounding it. He thus came to appreciate first-hand the important link between grief and rage, which impelled the Ilongot to seek revenge for the death of their loved ones. It would be tempting to assume that members of societies very different from our own are motivated by ideas and values that are alien to us, as researchers, and which will, therefore, defy academic explanation. However, as Rosaldo (1989) suggests, it could merely be the experience of the ethnographer, and hence her/his capacity to empathize and ultimately theorize, that is limited. He highlights: 'The relative youth of fieldworkers, who, for the most part, have not suffered serious losses and could have, for example, no personal knowledge of how devastating the loss of a long-term partner can be for the survivor' (Rosaldo, 1989: 9). Richard Shweder (1990: 252) advises the ethnographer to guard against the twin dangers of underestimating or overestimating the opaqueness of other cultures and the emotions that guide behaviour: '[I]t is ludicrous to imagine that the emotional functioning of people in different cultures is basically the same. It is just as ludicrous to imagine that each culture's emotional life is unique.'

So where does this leave us? The answer, in the form of the 'litany' which can be traced throughout this whole volume, is that we must be wary of slipping into making unwarranted assumptions. We need to analyze our data systematically for disconfirming as well as confirming instances of the arguments we wish to pursue. It is also essential that we engage reflexively with our data, deriving analytic purchase from our own emotional and intellectual reactions to events and comments arising during fieldwork. This requires us to acknowledge how our own views and behaviours have been shaped by our socialization and experience and what this tells us about the perceptions and life worlds of others.

HINTS ON USING ETHNOGRAPHIC METHODS

- Ethnography can be particularly challenging, but is also very rewarding in terms of the wealth of insights it can provide.
- Research design and sampling issues are important here, too, although it is essential not to take too rigid an approach. You may have less control than in other sorts of research but be aware of possibilities and constraints.
- A reflexive approach will yield many benefits, including a readiness to address issues as they arise, particularly with regard to re-negotiating access.
- Remain alert for new issues and explore these by asking relevant questions of informants.
- Try to anticipate analysis and maximize comparative potential through constantly reviewing your observational templates and fieldwork settings and the potential insights these afford.

FURTHER READING

Hammersley, M. and Atkinson, P. (1995) *Ethnography: Principles in Practice* (2nd edition), London: Routledge.

Wolfinger, N.H. (2002) 'On writing fieldnotes: Collection strategies and background expectancies', *Qualitative Research*, 2(1): 85–95.

EXERCISES

I have suggested two research questions that lend themselves to observational fieldwork.

Research Question 1: What role does gender play in participation at meetings?

This topic has been chosen because of the relative ease with which most of us can access a relevant fieldwork setting. Through rendering the everyday and familiar as strange (through engaging with a structured observational exercise), this should give some indication of what the ethnographic gaze might involve. It is, of course, likely that you will choose not to take such a structured approach. Nevertheless, this exercise should give some indication of the importance of defining categories to be employed and being systematic about recording data.

- Select three or four work-based meetings which you would normally attend in the course of your job.
- Decide what basis to use for selecting these (for example narrow or wide membership, or a combination of both).
- Use the provisional template presented in Table 4.1 to record your observations, thinking about what items you might wish to add.

  N.B. You are unlikely to start with such a detailed template for recording and I have included the timing of contributions merely to illustrate the sort of thing you might possibly elect to include as your interests and focus develop. Nevertheless, this should give you a taste of both the insights that observational work can afford and the discipline required to record relevant items.

Table 4.1   Provisional observational template

Purpose of meeting	Male	Female
Membership of meeting		
No. of contributions		
Length of contributions (timed)		
Initiating idea		
Re-presenting idea (with acknowledgement)		
Re-presenting idea (without acknowledgement)		
Summarizing		
Suggesting plan of action		
Delegating work		

There are likely to be other things you consider would be helpful in making sense of this interaction. Foremost among these might be:

1. Who is chairing the meeting – do male and female chairs exhibit different styles? Give more or less attention/time to men and women?
2. The relative seniority of the people attending the meeting. For example, is delegating predominantly done by those in senior positions or are any other individuals adept at suggesting that others do the work?

   - In reviewing the templates you have completed, what patterns emerge? What further questions does this raise? For example:

3. Do men and women behave differently? Do they employ any obvious strategies to put a point across, such as the approach I found myself having to resort to in one workplace where I had to angle to get a male colleague to repeat my suggestions before these were taken on board, or interrupting or deliberately misunderstanding?
4. What about meetings where only one gender is represented? Do individuals behave differently? Do the same individuals who have been observed in mixed gender meetings behave differently in single-gender meetings?
5. How does seniority influence the attention accorded to individuals' contributions? Is seniority more important than gender?
6. You might also become interested in recording 'small talk' preceding or following meetings, as this might provide important information regarding the nature of working relationships and the way in which gender impacts on these. For example, in a radio interview with Madeleine Albright, I was intrigued to hear her say that when she 'moved up a gear' to take up her post as Secretary of State she felt that she had to fundamentally alter how she behaved in meetings, abandoning what she characterized as a 'female style' of embedding formal interaction in more informal talk involving 'chat'.

Commentary

You might find that you become increasingly intrigued by the ways in which gender influences vocabulary and style of speech, in which case you might want to consider employing an approach that draws more explicitly on conversation analysis (CA). There is, of course, an ongoing debate about the utility and appropriateness of using such referents as 'gender' in CA, particularly if this is not a notion appealed to by participants. However, Stokoe and Smithson (2001: 236) observe that 'some researchers combine CA with social constructionism which sees common-sense and cultural knowledge as being negotiated and maintained in everyday talk'. It is in this spirit that I would recommend CA as a potential resource in developing an observational template and beginning to interpret your data. This is consistent with the broad licence and possibilities that I have claimed are afforded by employing a social constructionist approach at the outset of a qualitative study (as advocated in Chapter 1) with the potential to opt for a specific designated method at a later stage, once you have refined your interests and seen the sorts of data you are likely to generate.

Another paper, addressing the issue of gendered relations in a specific academic setting, and which might help you to develop your focus and potential analysis is:

Conefrey, T. (1997) 'Gender, culture and authority in a university life sciences laboratory', *Discourse and Society*, 8(3): 313–340.

Research Question 2: What processes of negotiation do parents and children become involved in during supermarket shopping? How do children exert 'pester power' and how do parents respond?

First of all, you will need to decide in which supermarket/s you wish to carry out your observations. Different chains cater to people in different socio-economic bands, so you might want to think about including more than one supermarket in order to maximize comparative potential.

You should also decide when to carry out the fieldwork. Obviously, if you carry out fieldwork on Monday to Friday during school hours, this will normally preclude observing parent–child interaction with older children.

You may find that different time-slots are likely to yield different combinations of parents and children – with, for example, fathers being more likely to be present at weekend shopping expeditions. This may also be when estranged parents – probably overwhelmingly fathers – may shop with their children. Think through the implications for inclusion and exclusion of your choice of time-slots.

In formulating your observational template, think about the categories and questions listed below.

Contextual details

- Is negotiation a feature of the entire shopping expedition, or does it surface in specific parts of the supermarket (i.e. in relation to particular types of product)?
- Is negotiation more likely to arise in relation to expensive items?
- Do your observations, so far as you can tell, cover extensive monthly shopping expeditions or 'top-up' shopping? You may wish to include both.

How do family characteristics appear to affect negotiation?

- Are specific family combinations more likely to give rise to negotiation, or to different types of negotiation (see also 'Observing the interaction' below)? (for example, a mother accompanied with two or more children, or children of differing ages or genders)

- Is negotiation or different types of negotiation more common with families of different socio-economic status (assuming that you are able to allocate families to useful groupings)?
- Do differing levels or types of negotiation appear to be associated with families who are overweight?

Observing the interaction

- What sorts of appeals do children make?
- What language do they use?
- Do they appeal overtly to advertisements for specific products?
- Do they invoke comparisons with their peer group?
- Does this differ by age, gender, social class or ethnicity (if appropriate)?
- Whether and how do parents counter these pleas or ploys?

Commentary

As you engage in further reading, you might decide to revise your question template. It is also possible that new theoretical directions are suggested, which may lead you to change your focus. The following papers may help you to further refine your question template:

Boden, S. (2006) ' "Another day, another demand": How parents and children negotiate consumption matters', *Sociological Research Online*, 11(2), http://www.socre-sonline.org.uk/11/2/boden.html

Eldridge, J. and Murcott, A. (2000) 'Adolescents' dietary habits and attitudes: Unpacking the "problem of (parental) influence"', *Health*, 4(1): 25–49.

Evans, J. and Chandler, J. (2006) 'To buy or not to buy: Family dynamics and children's consumption', *Sociological Research Online*, http://www.socresonline.org.uk/11/3/evans.html

5
INTERVIEWING

AIMS

- Taking the most commonly employed of all qualitative research methods, this chapter aims to encourage researchers to take a critical look at the assumptions underpinning its use.
- It advises the reader about the appropriate use of interviews, including narrative interviews.
- It provides detailed guidance on developing semi-structured interview schedules and using these (together with prompts) to generate the desired data in relation to both cross-sectional and longitudinal studies.
- It offers advice on phrasing and ordering of interview questions.
- It emphasizes the planning and preparation tasks as key components of research design.
- Hints are provided with regard to how to anticipate analysis.

INTRODUCTION

Often presented as virtually the 'gold standard' of qualitative research (Barbour, 2003), interviews nevertheless involve a somewhat rarified, in-depth exchange between researcher and researched. This chapter subjects interviews to critical examination, viewing them in a broader context which explores both appropriate and inappropriate use. Although many texts stress the importance of asking questions, it is also important for the researcher to listen actively. In addition to discussing the development of interview schedules and the challenges of the flexible use of question order in 'semi-structured' interviewing, the use of prompts is examined, and the accompanying exercises provide practice in using these to elicit data.

I view interviewing as both an art and a science. It is important that the researcher attends to both of these aspects of the research encounter if the full potential of interviewing as a means of eliciting relevant, valuable and analytically rich data is to be realized. This chapter will provide some hints with regard to developing necessary skills and capitalizing on your own inherent abilities.

Everyone thinks they know what an interview involves – we are used to seeing these carried out on television by chat-show hosts and political journalists, and several commentators have argued that we live in an 'interview society' (see Atkinson and Silverman, 1997; Mischler, 1986). Many pieces in our broadsheet newspapers are generated through the use of interviews in order to present us with the views of celebrities, whether actors, pop stars, well-known novelists and even the odd academic. Most of us will have been involved (perhaps even on both sides of the table) at job selection interviews. Many practitioners utilize interviews as a standard tool in their practice.

Whatever your involvement in this process – whether as an active participant or as a consumer of interview-generated copy – it is likely that you have reflected on the importance of thinking through beforehand the sorts of questions to be asked. This is enshrined in the checklists produced by professions in relation to diagnostic interviews, and we have all probably encountered – even thought up – somewhat formulaic job interview, questions which are designed to allow ready comparison between candidates. When we employ interviews for research purposes, however, we are usually attempting to add to the knowledge base either by questioning a new group of people about a topic, questioning people about a new topic, or both.

Indeed, this appears to apply to some other interview forms, such as journalism. A recent and unusually reflexive account from an individual (Pico Lyer) who has experience both as an interviewer and as an interviewee (by virtue of his own career as a novelist) bemoans the decline in thorough preparatory work by media journalists (*The Guardian*, 8 July, 2006: 21). He argues that internet search engines, such as Google, have both made such material readily accessible and, through their concentration on the most frequently requested items, have resulted in interviewing becoming a circular form, in which each new interviewer asks virtually the same questions as did previous interviewers.

What a perusal of the use of interviews in this wider context emphasizes is the role of the interviewer's style or personality. Although this reaches its peak in television interviewing (with some interviewers becoming celebrities in their own right) it alerts us, as academic researchers, to the need to pay attention to the match of individual interviewer and research method. Even where two researchers employ the same interview schedule, the data produced may vary – some interviewers are better than others at making even a list of pre-determined questions appear fresh and worthy of thoughtful consideration; some are more skilled at establishing rapport; and some seem to have a knack for encouraging interviewees to talk, knowing when exactly to prompt and when to leave room for the interviewee to mull over the question raised.

When researchers describe their work as involving interviewing, they may actually be talking about rather different approaches. Again, a broad spectrum is involved, ranging from the use of highly structured interview schedules with identically worded questions being put in exactly the same order to each interviewee through to very loosely structured encounters where the interviewee determines the content and order of the exchange.

DEVELOPING AND USING INTERVIEW SCHEDULES

There is a craft to formulating interview questions and to using these to advantage in the research encounter and, like so much in the qualitative research endeavour, this is not an exact science.

Before moving on to discuss the content of the interview schedule it is useful to consider the usefulness of pro-formas that can be designed to collect routine data on interviewees' demographic characteristics. It is often more efficient to collect such information by means of a short questionnaire prior to interviews as this ensures that all such details are recorded in the one accessible place. It also cuts down on potential transcription time – and costs. This sort of information is invaluable when we come to identify patterning in our data (see Chapter 10) and allows us to provide thumb-nail sketches (as provided in the exercise accompanying Chapter 10). This ensures that we routinely collect the same information from each interviewee.

In comparison to questionnaires, interview schedules are relatively short, but their brevity belies the amount of work that goes into developing these. Researchers who are well versed in survey research tend to produce long, detailed schedules with very precise wording. While this is a good discipline for designing questionnaires, it is not so useful for less structured approaches. It is useful to remember that in qualitative research we are not seeking to measure attitudes or specify the exact nature of relationships between variables, but are, instead, concerned with eliciting in-depth accounts from people with room for them to select which aspects they wish to emphasize. With quantitative approaches the onus is on the researcher to hone the instrument so that the maximum amount of pre-cise information can be collected from the respondent as efficiently as possible. With qual-itative research the interviewee is also invited to comment on the relevance of the questions posed and is encouraged to expand at length on the chosen topics.

A qualitative interview schedule may simply involve a series of headings or may have a few carefully worded questions which are usually open-ended to allow respon-dents to elaborate. However, accompanying prompts are helpful as a reminder to the researcher, should interviewees not flag up anticipated issues. In terms of drafting an interview schedule it is generally best to start with the least threatening questions and to move gradually through to those that probe a little more. An opening question might be along the lines of 'So can you talk me through how you came to be referred to the fertility clinic?' for the study of couples' experiences of sub-fertility and sub-fertility services. (See the excerpts presented in the exercises accompanying Chapters 10 and 11.) Such a question leaves room for the interviewee to select which parts of the story to stress and, importantly, where to start – some couples chose to talk about their relationship and how important having a baby was to them, while others began with the latest visit to their GP (where this was the referral route). Since this was a longitudinal study (with each couple taking part in up to four interviews, there was a lot of scope to develop the schedules as the project unfolded). This, however, was the list of topics that we provided for the ethics committee:

PROPOSED TOPICS TO BE COVERED IN INTERVIEWS WITH COUPLES

- When they first consulted someone about their fertility problems. Who this was (GP or other professional)
- What the triggers were to the decision to seek advice/help.
- Whether couples consider that they are subject to pressure to reproduce. The nature and source of such pressures.
- What information couples have about fertility services and treatments on offer.
- Sources of information – family, friends, media, further reading, etc.
- Their expectations of the clinic.

Additional topics to be covered in the second and subsequent interviews

- How satisfied couples are with the services provided.
- Whether they receive counselling and whether this is helpful. Which aspects are most helpful.
- Changes in their expectations or views about the different services and options on offer.
- Factors which contribute towards making particular decisions.

Interviewing as interaction

While none of the subsequent interviews strayed very far from these broad topic areas, this list gives little indication of the interactional richness and variety involved in the actual research encounters, as the researcher became familiar with the couples and their stories as these unfolded. The excerpt below is from the start of a third interview with a couple (Couple PFD23). With all of these sub-fertile couples, the interview involved a potentially emotive topic and the researcher was constantly engaged in moving between asking 'difficult' questions and trying not to be too intrusive. She frequently used her previous knowledge of the couples' situations in order to give her licence to raise these issues and this also served to remind couples that they had confided in her in the past (R = researcher; F = woman of the couple; M = man of the couple):

> R: How are you doing?
> F: I think we're both getting back to normal. (*Had conceived but miscarried.*)
> R: Sorry to hear about the miscarriage.
> (*Some general chat about the weather.*)

F: I'd managed to catch (i.e. conceive) myself, which was an absolute miracle, you know. After all this time I don't know why it happened then – I suppose it's just one of them things, and then to lose it was an awful thing. I've been told by the doctor to try until December time and then see. … So we'll see…

R: Do you feel quite encouraged, then, that you fell pregnant all by yourselves without having the treatment?

Fourth interview in series (Couple WBY36)

(*Exchange following a general enquiry as to how the couple was getting on*)

R: Last time I spoke with you, you'd just had the embryos implanted and you were saying that you felt as though you were about to have a period…?

F: Unfortunately. It was upsetting at the time, but we've come to terms with it now. Still, next time…

R: Are you going to try again?

Third interview in series (Couple BIH32)

R: How are you getting on now?

F: M. had to have another sperm test. The doctor's put me on, like hormonal tablets, because my bleeding was a bit irregular … so it's just wait and see now…

R: Last time I came to see you, you had to go for a hycosy and blood tests…?

F: Oh, right – hadn't I had that yet? Oh, right. That was an absolute nightmare. It was really horrible – I nearly fainted! (*She provides a lengthy account of this procedure and the researcher asks for information about the tablets the woman has been taking. After some discussion of this nature, the researcher then asked*):

R: How do you feel now – it's quite a long time since you started all this?

In another example the researcher had asked a couple being interviewed for the fourth time to talk her through what had been happening to them since she had last seen them. She then asked them to summarize for her, by asking, 'How would you describe how this last year has been?' After a vivid description of the various disappointments they had suffered and a slightly more upbeat interlude about a holiday the couple had been on, she raised the potentially difficult question, 'What are your expectations now?' However, the man of the couple relieved the researcher of the problem of how to end this interview on a positive note by responding 'Triplets!' This suggests that the couple were well-practised in accommodating other people's potential distress and highlights how each interview is actually a co-production between researcher and respondents. (For a further discussion of the role of such 'emotion work' see the commentary relating to the exercise at the end of Chapter 11.)

Another couple being interviewed for the fourth time, had held back until halfway through the interview the information that the woman was pregnant. This was interesting in that it highlights the active telling of stories for dramatic effect that is intrinsic to interviews (as well as other conversations) and also mirrors the sort of interactional strategy that might be engaged in when talking with friends (rather than taking part in a research interview). This can reflect the development of a relationship as part of the exchange between researcher and researched.

As qualitative researchers we are frequently exhorted to avoid asking leading questions. Despite our good intentions, however, we can get carried away from time to time and find ourselves making assumptions as we talk to interviewees. On one occasion I was involved in making a video for training purposes and this concerned an interview with a 'consenting' GP colleague about his views regarding the provision of primary care services for drug users. The following excerpt from the interview shows me slipping into the trap of asking a leading question:

CJ: As a GP there are two sorts of services we provide. One is general medical services, which we provide to everyone, which I'm quite happy with – that's not a problem. Then there's the more specialized drug abuse service – the prescribing of methadone and things like that, which we do provide in our practice – but I wouldn't say I'm happy about it. I wish we didn't have to. I wish there was another way this service could be provided ... but there isn't.

RB: So you see it as a ... sort of ... necessary evil?

CJ: Yes ... we...ell (*raising eyebrows and smiling*) ...

RB: Maybe that's putting it a bit too strongly?

CJ: I mean, it's a specialized area of work and we've had to develop some specialization in that. But there's a feeling that we don't have all the specialist knowledge that we should have.

This excerpt perhaps provides reassurance in that it demonstrates that our interviewees are not as passive as we – and some of the methods texts we read – suggest. The GP indicated that I had perhaps gone a bit too far and I was able to effect a 'repair'. While I would not necessarily advocate asking such questions, no real damage was done. Note, however, the non-verbal cues that indicated, in this instance, that I had perhaps made an unwarranted assumption. Had I been carrying out a telephone interview, this might have constituted more of a problem, as we then cannot pick up on such body language and facial expressions (Wiles et al., 2006).

Anticipating and eliciting richer data

Interestingly, the above example also illustrates the potential for using stimulus materials (more frequently reserved for focus group discussions) in the context of a one-to-one interview, although non-attributed material is likely to serve this end better than would a leading question. Such material, however, does not need to be neutral. Indeed, the more contentious it is, perhaps, the best it is in terms of stimulating discussion (see discussion on the use of stimulus material in focus groups in Chapter 6.)

It is a good idea not to make up all your prompts 'on the hoof', but to think about these beforehand. You may never have to use them if your interviewee is forthcoming. However, these are important as an *aide-mémoir* both for the researcher and the interviewee, who may leave something out not because it is not relevant for them, but simply because it has momentarily slipped her/his mind. One of the things that novice interviewers do find particularly difficult, however, is waiting an appropriate length of time before utilizing prompts. This is because it takes considerable practice to be able to tolerate silences. These may simply mean that an interviewee is carefully pondering the question, but may seem endless to the interviewer lacking in confidence.

In order to assist with the process of identifying and interrogating patterns in the data (see Chapter 10) I also like to include some 'contextualizing questions', such as 'Do you think that most people in your situation share your views?' and if not 'What is it about your situation/experience/circumstances that makes it different?' Similarly, rather than inviting a series of unspecific complaints, it can be helpful to invite people to consider structural (or even attitudinal) factors that may give rise to the problems they are experiencing. So, for example, when interviewing professionals and seeking to elicit data on the frustrations inherent in their work and their ideas as to how this might be usefully addressed, I might ask: 'What stops you from doing your job as you'd like to do it?' This enlists your interviewees in helping you to start to make sense of your data. Stay alert for distinctions being made by interviewees as these may furnish useful categories and sub-categories for use in your subsequent coding frame. It can be useful simply to ask them to reflect on whether their own views have changed over time, if such observations are not spontaneously offered. Summarizing the main points highlighted in an interview can also encourage respondents to reconsider whether they have left anything out and allows you to check on your own perceptions, since you will inevitably be putting your own 'spin' on the account as you feed this back.

It is always good practice – and potentially less distressing for interviewees – to end on a positive note wherever possible. I often try to do this by asking people to think about what advice they'd give to someone who has recently come to occupy the same situation or position as themselves: 'What advice would you give to someone starting out/who has just been diagnosed/who is just about to take up a similar job?'

Even where the topic is potentially distressing, such as caring for a terminally ill relative, this sort of question at least acknowledges someone's hard-won expertise.

Semi-structured interviews

The 'semi-structured' aspect is crucial as it refers to the capacity of interviews to elicit data on perspectives of salience to respondents rather than the researcher dictating the direction of the encounter, as would be the case with more structured approaches. Even within semi-structured interviewing, however, there is considerable variation in researchers' practice, with some relying more heavily on the prepared order of questioning than others, who use schedules in a much more fluid way. This is partly a matter of experience and partly a matter of personal styles. It can be intimidating for the novice interviewer when respondents appear to skip from one topic to another, presenting a challenge in ensuring that all questions on the schedule are covered. I would recommend that the interviewer consults the schedule throughout, marking off topics as they are discussed and highlighting those which could be overlooked as the discussion moves on. However, interviewees will often cover several of our initial questions in one concise excerpt and it is important to recognize when comments have rendered specific questions unnecessary or irrelevant – not only does this waste valuable time, it risks giving the impression that you are not really listening to the person's account! As a research project progresses and the number of interviews conducted accumulates, it is often helpful to re-order the questions on the interview schedule to more accurately reflect the general focus of interviews and the topics that appear to capture respondents' interest. This also highlights the potential of piloting, which helps ensure both that questions elicit the sort of data required and that the order is likely to facilitate a progression that is comfortable and that works for both interviewee and interviewer.

Embarking on semi-structured interviews can be a bit unnerving, particularly for those more used to relying on structured instruments. There is a bit of an art to asking questions that departs very markedly from the approach favoured in fixed-choice formats, where the researcher is cast as the expert. In qualitative research, with its focus on lay knowledge and understandings, we are frequently problematizing the taken-for-granted and end up using rather vague conversational gambits, and asking what I would term 'damn fool' questions, such as 'So, tell me, how did you come to suspect that all was not well?' Again, the rather rarefied nature of the one-to-one interview becomes apparent, and such questions are perhaps more akin to 'chat-up' lines than the tightly-worded tick-box type of questions that are a feature of survey research. As Bloor et al. (2001) observe in relation to focus group research, respondents may under-react to our questions and, should these be 'damn-fool'-type questions, this can be acutely embarrassing. The researcher who can overcome this discomfort without losing her/his nerve, however, is likely to reap the benefits of being able to engage interviewees in exploring and interrogating topics with them.

As several writers, including Rapley (2001), have pointed out, interviews are performances, involving a two-way encounter. It is essential that the researcher 'owns' the questions, which enables the interview to work in a way similar to a regular conversation.

Capitalizing on fresh insights

However, even with piloting and forethought with regard to the content and order of questions, there are likely still to be some surprises in store, provided that purposive sampling (as discussed in Chapter 2) has ensured a supply of interviewees with differing characteristics and experiences. There is a danger in assuming oneself as all-powerful as a researcher: interviews are two-way exchanges and we are not the only party with an agenda. As a social scientist researching at the interface between the clinical and the social, I have frequently been involved in interviewing people about issues that have a profound impact on their lives and, in such situations, an interview schedule may, on occasion, appear almost superfluous:

AN EXAMPLE FROM THE FIELD

When conducting some interviews for a project looking at couples' experiences of sub-fertility I arrived at one house to an enthusiastic welcome and a torrent of data before I even had a chance to remove my recording equipment from my bag, pull out my interview schedule and get set up for the interview. I listened to this couple's account, managing a series of gestures to my tape recorder and microphone to gain permission to tape the interview and, once we had moved on to discuss my areas of research interest, I took some time to recap with the couple the issues they had raised off-tape.

This particular couple told me that they had not shared their fertility problems with anyone except close family members and that they valued the opportunity provided by the research project to talk to someone who was not emotionally involved. They explained that they felt they had to temper their discussions with family members, due to the possible effect on them of the couple's problems and concerns. This involved them in carrying out 'emotion work' whereby they anticipated and managed the responses of others to their own predicament. (This aspect of social engagement was something also identified by Exley and Letherby (2001) in relation to sub-fertility and the experience of terminal cancer patients, but I was not, at this stage, aware of this work.) I resolved to include some questions about dealing with others' emotions in subsequent interviews.

It is important that, as interviewers, we don't silence such interviewees or stop them mid-account: not only might this be construed as disrespectful, it may also make them more guarded in their replies to later questions, when we might want them to be expansive. However, as researchers, we do always have our own agenda, and have in many cases been funded on the basis of producing findings in relation to specific questions. If we have given a clear explanation of the purposes of our research, then, with any luck, these flows of information are likely to be germane to our research interests. Not only is it helpful to bear in mind that people have given their time and energy to our projects and doubtless have their own reasons for agreeing to take part, but interviewees often have a real need to tell such stories and it may be best to acknowledge this, reconciling oneself to sometimes listening to accounts that may have little bearing on our research concerns, but which nevertheless may clear the way for more focused questioning at a later stage in the interview.

It is equally important, though, not to plunge in and go straight to what the researcher may think is the point, without first establishing the relevance of the issue for interviewees.

AN EXAMPLE OF RESTRAINED QUESTIONING

A PhD student was interested in studying the reproductive choices of women with epilepsy, starting from the vantage point of her clinical expertise in this topic area. Although she was keen to include questions about perceived risks of pregnancy for women with epilepsy, I advised her to leave epilepsy to one side and wait to see when and how the women mentioned it. Of course, they were aware that the researcher was interested in their views because they had epilepsy, but when questioned about decision-making with regard to whether and when to have a baby, their accounts were remarkably similar to those generated in other studies of women without epilepsy, and featured finding the 'right man', coming to a point when they felt themselves to be financially secure and prepared emotionally for motherhood, as well as considerations about age and 'biological clocks'. Leaving it up to the women to mention their epilepsy provided valuable insights into the relative importance of this factor in their decision-making. It emerged that, while risk was something which the women weighed up, it was not the central concern that might have been supposed from perusing the clinical literature. This may well be due to the fact that these women have often had epilepsy since birth and very few of us would probably mention first something which we have experienced as a constant – and therefore as unremarkable – in the context of making significant changes to our own lives.

NARRATIVE INTERVIEWS

Although biographical interviews and life-story research have a long pedigree in oral history, it is only relatively recently that these have come to be embraced by disciplines such as health services research. Several disciplines and sub-disciplines have latterly recognized the potential value of narrative approaches, in particular, and story-telling, in general. However, as Plummer (1995) points out, each discipline is likely to have a somewhat different 'take' on story-telling, which will colour not just what types of story they attempt to elicit and in what form, but also how they seek to use stories as 'data':

> 'Stories' have recently moved centre stage in social thought. In anthropology, they are seen as the pathways to understanding culture. In psychology, they are the bases of identity. In history, they provide the tropes for making sense of the past. In psychoanalysis, they provide 'narrative truths' for analysis. In philosophy they are the bases for new forms of 'world-making' and the key to creating communities. Even economics has recognised its 'storied character'. Everywhere, it seems, there is an interest in stories, and social scientists have now finally grasped this point. Sociologists may be the last to enter this field explicitly, although much of their work over the past century has in one way or the other implicitly been concerned both with the gathering of other people's stories … as well as telling their own stories. … But a clear 'narrative moment' has now been sensed. Sociology is bound up both with obtaining stories and telling stories … a sociology of stories should be less concerned with analysing the formal structures of stories or

narratives (as literary theory might) and more interested in inspecting the social role of stories: the ways they are produced, the ways they are read, the work they perform in the wider social order, how they change, and their role in the political process. (Plummer, 1995: 18–19)

Like Plummer, it is the use potential of stories for sociological research that most interests me, but you might want to ponder their usefulness in other contexts. Whatever discipline in which you are engaged, however, it is important to examine critically the assumptions behind your attempts to elicit and make sense of narratives or stories. Lack of attention to the context in which stories are told, the mechanisms through which they are recounted, the form and content of stories, the intentions, and practices of interviewers can lead to confusion for the researcher who seeks to casually adopt terms such as 'narrative interviews'.

At one point, almost all in-depth interview studies published in journals such as the *British Medical Journal* or *British Journal of General Practice* seemed to be given the label of 'narrative research'. While the interviews reported in these journals might well have involved an element of story-telling, very few actually bore the hallmarks of 'biographical narrative research': that is the telling of a story with a clear sequence (Riessman, 1993; Rosenthal, 2004) which seeks to locate experiences on a chronological continuum in relation to an individual's biography and life stages (perhaps also set against the broader backdrop of local or national history). At best, they might be more accurately described as 'personal experience narratives' (Denzin, 1989; Plummer, 1995), which may overlap with but are not exactly the same as biographical or life-story interviews.

One crucial difference relates to the extent to which narrative structure is imposed by the researcher. In some traditions, such as the narrative interviewing style advocated by Miller (2000) in life story-telling, the onus is on the interviewees to choose which aspects of their story to emphasize and which to leave out. Researchers involved in eliciting 'personal experience narratives', by contrast, are usually involved in setting the agenda as they ask focused questions with the aim of eliciting situated accounts on such topics as following (or not following) specific treatment regimes.

Seale (1998) has outlined two main traditions that are helpful in understanding the varying use to which researchers put interview data and these are helpful in teasing out different orientations to narrative interviews. These traditions are a view of interview-data-as-topic and one of interview-data-as-resource (see also Rapley, 2004). In the former camp would be studies that seek to 'bear witness' or 'give voice' to individuals with specific experiences and perspectives, through recording their 'authentic voices' (Harding, 2006). In the second, the data is likely to be interrogated with reference to both internal inconsistencies and relevant theoretical frameworks, rather than standing as an unquestioned record.

Atkinson (1997) has warned against what he sees as the dangers of 'romanticizing' our respondents' accounts and urges researchers to view these through a critical lens, just as we would do any other account. The extent to which one seeks to question respondents' accounts depends, ultimately, on the purpose of the research, but it is important that we, as researchers, acknowledge our starting point and that we don't slip into lazily referring to our work as narrative research in the hope that this absolves us from systematic and thorough analysis of data content.

Hodgkin and Radstone (2003: 2) remind us that memory is 'provisional, subjective, concerned with the present rather than fact and the past'. In other words, we should treat respondents' accounts as selective and potentially strategic. This is not to say that we disbelieve them, but simply that we are aware of the multiple functions of talk. As Harding (2006) argues, it is 'both possible and necessary to work between [the two] extremes', adopting wholesale neither the romanticized view of inherent authenticity nor seeing every utterance only through the lens of the ' "cultural" or "linguistic" turn in post-structural theory', whereby research encounters and the stories to which these give rise can be viewed *only* as vehicles for articulating situated and partisan cultural constructions.

Andrews et al. (2004: 112) suggests a way of bridging these two extremes while allowing the researcher to examine critically the influence of cultural and political referents:

> ...we perceive reality in terms of stories, and ultimately how we construct, interpret, digest, and recount for others our own experiences bears a strong relationship to the story-lines that are already 'out there'. As a researcher, what has fascinated me most are those situations in which people fashion stories that challenge – either implicitly or explicitly – those master tales, revealing alternative versions of how those stories we know best might be retold.

One of the reasons that I like this formulation is that it places the researcher centre stage in terms of making sense of the stories told. The task of the researcher is to look for recurrent themes, challenges or discrepancies. In other words, to examine in detail the constituent parts and patterning of the accounts presented by respondents. Bloor (1995) reflected on the routine hard-luck stories recounted by the rent boys he studied, which cast them as victims of brutal upbringings and bad luck. He thought that the remarkable similarities in the form and content of these accounts suggested that their life stories were well rehearsed, having been told before in a variety of different contexts, thus constituting a 'master tale' in Andrews' et al.'s terms. This might give pause for concern for the researcher who sees her/his task as eliciting an 'authentic' account, but this does not matter for the researcher who is interested in the reasons for couching stories in this way and for what this tells us about experiences over and above the 'face value' of the tales we are told.

Sometimes in the course of a research project, we come to suspect that we are being told apocryphal tales, but it can be difficult to decide exactly how to use such data. Researchers may experience conflicting feelings of disciplinary excitement tinged with guilt when they come to question responses produced 'in good faith' (Barbour, 1998b). Rosaldo (cited by Brettell, 1993: 16) refers to similar concerns with regard to anticipating how research reports are likely to be perceived by those about whom we write, commenting that some anthropological writing can appear 'parodic' rather than 'perceptive'. Several of the professionals I interviewed in the course of a study looking at the demands made of them by HIV/AIDS provided examples of their encounters with clients which reflected their grudging respect for clients, and showed an appreciation of their inventiveness and resourcefulness, while stopping short of condoning their illegal activities. What exercised me, however, was coming across the same story, presented each time as a personal experience, but which could not have happened in exactly the same way to all the people who claimed first-hand involvement:

> [This was] a story about a client who was not too bright and who supplemented her meagre income 'on the game' [i.e. selling her sexual services]. [She was said to have told the worker recounting the story] … that she had also been removing coins from the gas meter installed in her flat [and explained] that she had avoided detection by providing sexual favours to the 'gas man' who came to read the meter. The punchline [of the story] however, is that her flat was all electric. (Barbour, 1998b: 191)

Some stories will out, regardless of research methods, because those we study have a need to tell them as they seek to make sense of their experiences. A good example of this appears in Barbour and Huby (1998), which has the express purpose of unpicking some of the myths involved in HIV/AIDS research, and therefore afforded researchers licence to question both the stories told to them and those that we tell each other. The example relates not to interviews but to a piece of observational fieldwork conducted with drug users in Scotland. Having carried out extensive fieldwork, Clive Foster (1998) became interested in the stories told to him by drug users as he realized that many of these were both dramatic and amusing. My own personal favourite relates to a tale of how drug users (with a sideline in dealing drugs) were decorating their house when a police raid was carried out. Thinking quickly and laterally, the protagonists in this tale, it was alleged, tipped large quantities of heroin into the paste bucket and carried on calmly wallpapering as the drugs squad searched in vain for illegal substances, apologizing to the officers for their immersion in this task and the need to complete it before the paste dried out. Recounting this story usually culminated in the drug users present speculating as to whether the property involved has since been redecorated and whether it might be worth returning to lick the wallpaper. However, Foster realized that these stories celebrated not only the skill and wit of the raconteurs. The eagerness with which they were embraced alerted Foster to the possibility that they simultaneously served another function. He develops the following theorized explanation, paying particular attention not just to what is included in the stories, but also to what is omitted:

> What is being brought into play here [regarding the above story and others presented in this published account] is the way that metaphor can hide certain

aspects of reality, aspects which, were they not removed, would deny the individual this ability to reconstruct identity. These stories of one-upmanship conveniently forget the fear and panic as the fourteen-pound sledge-hammer crashes into the front door and the drug squad rush through the flat, bursting into each room and tearing it apart in their efforts to find the stash of heroin before it is disposed of. They also forget the aggression and violence, the prison sentences, the awful invasion of self and the final humiliation and reduction of that self into a prison number. It is the good times the metaphor remembers, the heroic times, the times when 'we won and they lost'. These metaphors serve a very positive function, for it is this selectivity of their construction that serves to inform the idioms from which the present is reflected and managed, and suffering and deprivation endured. (Foster, 1998: 158)

Foster also discusses the importance for drug users of celebrating the 'glory days' of heroin and 'derring-do', which have more recently been eclipsed by the widespread switch to legally prescribed methadone.

Although this might make the process of eliciting data appear very easy, with such gems apparently falling into the researcher's lap, not all stories are equally compelling or likely to be told to us as researchers. The ease with which Foster's research participants apparently shared their tales with him belies the effort involved in establishing trust and reciprocity through sensitive fieldwork. In many other situations, researchers may have to coax interviewees to recount the types of story that they are interested in hearing.

ANTICIPATING ANALYSIS

Since we are generally aiming to aggregate one-to-one interview data (Barbour and members of the Wolds Primary Care Research Network (WoReN), 2000), it makes sense to attempt to include similar questions in our schedules in order to facilitate comparison between transcripts (or annotated recordings). This is why a set of questions is invaluable as an *aide-mémoir*. As we carry out successive interviews we sometimes augment this list with new questions arising from issues or even distinctions or qualifications made by interviewees. Even where we have not asked a question, however, retrospective analysis often identifies a passing reference to something that is discussed more extensively in later transcripts. However, explicit questioning helps us, as researchers, to decide whether this may, in the event, be an issue or concern that is more salient for some of our respondents than it is for others. We can even explicitly interrogate silences in the data – particularly if we pick up on these during interviews.

Therefore, analytic possibilities are shaped to some extent by the nature of our questioning as we generate data and it is important that we use to the full the capacity of semi-structured interviews to uncover surprises and take our analyses in new directions. Even as we generate our data, we are engaged in anticipating analysis.

However, as Collins (1998) and Rubin and Rubin (1995) point out, we may place too much emphasis on how we ask questions (concentrating on our own agendas as researchers) and neglect to *listen*. Collins (1998: 1) also talks about the unfortunate tendency to see the one-to-one interviews as an opportunity for what he calls 'data grabbing': 'There is a tendency at the outset for students to see the interview as a kind of smash and grab opportunity in which they accost some innocent bystander and relieve them of whatever useful "data" they may have.' A further implication of this sort of approach is that the researcher may be content with simply recording the responses rather than engaging in active listening and further questioning. This can result in the 'reification' of data and is apparent even in some versions of 'grounded theory' (Barbour, 2003).

Workshop participants engaging in an interviewing exercise about the provision of primary care services to drug users could be seen to have different orientations towards drug use, which could colour their responses. While some (notably the two GPs) talked about the goal, in working with drug users, being to stabilize their lives and drug use (through methadone), others identified the aim as getting users to the point where they were 'drug free'. And one interviewee (not a practitioner) talked about 'curing' them of their addiction. One of the GPs commented: 'Every one of them that comes to us says that they want to come off the drug. They're all lying. Most of them don't want to come off the drug at all – they want to stabilize themselves, and it may be that – once they're stable – they can start to think about coming off.'

This demonstrates the analytic potential of apparent contradictions and the need to remain alert to these, even as we generate our data. In the excerpt quoted above, the GP is drawing simultaneously on his professional standpoint and experience, but alludes at the end to a lingering hope that it might sometimes be possible to achieve abstinence. In effect, this allows him to 'have it both ways'. This tension, however, may be key to understanding some of the difficulties that GPs experience in their interactions with drug users visiting their surgeries. Indeed, this was a feature in the accounts generated through our enhanced case records utilized in another study of GPs' views and experiences of prescribing methadone (as discussed in Chapter 2).

Realist approaches to producing data would view silences as a problem to be addressed by more sensitive interviewing (Collins, 1998). Of course, some silences may be the product of the researcher foreclosing discussion or omitting to ask key questions. Not only may the researcher be held responsible, but blame can also be apportioned to the participant. Poland and Pedersen (1998: 301) highlight the often implicit assumptions of some qualitative researchers as to what constitutes a 'good' respondent:

> …the expectation is that the good respondent is one who visibly ponders the questions posed, who gives the appearance of genuine self-reflection by the use of suitably analytic terms, and who offers appropriately thoughtful rationales or explanations for behaviour and experiences.

Although the interviewees are centre stage (and many enthusiastically seize the opportunity to tell the story as *they* see it), this does not preclude asking them to account for their views. This does not necessarily mean coming into conflict with interviewees as they expound their views and provide their accounts of how things happened. However, the attentive interviewer may focus on the use of a specific word – for example, 'I'm interested that you used the word "abandoned". Do you think that service providers could have provided you with more … information, support …?' Sometimes interviewees will contradict themselves and, provided that the researcher brings this up in a way that conveys interest rather than disapproval, encouraging interviewees to question this alongside the interviewer can tap into a rich vein for exploring the distinctions involved. For example, an interviewee may have categorically stated that s/he would 'never' advocate euthanasia, but then talk sympathetically about the plight of an individual who has been charged with assisting his terminally ill wife to die. Exploring with the interviewee the situational factors that encourage these somewhat different responses can be illuminating. It may emerge, for example, that in the first case, the interviewee is thinking about the involvement of health care professions, but that s/he takes a different view when considering the domestic context and personal relationships. It may even be that the place of death serves to 'frame' this issue, with home deaths being viewed differently from hospital deaths.

HINTS ON USING INTERVIEWS

One-to-one semi-structured interviews are possibly the most commonly used qualitative method and have become almost the 'gold standard' approach, against which other data are frequently compared and found wanting. However, surprisingly little attention has been paid to questioning the nature of the interview encounter. Far from replicating commonplace social encounters, one-to-one interviews involve an intense exchange which is seldom seen outside therapy sessions or the early days of 'courtship'.

- Give some thought to the ordering as well as the content of your interview schedule.
- Be prepared to modify your questions or augment these as new issues arise as you generate data through interviews.
- Remember that this is a two-way interaction and think about why the interviewee is telling a particular story and why s/he is selecting certain aspects of this.
- Anticipate the analysis even while generating data through exploring distinctions, qualifications, contradictions and tensions alluded to.
- Ask some contextualizing questions.
- Give the interviewee an opportunity to raise any other issues salient to her/him.

FURTHER READING

Barbour, R.S., Featherstone, V.A. and members of WoReN (2000) 'Acquiring qualitative skills for primary care research: Review and reflections on a three-stage workshop. Part 1: Using interviews to generate data', *Family Practice*, 17(1): 76–82.

Barbour, R.S. and members of WoReN (2000) 'Acquiring qualitative skills for primary care research: Review and reflections on a three-stage workshop. Part 2: Analyzing interview data', *Family Practice*, 17(1): 83–89.

Britten, N. (1995) 'Qualitative interviews in medical research', *British Medical Journal*, 311: 251–253.

Rapley, T. (2001) 'The art(fulness) of open-ended interviewing: Some considerations on analyzing interviews', *Qualitative Research*, 1(3): 303–323.

Rapley, T. (2004) 'Interviews', in C. Seale, G. Gobo, J.F. Gubrium and D. Silverman (eds) *Qualitative Research Practice*, London: Sage, pp. 15–33.

Rubin, H.J. and Rubin, I.S. (1995) *Qualitative Interviewing: The Art of Hearing Data*, Thousand Oaks, CA: Sage.

EXERCISE

You could generate interview data on the same broad topics as were suggested for the exercises in the previous chapter. Obviously the research questions would have to be modified slightly in order to make them amenable to being studied using interviews, but you could carry out interviews on the following topics:

- **Interview Topic 1: How do you think that gender affects your experiences at work?**
- **Interview Topic 2: What are your views and experiences of making choices when shopping for family food for and with your children?**

These topics have been chosen so that you should be able to practise on friends – perhaps even fellow students – if you are using this textbook in the context of a taught methods course.

NB: The coding exercise at the end of Chapter 9 relates to focus group transcripts, but should your interest be in interviews in particular, you might wish to record and transcribe your interview and use this to develop a coding frame and gain some hands-on experience of coding, once you have read the guidance provided in Chapter 9. Should you be engaging in these exercises in conjunction with a taught course, you could, together with fellow students, generate a small dataset that would yield a number of transcripts on the same topic. This would effectively allow you to engage in a mini-project, using your individual transcripts comparatively and perhaps exchanging these as you work to refine your coding frame (see Chapter 10).

First, you need to develop an interview schedule, listing either broad topic areas or more detailed questions you wish to ask. Although you will not be able to directly observe behaviour, you can ask interviewees to reflect on similar experiences to those which are the focus of your earlier observational fieldwork. So, for example, when addressing **Interview Topic 1** you might decide to ask interviewees to think about meetings they've attended and whether the gender of those attending made a difference to the content and outcome of discussions – both in general and in relation to their own contributions or decisions which affect them directly. This is quite a mouthful and I'm not suggesting that you ask such a question in a breathless rush. You might want to think, though, about formulating a series of questions and suitable prompts to ensure that this ground is covered.

Other questions might relate to perceptions about the influence of gender on promotion prospects, both in the individual's current workplace and possibly also in relation to previous jobs or potential future posts. Some questions you might like to use include:

- **What is the gender balance in your workplace?**

  - Is this something you're usually aware of?
  - When (if at all) is this likely to become an issue for you?

- **How do you think gender influences:**

  - senior appointments?
  - promotions?
  - reputations?
  - management styles?
  - your interactions with co-workers?
  - behaviour at meetings?
  - inclusion and exclusion from decision-making?

An interview schedule for **Interview Topic 2** might begin with a few questions designed to collect demographic details, including the number, ages and gender of any children (unless, of course, you already know this). However, even if you do know about someone's family composition, getting them to think about this at the outset may help sensitize them to the sorts of comparison you will be asking them to think about.)

Next you would probably want to ask about who does most of the family food shopping, when they do the shopping, and whether this is in the company of the child/ren or not.

Further suggested questions are:

- **Do you ever feel under pressure to buy particular items of food?**

If so, where does this pressure come from?
Prompts:

- *Your own children?*
- *Your own children via their peer group?*

- *Your own parental peer group?*
- *Your own parents?*
- *Other people?*
- What sorts of items are usually involved?
- Are there any items of food that never seem to give rise to arguments or negotiation?

- **What is it about such pressure that makes it difficult?**
  Concerns about:
  - *Cost?*
  - *Nutrition and health?*
  - *Providing adequately for your children?*

- **What sorts of arguments do your children put forward when trying to persuade you to buy items?**
- **Do you think that your children understand your concerns?**
- **Do you discuss these issues with other parents?**
  - Do you think other parents think the same way about these issues as you do?
  - *Why/why not?*
- **Do you think that things have changed since you were a child yourself?**

It is unlikely that you will have to use all of these prompts (or, indeed questions) since this is likely to be a topic that generates lively responses.

As with the observational fieldwork exercise, however, you may wish to add some further questions suggested by reading other research reports.

6
FOCUS GROUPS

AIMS

- This chapter provides guidance as to when it is appropriate to use focus groups.
- It will equip the reader to effectively plan focus group studies, paying particularly attention to the practicalities involved, including the use of recording equipment, hints on transcription, choosing settings, sampling and group composition.
- It offers detailed advice on the development and use of focus group topic guides, group exercises and stimulus materials.
- It explains the importance of planning and recommends pilot work, in relation to both selecting questions and stimulus materials.
- It provides specific guidance on how attentive moderating can help to anticipate challenges in analyzing focus group data.
- Finally, it demonstrates the potential of focus groups to advance theoretical explanations (through employing second-stage sampling) and shows the reader how to build such possibilities into the research design.

INTRODUCTION

In contrast to ethnography and interviewing, which are associated with particular philosophical approaches to research, focus group use has developed independently of particular qualitative paradigms. While this has provided considerable scope for the imaginative use of focus groups, it has more often effectively curtailed the extent to which they have been used imaginatively. Focus groups are often employed as a 'method of least resistance' and are viewed as a poor relation of ethnography or one-to-one interviews, being employed in situations where it is not deemed possible to use these other more desirable methods. However, focus groups have unique advantages and, if used appropriately, can provide extremely rich data with enormous potential for comparison and, hence, can afford analytic purchase with regard to a wide range of research questions. This chapter discusses appropriate and inappropriate uses of focus groups and provides guidance on how to anticipate the particular challenges which they throw up. In common with the discussion on other methods, it advocates turning what might, at first glance, appear to be weaknesses into resources to be capitalized upon during the process of analysis.

RATIONALE FOR USING FOCUS GROUPS

Focus groups have enjoyed a massive surge in popularity in recent years. However, with this comes the associated danger of inappropriate use. Many of the advantages that they might, at first glance, appear to offer may be illusory. One of the most common fallacies is that they offer economies in terms of researcher time and costs. Sampling decisions (see discussion below) require more careful thought than do one-to-one interviews, for example, since there are important ethical issues to be considered. The logistics involved in bringing individuals together in a set place and at a specific time should also not be underestimated; travel costs will need to be calculated and you may have to pay for room hire.

Although I suspect that some researchers use focus groups in preference to one-to-one interviews due to misconceptions of the sort outlined above, the methods are not necessarily interchangeable. Narratives are much easier to elicit and clarify in one-to-one conversations and some individuals may also be reluctant to take part in group discussions. Sometimes focus groups are used in order to access views or attitudes of participants. This is not the forte of the method, however, which, as David Morgan (1988) has emphasized, is to uncover *why* people think as they do. While interviewees may well provide commentaries (either spontaneously or at the request of an attentive interviewer) which are helpful in clarifying apparent contradictions, focus groups are likely to give rise to lively debate resulting in what may be dramatic changes of heart. This is good news if you are using focus groups – appropriately – to study how views are created and modified *through* group interaction, but bad news if you are using the method as a back-door survey route. This latter temptation should be avoided as any attempt to fix meanings and measure attitudes via focus group discussions is doomed to failure and is the province of survey methods. Again, the influence of the researchers' own disciplinary background and 'take' on methods becomes particularly evident and this is something that may have to be debated within multidisciplinary teams.

Bloor et al. (2001) argue that focus groups are the method of choice only when the purpose of the research is 'to study group norms, group meanings and group processes'. Focus groups are, therefore, extremely valuable tools to understanding decision-making processes and are especially effective in studying professional practices. They allow the researcher to access the process through which collective meaning is negotiated and through which group identities are elaborated (Wilkinson, 1999). They also allow researchers to invite participants to 'problematize' taken-for-granted assumptions, as with the potential research questions featured in the exercises accompanying these chapters. These have been selected by the author and, given my own enthusiasm for focus group methods, this also serves to highlight the conjunction between individual dispositions and choice of research questions. Focus groups can also encourage people to collectively address topics to which, as individuals, they may have previously devoted little attention. Group discussions can be helpful in reproducing or creating rationales for issues such as non-take-up of services and do not put individuals 'on the spot' as might one-to-one interviews on the same topic. If, when formulating your research question, you find yourself asking 'Why not …?', then you should perhaps consider using focus groups.

Focus groups are often used in order to access groups who are viewed as hard-to-reach, including people who are out of touch with services, members of minority ethnic groups, and children (Kitzinger and Barbour, 1999) and, in some instances, may be less intimidating to potential participants. However, careful thought should be given to the implications of utilizing pre-existing networks (which provide invaluable insights into peer group dynamics) since the discussion, and any revelations made by individuals, may well impact on future relationships. Of course, if peer group dynamics is the focus of your research, then this suggests that focus groups may well be the way forward.

Group discussions provide a little more leeway for participants in that they do not, like the one-to-one interview, carry the unspoken expectation that each person will answer every question. For this reason, they may sometimes hold promise for researching sensitive topics (Farquhar with Das, 1999), although other researchers take the view that such topics can best be addressed in interviews. Again, there are no hard-and-fast rules, and, in the event, the best option may be to give respondents the choice. Some may value the safety provided by numbers and prefer to discuss 'difficult' topics with others in a similar position, which may afford permission to share such revelations. Others may feel less comfortable with discussing feelings in public.

There are also important cultural patterns that need to be taken into account. In some cultures or subcultures, for example, focus groups may be more attractive to women than they are to men, while in others traditional patterns of interaction may preclude engaging in interaction with members of the opposite sex. Pre-existing cultural patterns may lead to the superimposing of a style of interaction that more closely resembles an interview, with the researcher effectively taking centre stage and speaking more than any one participant. As with interviews, this is a two-way process and our focus group participants will adapt the method and their engagement to fit with their own mores and expectations. Strickland (1999) observed that, when running focus groups with Pacific Northwest Indian people, their custom was for the respected elders of the group to wait until the very end of the session before they contributed to the discussion.

Focus groups have been described as 'structured eavesdropping' (Powney, 1988) and this captures very well both the potential and challenges of the method. Such discussions can encourage animated and spontaneous exchanges between participants, with the moderator taking a back seat, thus approximating naturalistic fieldwork settings. The added benefit, however, is the greater degree of control over the composition of the group and the potential for the researcher to guide the discussion in terms of focus. This is the 'structure' part of the equation and requires considerable planning and attention to practicalities.

PLANNING AND PRACTICALITIES

Once you have decided that focus groups are an appropriate approach likely to yield the sort of data you wish to elicit, you will have to consider issues concerning access and sampling. Again, as with all qualitative methods, the main concerns here relate to the dual imperatives of ethics and maximizing analytic potential through affording comparative possibilities.

You may need to be creative with regard to sampling strategies and identifying gatekeepers who might be helpful in affording access. Umaña-Taylor and Bámaca (2004) highlight the importance of making use of local community organizations, including, somewhat unusually, Consulates, to make contact with members of the various Latino populations in a US context. However, using recruitment strategies that rely on managers as gatekeepers can introduce problems in that such individuals may inadvertently exclude some individuals or groups or may even seek to manipulate selection so as to confirm their own views of an organization and people's behaviour within it. This can serve to mute certain voices and is of particular concern if you are committed to inclusive and participatory research practice. At the very least this can lead to a partial and possibly theoretically impoverished analysis.

Two questions always arise in relation to sampling for focus groups: these are 'How many people should I recruit to each focus group?' and 'How many groups do I need to run?' While some marketing research texts advocate convening groups of 10-12 members, for social science research projects this is likely to be unwieldy as we are likely to want to pay closer attention to the type and content of interaction. Importantly, you are likely to wish to transcribe the discussions. For these reasons, most focus group researchers recommend aiming to recruit a maximum of 6-8 individuals, although it is possible to run focus group discussions with smaller groups (Kitzinger and Barbour, 1999). This is, of course, not an exact science, and it is sensible to over-recruit slightly as there are likely to be 'no shows' on the day.

The number of groups is likely to be determined, in part, by the level of funding available and the resources you have for transcription and analysis. However, it is useful to think about the comparisons you want to make. Groups are usually convened on the basis of some shared attribute, such as professional role, or locality (which it may also be necessary to build in due to logistical considerations). Members may also be recruited on the basis of some shared experience, such as having a specific chronic illness. However, you may also 'hypothesize' that personal characteristics may be relevant and seek to group people in terms of age, gender, ethnicity, or social class (with locality perhaps serving to assist in sampling with regard to the last of these). If this is sounding familiar, then it is because purposive sampling (as outlined in Chapter 2) also informs the selection of focus group participants. Particular consideration should be given to the implications of bringing people together in particular combinations. You should think carefully, for example, about the possible repercussions of exposing newly diagnosed individuals to a group situation that provides harrowing insights into the longer-term consequences of illness as evidenced by others further along the disease trajectory.

In theory, it is, of course, possible to select the same individual into a number of different groups, by virtue of the combination of characteristics s/he possesses. Your sampling decisions will be governed by the focus of your research and the comparisons you wish to make. If you are interested in how individuals make decisions in multidisciplinary teams, for example, it makes sense to convene some mixed professional groups, but there may also be some mileage in convening single professional groups too, so that you can access peer group constructions of the decision-making process and the role of other professional groups. Certain ethical considerations may militate against employing what would in research terms constitute an 'ideal' sampling strategy, but this is something that has to be accommodated. It is impossible, in any case, to make the 'right' sampling choices, but you are also unlikely to end up with a situation where there is no room for discussion or comparison. It is not possible to know in advance everything about your participants that might have been useful in deciding to which group to assign them, but you are unlikely to end up with a group where everyone agrees about everything.

The absence of lively debate and discussion is probably every focus group researcher's worst nightmare. Morgan (1988) provides the useful reminder that focus groups should be homogeneous in terms of background and not attitudes. However, it may sometimes make sense to exclude any individuals who are known to hold very strong opinions and who may severely limit the capacity or willingness of others to join in discussions. It was for this reason that we opted to carry out one-to-one interviews with some individuals who were known to be active and vocal with regard to the issue of living wills (Thompson et al., 2003a, 2003b).

It is particularly important to use good-quality recording equipment for focus group discussions in order to capture what are – literally as well as conceptually – multiple voices. Some focus group researchers do not bother to distinguish between individual participants in their transcripts, arguing that this is unnecessary, since the focus of the analysis will be on making comparisons at group level. Certainly, it is not advisable to use focus group discussions as a 'back-door' route to interview data and to try to piece together individual accounts. This is laborious and is essentially a waste of interactive focus group data. I would recommend, however, that you take notes on the sequence of talk, since this can be invaluable later in explaining differences between groups. This is a function best carried out by an assistant moderator, who need not be an experienced researcher, since such notes need to focus on sequencing rather than content and it is important that the note-taker remains focused on this specific task.

Although it is possible to take some notes during discussions, it is unlikely that the moderator will be able to take extensive notes as it requires considerable effort to engage with several participants, picking up on distinctions and qualifications, trying to deal with interruptions and seek clarification about meanings (as with one-to-one interviews), but with the task magnified both by dint of greater numbers and the complexities of the interactional process). It makes excellent sense to do some of your own transcribing. Not only does this serve to help you reflect on your own performance and allow you to become a more attentive moderator in the future, but it also highlights the skills involved in transcribing and encourages a helpful dialogue with the audio typists who may be enlisted to do the rest of your transcribing. It is also especially important to listen to the original recording and to add any additional information (as discussed in relation to interview transcripts, but with the added challenges associated with multiple participants). Again, fieldnotes should be made directly after each group as this will provide an invaluable source of additional contextual information to aid analysis.

Although focus groups are often used in order to 'brainstorm', careful forethought can yield greater dividends. It seems a pity to invest considerable time and resources in setting up groups without paying attention to developing appropriate topic guides which will allow the discussion to be focused, as suggested by the method's name.

DEVELOPING AND USING FOCUS GROUP TOPIC GUIDES

Focus group topic guides can appear disarmingly brief and it can be hard to trust that these will really give rise to the fulsome debate that you hope to encourage. The brevity of such documents, however, belies the amount of preparation involved. It is helpful to pilot your questions and any 'stimulus materials' (i.e. materials used to encourage discussion) in order to ensure that they will elicit the sort of data that is of interest for your project. They should, for example, encourage discussion between group members, involving them in comparing notes or formulating a collective response. If your questions give rise to extensive talk between individual group members and the moderator, then you would be well advised to rework your topic guide.

Our experience on a current project serves to provide a detailed example of the process behind developing a focus group topic guide. With one-to-one interviews with patients with dysarthria under way, a member of the research team produced the following list of questions, which outlined all the areas which we were interested in exploring in focus groups with carers. However, it was considered that the topic guide needed to be shortened considerably and reformulated. You might want to take a look at this and have a go at reformulating it, bearing in mind the guidelines discussed earlier.

FIRST DRAFT: QUESTIONS TO BE COVERED IN FOCUS GROUP DISCUSSIONS

Question Set 1: BACKGROUND/EARLY STAGES

Now, all the people who you care for have had difficulty speaking after their stroke …

A)   Can you tell us when you <u>first</u> knew speaking was going to be difficult for the person and how you knew this?

B)   Which health professionals <u>first discussed</u> this speech difficulty with you and what did they say? What did you know about why the person's speech was affected by the stroke?

C)   What were the <u>other kinds</u> of difficulties that the person had soon after their stroke? How much did the speech difficulties concern you <u>compared</u> to these other difficulties?

D)   At the time, how would you sum up your <u>reactions</u>? How much did you think the speech difficulty would affect the person's life <u>in the future</u>?

E)   What <u>concerns</u> did you have about the future?

F)   Did you have any immediate thoughts about what you could do to help to make the speech better?

Question Set 2: RECOVERY PHASE

A)   When the person with the stroke left the hospital, in those first few days, can you tell me what you <u>expected</u> to happen to their speech? How <u>quickly or easily</u> would the speech come back? What did you think <u>could be done</u> to help this happen?

B)   How would you say the person progressed during the first couple of months? What were their reactions to what had happened to them? What were <u>your feelings</u> at this time?

C)   In the first few weeks, what kinds of things did the <u>speech therapist</u> at the hospital do with the person who had the stroke? What <u>involvement</u> did you have in these sessions/exercises?

D)   What other kinds of things did you do <u>to try and help</u> the person with their speech? <u>Why</u> did you think these would help?

Can you remember when you first went out with the person with the stroke to the shops or the pub – somewhere where there was other people?

E)   How easy did <u>other people</u> find understanding the person you care for? How would you say they reacted to the person with the stroke? (<u>How</u> did you know this?)

F)   What do you think <u>they had difficulty</u> with? Did you expect this to happen? What things did they do to make the person with the stroke <u>feel better</u> or communicate better? What things did you do to try and <u>make things easier</u>?

G)   Were there any types of <u>social situations</u> that you would deliberately try to <u>avoid</u>?

H)   What were your thoughts and reactions about the <u>longer term</u> at this stage? How did the patient's other difficulties affect these thoughts?

Question Set 3: LONGER TERM

Thinking now over the weeks and months after the person with the stroke left hospital...

A)   What were the <u>main changes</u> you saw in the person with the stroke?

B)   How did the speech <u>change over time</u>? <u>What</u> do you think helped it change?

C)   How did changes to the speech *tie up* with what you had expected to happen?

D)   What kinds of things did you do <u>differently</u> to help the speech compared to at the beginning?

On the other times you went out with the person with the stroke ...

E)   What <u>changes</u> were there in how people reacted to their speech? What do you <u>do now</u> to help make situations easier?

Question Set 4: QUALITY OF LIFE

A)   Overall, how would you say the speech difficulty <u>has affected the person's life</u>? How would you say it has affected *your own life*? What are your <u>hopes</u> for the future?

Research tells us that caring for someone with a stroke can be hard work for carers ...

B)   What were the <u>main challenges</u> for you in providing care for the person? How did these <u>change over time</u>? What were your own personal thoughts about <u>becoming a carer</u>?

C)   How did you <u>feel</u> in social situations in which the speech was difficult?

Question Set 5: SUPPORT

A)   How do you think health professionals can give more support to the carers of people who have speech difficulties after stroke?

B)   What were the things that the health professionals did that helped YOU most?

C)   What were the things that other people who knew you did that helped YOU most?

While this set of questions covers all the relevant ground, it is more suited to carrying out one-to-one interviews because of its temporal organization (i.e. it is ideal for eliciting individual narratives) and attention to detail. Little would be gained from using this schedule in a focus group setting, as it would tend to give rise to individual accounts, while discouraging discussion of commonalities or differences. I subsequently produced a revised version more suitable for use in a group setting. One of the most noticeable features is its brevity and suggested prompts (*in italics*) to be used *only* if discussion does not spontaneously develop with regard to these highlighted issues.

SECOND DRAFT: AMENDED FOCUS GROUP TOPIC GUIDE

(Following preamble regarding purpose of the research and assurances of confidentiality.)

Thanks for coming along today. Can I first of all ask you to introduce yourselves and tell us who it was in your life who had the stroke and how long ago this happened?

1. You've all been invited along to this discussion group because you're involved in caring for someone who has had a stroke and has since had difficulty with speaking. I'd like you to tell us what this has meant for you.

Prompts:

In particular, how have the speech difficulties affected you/your ability to provide care?

2. Were there any surprises with regard to how the stroke affected this person?
   What did you know about strokes before this happened?
   Did you have any experience of strokes?
   Has it got any easier dealing with this as time has gone on?/Would you say there are different stages involved? How has it changed over time?
   How do you see the future now?

3. How has the stroke, and particularly the speech difficulties, affected your daily life with the person you're caring for?
   What impact has it had on your interests/socializing (with and without the person with the stroke)/ relationship with the person you're caring for?

4. What ways have you developed for dealing with problems? What do you do to make things easier?
   What sort of things do you do?
   Are there any situations you avoid?
   Have you developed these things yourself – or have you been given useful advice?

5. What sort of things have helped you, as carers?
   Health care professionals? (Especially speech therapists)
   Information – sources?
   Social networks/support?

6. Looking back on your own experiences, what advice would you offer to someone who is about to start caring for someone with speech difficulties following a stroke?
   Useful hints?/Things you've done that have helped?
   Useful hints – mistakes you've made?

7. Are there any changes you'd like to see made to service provision for carers/people with speech difficulties following a stroke?

Murphy et al. (1992) provide some useful advice about running focus groups and dealing with issues such as dominant members and individuals who may be reluctant to speak. However, it is important not to overstate the potential problems in this respect: focus group members often share the moderator's commitment to participation and may act to restrict the contributions of an overly dominant member or to encourage the reticent. Sometimes such patterns are data in themselves, especially if you are looking at peer group relationships where the muting of certain perspectives may be highly relevant. You can, of course, always elect to combine focus group discussions with one-to-one interviews if you wish to access private as well as public accounts or performances (see, for example, Michell, 1999).

STIMULUS MATERIALS

Sometimes focus group researchers imagine that materials have to be cleverly constructed, but while this may sometimes be the case, there is not necessarily any great mystery to selecting stimulus materials: their purpose is simply to stimulate and focus discussion. Ready-made materials, such as video clips, cartoons, or health promotion leaflets (as used by Crossley, 2002) may be useful, depending on what sort of data you wish to generate. This, again, is the key to deciding what will or will not work in the context of your own particular project.

I have also used a book written for children in order to run focus groups on the topic of how to deal with children's curiosity regarding reproduction and sexuality. This was *Mummy Laid an Egg*, written, and imaginatively illustrated, by Babette Cole. One of the things that alerted me to the potential of this material was the heated debate that the publication of this book had engendered – at least in relation to book review sections of broadsheet newspapers. Opinion was divided between those who thought this a refreshingly frank and amusing take on a perennially delicate subject and those who thought it was disgusting, inappropriate, and even dangerous. Some critics mentioned that Cole herself was not a mother and had therefore completely misjudged the situation. This 'stimulus material' gave rise to extremely rich focus group data, encompassing issues covering intergenerational differences, cultural and religious values and practices, ideas about children's cognitive abilities, gendered considerations, and specific situational contexts, such as that of step-fathers.

Some ready-made stimulus materials can backfire, however, as the context in which these were developed can sometimes prove to be a more compelling topic for participants than your particular research question. I discovered this when I used a newspaper clipping referring to the then under age Prince Harry's bad behaviour in relation to alcohol and drugs in order to explore views of the challenges of parenting. What I had not foreseen was that this audience was much more intrigued by the other royal story simmering in the background at that time – whether Prince Charles and Camilla Parker-Bowles would eventually marry! This highlights the importance of piloting your stimulus material in order to establish that it is likely to give rise to the sort of discussion you want to elicit.

Appropriately chosen stimulus materials can give permission to participants to raise potentially awkward topics. One of my colleagues recently recounted her experience of running focus groups with professionals involved in working with drug-using parents. The unmentioned spectre at the back of everyone's mind – 'the elephant in the room', as the researcher called it, which no one spoke about, but which coloured contributions – was the recent raw experience of a staff member in that area having been disciplined following an enquiry into the death of a child. While it is difficult to envisage introducing this topic in this particular situation, we often wish to tap into people's worst-case scenario-type fears. When conducting focus groups with professionals about work which spanned maternal mental health and child protection issues, we used a newspaper clipping to facilitate such discussion (Barbour et al., 2002). This story, with the headline 'Mother threw baby off bridge' (*The Guardian*, 25 February 1997), recounted how a young mother had thrown her baby to his death. We chose this item because it contained several elements which we wished to explore, including the calculated risk that the social worker had taken in allowing the child to return to the mother's care, the 'benefit-of-hindsight' allocation of a 'personality disorder' (Stanley et al., 2003) diagnosis, and the explicit criticism of all the professionals involved.

As well as employing ready-made stimulus materials, however, you might consider engaging participants in more imaginative exercises. It is, however, important to construct these carefully to ensure that they address the issues with which your research is concerned and that you do not simply use exercises for the sake of it (Kitzinger and Barbour, 1999).

An instructive example is provided by Sparks et al. (2002: 116), who were interested in studying the 'ways in which the moral and practical dilemmas of punishment are debated and deliberated upon in discussions among nine-year-old children'. They employed a Hobbesian-inspired make-believe gambit to encourage children to consider a world in which adults had disappeared. They explain:

> We tried a number of different stimuli to start the discussions off, but the most fertile was a short introduction that posed a situation in which the children awake one day to find that all adults have disappeared in the night. A letter explains that the adults (mysteriously) had no choice, but that the children are to manage things as best they can until the adults return. In this sense, the children are the guardians of society and can organize and administer it as they choose. The discussion is therefore rooted in the children's own time, location and material infrastructure: this is not a 'Lord of the Flies' situation. Almost all the children engaged with this situation with imagination and interest. It also provoked a range of responses from wild excitement to earnest and careful thought. It allowed the children to comment on their own experience while they pondered the challenges and opportunities of an adult-free world. Each group took the discussion in a slightly different direction, covering the mundane and the profound as well as (occasionally) the fantastical.' (Sparks et al., 2002: 118–119)

CHALLENGES IN ANALYZING FOCUS GROUP DATA

Analysis of focus group data does present a range of challenges. However, as with other methods, some of these can be circumvented by careful preparation and others may be recast as advantages. Sometimes researchers find it difficult to make meaningful comparisons between groups since discussion may have focused on different issues. However, careful preparation in the form of honing topic guides and employing stimulus materials can allow you to anticipate and minimize such problems. In terms of making comparisons, silences or omissions can be as revealing as comments relating to specific concerns – but only if the participants have been given the opportunity to comment on these.

The rapid-fire exchanges that are often a feature of focus group discussions can also present a challenges for analysis. However, it is possible to ask individuals to return to earlier comments and to complete their intended contributions and an attentive moderator can seek clarification. Sometimes, of course, participants themselves provide commentaries and may even engage as 'pseudo-assistant moderators', asking questions of each other and starting to do some of the work of analysis. The insights provided by participants are an important resource that can be harnessed in focus group discussions, provided, as always of course, that one does not simply take these at face value.

Although you are likely to be making comparisons between groups rather than between individuals, this necessitates knowledge of the make-up of groups. Provided that you have given forethought to your rationale for convening groups, you should have, as a basis for comparison, groups made up of individuals selected on the basis of some shared characteristic or attribute, but which differentiates them from other groups. However, in the flurry of debate and discussion many other factors come into play, and these may be seen by the researcher, eager to make broad cross-group comparisons, as irritating 'noise'. It is also important to pay attention to individual voices.

Several commentators (for example Sim, 1998) have highlighted the tendency of focus groups to produce consensus and this can also be a product of researchers' attempts to make inter-group comparisons while overlooking intra-group comparisons. The propensity of focus groups to generate consensus, however, depends both on the topic and the form of discussion. Some focus group applications capitalize on the capacity for co-producing consensus in order to develop guidelines (e.g. see Fardy and Jeffs (1994), who reported on a study that used focus groups to develop consensus guidelines for the management of the menopause in general practice). Other writers, such as Waterton and Wynne (1999), point out that many focus groups do not achieve consensus and a well-prepared moderator can always encourage discussion that interrogates rather than produces consensus.

SECOND-STAGE SAMPLING AND DEVELOPING EXPLANATIONS

In common with all the methods discussed here, focus groups rely on the iterative process in order to achieve their full potential in terms of furnishing explanations. The original formulation of 'grounded theory' advocated that the researcher return to the field in order to test out emergent hypotheses. In the current climate of tight deadlines and the additional restrictions that the ethical review process may impose, this is rarely possible. However, focus groups can yield unique opportunities in this respect in the form of additional sessions, convened not with new groups of participants, but with participants drawn from the same pool, the difference being that this time they are allocated to groups on the basis of different common characteristics. This relies, of course, on the researcher having carried out a preliminary analysis in terms of seeking to identify patterning in the data, and depends, crucially, on being able to identify individual speakers in focus group discussions (see the discussion above).

In a study of GPs' views and experiences of sickness certification (Hussey et al., 2004) we had noticed that certain group members appeared to be exercised by rather different issues. We had convened groups based on locality (due partly to logistical considerations) and had also sought to obtain a range in terms of length of experience of GPs, seniority, gender, and size of practice (in terms of numbers of patients and GPs). It appeared that GP Registrars (relatively recently qualified), GP locums (who moved between practices offering relief labour) and GP Principals (with management responsibilities and long-term commitment to specific practices) viewed the challenges of sickness certification in ways that were sometimes at odds with those of their colleagues. In order to explore this hunch we decided to convene a further set of focus groups, this time bringing together members of these specific posts in separate groups.

We also decided to develop new materials for use in these groups to facilitate exploration of our emerging ideas about the factors that affected GPs' responses and conceptualizations of sickness certification. In the course of the initial set of focus groups, we had elicited examples of GP statements that formed a spectrum, from those which referred to acquiescing automatically to all patient demands (at one end) to those which advocated not believing a word patients said and reporting them to the authorities (at the other end). Several of the group participants had seemed to rather relish their role in stimulating debate, and we doubted whether any of them applied such extreme measures with the consistency implied. However, in the course of convening these groups we noted that such comments had effectively given other participants permission to admit to – or at least to consider – such responses and to locate their own position with reference to this notional continuum.

ADDITIONAL PROBES DERIVED FROM FOCUS GROUPS

Probe set 1

GP1: My line is, if I've got somebody who I think is … is doing the system, I examine them always – each time if I can. It's time-consuming for me, but keeps my conscience happy. … I've got some sort of objective proof rather than just a hint, or a feeling that someone is swinging the lead.

GP2: … so, I've just given up worrying about whether I'm acting as the gatekeeper to the DSS [Department of Social Security] system or the benefits agency system, or whatever it is. Too many other things to think about; too many other priorities. Terribly sorry – I just don't give a moment's thought. Patient wants a line – that's fine, here you are.

GP3: After the benefits agency fraud hotline was put out about 18 months ago I made a few 'phone calls (I did the 141 before dialling). I reported information that I had got, circumstantially, you know, third-party information to the effect that this person should have a review of their DLA [Disability Living Allowance].

Other examples which occupied the middle ground were also utilized as stimulus material in the second round of three focus groups with, respectively, GP Registrars, locums and GP Principals.

ADDITIONAL PROBES DERIVED FROM FOCUS GROUPS

Probe set 3

I once got myself into a real difficult situation where a patient didn't come to me for ten years because of me refusing her a sick line. She was wanting to extend her sickness period because of back pain and I couldn't find any evidence of that. At that time I was a young – I suppose, what you would now call a GP Registrar and, eh, full of this, 'Oh, this is the right thing to do – I don't think I can sign you off', which just destroyed the relationship. She was aghast. She couldn't believe it. 'I can't believe it. You're telling me I don't have back pain, but I do have back pain.' 'Well', I said, 'I can't find any great evidence of this, that would stop you working' and she never came to see me for ten years.

Probe set 5

I had a lady just before lunch time, one time, who came in and was absolutely academy award performance: she couldn't sit down, back pain agony, furrowed brow, you know, almost out in a cold sweat, and straight leg raise – the whole lot. I couldn't, couldn't trip her up. So, anyway, I had to give her the line. So, this was about five to one. I was just going home for my lunch about 10 minutes later – I saw her walking at a rapid pace up the back – fitter than Linford Christie, you know, and she'd pulled the wool … and I just laughed. But she won't do it again, I mean, obviously. That was her one and only dupe on me.

Further information on the probes used in these focus group discussions (together with a full list of coding categories developed) can be found on the *British Medical Journal*'s website, which allows for the deposit of supplementary materials. This can be accessed electronically by a link from the original article – Hussey et al., 2004.)

HINTS ON USING FOCUS GROUPS

- Focus groups are useful in accessing group norms, meanings and processes.
- They should be used, above all, to study interaction between participants.
- Careful preparation and planning can maximize their potential both to generate relevant data and to facilitate analysis.

- Sampling is key to the comparative potential of focus groups, but ethical considerations are also of paramount importance.
- Topic guides and stimulus materials should be carefully developed and selected and it also pays to pilot these.
- Anticipate the analysis through attentive moderating.
- Identify and interrogate patterning in the analysis of focus group data
- Consider the potential of second-stage sampling and the development of new materials to further explore any emergent explanations or theories.

FURTHER READING

Barbour, R.S. (2007) *Doing Focus Groups*, London: Sage (a book in *The Qualitative Research Kit*).

Barbour, R.S. and Kitzinger, J. (eds) (1999) *Developing Focus Group Research: Politics, Theory and Practice*, London: Sage.

Bloor, M., Frankland, J., Thomas, M. and Robson, K. (2001) *Focus Groups in Social Research*, London: Sage.

Murphy, B., Cockburn, J. and Murphy, M. (1992) 'Focus groups in health research', *Health Promotion Journal of Australia*, 2: 37–40.

Wilkinson, S. (2003) 'Focus groups', in J.A. Smith (ed.) *Qualitative Psychology: A Practical Guide to Research Methods*, Thousand Oaks, CA: Sage, pp. 184–204.

EXERCISE 1: SELECTION OF STIMULUS MATERIAL

You could consider what sources you might use as stimulus materials if carrying out focus groups to address the research questions suggested elsewhere in this book. You might even try some of these out with friends or fellow students to see whether they give rise to the sort of discussions you want to elicit.

Potential research question 1: Do people view risk differently when they travel?

You might consider newspaper reports, for example.

Potential research question 2: Are our notions shifting with regard to how long we think adolescence lasts?

Again, newspaper coverage might be useful. As I prepare this book in the wake of England's ignominious departure from football's World Cup, the newspapers are full of discussions about Wayne Rooney, including some pleas along the lines of 'He's only nineteen!' This, of course, has the potential to 'backfire', particularly if your participants are football aficionados and likely to stray into discussing the finer points of the game.

Problem pages might also yield stimulus material. In recent editions of *The Guardian* Money supplement I have come across examples of parents writing in for advice in relation to sons aged, respectively, 22 and 25 years.

Potential research question 3: What impact does media coverage of fertility treatment have on public perceptions of appropriate provision?

There should be no shortage of potential materials in relation to this topic, as there always seems to be some coverage of women in their 50s giving birth.

Potential research question 4: What do people think about fathers' attendance at deliveries?

If you have access to a group of midwives or obstetricians you might consider using some excerpts from the study I've referred to in Chapter 2 to explore their ideas about whether fathers' attendance makes their job easier or more difficult; whether they have seen others, or even admit themselves to, having co-opted fathers in the pursuit of their professional goals; how they respond to the idea of 'a good birth' as involving making some value judgements about the couple involved.

Potential research question 5: What are the challenges of parenting?

EXERCISE 2: GENERATING FOCUS GROUP DATA

I would recommend that you generate some data in relation to question 4: What do people think about fathers' attendance at deliveries? It is a topic that I have used in many workshops and it has always made for lively discussion. It seems to be an issue on which everyone has a view – regardless of whether they are parents themselves or not.

Suggestions on how to run this exercise

The focus group topic guide I've provided is very short and relies on two main questions. In workshops I have used as stimulus material two cartoons from Claire Bretecher's (1995) book *Mothers* which address these two topics humorously and succinctly. (The excerpts reproduced in Chapter 9 come from focus groups which used these cartoons.) You could, however, simply provide two short scenarios to precede each of the questions:

Scenario 1

A young man is talking to a group of women friends (including his partner) about the impending birth of their baby and is adamant that he is not going to be there for the delivery. The response is one of incredulity and disapproval. One of the women concludes the discussion by asserting that this is nonsense and that he 'wouldn't miss it for the world'.

Scenario 2

The partner of a woman in labour enters the delivery room with a film crew and proceeds to set up his shot, exhorting the woman to push, as he's in danger of running out of film. The midwives have to squeeze past him and film crew members in order to attend to the woman. In the event, the baby's head appears as the partner is engaged in changing a roll of film. He voices his disappointment to the newly delivered mother, who is now lying exhausted and clutching the baby, 'It's ridiculous, darling, we won't even have a souvenir'.

Suggestion on how to run this exercise

Although there are a few prompts, you may well not have to use these. In workshops I've usually limited this exercise to 25 minutes or so (indicating when participants are halfway through their allotted time, so that they can move on to the second scenerio and question) in order to keep transcription within manageable limits. You may, however, want to hold longer discussions. (Excerpts from transcripts generated in short sessions on this same topic are included in Chapter 9 to provide you with an opportunity to try out a coding frame and gain some experience of marking up a transcript. However, you may decide to take notes on your own data generating exercise, or even to fully transcribe this, in order to provide further comparative material to use in this later exercise.)

FOCUS GROUP TOPIC GUIDE: FATHERS' ATTENDANCE AT DELIVERIES

Should fathers be encouraged to attend deliveries?
(Show participants Scenario 1)

Prompts:

- *Do fathers serve a useful function in the delivery room?*
- *Is there pressure on them to attend? Too much pressure?*
- *What are the implications – for men and women?*
- *Is it always appropriate?*
- *What about other birth partners?*
- *Changes in expectations over time?*

Do fathers serve a useful function in the delivery room?
(Show participants Scenario 2)

Prompts:
- *Are they able to provide support?*
- *Are they able to act as advocates?*
- *What are the implications for couples' relationships?*
- *Do all women like to have their partners present?*
- *Is it a pleasant experience for all fathers?*

SECTION 3
COMPLEX RESEARCH DESIGNS IN PRACTICE

Esoteric discussions about the epistemology and ontology of qualitative research notwithstanding, our studies are carried out in the real world, where the funding climate, the structure of academic careers and publishing requirements inevitably colour our endeavours and outputs. Moreover, many of those who employ qualitative methods are charged with the responsibility of bringing about change – either political or professional. For those of us who are seeking to carry out research that is relevant to practice, the use of mixed methods designs can be attractive. Such an approach may also find favour with research commissioners who are keen to fund research that can be seen as making a contribution to the 'evidence base' in addition to addressing the more theoretical concerns that may engage us as academics. Chapter 7, in this section, addresses mixed methods designs and Chapter 8 considers action research, which frequently employs mixed methods designs, but which can raise additional challenges.

7
MIXING METHODS

AIMS

- This chapter equips the reader to make appropriate decisions regarding the design of mixed methods studies.
- In particular, it helps the researcher to capitalize on the possibilities of mixing methods by suggesting helpful combinations in terms of the relationship between methods and their sequencing (whether this involves combining qualitative and quantitative methods or different approaches to generating qualitative data).
- It helps the mixed methods researcher to anticipate challenges and to take appropriate steps to minimize problems while maximizing the potential for useful comparison.
- Some recommendations are also provided with respect to mixing the disciplinary backgrounds and expertise of research team members.

INTRODUCTION

This chapter will outline the various reasons for combining methods within one study. These include using qualitative methods in order to inform development of a survey instrument, which is probably the most common approach to mixing methods. Mixing methods are also often employed in order to compensate for the perceived shortcomings of stand-alone methods, with the aim of either providing a more complete picture or enhancing coverage. This chapter will also examine the potential afforded by employing qualitative methods later in a project, for example, using quantitative work to furnish a sampling pool for more in-depth qualitative work. It is also argued that focused qualitative work can make a valuable contribution in providing an explanation for some of the more surprising or anomalous results of quantitative studies.

Each of these justifications for mixing methods will be explored in turn, and examples will be provided of studies which have utilized these different rationales for using a mixed methods design. Detailed examples will provide insights into the process of producing and refining successive drafts (including development of research questions and explanations as to how various research methods will fit together). Recognizing the importance of the research team members' individual disciplinary backgrounds and the skills they bring to the enterprise, attention is paid to the possibility of developing hybrids (e.g. the innovative use of enhanced case notes, diaries, or artwork).

The debate about 'triangulation' is presented, both with regard to combining different qualitative approaches and to combining qualitative and quantitative approaches within one project. It will be stressed, as always, that the key to successful research design is achieving a match between research questions and aims, and the approaches or combination of approaches selected. Rather than simply applying several methods in the hope that they will, somehow, afford a multidimensional insight into the topic being studied, it is important to have a well thought-out rationale for using methods in particular combinations. Again, this relates to having an understanding of the assumptions underpinning the various methods and, hence, their potential and limitations (as discussed in Chapter 1).

Although some commentators have asserted that mixing different qualitative methods is less problematic, since they stem from the same paradigm, I have questioned this, arguing that there are, in effect, several distinct qualitative paradigms, each of which has differing ideas about what sorts of questions to ask, how to generate data, what constitutes data; how to analyze and use data, how to present findings and to which audiences (Barbour, 1998b). Whereas disciplines such as anthropology take as their starting point relatively unstructured observational fieldwork in naturalistic settings and involve the researcher in spending perhaps two years in the field, other qualitative approaches involve tightly orchestrated encounters which closely reflect the researcher's agenda and which take place within a very short timescale. Qualitative approaches also vary with respect to the salience which they accord to social structure: some, such as conversation analysis, or even phenomenology, may be more 'self-referring', paying little attention to the broader social context in which encounters are played out, while others attempt to place these within their wider social, cultural and even historical context, including policy documents as data and using the same sorts of variable as are commonly associated with quantitative approaches in order to sample and facilitate comparison. Here, I'm thinking about the stance of some researchers who describe themselves as working within a social constructionist or critical realist paradigm.

DECISIONS ABOUT MIXED METHODS DESIGNS

The resulting research design is usually the product of many discussions between the research team and also takes account of the funding body's research brief (including the amount of money available and the anticipated timescale). Decisions are also, hopefully, informed by the available methodological literature, a re-reading of which may suggest particular combinations that are especially well suited to the research question at hand. One common rationale for mixing methods relates to the development of research 'tools' and usually involves using qualitative methods for the initial exploratory phase.

Mixing methods to develop research 'tools'

In designing a study which focused on professionals' perspectives on work, where concerns about both maternal mental health and child protection were involved (Stanley et al., 2003), we opted to use three mixed professional focus groups in order to develop a questionnaire to be sent to a sample of professionals in two contrasting geographical areas. The focus groups were held in another area not included in the main study and utilized a brief topic guide and stimulus material. We also used the group discussions in order to pilot the wording of two particular questions we hoped to include in the questionnaire. The focus groups were intended to sensitize us to the issues that arose for professionals and to help ensure that we asked relevant and meaningful questions without omitting important areas of concern.

A study of the role and responsibilities of midwives in Scotland used observational fieldwork to inform development of interview schedules and then used preliminary analysis of these qualitative datasets in order to design a questionnaire.

In addition to using qualitative methods in order to develop quantitative 'tools', some studies augment qualitative data by seeking to capture some quantitative information to provide a context against which qualitative data can be interpreted.

Developing research 'tools' to contextualize qualitative data

Our study of the introduction of methadone prescribing relied on interviews (with both GPs and methadone users) as the main method for generating data. However, we also collected detailed information on the number and content of consultations utilizing pro-formas designed to record routine data on patients, such as age, employment details, medical conditions, length of drug misuse, and reason for the consultation. This was supplemented by 'enhanced case records'. These were included as anecdotal evidence that suggested that the GPs found the consultations with drug users particularly problematic, but little information was available regarding why such consultations were difficult. The 'enhanced case record' (as advocated by McKeganey and Boddy, 1988) was developed to allow GPs to record such details and allow us to identify any patterns associated with especially difficult consultations. While we asked for patients' NHS numbers, we of course did not have the facility to de-code these, but reasoned that it might be useful to see whether the same patients cropped up in records produced by different GPs (in the event they did). We also wanted to collect some routine demographic details relating to patients, and to the purpose and length of the consultation. However, we left it up to GPs to decide when they wanted to complete a form in relation to a difficult consultation and relied on free text to allow them to express their frustration. Not only did the enhanced case records give us an idea of the frequency with which GPs were dealing with problematic methadone-related consultations, but they also indicated why GPs experienced these as problematic and afforded us the chance of exploring issues identified in these pro-formas when we carried out follow-up interviews with the GPs. The enhanced case record is reproduced below (NB: The space for free text continued on the lower half of the second side of the document (not reproduced here) with the top half left blank).

EXAMPLE OF AN ENHANCED CASE RECORD

DATE OF CONSULTATION: ....   **GP Identifier:** ....
Patient's NHS Number: .... **Length of Consultation:** .... mins.

Purpose of Consultation: (*Please tick ALL that apply*):-

[ ] To acquire methadone prescription **and** Dose requested: .... (*if applicable*)

[ ] To acquire prescription for other psychotropic drugs

[ ] To acquire prescription for other drugs

[ ] To seek advice about drug use

[ ] To seek advice about drug-related health problems

[ ] To seek advice about other health problems

[ ] Other (*Please specify*):- ....

Outcome of Consultation: (*Please tick ALL that apply*):-

[ ] Issued methadone prescription **and** Dose: ....

[ ] Issued prescription for other psychotropic

[ ] Issued prescription for other drugs

[ ] Provided advice about drug use

[ ] Provided advice about drug-related health problems

[ ] Provided advice about other health problems

[ ] Referred for investigation/treatment (*Please give details*):-
....
....

[ ] Other (*Please specify*):-

N.B. THE TEAR-OFF SLIP BELOW WILL BE REMOVED AND WILL BE STORED SEPARATELY FOR RESEARCH PURPOSES

Patient's NHS Number: .... Date: ....

Was this consultation...? (*Please tick **one** box*):-

[ ] Very Difficult?   [ ] Difficult?   [ ] Neutral?   [ ] Easy?   [ ] Very Easy?

Please comment (if you wish) on the reasons for ticking this box or add any other observations about this consultation:

....

....

....

....

....

.... P.T.O.

Mixing qualitative methods to generate parallel data: providing multiple perspectives and the potential for comparison

Mason (2006: 10) provides a compelling rationale for using mixed methods in order to access multiple perspectives and dimensions: She argues that 'social experience and lived realities are multi-dimensional and … our understandings are impoverished and may be inadequate if we view these phenomena only along a single continuum'. This highlights the potential both of using different methods in order to provide parallel insights into the experiences of different stakeholders (e.g. the GPs and drug users interviewed in our study of the implications of the introduction of methadone prescribing, described above) but equally that of using complementary methods in order to illuminate the different aspects of the experience of the same group of people. My PhD study of professional socialization for social work combined participant observation with a series of interviews with students at different points during their course. Rather than being a staged approach, the two methods were employed in tandem.

Writing some time ago, Becker and Geer (1957) argued that participant observation, as a method, is far superior to interviewing. The main faults in interviewing, they claimed, are the underlying assumptions that word meanings are common to interviewer and interviewee, that the interviewee will talk about the chosen topics, and that the interviewee's account will be more or less accurate. However, embedding interviews within a study which utilizes participant observation satisfactorily addresses all of these objections. The interviewer/participant observer can phrase questions in the language and concepts used by the group under study. During the course of the interview s/he can clarify meanings with respondents with reference to shared experiences. Although co-operation cannot be guaranteed, the participant observation component of the research gives more scope for coaching potential interviewees about the interviewer's research interests. Ongoing contact and developing friendships with respondents will probably result in them being more favourable towards the research project, as, indeed, will their own investment in terms of time. Interview questions can also be informed by fieldwork, as the researcher is well placed to determine which topics are currently regarded as important by the group being studied. Misleading impressions are not so easy to sustain when interviews are taking place alongside participant observation, which involves close daily contact. Should any contradictions be uncovered these have value as data in their own right and can always be explored with interviewees, provided that this is done sensitively.

Given, during fieldwork, that the number of statements volunteered (see Chapter 9) in relation to one theme may be relatively small, interviews can establish whether a perspective is shared by most members of the group. A series of interviews is also particularly useful in monitoring change in individuals over time and allow the researcher to enlist the help of respondents in accounting for such shifts. Interview schedules can incorporate issues arising in the field and give the researcher the opportunity to probe. After all, interviewees expect to be asked questions, whereas explicit or repeated questioning in the field might well give rise to discomfort, resentment or suspicion amongst research contacts.

Likewise, combining interviews and focus groups can provide access, and the potential for comparison between, public and private accounts. Here it is important, however, to recall the caution voiced by Rapley (2001) with regard to how much significance we attach to 'off the record' comments after interviews. A similar degree of scepticism is needed in this instance if we are to avoid the dangers inherent in viewing one type of data as 'more authentic' than another. However, if the researcher can be content with utilizing the multiple perspectives accessed in order to develop a fuller account, then mixing methods can play a valuable role in providing a multifaceted account or explanation of the phenomena we seek to study.

Utilizing records, questionnaire or survey data to furnish a sampling frame for qualitative work

Although it is more common for qualitative methods to be seen as a precursor to quantitative work, there is much to be gained by capitalizing on existing quantitative data (either in the form of records or survey responses) to furnish a sampling frame for qualitative work. This overcomes the problems associated with convenience sampling, which relies on chance to provide diversity that can be further explored during the process of data analysis. Unless the researcher or project is officially linked to an organization or larger study, however, it can be difficult to obtain access to such a resource and, in this case, the best option may be to collect one's own quantitative data.

Rather than defensively insisting on convenience sampling, for example, qualitative researchers might use the detailed information about respondents afforded by a survey in order to purposively sample interviewees. This was the approach taken by Cawley (2004), who conducted a community survey investigating the links between obesity and psychological health. She included a number of pre-validated scales measuring self-esteem, body image, physical health status and psychological health in order to provide data for quantitative analysis. However, these were also useful in providing a sampling pool for interviews. The advantage of using pre-validated scales is that, in a given population, they are likely to provide a range of scores (which in this case were also used as a criterion for qualitative sampling). However, pre-validated scales may not necessarily cover all of the issues which are likely to be relevant for you in selecting a sample for in-depth study and, with this in mind, Cawley's questionnaire also contained some questions about health beliefs, including, importantly, respondents' perceptions of the role of heredity in obesity, whether they subscribed to a version of weight management as within individuals' control, or whether they were essentially fatalistic. This information (for respondents who had given permission for the researcher to re-contact them to arrange for one-to-one interviews) allowed her to purposively select a sample which included both women and men, some individuals who could be described as 'fat but fit', some with a previous history of eating disorders, depression, diabetes, and people with differing views about the role of heredity and fatalism.

Relationship and sequencing of different methods

The example of a project timetable reproduced in Chapter 2 draws attention to the relatively tight timescales within which we are often required to carry out our research. It is imperative that researchers pay attention to the sequencing of methods, and the backdrop against which these are being employed, to ensure that they can inform each other and successive phases of the project in the way intended. Although funding periods can sometimes be more generous, this does not necessarily allow room for complacency. In one project involving a pilot study of changed management arrangements for community nurses, the research team (myself and a research assistant) were appointed only two months before the new management arrangements were due to begin, so we needed to collect baseline data quickly before changes started to have an impact. With little time to spare, we capitalized on the capacity of focus groups to provide in-depth and timely data in order to establish how teams worked, how they allocated responsibilities and conceived each others' roles and remits. However, the method was fairly novel at this point in time (at least in health services research) and we had to contend with some resistance and scepticism on the part of the steering group (for a fuller discussion see Barbour, 1995).

Another study which involved a mixed methods design provides some insights into the rationale for combining methods, the sequencing of methods, how we envisaged these complementing each other and how we went about putting the design into practice.

MIXING METHODS TO STUDY MATERNAL MENTAL HEALTH AND CHILD PROTECTION

The research objectives of this study were:

- To explore the experiences and perceptions of health, social services and voluntary sector practitioners working with families where mothers have severe mental illness and there are identified child protection concerns.
- To identify barriers to effective communication and collaboration between professionals and agencies.
- To elicit the views of mothers with severe mental health problems regarding both their own and their children's needs and how these could most appropriately be met.
- To establish what services and resources are available and how these are viewed both by professionals and service users.

This study design had three separate, but related, phases:

Phase 1 involved three multi-professional focus groups held in a neighbouring authority (not included in the other two phases). The focus group discussions were originally intended to assist us in developing a questionnaire to be sent to professionals involved in work where these two issues might coincide. The focus groups involved us in using a short topic guide, a newspaper clipping (as stimulus material – see discussion in Chapter 6 on focus groups) and two draft questions for inclusion in our survey instrument, selected because of the challenges we were experiencing in drafting these. (We had started drafting a provisional questionnaire while setting up the focus group sessions.) However, these focus groups elicited such rich data that we subsequently analyzed these in their own right (an option we were able to exercise since we had taped the discussions) and published our findings separately (Barbour et al., 2002).

Phase 2 involved a postal questionnaire which covered two geographical areas in order to furnish a larger pool of respondents and to provide a basis for comparison. A total of 500 questionnaires were completed by professionals drawn from health, social services and the voluntary sector (327 in Hull and 173 in North Tyneside with an overall response rate of 50.5% and a fairly even response rate from different professional groups). The questionnaire utilized feedback from the focus groups to produce reformulated questions and covered a range of questions on the following topics: experiences of such work, perceptions of roles and remits, the role of the key worker, communication with other professionals, requirements of service users, and gaps in service provision.

The questionnaires also incorporated a set of 'risk scenarios', derived partly from the literature but also informed by issues raised in focus group discussions and by the professional experience of one of the collaborators, and respondents were invited to assess the level of risk involved in each short description.

Phase 3 consisted of a set of interviews with women with severe mental health problems and whose child/ren had been the subject of a child protection case conference in the past 18 months. These women were identified to the researcher team by health and social services staff in the two localities. The guidance provided to these 'gatekeepers' was that the diagnosis could be provided by any health professional and could include diagnoses of personality disorder and repeated episodes of self-harm, but not diagnoses of substance abuse alone. This resulted in a total of 11 women being recruited into the study. The diagnoses (as reported by the mothers) related to: depression (3); manic depression (2); psychotic disorder (3); personality disorder + schizoid disorder (2) and 'mental health problems' (1). Interviews established that all had experience of in-patient psychiatric care. In order to try to capture some idea of progress through services, each woman was interviewed twice; the first interview utilized a structure interview schedule, while the second (conducted 5–6 months later) was less structured. Interviews were carried out by a qualified psychiatric nurse with research experience.

Alongside the willingness to innovate and explore new ways of working across paradigms, there is considerable pressure from funding bodies – and, indeed, ethics committees – to timetable sequentially, demonstrating how different methods fit into the overall study design. Although this can sometimes hamper the development of new ways of working together, with room for trial and error in the field, most mixed methods proposals can be strengthened by paying attention to the potential for linkages between datasets – either through utilizing their capacity to address the same questions using different means, or considering whether a shared coding frame might be developed and used to guide analysis. The next section considers in detail some of the challenges involved in analyzing mixed methods datasets.

THE CHALLENGES OF MIXING METHODS

One of the pitfalls in mixing methods is the temptation to downplay the contribution of other paradigms, traditions, and methods and to reduce these – perhaps inadvertently as we, ourselves, grapple with new approaches – to a set of techniques. I've argued that this can be an invidious practice, leading to a situation where technical fixes rather than research questions are driving the way in which research is conducted – what I've also termed 'technical essentialism', where, in fact, the 'tail is wagging the dog' (Barbour, 2001). It can be challenging to take on board other versions of the research process and criteria for rigour, and the temptation to stick to our own is strong, even where this is clearly inappropriate.

The question of emphasis is an important one. Certainly mixed methods designs which accord equal weight to quantitative and qualitative data gathering and data analysis are relatively rare and it may be more realistic to settle for designs which are predominantly quantitative, but which involve a qualitative component and vice versa. However, the imbalance in terms of the weight accorded different methods can very easily lead to tokenism unless we are genuinely open to modifying our own approaches to take advantage of some of the added benefits of mixed methods. This can also apply to studies that seek to combine different qualitative methods, as we all have our own preferences and enthusiasms and may be less committed to other approaches, perhaps including such methods somewhat reluctantly at the behest of collaborators, reviewers or funding bodies.

Challenges in combining qualitative and quantitative methods

Although it is undoubtedly an over-simplification, it is probably fair to say that there are important differences with regard to the quantitative and qualitative research process. Here I've characterized quantitative research as involving a linear approach and qualitative, an iterative approach. I recently read a chapter by Brian Doig (2004) which argues that quantitative research, in effect, works backwards, focusing on how results are to be reported, rather than selecting an analytic approach and making a decision as to how to collect data so that they are amenable to analysis in this way. Qualitative research is generally viewed as being more flexible, with interview schedules and focus group topic guides being revised as they are employed and with the research question even being subject to modification in the course of the research. The two paradigms differ perhaps most significantly with regard to when the most conceptual work is done. The scale of quantitative studies – and the financial implications – require much of this work to be done up-front. One of the challenges of seeking to mix quantitative and qualitative methods concerns the extent to which it is still possible to be flexible, while taking account of these very different requirements.

One compromise has involved restricting the use of qualitative methods to the exploratory phase of research, where these are used to inform development, for example, of survey instruments. At the other extreme, relegating qualitative methods to a later stage in the research project may mean that we are invited to collaborate, but only after important decisions have been made regarding the study design. Not surprisingly, this can seriously hamper our contribution.

There are, however, more ambitious possibilities, such as the cross-over or integrated designs described by Greene et al. (2004), who contend that there are three distinct approaches to mixing quantitative and qualitative paradigms:

- A-paradigmatic stances, which argue that philosophical assumptions are useful conceptual tools but that they should not drive practice.

- Pragmatic stances, which advocate an alternative inclusive philosophical frame-work which de-emphasizes differences in philosophical traditions. Taking this approach, multiple assumptions and diverse methods can comfortably co-exist.
- Dialectic stances which intentionally mix philosophical assumptions and methods. In this version, possible tensions and dissonances from different sets of assumptions are especially welcomed as a resource likely to be generative of new insights and fresh perspectives. (adapted from Greene et al., 2004: 275)

However, as these authors themselves concede, practice is always much more com-plex than theory and, like any typology, this needs to be critically examined. For the purposes of illustration, they have matched particular authors with each of these approaches. However, I wonder whether one can subscribe to only one paradigm, or whether one can shift in the course of one's research career, or, indeed, whether these stances are necessarily mutually exclusive? Also, do all team members need to take the same stance, or is it possible to work together constructively while adhering to differing rationales for combining methods? Does a particular stance need to be maintained throughout or only for some parts of analysis or in relation to specific papers, with the option of taking another stance with regard to others?

Other advice, such as thinking about the relationship between and sequencing of different methods can be useful in making us think carefully about how methods can complement each other rather than simply throwing together lots of methods in a spirit of optimism. However, the challenge lies in being able to plan studies and the respective contributions of different methods, while remaining open to new possibilities as these unfold. As Greene et al. (2004: 277) argue: "Flexibility, creativity, resourcefulness - rather than a prior methodological elegance - are the hallmark of good mixed method design."

Challenges in analysis

Anticipating potential overlap between coding frames would facilitate the approach advocated by Moran-Ellis et al. (2006), who describe how they identified key themes and analytic questions and then engaged in 'following this thread' in looking across their various databases.

Moran-Ellis et al. (2006) caution against reducing qualitative data to broad cate-gories, viewing this as involving an attempt to transform one type of data into another, and thus as inherently problematic. However, I would argue that there can be a place for carrying out such an exercise, provided that it is not viewed as a definitive end-point.

AN EXAMPLE OF HARNESSING QUANTITATIVE METHODS TO IDENTIFY PATTERNING IN QUALITATIVE DATA

I carried out an interview study of HIV/AIDS workers in four Scottish cities in the early 1990s, at a time when services were having to formulate rapid responses to escalating incidence and associated multifaceted health and social care demands. Although this was a 'stand-alone' interview study, the challenges raised by the analysis led me to explore the potential of a limited application of SPSS.

A total of 153 interviews were conducted with staff members of varying professional affiliations, and the occasional volunteer and ex-member of staff. The analysis relied on the package Ethnograph, which was not, at that point in time, very sophisticated. It did not allow, as do latter-day packages, for the researcher to identify patterning in the data or to begin to build conceptual models. Instead, I used Ethnograph for data retrieval purposes and resorted to coloured pens and paper in the time-honoured fashion embraced by many qualitative researchers (Kelle, 1997). However, dealing with such a large number of interview scripts posed considerable problems with regard to 'getting a handle' on the huge amount of text involved. As I wanted to guard against impressionistic selection of quotes from particularly vocal interviewees, I needed to devise an approach that allowed me to interrogate my data systematically and thoroughly.

It was with this aim that I decided to attempt to reduce my data to broad categories, and to enter my newly produced data into SPSS with a view to producing cross-tabulations that would identify the existence of patterns, allowing me to look at the relationship between variables. Since I had interviewed virtually all the specialist HIV/AIDS workers in Scotland and had augmented this sample by the 'snowball sampling' of key professionals with generic posts but high involvement in AIDS work, I decided (with the advice of a statistician) to pursue some quantitative analysis of the data, presenting – unusually for me – pie-charts and tables showing statistical significance (Barbour, 1995). However, this was a by-product and, essentially, what this exercise did was to provide direction for the further interrogating of my data, using the standard pen-and-paper-approach, utilizing Ethnograph to retrieve relevant coded excerpts.

Thus, although I had reduced my qualitative data to very broad coding categories amenable to analysis using SPSS, this transformation was strategic and, most importantly, temporary – as means to an end. I would argue that Moran-Ellis and colleagues (2006) are right to warn against the casual transformation of data. However, I would suggest that carrying out a similar exercise within a context that affords the opportunity to re-interrogate the data in its original form can reap dividends. It is not, perhaps, the practice that should be condemned, merely the unthoughtful and unimaginative translation of data. Perhaps, indeed, Moran-Ellis et al. would agree, as what they criticize is research practice 'where one type of data is transformed into another paradigmatic format for *single* analysis' (Moran-Ellis et al., 2006: 56, my emphasis).

Although many questionnaires include open-ended questions, they frequently serve more as a public relations exercise rather than at attempt to generate data for in-depth analysis. Very often such data – if it is analyzed at all – is simply translated into a few broad quantitative categories and analyzed accordingly. However, there is considerable potential to capitalize on such material as qualitative data, by employing standard approaches to analysis, even when it is generated under the auspices of a survey.

I have recently been involved in a Scottish Needs Assessment Project (SNAP) which has been examining the views, experiences and responses of a variety of professional groups in dealing with children with behavioural or psychological problems (Barbour et al., 2006). Although this study employed a pre-coded questionnaire, it also utilized two open-ended questions which invited respondents to write about (a) their most difficult and (b) their most rewarding case. The research team involved a wide range of clinicians in health and social care (general practitioner, social worker, clinical psychologist, child and adolescent psychiatrist), of whom two had previous experience of analyzing qualitative data and, encouragingly, there was a commitment to carrying out a close-grained analysis of this textual data, looking, for example, at the language used and the intervention models implied in this talk.

Moran-Ellis et al. (2006) distinguish between approaches that seek to 'combine' methods and those which aim to 'integrate' different methods, acknowledging, however, that most studies defer integration to the point of analysis or theoretical interpretation. An important exception, also cited by Moran-Ellis et al., is the work of Kelle (2001), who reflects on his experience of being involved in a study which employed separate methods but sought to carry out an integrated analysis.

AN EXAMPLE OF INTEGRATED USE OF QUANITITATIVE AND QUALITATIVE DATA IN ANALYSIS

Kelle and colleagues carried out research in two German cities in order to study the passage from school to the labour market. This panel study involved administering a series of four structured questionnaires (over a period of eight years) to all school-leavers in these two localities who had embarked on vocational training in identified occupations selected to cover craft, office and technical-industrial work.

Statistical data highlighted that two of the chosen occupations (industrial mechanics and car mechanics) were almost exclusively male, while the majority of hairdressers were female. Analysis of survey data also showed a strong relationship between access to training and gender. Data generated in interviews with a sub-sample served to illuminate the processes through which such exclusions and gender discrimination in companies takes place.

Multivariate modelling with the quantitative data suggested that the high proportion of bank executives returning to education could be explained by their previous higher levels of success in terms of achieving high school qualifications. However, industrial mechanics were less likely to return to the educational system regardless of their previous qualifications. By analyzing in-depth responses in successive interviews, which focused on work experiences, aspirations and reflections on careers, the researchers were alerted to the presence of different modes of coping with the constraints and opportunities afforded by their occupational situation. Kelle (2001) summarizes:

Industrial mechanics who stayed in their occupation often developed a mode of action orientation which can be called the 'workmen's habit': they regarded good working conditions and good salary as the most crucial things in their work. Their attitudes towards their job and concerning careers opportunities were rather sober: they did not see work as a means of self-fulfilment but as a way of bread-winning and developed strategies to avoid being exploited and worn out.

Kelle concludes that neither quantitative nor qualitative data on its own could have provided sufficient information to allow for adequate explanations of the social processes under scrutiny.

The challenges of collaboration

Although we've been talking about mixing methods, the other dimension involved is that of mixing disciplines. I thought it might be helpful to try to visually depict the scale and nature of the challenges involved and have produced what I suppose might be called a tartan diagram, where the challenges intensify as the colour used deepens (Figure 7.1). Although, of course, you don't have to be mixing methods to experience tensions, such difficulties are exacerbated when we approach research from different disciplinary standpoints. Nor are challenges exclusive to those situations in which we seek to mix quantitative and qualitative paradigms.

	Mixed quantitative	Mixed qualitative	Mixed quantitative and qualitative
Single discipline			
Mixed sub-disciplines			
Mixed disciplines			

FIGURE 7.1   DIAGRAMMATIC REPRESENTATION OF VARYING DEGREES OF DIFFICULTY IN CARRYING OUT MIXED METHODS RESEARCH

As Fenton and Charsley (2000) have pointed out, epidemiology, for example, has a narrower focus than other quantitative applications, concentrating, as it does, on the three core elements of disease, population and a set of determinants. Even within disciplines such as sociology, there may be sub-disciplines, each with its own distinct history and particular 'take' on the application of a method. Here, too, the history or origins of methods also impact on the ways in which these are conceptualized and pressed into service. For researchers, language can also constitute a barrier and Robert Alford (1996) has described mixed methods research as involving 'tribal languages of modes of enquiry'.

Layer on to this diagram the dual, but not necessarily co-terminous, categories of experience and seniority and the picture becomes even more complex. Who is in the driving seat with regard to a project and what is the funding source? Take, for instance, the position of a social scientist in a clinical department, such as epidemiology, public health, or primary care. Occupying the somewhat uncomfortable position of 'cuckoo in the nest' (Barbour, 2003), one can find oneself the sole representative of qualitative methods – and, indeed, of one's own discipline – in an environment which downplays disciplinary expertise and privileges methods, or techniques. Although one may, in theory, be in a relatively powerful position as supervisor or consultant, this can give rise to considerable frustration.

Even when employing a participatory method such as focus groups, it is possible for the researcher to 'play his cards close to his chest' preferring this approach to one where we would seek to harness the insights of participants and share with them the objectives of our study. (I am sure that quantitative researchers might be equally perplexed by my own possibly blinkered approach to using quantitative data descriptively, rather than using it to address what are, for them, burning and obvious questions.)

Epistemological differences become evident when we examine the role of theory in different research traditions. This applies to the epistemological underpinnings of individual methods, constellations of methods, and to the differing rationales for combining methods. The task of formulating, interrogating or refining existing theoretical frameworks is a much higher priority for some modes of research enquiry than it is for others. Much mixed methods research comes under the broad umbrella of health services research or action research, both of which have also been criticized as being a-theoretical (e.g. Harding and Gantley, 1998). Perhaps we should ask, however, whether it is possible, or even desirable, for studies grounded in practice to aspire to engaging with theory in preference to making recommendations about service provision. There is no simple answer to this question, but, depending on the make-up of the research team, it may be possible to address both aims, although it is likely that the findings relevant to practice are likely to take precedence, at least with regard to the sequence of publication and dissemination.

One of the added advantages of mixed methods approaches is that it is often possible to subsequently mine rich qualitative datasets in order to write more theorized accounts which can engage with our own disciplinary concerns as social scientists. While some researchers have pointed out that claiming to have a monopoly on theorizing has been a powerful tool for sociologists in boundary disputes within the contested arena of health services research, charges of 'sociological imperialism' (Chapple and Rogers, 1998) may be overstated. There may, however, be a middle ground, which goes some way towards addressing how we can begin to integrate qualitative and quantitative approaches.

I recently came across a cartoon which, for me, summed up one of the important but often overlooked challenges of team-working in the context of mixed methods designs. It showed a dog balancing precariously on a high wire above a circus ring. The caption referred to the hushed and anticipatory crowd and the dog's discomfort, as he reflected that 'He was an old dog and this was a new trick'. I like this cartoon precisely because it emphasizes that mixed methods research requires individuals to leave behind their zones of comfort and that this can be an unnerving experience. The reference to 'tricks' also highlights the tendency, in some quarters, to reduce the contribution of other paradigms, or indeed disciplines, to a set of tricks. In a paper with the wonderful title of 'Don't mind him: He's from Barcelona', Dingwall (1992: 161) argues:

> One of the great methodological fallacies of the last half century in social research is the belief that science is a particular set of techniques: it is, rather, a state of mind, or attitude, and the organizational conditions which allow that attitude to be expressed.

An associated misconception is that methods achieve consistent results. However, what might appear a relatively straightforward tool (for example, the interview) can be a very different beast when carried out by someone used to administering structured question-naires or someone more attuned to doing ethnographic fieldwork. Even when using the same interview schedule, individual researchers can conduct encounters which are quite different in tone and content, depending on the extent to which they pick up on cues, change the order of questions, and the use they make of prompts. Perhaps we have gone too far in de-mystifying the research process and it is now time to reinstate skills. Of course, researchers working from different epistemological assumptions may have very different perceptions of the role of the researcher. Whereas some researchers content themselves with acting as a cipher or bearing witness for respondents, others accept the responsibility of providing an overview.

I'd argue that multidisciplinary teams reflect wider disciplinary disputes and also are dependent for their very existence on the funding climate. This determines to a con-siderable degree the research questions we can ask and the preferred ways of tackling these. However, one of the difficulties is that what constitutes one discipline's source of pride can so readily slip into a denigration of the methodological approaches of other disciplines. Some combinations are likely to be more problematic than others, depending on whether the underlying assumptions and focus can be conceived as being adversarial or co-operative. Are epidemiology and sociology, for example, as Fenton and Charsley (2000) have argued, 'incommensurate games'? Certainly, as they point out, sociology traditionally interrogates the categories deployed by epidemio-logical and quantitative methods. Fenton and Charsley cite the variable of ethnicity as a prime example of such interrogation. Another comes from the field of HIV/AIDS, where sociological studies shifted the focus from risk groups to that of risk behav-iours. Whether this is viewed as an obstacle or as a resource depends in large part on the willingness of research teams to engage in what can be challenging debates.

CONCLUSION

Advocates of mixed methods approaches frequently assert that this results in a better understanding of the phenomenon under study – but better for whom? For the funders, the researchers, the participants, or the audience of policy-makers, clinicians or one's own disciplinary peer group?

It is easy to highlight the differences between approaches and downplay the commonalities. For instance, a qualitative research project will usually have drawn on the quantitative research literature in formulating a research question, summarizing the state of play and demonstrating what the proposed study will add (see, for example, the discussion about supervisory advice in Chapter 2). This could serve either to dissipate or fuel tensions, of course, depending on how this is presented to quantitative collaborators. However, I do wonder, given the coverage of databases such as Medline (Barbour and Barbour, 2003), whether quantitative researchers are equally likely to have identified or familiarized themselves with a relevant body of qualitative work.

Perhaps because of the constraints of tight timetables, or even as a result of irreconcilable differences between team members espousing different approaches, the end-product of many mixed methods studies involves separate publication of quantitative and qualitative findings. This separation is often further compounded by publication in a range of journals that allows respective contributors to gain the necessary academic 'brownie points' at the possible expense of the reader, who is unlikely to access the papers in specialist journals.

Moran-Ellis et al. (2006: 56) conclude:

> As the warrant for methodological pluralism has become more widely accepted, the recognition of the value of using different or mixed methods needs to be accompanied by a recognition of the pragmatic and epistemological implications of how these methods are to be brought into relationship with each other in a particular study.

Despite injunctions to use mixed methods approaches – and their current popularity with funding bodies – it is still possible to make a strong case for stand-alone qualitative studies. This is not a decision, however, that should be taken lightly and paying even passing attention to the potential of mixing methods may result in better thought-through rationales for selecting specific methods. It is easy, with the heady talk of the increased potential of mixed methods studies, to lose sight of the equally important strengths of qualitative methods, but these need to be highlighted and built into our research designs and proposals, rather than being implicitly referenced. This means being transparent and 'up-front' about how we are going to sample and develop coding frames and interrogate our data – topics which are discussed in detail elsewhere in this book. Although commentating in the context of mixed methods studies, the following comment from Moran-Ellis et al. (2006: 56) is no less relevant for 'stand-alone' qualitative studies: '…it is in the *practices* of social research that the potential of epistemological claims are created: in the practicalities and the pragmatics of generating, analyzing and interpreting data.' (my emphasis)

HINTS ON USING MIXED METHODS

In planning and conducting mixed methods studies it is important to pay attention to the following:

- Think about the rationale for mixing methods. Why does this offer added value?
- Capitalize on how methods can complement each other and spell out the advantages. These are not self-evident or automatic.
- Give thought to developing imaginative and resourceful sampling and analysis strategies that draw on the strengths of the various methods employed.
- Consider, in particular, how you propose to integrate your analyses, paying attention, as always, to maximizing the comparative potential.
- Do engage in debate within the team and use the multidisciplinary make-up and differences of opinion as a resource.

FURTHER READING

Barbour, R.S. (1998) 'Mixing qualitative methods: Quality assurance or qualitative quagmire?', *Qualitative Health Research*, 8: 352–361.

Barbour, R.S. (1999) 'The case for combining qualitative and quantitative approaches in health services research', *Journal of Health Services Research and Policy*, pp. 39–43.

Brannen, J. (2004) 'Working qualitatively and quantitatively', in C. Seale, G. Gobo, J.F. Gubrium and D. Silverman (eds) *Qualitative Research Practice*, London: Sage, pp. 312–326.

Kelle, U. (2001) 'Social explanations between micro and macro and the integration of qualitative and quantitative methods' [43 paragraphs], *Forum Qualitative Sozialforschung/Forum Qualitative Social Research* [online journal]. 2(1), Available at: http://www.qualitative-research.net/fqs-eng.htm [Date of access, 11/01/2006].

Moran-Ellis, J., Alexander, V.D., Cronin, A., Dickinson, M., Fielding, J., Sleney, J. and Thomas, H. (2006) 'Triangulation and integration: Processes, claims and implications', *Qualitative Research*, 6(1): 45–59.

EXERCISE

Re-work your research design produced in the exercise at the end of Chapter 2 to that of a mixed methods approach (if it is not already). Give particular thought to the following:

- Justifying the rationale for using mixed methods.
- The sequencing and timetabling of the different methods.
- How you propose to approach analysis.
- What the challenges are likely to be.

8
ACTION RESEARCH

AIMS

- This chapter equips the reader with an overview of the distinctive features of action research through locating current debates in relation to its origins.
- It provides a template of different models of action research, alerting the researcher to the areas of potential overlap/problems and helps her/him to anticipate and perhaps avoid difficulties.
- It gives advice on planning action research projects, paying close attention to the 'cycle' or 'spiral' involved.
- It concludes, however, by encouraging the action researcher to learn from other types of research and to explore helpful parallels rather than focusing on those features of action research that may make it distinctive.

INTRODUCTION

With increasing numbers of practitioners becoming involved in qualitative research, there is considerable potential for these methods to be employed in relation to action research, where the intention is to engage with research respondents in a collaborative project to facilitate and bring about changes which have been agreed upon by both parties. This type of research is particularly demanding, especially as it requires practitioners to step back from their occupational roles and take a critical look at their own taken-for-granted assumptions. Such research takes place against a constantly evolving backdrop, with many factors impinging on the research process, and outcomes being largely outside the researcher's control. Such work, moreover, is frequently highly political in nature, which gives rise to a further set of challenges. Again, flexibility is the key to carrying out action research and it is characterized by the use of a very wide range of methods, often combining quantitative and qualitative approaches. Action research tends to draw on two contrasting models: that of community development (associated with the anthropological tradition but more overtly political in focus) and that of professional research and development. The former tends to favour a 'bottom-up' approach, while the latter more frequently is embedded in an organizational 'top-down' environment. Depending on the precise occupational or practice setting, the use of these two models can become conflated and this can result in further tensions. Examples are provided of action research projects in a variety of fields and settings, and the discussion is linked to issues debated in Chapters 1 and 7 in particular.

ORIGINS OF ACTION RESEARCH

The social psychologist Kurt Lewin is generally credited as having been the person to coin the term 'action research' in 1964 (Hart and Bond, 1995). However, as Hart and Bond observe, Lewin is likely to have distilled, developed and even popularized an approach that was already emerging and gaining ground in a variety of applied research fields.

Hart and Bond (1995) explain that action research developed out of several complementary, but relatively independent strands. One of these was organizational research, particularly as practised, from the 1940s onwards, by researchers at the Tavistock Institute in London, who based their work on psychoanalysis and social psychology. Employing a consultancy model, and not using the term 'action research' until some twenty years later, their work, from the outset, nevertheless had many of the features we have come to associate with this approach:

> The Tavistock's work included a problem-centred approach, a commitment to establishing relationships with clients over time, a focus on client needs and an emphasis on research as a social process. ... [This approach] was designed to enable an organization to work through conflict by a therapeutic process underpinned by action research. (Hart and Bond, 1995: 24)

Meanwhile educational research had witnessed similar developments, both in the UK and USA, with action research coming to be seen as a means of encouraging self-reflection, with collective involvement of practitioners seeking to understand and improve their practice (Kemmis and McTaggert, 1988). More recently a more radical form of organizational research has developed which involves Participatory Action Research (PAR). Whyte (1991: 20) describes this as:

> ... *applied* research, but [which] ... also contrasts sharply with the most common type of applied research, in which the researchers serve as professional experts [as did the Tavistock researchers], designing the project, gathering the data, interpreting the findings, and recommending action to the client organization. ... [T]his is an elitist model of research relationships. In PAR, some of the members of the organization we study are actively engaged in the quest for information and ideas to guide their future actions.

A parallel response was sparked in the late 1960s when the 'rediscovery of poverty' led academics working within the social policy field to engage with community development projects in order to challenge explanations of poverty that relied on an individual pathology model (Hart and Bond, 1995). This involved working in an overtly political manner and it is perhaps not surprising that these projects tended to fizzle out – particularly when one reflects on the somewhat tenuous position of statutory workers who formed part of such initiatives. More recent community development initiatives have involved researchers from a number of disciplines, including anthropology, and have drawn explicitly on the work of the Brazilian educationalist Freire (1972) and his 'dialogical research methods'. This approach is described as a method involving extensive preliminary fieldwork, with emergent hypotheses being explored through group discussions in order to identify barriers to change. 'The essential role of the investigators in dialogical research is to facilitate the production of knowledge by and for the subjects' (Padilla, 1993: 158).

Organizational and educational researchers continue to be enthusiastic exponents of action research, as demonstrated by the number of published papers produced by members of these disciplines, both in mainstream academic journals and in specialized journals, such as *Action Research*. More recently, action research has been embraced by nurse researchers who have recognized its potential to develop professional practice, by bridging the gap between theory and practice and by offering an alternative to hierarchical and exploitative ways of working with people (Hart and Bond, 1995: 33). Educationalists and nurse researchers, in particular, have been keen to endorse what has been termed 'new paradigm' research, in which 'the distinction between researcher and researched disappears and all who participate are both co-researchers and co-subjects. Co-operative enquiry is, therefore, also a form of education, personal development, and social action' (Reason, 1988: 1).

Whatever its precise provenance, action research, in its many applications and guises, can certainly be seen as having been born of disenchantment and a desire for change. This disenchantment related to large-scale quantitative research – and even, in some quarters, qualitative approaches (see Meyer, 1993a for discussion of this point) – which was viewed as undemocratic, exclusive and exploitative of participants. Carr and Kemmis (1986), for example, criticize interpretive research for its failure to address problems of social conflict and social change. A parallel strand of dissatisfaction has related to the perceived lack of relevance of academic research for practitioners (Greenwood, 1994).

DEFINITIONS AND FEATURES OF ACTION RESEARCH

Despite the well-documented disenchantment of some professionals with traditional research (however they choose to define this) there is, nevertheless, a long tradition of the 'reflective practitioner' in the fields of education, social work and nursing. Some commentators would include at least some variants of reflective practice in their definition of action research (viewing this as first-stage involvement (Heron, cited by Ladkin, 2004). Carr and Kemmis (1986: 162), for example, explain: 'Action research is simply a form of self-reflective enquiry undertaken by participants in social situations in order to improve the rationality and justice of their own practices, and the situations in which those practices are carried out.' Others, however, argue that reflective practice is distinct from action research, since it does not incorporate the hallmark of action research, which involves 'a deliberate and planned intent to solve a particular problem (or set of problems)' (McMahon, 1999: 167). McMahon continues:

> By its nature, action research involves *strategic action*. Such strategic action is not integral to the reflective practitioner model of learning and teaching (though, of course, it may result). That the reflective practitioner model involves going through part of the action research spiral … does not make it action research. (McMahon, 1999: 167)

Although most accounts of reflective practice draw implicitly on theoretical models and research methods, there is a growing trend for practitioner-researchers to utilize qualitative research methods in critically examining their own practice. An example is provided by Suoninen and Jokinen (2005), who use conversation analysis techniques to critically examine their own professional practice in social work interviews, leading them to theorize about the strategies of persuasion that are involved. A recently launched journal, *Communication and Medicine,* provides an academic forum for presenting findings from studies into medical consultations, with researchers generally employing approaches to analysis informed by conversation analysis. This sort of activity seems to place such 'self-researching practitioners', at the very least, at the intersection between reflective practice and action research, since such practitioners have the potential to engage others, should they choose to use such methods in their teaching and supervision within their teams and organizations. Indeed, such involvement would constitute a second-person rather than first-person approach, in terms of Heron's typology (cited by Ladkin, 2004).

Although there have been, and continue to be, many attempts at defining action research, most versions include the aspects covered in the following definition, provided by Reason and Bradbury (2001: 1): 'Action research is a participatory democratic process concerned with developing practical knowing in the pursuit of worthwhile human purposes, grounded in a participatory worldview.' Reason and Bradbury's definition reflects both action research's strength and its weakness, as consensus as to what constitutes a 'worthwhile' purpose is likely to be elusive at best, and differing value positions can be divisive, at worst. As McTaggert et al. (1997) observe, the drive to improve people's circumstances via active engagement in generating knowledge, which characterizes the action research enterprise, is inextricably interrelated to *moral* considerations. This is an important factor in terms of how action research is conducted, experienced, received and evaluated, although the moral dimension is frequently implicit rather than being explicitly stated.

Waterman et al. (2001) summarize the key aspects of the action research endeavour as involving the following:

- It seeks to explain social situations while implementing change.
- It is problem-focused, context-specific and future-oriented.
- The whole group is actively involved in the change process.
- It aims to be educative and empowering.
- It is an approach in which problem identification, planning, action and evaluation are interlinked.

This last bullet point refers, of course, to the notion of the action research cycle, first introduced by Lewin and still a central feature in the design of most action research projects. Although sometimes accorded different labels, the components of this cycle are generally described as involving something similar to Figure 8.1, moving through the stages of identification of problem, planning of intervention, implementation and evaluation of change. The essence of this 'cycle' involves an iterative process, which has no natural end-point – rather the capacity to start the cycle again – and, it is for this reason that Carr and Kemmis (1986: 162) have described the action research process as, perhaps more accurately, involving a 'spiral of cycles'. Thus, the last arrow in the figure leads back to identification of the problem.

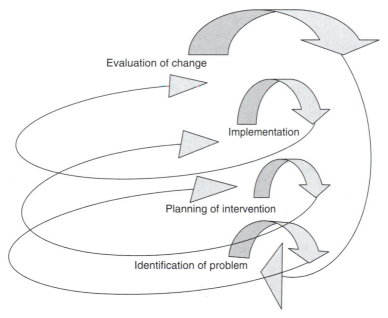

Evaluation of change

Implementation

Planning of intervention

Identification of problem

FIGURE 8.1   THE SPIRAL OF ACTION RESEARCH

The action research literature abounds with typologies, which can be confusing. The one that I have found most useful is that provided by Hart and Bond (1995: 40–44). They distinguish between four main orientations to action research – experimental, organizational, professionalizing and empowering – placed along a continuum which reflects the model of society implied in these various approaches (i.e. a consensus model relying on rational social management or a conflict model emphasizing structural, or even political, change, with gradations in between these two extremes). As Hart and Bond are at pains to point out, this should not be conceived as a rigid set of rules and there are many projects which span more than one of these descriptions. Indeed, some projects may involve different approaches to action research at different stages (Hart and Bond, 1995: 46). I have adapted and simplified Hart and Bond's diagram, and have also indicated (with arrows) where such 'grey areas' – or overlaps – are most likely to feature (see Figure 8.2).

Consensus Model ←			→ *Conflict Model*
Key aspects **Experimental**	**Organizational**	**Professionalizing**	**Empowering**
Change envisaged	Re-education/ change towards consensus	Enhancing management ↔control/overcoming resistance to change	Development of reflective advocacy	Empowering of oppressed ↔Shifts in power Consciousness-raising
Research question	Researcher or funder-determined Disciplinary focus	Defined by sponsors/ managers/clients	Emerges from ↔professional practice	Co-produced ↔Negotiated Acknowledges multiple agendas
Role of researcher	Outside expert	↔Consultant	Practitioner-researcher	↔Co-researchers
Recruitment/ involvement	Fixed Determined by research methods/ measurements	Selected work groups/teams or mixed groups of managers and workers	↔Shifting membership of professional group Negotiated boundaries	↔Negotiated/fluid membership
Process	Scientific identification of causal factors Research-dominated	Top-down action and research	Problem-led	↔Bottom-up Fluid and pluralistic

FIGURE 8.2   VARIANTS OF ACTION RESEARCH (ADAPTED FROM HART AND BOND, 1995: 40–44)

One consequence of over-reliance on templates and typologies is that researchers often do not pay adequate attention to the occupational and organizational setting in which the work is being carried out. This overlooked dimension shapes action research in important respects. As Greenwood (1994) has pointed out, for example, teachers enjoy considerably more autonomy in the classroom than do nurses on the ward. Perhaps this is one reason for the proliferation of small-scale studies in nursing noted by Meyer and Batehup (1997).

The funding climate also plays a significant role in determining the scope of action research. As Meyer and Batehup (1997) observe, funding bodies may not favour action research and this may lead researchers to focus on the development potential of Research & Development as an interim step in pursuing their interests, since it has historically been easier to secure funding for such activities. However, this can have the consequence of heightening the emphasis on action at the expense of theory that is bemoaned by many commentators on action research (including Greenwood, 1994).

Good intentions on the part of the action researcher may not be enough to withstand the powerful influence of professional and organizational imperatives in the field. Action research, as we are constantly reminded, takes place in the 'real' world, but this does not guarantee that researchers can pursue their aims unimpeded by policy and political considerations. For example, in the course of carrying out action research, empowerment may become incidental to the facilitation of change, as noted by Waterman et al. (2001) in their review of action research in the UK. This highlights the potential for action research projects to veer towards the organizational end of the continuum (represented in Figure 8.2), which privileges the achievement of managerial goals and which views resistance to change as a problem to be overcome, rather than working with participants to develop shared goals. This also underlines the potential for action research to be co-opted by professional interests and concerns, and thereby to formulate research questions and tailor research according to the professional's or manager's, rather than the activist's or academic's, gaze. As Hart and Bond and many other commentators have pointed out, the various stakeholders involved in any one action research project are likely to have very different and possibly conflicting agendas.

ACTION RESEARCH DESIGN AND METHODS

Due possibly to its focus on initiating change – putting 'action' before 'research' – action research, particularly participatory action research, has been described as being rather 'short on methodology' (Reason, 1994). Since it is difficult, and probably misguided, to attempt to produce a tight schedule in the face of the constantly evolving backdrop that is action research, with all its attendant uncertainties and surprises, some action researchers have apparently espoused the notion that 'anything goes' (Reason, 1994). However, as with all research endeavours, it is useful to consider at the outset the methods or combination of methods that might be used to advantage in generating the sort of knowledge required. Thus, it may be helpful to include some quantitative data collection methods alongside those which illuminate the processes involved, particularly if one is keen to persuade managers and policy-makers of the impact, utility and even cost-effectiveness of the changes being studied (Lilford et al., 2003).

Action research is frequently local and small-scale, thus lending itself to qualitative approaches, which excel at capturing process and illuminating context (as was argued in Chapter 1). Harding and Gantley (1998: 79) contend that qualitative research can offer 'an understanding both of social processes and how they may be modified in the pursuit of desired ends'. This suggests not only that qualitative methods are likely to be useful in allowing the researcher or research team to generate relevant data and knowledge, but that they can also provide an avenue for initiating and implementing change.

Group methods, in particular, have a ready appeal for action research, which generally has a collective focus, leading some commentators to advocate their use on account of their transformational potential (Chiu, 2003). It is for similar reasons that focus groups have proved so popular in developing guidelines for professional practice (Barbour, 2007). For example, Fardy and Jeffs (1994) employed several methods, including focus groups, to develop a consensus guideline for the management of the menopause in general practice. This usage may not be that far removed from action research, at least in terms of *how* such professional peer group research teams go about engaging with people. Hart and Bond (1995: 3) highlight the convenient fit between the action research cycle and professional practice, arguing:

> … the combination of enquiry, intervention and evaluation which powers the action research cycle mirrors the iterative processes employed by professional staff in assessing the needs of vulnerable people, responding to them and reviewing progress. Thus many practitioners will already be familiar with an action research approach, even though they might not explicitly label what they do as such.

Focus groups can be a valuable tool in charting organizational change, due to their capacity to provide a window on collective identity (Callaghan, 2005; Munday, 2006) and to elicit commentaries on process as it unfolds (Barbour, 1999a).

Ethnographic methods, particularly observational fieldwork, are also well suited to action research as they afford the opportunity for the researcher as 'outsider' to familiarize her/himself with a new environment and for the researcher as 'insider' to render the familiar strange through encouraging practitioners, for example, to step back from their everyday engagement and look at their practice through a different lens. Meyer and Batehup (1997) argue that action research can address the unintentional as well as the intentional consequences of change interventions. However, critical ethnography can also do this, whether or not it is located within an action research framework.

Qualitative research, in common with professional practice, as described by Hart and Bond (1995), relies on an iterative process and is thus much more likely than are other approaches to facilitate an understanding of the complex and constantly evolving phenomenon that is action research. Allowing for flexibility in the research design can facilitate the development of appropriate methods (by modifying existing methods or by using approaches in novel combinations) to engage with the various stages of the action research cycle. Thus, observational fieldwork might provide a useful introduction to the topic area, setting and people involved, while focus group discussions, delphi groups or expert panels (depending on the focus of the research), might afford a more focused way of approaching key tasks identified in the course of the research, and one-to-one interviews might be useful in exploring individual perspectives on sensitive issues or those giving rise to conflict (although many action research approaches would see the harnessing and addressing of conflict as a key area for intervention rather than simply as data to be recorded).

Action research is inherently flexible and many researchers working within a medical environment have appropriated the tools of rapid appraisal popular in this setting and have used these as part of an action research strategy (Ong, 1993). Ong argues that rapid appraisal can be used to engage users in the development of health care policy and practice (Ong, 1996). Action research borrows from a wide range of qualitative (and quantitative) approaches to carrying out research. In so doing, however, each occupational group is likely to rework the methods to reflect its own preoccupations, style and abilities, and the impact of cultural clashes – some fortuitous, others more problematic – has led to a proliferation of approaches to action research. The demands of specific projects may lead us to 'inhabit each others' castles' in borrowing or adapting methods developed in another setting or undertaking research in multidisciplinary teams (Somekh, 1994).

Perhaps because of the 'outward-' rather than 'inward-looking' focus of action research, the genre has not produced a great deal in the way of methodological papers and the details provided in reports may be fairly scanty. In their review of action research in the UK context, Waterman et al. (2001) observe that most used more than one method and that seven out of ten utilized qualitative methods. However, many of the action research reports reviewed in this exercise provided only very brief details of the methods used and methodological approach followed. One might argue, of course, that this does not matter, since action research should be judged by its achievements and not by its methodological sophistication (Hilsen, 2006). However, I would argue that the two concerns are not necessarily mutually exclusive and that a greater awareness of methodological issues and traditions can help researchers to make sense of the challenges and dilemmas they encounter in the field. Methodological engagement can also ultimately strengthen the conclusions and recommendations of action research projects.

Notwithstanding the many texts on action research, and some attempts to portray it as a distinctive methodology, it is probably more useful to view it, as do Reason and McArdle (2003), as an *orientation* towards research. What the preceding discussion has highlighted is the interrelatedness of personal, professional and political values, ethics, and convictions in the making of research design choices in the action research arena. Research practice can be enhanced by a greater understanding of how these decisions come to be made and their consequences both for the research process and outcome of action research endeavours.

PROCESS AND CHALLENGES

Many research projects rely on a design involving a number of interdependent stages and this can constitute quite a timetabling challenge – particularly when the initiation of one stage depends on the successful completion of the one before. Add to this, in the action research context, the possibility that different stakeholders or parts of an organization (including the members who make up the research team) may be ready to move to the next stage at different times and that some may never progress beyond a particular stage and the picture becomes even more complicated. The notion of cycles, although encompassing flexibility and movement, is nevertheless 'inherently messy' (Ladkin, 2004).

Some commentators have highlighted the emphasis on addressing the resistance to change in those variants of action research that tend towards an organizational model based on a belief in rational management, but this issue is a perennial one for action researchers whatever their orientation. All action research projects, by definition, involve the potential for change and, in most cases, some of the players involved are likely to fear or resist change (regardless of what that change involves). When carrying out observational fieldwork in an organizational or professional setting, the spectre of the 'time and motion man' is always in the background, as a focus on practice means that this may ultimately be found wanting. The desire to improve practice carries with it the potential to uncover bad practice. Although some action researchers, such as Meg Bond, who carried out an audit of medication procedures in the home for older people that she managed, may include themselves in this critical gaze and share responsibility for any shortcomings uncovered, there is no guarantee that other members of staff will not feel threatened.

Action research projects can provide insights into the perspectives and experiences of a range of stakeholders, as did the work of Bridges et al. (2003), who evaluated the introduction of a new co-ordinator's role and the organizational issues raised.

EVALUATION OF A NEW INTERPROFESSIONAL CARE CO-ORDINATOR ROLE AND ORGANIZATIONAL ISSUES

This project sought to evaluate the impact of the introduction of a new role of Interprofessional Care Co-ordinator (IPCC). This role (taken on by four new appointees, all of whom had a background in administration rather than clinical practice) required IPCCs to act as the central point for communication and co-ordination of the various professionals involved in the care and discharge of elderly patients in a specific context. The new initiative was designed to address the situation where elderly patients without a specific diagnosis do not fulfil criteria for admission to a specialized service and who may end up being cared for by the General and Emergency Service, due to a shortage of beds in the Care of the Elderly Unit. The remit of these post-holders was to ensure that elderly patients' acute stay was 'no longer than was clinically necessary'. (A pilot project had already been carried out and had involved interviews with four managers, six charge nurses, and three care co-ordinators. In the course of this exploratory phase, researchers had also shadowed two of the co-ordinators and had generated observational data through this activity (Reeves et al., 1999).

The researchers chose a mixed methods approach, which covered:

- 37 interviews with IPCCs, managers and other team members
- 16 focus groups with the same groups of staff
- structured observational fieldwork (involving 24 half-days)
- general observational fieldwork over a two-year period
- documentary analysis of job descriptions and policy documents
- Profile of 814 patients admitted over a 12-month period.

The findings of the project were as follows:

The role was highly valued within the service, but some uncertainties remained. Managers valued the new roles because they were shown to reduce the length of hospital stay and team members saw the incumbents of the new posts as providing useful information and freeing up their own time by taking over some of the administrative burden.

There was, however, a mismatch between the job description and the daily work covered. IPCCs became involved in substituting the core professional activities of other team members, giving rise to some ambiguity, particularly with regard to nursing duties.

The new role did not fit with the established hierarchy of the hospital, since it ranged from providing support work to leadership. Managers accorded the IPCCs informal power and encouraged development of leadership roles because this was expedient and was seen to be an efficient use of resources.

There was a lack of clarity with respect to accountability – especially with regard to relationships between IPCCs and nurses. There was a lack of supervisory arrangements and procedures for IPCCs and no agreed training pathway.

These issues were raised with the Trust, which responded by reviewing existing arrangements and job descriptions, and trying to achieve greater clarity in terms of matching competencies to practice.

The research project was ambitious in terms of coverage and clearly required considerable funding. However, the Trust had already committed resources to this initiative, so researchers in this situation can find themselves in a favourable position. However, this begs the question as to what the response would have been had the research established that the idea behind the new posts was fundamentally flawed and needed to be abandoned rather than suggesting a rethinking of some of the details.

As the experience of Meg Bond (Hart and Bond, 1995: 163–182) demonstrated, a project can simultaneously be perceived as 'top-down' by those in the research setting (in her own case the staff of a home for older people, for which Bond was the manager) and 'bottom-up' by the wider organization, which dismissed the work being carried out and did not take the opportunity of engaging with the action research team in a highly relevant consultation exercise being run at the same time as the action research was being carried out.

Although action researchers can find themselves in an uncomfortable position as the 'bearer of bad tidings' to management and 'coal face' workers alike, it is also sometimes useful to examine the motivations of 'would-be' action researchers. Involvement in research may, for example, contribute towards enhanced promotion prospects. Colleagues and co-workers are likely to be well aware of such possibilities and this, in turn, may affect their willingness to participate in action research initiatives.

Research that is carried out at the intersection of organizational and professional agendas is particularly likely to give rise to such challenges in terms of the varying or fluctuating commitment of key individuals. As Ladkin (2004: 547) points out:

> … real researchers engaged with these approaches, must tussle with a range of 'confounding' factors, including various levels of commitment and engagement from co-inquirers who promised unerring support at the beginning of a project, political machinations within organizations that can turn an agreed-upon project topsy-turvy, the discovery that the focus of an inquiry that has taken up a considerable amount of time is completely wrong, or even internal battles within the researcher her or himself as she or he encounters that implications of new insight. Furthermore, the action researcher is encouraged not to see these as 'inconveniences' to be 'got round', but as key contributing factors within the research frame itself.

For the practitioner-researcher, in particular, there are many challenges. Meyer (1993a) carried out observational fieldwork on a general medical ward in a teaching hospital, which had undertaken to develop user and carer involvement. She reflects on the tensions between being a colleague and being perceived as an 'expert', and describes very well the tensions and competing loyalties involved. Her research demonstrated the yawning gap between affirmed acceptance of the principles of lay involvement and how this was inhibited in the practice setting, where the concept was paid only 'lip service'. Meyer also highlights that, for the practitioner-researcher, leaving the field never involves a clear-cut break, as it might for the more traditional ethnographer.

Not all the challenges reported by action researchers, however, are a direct result of the inherent difficulties of engaging in this type of work. Many reflect the problems encountered by all novice qualitative researchers – and, in particular, of practitioners embarking on research. Many new action researchers do not have the opportunity, as did Meyer (1993a), to hone their skills and to theoretically embed their research during an extended period of study for a PhD. New skills include addressing the formulating of research questions, designing the research, ethical issues, carrying out fieldwork, negotiating access, engaging with the practicalities and politics of observational fieldwork, developing interview skills, carrying out data analysis, feeding back findings, writing up and publishing. This textbook, therefore, aims to provide guidance for action researchers through addressing these issues as they arise in relation to specific research methods, settings, and communities of interest. Although the *constellation* of challenges raised by action research may be unique, most are shared by other researchers not explicitly engaged in action research.

It is not only action researchers who agonize over how their findings are interpreted and used by policy-makers and practitioners. Nor does one have to be working explicitly on an action research project for one's research questions to have been framed in relation to deep-seated discomfort relating to perceived inequalities or injustices. Other researchers also seek to disseminate their findings, publishing in professional as well as academic journals, and may contribute to professional training programmes as an adjunct to their research rather than as part of the original research design. It would, however, be unusual for them to actively engage in evaluating the impact of such programmes and their input to them, as would be indicated by an action research approach. Such research, nevertheless, could be undertaken by others, since we all contribute incrementally, both to the knowledge base and practice developments. With their talk of cycles of action research and their emphasis on outputs and effecting change, action researchers are, perhaps, particularly hard on themselves.

Most action research projects are funded on a short-term basis and, as Waterman et al. (2001) point out, may underestimate the time required to effect change. A broader appreciation of the many other contributions that action research projects can make to enhancing our understanding of social phenomena and social change may provide a useful counter-balance.

CONCLUSION AND THOUGHTS ON THE CONTRIBUTION OF ACTION RESEARCH

We have already seen that disenchantment with what are perceived as more traditional research approaches has been an important driver for action research.

Comparing action research with standard academic endeavours, several commentators have highlighted that outputs can be simply a change in the situation rather than a more formal report (Ladkin, 2004). Hilsen (2006: 29) argued that '[action] research *is* what research does'. However, others have urged for the use of less harsh criteria in judging the contribution of action research:

> …although action research lends itself well to the discovery of solutions, its success should not be judged solely in terms of the size of change achieved or the immediate implementation of solutions. Instead, success can often be viewed in relation to what has been learnt from the experience of undertaking the work. (Meyer, 2000: 179–180)

Projects that seek to encourage new orientations to the work of professionals may simply kick start a very long-term process of change, and should perhaps be evaluated with regard to their more wide-ranging or longer-term impact rather than by reference to tightly defined, short-term objectives.

SERENDIPITY - UNINTENDED POSITIVE OUTCOMES OF A GROUPWORK ACTION RESEARCH PROJECT

While employed as a researcher in a local authority social service directorate, I became involved (in collaboration with the groupwork director) in an action research project that sought to challenge the automatic response to clients in the form of providing casework, and to promote groupwork as a viable alternative. We were fortunate in having acquired the services as project consultant of an academic with expertise both in groupwork and in relevant research, and we held several study days with area social work teams who had been recruited to the project. Notwithstanding the enthusiasm and commitment of participants, there were many problems to be overcome – not least the pressure of work and statutory commitments.

As part of the research design, we held group discussions with each practice team, where we asked individual social workers to present their caseload and to identify any individuals who might benefit from groupwork. This did identify several potentially fruitful avenues for developing group-based approaches, including work with unemployed (and sometimes violent) fathers on childcare and parenting problems. Although some groupwork sessions were subsequently planned and run (with varying degrees of success), an unanticipated bonus was that social workers realized that, despite exchanging gripes about their work and asking for the odd piece of advice, they had previously had little knowledge of the entirety of each others' caseloads.

As a result of our exercise, which was intended solely for research purposes, they decided to include such presentations as part of their regular team meetings. Another unexpected outcome of the project was the local authority's response to our identification of the individually-focused referral form as an obstacle to routine assessment of clients regarding their suitability for groupwork interventions. As the lead in-house researcher on the project, I was single-handedly charged with this responsibility, which I did to the best of my (non-practitioner and non-administrator) ability, my pleas for input from other sources having fallen on deaf ears. Clearly, this task was not viewed as prestigious or desirable, judging by the reluctance of colleagues and the several committees I approached to dedicate staff time to designing a new form. As far as I know, the social services directorate in question may still be using my form!

Other practical outputs can include development of appropriate materials, such as the breast-screening pack produced by Chiu (2003). Outputs can also be in the form of quantitative research findings, which may be more likely to convince managers, as Lilford et al. (2003) point out. Hampshire et al. (1999) report that, although they were unable to demonstrate a statistically significant difference between the two groups of general practices recruited to their action research project, this nevertheless involved a high level of self-reported change among professionals, with ten of the twenty eight practices having voluntarily undertaken an audit of their child health surveillance. The project also produced a standard for child health surveillance.

Certainly not all action researchers feel compelled to publish their findings in peer-reviewed journals, but where they do, action research is not alone in wrestling with journal formats and tight word limits (as described, for example, by Waterman et al., 2001).

I have argued that many of the challenges viewed as part and parcel of action research may be more helpfully understood as arising as a result of the relative inexperience of novice action researchers, many of whom have no prior involvement in research. Some of the other perceived problems may also arise as a result of the lack of theoretical underpinning for the interventions proposed. While 'grassroots' or co-produced proposals for change in organizational or professional systems sound persuasive and inherently more egalitarian, they can be dangerous – and even unethical – in practice. (Of course, many interventions studied by action researchers are likely to have been initiated by management or organizations in any case, but I am not referring here to opportunistic research that seeks to evaluate the impact of these imposed rather than negotiated changes.) Rather than subscribing to the widely held antipathy to theory that characterizes much action research practice, we should, instead, be arguing for an enhanced role for theory – not so much as an outcome of the research, although this is often a feasible aim, but as a prerequisite. This does not preclude grassroots involvement: rather it serves to restate the challenge, which is to render theoretical models accessible to everyone involved in the research and to work to interrogate these together in formulating potential solutions.

It is difficult and probably misguided to make a virtue out of 'grassroots' involvement and bottom-up approaches without ensuring that the proposed changes and their potential consequences are well understood – at least by the research team. To seek to implement changes without paying due attention to the existing knowledge base locates action research not just at the experimental end of the spectrum so often denounced by action researchers, but positions it as an experiment without evidence, which is also difficult to justify on ethical grounds. Of course, even where interventions are based on a sound rationale, there may be surprises and unintended consequences along the way, but this is not an excuse for neglecting to embed action research within its relevant theoretical context. As with any research project, such considerations can ultimately ensure that the research design takes into account those factors that are likely to impact on change and allow for these to be systematically studied. This does not preclude being responsive to changes as these unfold, but here again action research is not alone in seeking to provide an understanding of social processes against a constantly evolving backdrop.

Through emphasizing what is distinctive about action research, its many proponents may miss out on the opportunity to learn from other types of research, resulting in projects with sub-optimal research designs, inadequately prepared researchers, and research that does not achieve its full potential both in terms of informing the action research literature and, ultimately, improving the lot of those whose interests it purports to champion.

FURTHER READING

Hart, E. and Bond, M. (1995) *Action Research for Health and Social Care: A Guide to Practice,* Buckingham: Open University Press.

Ladkin, D. (2004) 'Action research', in C. Seale, G. Gobo, J.F. Gubrium and D. Silverman (eds) *Qualitative Research Practice*, London: Sage, pp. 536–548.

EXERCISE

Imagine that you are tasked with designing and carrying out an action research project building on findings of two research projects with which I have been personally involved. Both studies have highlighted the differing 'mindsets' and lack of understanding of each others' roles of the different professionals working at the intersection of mental health issues, childcare practice and child protection concerns. In particular, these studies have shown the discrepancies between the thresholds of risk employed by childcare social workers and those who had a psychiatric training (Barbour et al., 2002). Other tensions were evident in relation to the conflicting priorities of those employed in child- and adult-focused services and between those working in the social service and health service context (Stanley et al., 2003).

A more recent study of professional responses to children and young people with psychological and behavioural problems (Barbour et al., 2006) has again focused on problems of inter-agency and inter-professional communication. This study has also identified the demands and expectations of differing work settings, the lack of appreciation of each others' roles and remits; and potentially conflicting professional models and priorities as giving rise to difficulties and barriers to developing effective multidisciplinary responses. It would appear from these studies that these differing 'mindsets' are formed early in the process of professional socialization, that these 'run deep' to the extent that they are taken for granted, and are not readily acknowledged as influencing decision-making, inter-agency and multi-professional work practices.

One action research response might be to develop, implement and evaluate a pilot joint training module. How would you go about this? Can you write a research proposal including a detailed research design?

In drawing up this research plan it will be useful to consider the answers to a range of questions. Waterman et al. (2001: 44–48) offer a set of 20 questions for use in assessing action research projects. As with all such checklists, its usefulness lies not so much in providing a set of criteria that must be fulfilled in each and every piece of work, but in furnishing an *aide-mémoire* (Seale, 1999) for the researcher. This set of questions is also helpful in planning action research and, in particular, in anticipating and perhaps avoiding some of the common pitfalls. I have also drawn extensively on the toolkit provided by Hart and Bond (1995: 186–190), which provides some more detailed guidance as to how to go about addressing some of these questions.

What is the problem as you see it? (Hart and Bond, 1995) What are its causes? What do you feel lies at the heart of the problem? (Hart and Bond, 1995) By what means might you do some fact-finding about the problem? (Hart and Bond, 1995)

This would involve exploring the evidence provided by the two studies and carrying out a further literature search to identify the main areas where differing professional 'mindsets' give rise to problems or lack of communication in these fields of practice. This might lead you to concentrate on specific aspects of training relating to particular tasks (for example making referrals or assessing risk).

What is the purpose of the proposed project? (Hart and Bond, 1995)

Presumably, the purpose of this research would be to reduce the potential conflict between professionals and to generate a better understanding of each others' roles and remits and the constraints within which others work. This also raises the question as to how to measure or otherwise evaluate the extent of change achieved. You would have to decide whether to include all professions in the training initiative or whether to concentrate on those where you can demonstrate that significant problems occur. You would also have to consider whether it is most appropriate to initiate joint training for people entering the professions involved or to include qualified professionals who are undertaking continuing professional development activities. You would also have to think about whether this would be purely a taught course or whether it might also involve placements or shadowing of other professionals. The source of funding would also determine whether your focus would be local or national and perhaps which professional groups to involve.

(Are) the participants and stakeholders clearly described and justified? (Waterman et al., 2001)

Since action research aims to be inclusive and responsive, it is a reasonable expectation that new groups of stakeholders may well be identified in the course of a project, or that the change process is seen to have a greater relevance, as it unfolds, for stakeholders not originally centrally involved. Hart and Bond (1995) advise forming a project group and making alliances with others who share your point of view. You should also consider the merits of including 'representatives' of particular constituencies in your research team and give consideration to the research skills and access potential provided by such individuals. **Do you need specialist skills, such as financial, statistical or research expertise? If so, who can you go to for help? Do you need an outside person? (Hart and Bond, 1995)**

What might the problem look like from different points of view? What is each interest group's perspective? (Hart and Bond, 1995)

Hart and Bond suggest listing the stakeholders in rank order according to the power they hold. In the case of the proposed research these would include the institutions and individuals already charged with the responsibility of providing professional training and in-service training, and would also include professional bodies who accredit and licence practitioners. Any active user groups in the area are also likely to have a view about the proposed development and, depending on the topic areas selected for the joint training initiative, they might also be involved in the provision of training. Hart and Bond also suggest (literally) mapping out the spheres of influence of 'allies', 'opponents' and 'neutrals' in order to identify potential areas of conflict and support.

(Is) consideration given to the local context while implementing change? (Waterman et al., 2001)

This is an important consideration, as there may be a local history – either of good joint working or antipathies between particular professional groups or agencies – about which you need to be aware. You should establish whether there have been any previous joint training initiatives, as participants' recall of these might colour their response to your own project.

(Is) the relationship between researchers and participants adequately considered? (Waterman et al., 2001)

Are you (or other team members) a member of an identifiable professional group yourself? How are you likely to be perceived by participants? Have you thought about how to involve participants in shaping the training initiative by identifying their needs and concerns? **(Are) ethical issues encountered and how (will they be) dealt with? (Waterman et al., 2001)**

(Are) the phases of the project clearly outlined? (Waterman et al., 2001) Is there a clear statement of the aims and objectives of each stage of the research? (Waterman et al., 2001)

While these questions obviously refer to the cycle that forms a crucial aspect of action research design, many other qualitative research projects involve staged approaches, and some application forms (see, for example, the Key Milestones in Table 2.1 on p. 51). 'It is difficult to specify, in advance, specific activities or cycles, because the outcomes of each phase inform the next.' (Waterman et al., 2001: 45). However, I suspect that with action research projects, if these are genuine collaborative ventures, then aims may be modified over time, which, presumably, is what leads Waterman et al. to distinguish here between the research proposal and the final report.

How might you generate evidence of different kinds (quantitative and qualitative)? (Hart and Bond, 1995)

You may decide to concentrate on professionals in training, but if you were to provide a pilot training module for professionals in the context of continuing professional development, you could perhaps study the impact of training on outcome of work carried out after the course had ended. What information is available to you through existing records (for example information about case conferences) and how might you gain access to this? Alternatively, you could carry out follow-up interviews with the professionals who have taken part in the training (and perhaps selected colleagues with whom they work closely).

(Is) the action research relevant to practitioners and/or users? (Waterman et al., 2001)

This should be covered by the data you collect on the impact of your intervention for different stakeholders.

Further questions put by Waterman et al. (2001) relate to evaluating a piece of action research reports. However, they are also useful to consider at the planning stage. These all relate to issues covered elsewhere in this book (in relation to Chapter 2 on research design, Chapters 10 and 11 on analysis; and Chapter 12 on presenting and writing up qualitative research).

Was the length and timetable of the project realistic?

Was the study design flexible and responsive?

Were steps taken to promote the rigour of the findings?

Were data analyses sufficiently rigorous?

Do the researchers link the data that are presented to their own commentary and interpretation?

Is the connection to an existing body of knowledge made clear?

Are the findings transferable?

Have the authors articulated the criteria on which their own work is to be read/judged?

(adapted from Waterman et al., 2001: 44–48)

SECTION 4
ANALYZING AND PRESENTING QUALITATIVE DATA

Throughout this section of the book, the process of qualitative data analysis is presented as one that involves producing 'findings' rather than 'results'. This formulation emphasizes the agency of the researcher and avoids the reification of data (as an independent entity) which is apparent in some approaches. A further aspect of the agency of the researcher in generating data is that this affords an opportunity to begin to address the process of analysis. It has been mentioned earlier that the qualitative research process is iterative rather than linear, and it is argued that analysis – or, at least, analytic thinking – begins as soon as the first interview or focus group discussion has been held. The attentive observer, interviewer or moderator will be alerted to distinctions or qualifications made by individuals in discussing their views or reactions. Indeed, some respondents may well do some of our initial theorizing for us. It is not uncommon for focus group participants, for example, to ask questions or each other, thus assuming the role of co-moderator and, perhaps, teasing out differences in the meanings attached to certain concepts, or assumptions being made. Qualitative researchers do not need to wait before commencing their analysis or until they have amassed all of their data. By employing 'active listening' it is possible to harness the insights of respondents both *in situ* and after the event to gain analytic purchase on the data generated.

The chapters in this section address, respectively, the storing, coding and retrieving of data (Chapter 9); the systematic interrogation of data in order to identify patterns (Chapter 10) and the use of theory in qualitative data analysis (Chapter 11). Chapter 12 explores both challenges and the potential for innovative approaches to presenting qualitative research.

9
ANALYSIS GROUNDWORK – STORING, CODING AND RETRIEVING DATA

AIMS

- This chapter equips the researcher to make decisions about recording, note-taking and transcription, which will, in turn, ensure that many of the common pitfalls are avoided.
- Crucially, problems can be avoided through anticipating analysis and hints are provided with regard to forward planning.
- It outlines the advantages and disadvantages of using computer software packages and allows the reader to make an informed decision as to whether to pursue this option.
- The principles of coding are introduced and the researcher will learn how to assign codes and sub-categories to transcripts in order to aid meaningful data retrieval.
- The reader will also acquire skills in developing and refining a provisional coding frame.

INTRODUCTION

Although qualitative research can seem – from the outside – a glamorous option, many of the tasks involved are mundane. The key to effective qualitative research is being systematic and thinking ahead to the challenges one is likely to encounter in analysis. This chapter deals with 'housekeeping' issues, including note-taking, recording and equipment, taking notes on the sequence of talk (in focus groups), keeping a fieldwork diary, producing 'thumb-nail sketches' of respondents, assigning coding categories (use of memos) and techniques for collecting supplementary information, transcription, and computer analysis. Despite its necessarily somewhat pedestrian focus, the first part of this chapter will pose some fundamental questions, such as 'Is transcription always necessary?' and 'Must a computer package be employed?'

NOTE-TAKING AND MAKING DECISIONS ABOUT TRANSCRIPTION

In ethnographic studies the notes taken constitute the data, but keeping a fieldwork diary is an excellent habit to cultivate, even when methods other than observation are employed. These serve several important functions, some anticipated and other serendipitous. As discussed in Chapter 6, practical measures such as taking notes of focus group seating plans can be very helpful in identifying speakers, and taking notes on the sequence of talk can help distinguish individual speakers when discussions are transcribed. Other contextual details can assume significance at a later stage (notably during analysis) and so it can be invaluable to jot down a few comments about the general tenor of the interview or group discussion, such as information about the setting, or events occurring immediately before or after the specific research encounter. Although some researchers describe their interview studies as being 'ethnographic', I would argue that it is only where such notes have been made (and drawn on as a resource in analysis) that this is a reasonable claim. Of course, it is not always possible to predict which features of rich fieldwork experiences are likely to be relevant, but researchers' recall is surprisingly vivid – as evidenced by my own recall of incidents recorded nearly thirty years ago and presented as examples of ethnographic fieldnotes in Chapter 4. Fieldwork diaries can also help to record the changing focus of our interests, preliminary speculations and 'embryo theorizing', details of the books and papers we have been reading and can, ultimately, assist us in piecing together the whole story of the project.

Like many other issues involved in the qualitative research endeavour, transcription is a topic about which researchers can be 'precious'. Advocates of full verbatim transcripts, for example, sometimes refuse to acknowledge that there can be other ways of recording data to facilitate analysis. While a verbatim transcript is a useful resource that allows the researcher to return to the data at a later stage to carry out further analysis, allowing for such a possibility is not always at the top of our list of priorities. Many research projects are carried out within tight timescales and verbatim transcription may be a luxury. Moreover, I am not convinced that full transcripts are always fully mined in analysis. My own view is that it is perfectly acceptable to rely on indexed recordings and notes, provided that these have been systematically produced through thorough interrogation of the data, noting any contradictions or exceptions. It is the *researcher*, not the method of transcription that ensures rigour in interpreting data.

Transcribing qualitative data, however, is a more subtle art than at first it might appear. Good transcriptions don't just magically appear: like all other aspects of the qualitative research process, they are the product of forethought, careful planning and attention to detail. It is important to talk to the audio-typist employed to carry out transcription to ensure that there is a shared understanding of requirements and that helpful notes are provided to accompany the tape, mini-disc or digital recording. Good audio-typists are worth their weight in gold, especially when it comes to transcribing focus group discussions. It pays to work with the same audio-typist over time and some develop an almost preternatural awareness for asides and *sotto voce* utterances. Notes on the sequence of talk can also help the focus group audio-typist to identify individual speakers, which can, in turn, aid your analysis.

Even though we should know better, many qualitative researchers slip into the assumption that the transcript cannot lie – especially if it is a verbatim one. However, as conversation analysts would point out, the transcript itself is a product:

> …transcription is a transformational process, taking live conversation and changing it into a textual representation of talk. Hence, transcripts are silent in several ways. They are, for instance, silent about body language, such as gestures, facial expressions … and positioning …. (Poland and Pedersen, 1998: 302)

The surprise best-seller by Lynn Truss (2005) apparently touched a dormant nerve among those who have been at the receiving end of misleading punctuation. Her title highlights the world of difference punctuation can make, employing the example of 'Panda: Eats shoots and leaves' (as would characterize a descriptive dictionary definition) and the contrasting narrative extract: 'Panda eats, shoots and leaves'. Although most of the English-speaking world must by now be familiar with this example, this heightened awareness has yet to permeate thoroughly the world of qualitative research and production of transcripts.

Along with punctuation, it is important to pay attention to emphasis and tone, which can significantly alter the meaning of an utterance. While putting together an edited collection on *Developing Focus Group Research* (Barbour and Kitzinger, 1999), Jenny Kitzinger and I held a two-day workshop with contributors. This somewhat self-indulgent exercise culminated in us producing a transcript of focus group researchers talking, in a focus group situation, about using focus groups as a method. When we read this document, however, we received a very immediate and salutary lesson, as we saw our own ponderings and attendant inarticulacies reproduced in black and white. A subsequent editorial meeting found us both insisting that we had, for example, said something ironically, in inverted commas, and bemoaning the potential for misrepresentation. Kitzinger herself (Kitzinger and Barbour, 1999) – and other commentators, including Rapley (2004) – advise researchers to read transcripts that have been produced 'second-hand' by an audio-typist while listening to a recording of the original discussion, noting aspects such as the tone, stresses, facial expressions and body language, all of which may be relevant in conferring and conveying meaning. Digital recording packages have now, of course, made it much easier to simultaneously access transcripts and audio or even video footage.

In order to illustrate the importance of emphasis and tone I have asked workshop attendees to think of the different ways of conveying and interpreting the last comment from Carolyn in the following excerpt. This extract is from a workshop-generated focus group transcript and the topic was fathers' attendance at deliveries:

Mod: OK. I wonder if anyone's had a recent experience of … of a birth
            with either the father present or not present?
Carolyn: Yes, well, I've had a baby recently – two in the last three years.
Mod: Oh really?
Carolyn: So, and my husband was there for both and it wasn't an issue – he was
            gonna be there.

Think about how changing the stress put on particular words could alter the meaning. Carolyn could, for example, be conveying that her husband would brook no disagreement about his attendance, as in '… it wasn't an issue – *he* was gonna be there'. Reading the transcript in its full context (and with the benefit of later comments) shows that, in fact, the speaker was commenting on the lack of choice that *she* had given her husband. Listening to the recording, the speaker's intent is clear at the time of the first comment (which was followed by a rueful laugh, which is included in the full transcript). However, the perceptive moderator (mindful of the limitations of the written word) has taken the opportunity to make this evident. This is the fuller version of the excerpt:

Mod: OK. I wonder if anyone's had a recent experience of … of a birth
            with either the father present or not present?
Carolyn: Yes, well, I've had a baby recently – two in the last three years.
Mod: Oh really?
Carolyn: So, and my husband was there for both and it wasn't an issue – he was
            gonna be there (laughs).
Mod: It wasn't an issue?
Carolyn: Yes, yes. I didn't even ask him whether he wanted to be there or not
            and I don't know whether it was just, sort of, me deciding that was
            how it was going to be …
Gail: I think I put enormous pressure on my ex-husband to be there at the
            birth ….

Although subsequent talk is likely to clarify the speaker's intention, this may not happen – especially in animated focus groups, where interruptions may mean that the topic is not revisited. Real speech is so information-rich that it frequently defies accurate transcription – except perhaps that carried out using conversation analysis symbols. Even then, some additional information – akin to the stage directions that feature in theatre and film scripts – may be necessary in order to convey the full context. This, of course, presents quite a challenge for analysis, particularly if the person doing the analysis was not present at the actual focus group or interview. Traulsen et al. (2004) have suggested an approach that involves interviewing the moderator immediately after a focus group session in order to capture this otherwise elusive contextual detail.

However, this does presuppose that it is possible to determine in advance exactly which aspects of the reported speech will be of relevance during the process of analysis. My own recommendation would be to ask interviewers and moderators to keep a field diary in which they record *in vivo* observations about research encounters, but to ensure, wherever possible, that the original interviewer or moderator attends research team meetings so that s/he can contribute to the analysis as it proceeds and provide what can be pivotal supplementary observations (Barbour, 2007).

MAKING DECISIONS ABOUT ANALYSIS

Whether doing manual or computer analysis, the conceptual journey you have to make is the same. Some of the most common problems encountered by novice qualitative researchers arise simply because they are simultaneously learning how to do qualitative analysis and how to use a specific computer package. It is essential, I would argue, to learn the principles of qualitative data analysis before exploring any of the available computer packages. If you do not do this, then there is a very real danger that your analyses are driven by the properties of the package rather than the other way around. Some packages claim to help with theorizing, but can do so only by alerting the researcher to similarities contained within the data. Importantly, this relies on the coding scheme which the researcher has imposed on the data. No package can generate new codes or ideas. Computer packages do 'not absolve the [researcher] from his or her theorized account' (Coffey et al., 1996). Even when computer packages are employed many researchers use these alongside pencil and paper, as Kelle (1997) concedes.

Although computer packages, like much else in the qualitative research endeavour, inspire their passionate advocates and detractors, it does not greatly matter which package you use. The most commonly used are probably N-Vivo and ATLAS-ti (which I've used for the figures reproduced in this chapter and in Chapter 11). There is, however, little point in learning to use a new package if you are already familiar with another, unless you plan to work with other team members, in which case you might favour one over another, either due to force of preference of team members or perhaps because of the facilities it offers. However, packages evolve all the time and it is therefore important not to dismiss a particular package due to perceived shortcomings without checking this out. Although the references provided at the end of this chapter may be useful in helping you to work out what your requirements are, it is important to remember that most packages will have developed new features since these reviews were written. Indeed, packages evolve, in any case, at a faster rate than the accompanying literature, however recent. Most packages are quick to respond to users' queries and problems in terms of developing 'patches' to address any shortcomings and also have very helpful support provision, via websites, which often include online discussion groups.

The exercises which accompany these chapters on analysis all rely on printed materials and the only equipment necessary to engage in these is a large table – as in the advice provided by the anthropologist Bowen (1967). An invaluable addition to this would be a stock of coloured pens. It may sound silly, but if you have coded something in green all the way through your transcripts, then it is much easier to retrieve these relevant data excerpts. Of course computer packages do this work too, and some also notably rely on colour in order to label sections of text.

Don't forget about the potential for coding notes from your own reading of the relevant literature (see examples provided in the exercise on theorizing in Chapter 11). This can be a useful, and illuminating, source of 'pseudo data', allowing for the constant comparative method to include consideration of parallels and disjunctures between the researcher's own findings and those of other studies. It also facilitates the placing or contextualizing of your own findings within the wider research literature, and hence helps in establishing its transferability). However, this material is important in another respect. Together with a conscientiously-kept fieldwork diary, this can provide a helpful backward glance, which reminds the researcher precisely why s/he was pursuing specific ideas or theoretical frameworks at a particular stage in the research.

The main message to be conveyed through all of this is that computer-assisted analysis is not necessarily any more rigorous than manual analysis. It is the researcher and not the medium of analysis that ensures that analysis is systematic and thorough. Rigour is strengthened and enacted through utilizing an iterative process and the three analysis exercises all engage the reader in moving back and forth between provision and revised coding frames and transcripts or coded extracts in order to interrogate themes and build up explanations.

CODING

This section presents the processes involved in coding, balancing, as Seale suggests, the requirement to provide a preliminary model for understanding the content with the capacity to revise this as the argument is successively built up:

> Coding is, of course, an attempt to fix meaning, constructing a particular vision of the world that excludes other possible viewpoints. … However, coding that fixes meanings too early in the analytic process may stultify creative thought, blocking the analyst's capacity for seeing new things. The early stages of coding are therefore more appropriately called 'indexing', acting as signposts to interesting bits of data, rather than representing some final argument about meaning. (Seale, 1999: 154)

'Grounded theory' (Glaser and Strauss, 1967) is a concept that you are likely to encounter early in the process of engaging with the tasks of qualitative data analysis. Like so much else in the 'received wisdom' of qualitative method approaches, a lot can be lost in the telling. It is important to remember that this idea originated as a riposte from empirical researchers, whose work had been cast by theoreticians as being devoid of theory and thereby academically inferior (Melia, 1997). It means, in essence, that it is possible, even desirable, to derive theoretical propositions and frameworks from the raw data generated in qualitative research encounters. This means that the researcher should be attentive to the concepts and terms employed by respondents and that s/he can draw on their explanations in developing explanations. However, somewhere along the way, this has been translated by many aspirant qualitative researchers into the maxim that you should approach your data without recourse to any preconceived theoretical frameworks. Regardless as to whether this is desirable, in the first place, it is simply not possible, as our approaches to qualitative research and even the questions we ask are inextricably embedded in our own disciplinary and cultural assumptions (see Chapter 1). These form a constant implicit backdrop to all our research endeavours and cannot be put to one side. What is more important, however, is that we recognize what our reference points are and make these explicit in our analysis, even allowing ourselves to interrogate these, as we interrogate the theoretical assumptions of others. Melia (1997) points out that most practising researchers use a modified version of grounded theory and that is what I would advocate you aspire to as well.

Another reason for the popularity of 'grounded theory' is, I suspect, the hope that this absolves the researcher of reading the relevant literature. This is also unrealistic and you are unlikely to secure funding unless you can demonstrate a thorough knowledge of the existing state of knowledge and what exactly your research will add.

All too often qualitative researchers make a virtue out of having developed 'grounded theory' or '*in vivo*' (Kelle, 1997) codes, allegedly derived from participants' words and concepts, but which bear all the hallmarks of having originated in the researcher's *a priori* categorizations. '*In vivo*' codes should require some explanation and are often characterized by colourful phrases, such as the soundbites beloved of tabloid journalists. In one focus group workshop on the topic of the challenges of parenting, one participant recounted how as a child she had spent whole days off on her bike, picking bluebells in the woods, and compared this unfavourably with the restrictions on today's children in the face of fears about traffic dangers and the threat posed by paedophiles. She laughed as she said this and other participants joined in. They acknowledged their tendency to exaggerate the freedoms they had enjoyed and to wax lyrical about these while perhaps overstating the constraints placed on our own children. This comment related also to the tension experienced by parents in allowing their children a reasonable amount of freedom, while ensuring their safety. In the rest of this focus groups discussion the participants adopted the phrase 'picking bluebells' in order to refer to this complex set of contradictory imperatives. All too often, however, the '*in vivo*' codes provided by researchers do not have this ring of authenticity and can be rather pedestrian, suggesting that they are researchers' rather than participants' constructs.

DEVELOPING A PROVISIONAL CODING FRAME

In order to provide an illustration of the incremental and iterative process of refining a coding frame, I have drawn on my analysis for my own PhD (on professional socialization for social work).

Early coding categories (used with regard to both interview transcripts and observational fieldnotes) reflected closely the questions included in interviews (i.e. 'a priori' codes) and included the following:

- Reasons for choosing social work as a career
- What social work is about
- Expectations of the course
- Aims of social work intervention.

As fieldwork progressed, student perspectives shifted and various new themes evolved. These were incorporated into the coding system, together with their corresponding 'negative categories', where appropriate. This reference refers to the central tenet of *analytic induction*, which refers to utilizing the analytic potential of exceptions, or comments that appear to contradict ideas expressed elsewhere. As you analyze your data you should note any such instances and attempt to modify your explanations to take account of these. It is not acceptable to simply sweep these under the carpet. Indeed, these uncomfortable grey areas are what ultimately allows us to refine our theoretical frameworks. (For a detailed account of using analytic induction to analyze focus group data, see Frankland and Bloor, 1999.)

Interview transcripts and fieldnotes were coded by means of symbols (which was more manageable, given that I relied on manual analysis), these being continuously amended as research interests changed and new themes came to my attention. The one disadvantage of this approach has been that it is not possible to reproduce these in a computer-friendly mode, so I have chosen to use a print-out that has been produced using the package ATLAS-ti. This allows the codes and corresponding segments of text to be clearly shown. It is important to stress that the process (although not the form) was exactly the same in both cases. (Figure 9.1)

Computer packages allow the user to store notes about the definition of their codes and to retrieve segments of data that have been assigned different codes, allowing you to gather together all instances of a particular code in order to compare these. When carrying out my analysis in the pre-computer age, I relied on index cards, an example of which is reproduced in Figure 9.2.

I assigned one card for each sub-code, using numbers 1–9 to indicate the page number (for example page 01–99) and giving each student a number. The quote given the label 17(4) occurred on page 17 of the third interview with student number 4. On the reverse of the card I reproduced the relevant quotes.

001 Fieldnotes: : Pages 405 & 406; 8th February, 1979
002 (Class on Situational studies – cont./...)
003
004 Colin: What does it men to say you applied a theory? I mean …I think I use
005 theories implicitly… like … that the past influences the present. Maybe we use
006 small theories rather than big theories …?
007
008 Jim (lecturer): There are all different schools of thought about knowledge in
009 social work. Some people would even say that every mother was a social
010 worker. It's using ideas to understand behaviour.
011
012 Kathleen: I don't know how I'd explain what I did in terms of theories. The girl
013 I worked with …… I know I was trying to stretch her … take her out shopping
014 and things. But I don't know that that's a theory ……?
015
016 Jim: Well … that could be theories about maturation … you know … the
017 latest BASW (British Association of Social Work) document which is
018 concerned with what social workers do and what they're about. It seems to me
019 that they're just things which apply to any area of life. A lot of it's just
020 common-sense. You know., there was a youngster who absconded from a
021 setting where we had psychiatrists, social workers, analysts … you name it …
022 We finally tracked him down and he'd teamed up with a farmer who'd offered
023 him a job. He's still there. We obviously – with all our training – couldn't hold
024 a candle to that farmer … (Students present – Christine; Kathleen; Colin;
025 Maggie and Jenny – all nod and smile approvingly) I'd also say, 'If a theory
026 seems likely to work, use it – wherever it comes from' – when you're in the
027 situation and you have to do something.
028
029 Jenny: I worked with a girl truanting from school. She had a bad background
030 which was causing problems. There were three generations involved. I(draw
031 form lots of different theories. I just use whichever theories are handy – even
032 Freud. I even used Freud, although I don't know if I'd really go along with it
033 … but I used it as a student on placement. I don't know if I'll use that case for
034 my situation study or not.

◈◈ Relating theory to practice~ ◈◈ Sounding out re theory and practice~

◈◈ Social work knowledge

◈◈ Sounding out re theory and practice~

◈◈ Social work knowledge

◈◈ Anec.

◈◈ SW skills inherent

◈◈ Use of amalgam account~

◈◈ students' ideas about causes of client problems
◈◈ Use of amalgam account~

035
036 (The tutor then winds up the class, asking students to think about their essays in
037 some detail for the next class and to bring along anything they have written.)
038
039 (Lunch with Sarah)
040
041 Sarah: are you still going to be coming to classes?
042
043 Observer: I'd be interested in coming to some of the options, but I'm not sure
044 what form they'll be taking. I'll just have to wait and see and sort out my
045 timetabling to see if I can fit in all the ones I'd like to go to.
046
047 Sarah: (Picking up my library books and leafing through them) It's all jargon.
048 That's what I hate about sociology. They all just write thing like this just for
049 their own good and get publications so that they can get a teaching post and get
050 a name for themselves. They don't care about anything else.
051
052 Observer: Yes, well, I suppose academic's life's just as competitive as other
053 areas…
054
055 Sarah: Do you have a note of what options we said we wanted at the end of last
056 year?. I'd just like to know if they're the same as what they're offering us now.
057 Do you have a record of what we asked for?
058
059 Observer: I don't know off-hand, but I should have. I'm not too sure where it'll
060 be, but I could have a look …
061
062 Sarah: It doesn't really matter, but it might be interesting just to see if they've
063 kept their word.
064
065 (Meeting with Jenny in the Library)
066
067 Jenny: I'm going to do some work on my situation study. I'm thinking of doing
068 it on an old woman that I met as a client. She was a fascinating person. She

Research relations

Anti academic perspective

Us and Them~

069 was really intelligent. She was fighting against being treated as old and stupid.
070 They had defined her that way, you see.
071
072 Observer: Who?
073
074 Jenny: Oh, the psychiatrists and doctors and social workers – the hospital social
075 workers. They said because she was fighting against it she was paranoid. They
076 just saw it in clinical terms, you know, the typical medical attitudes. So, you
077 see, she couldn't win either way. They wanted her to go into a home and she
078 didn't want to go. She said she was just going to play along with the social
079 workers and fill in the forms for admission to homes and all that, although she
080 wasn't going to go. Do you think that'd be a good thing to do for my situational
081 study?
082
083 Observer: it seems feasible enough to me. Are you going to relate it to theories
084 of old age at all?
085
086 Jenny: yes, but I'd have to do some reading on it. I don't know anything about
087 it at all.
088
089 (We decide to go for a coffee and are joined by Gavin, David, Colin and
090 Christine, who leaves shortly afterwards.)
091
092 Jenny: (Talking about her last supervisor) She was great … she's dead set
093 against theory. She's very direct with clients and confronting them with things
094 …. They have to face her.
095
096 David (on the same social worker) She always ended up with the most difficult
097 kids and she really seemed to get things done.
098
099 Colin: yes, she's just the sort of person who could go into a house where there's
100 child abuse or something and tell them what to do. She's marvellous. It makes
101 you wonder … I mean … she just seems to have it naturally.
102

Coding annotations:
- Other professionals
- Criticism of social workers
- Client Vs Social work~
- Relating theory to practice~
- qualities of SW desc. as skilled
- Anti theory applied to practice~
- SW skills inherent

FIGURE 9.1   CODED FIELDNOTES ATLAS-TI

Interviews 1st – 4th   **CODE: Composite Role Model**

	0	1	2	3	4	5	6	7	8	9
1st										
2nd		31(5) 101(18)	22(4) 82(15)	13(3) 43(7)			56(10) 106(19)	67(12) 77(14)	88(16)	
3rd	40(7) 140(14)	121(12)		33(6) 153(16)	4(1) 164(15)			17(4)		9(2)
4th		101(11)		163(18)			176(19)			

FIGURE 9.2   EXAMPLE OF AN INDEX CODING CARD

13(3)   …I'd maybe take bits from other people too, if I thought I could handle them.

101(18)   I'll piece together my own way of working, taking a bit from each of them.

The 'composite role model' code was derived from an earlier, broader code of 'role model'. Related sub-codes subsequently developed alongside the 'composite role model' code included 'single role model', 'anti-role model' and 'non-committal role model'. Interestingly, although these are conceptually separate, and potentially contradictory, some students appealed to more than one model at different stages in their training, and on occasion within the course of one interview or observational fieldwork session.

EXERCISE ON DEVELOPING AND REFINING A PROVISIONAL CODING FRAME

This exercise on developing a provisional coding frame is linked to the focus group data you generated in the exercise in Chapter 6. If you have transcribed this discussion, you can use your transcript to identify relevant themes or codes. If not, don't despair, as it's perfectly possible to develop a provisional coding frame without recourse to a verbatim transcript. Indeed, it can be helpful to set this process in motion even while you wait for transcripts to appear.

You should ask the following questions:

- **What are the themes that emerge?** This involves drawing on your own a priori codes – in this case you will probably want to include items such as 'pressure' and 'role of fathers' as starting points. *A priori* codes often reflect the wording of a question in our interview schedules and topic guides and we would certainly be dismayed if the data we generated did not address our central concerns. However, you should also be alert for 'picking bluebells'-type phrases, which may sum up complex and intriguing ideas.

- **How are these themes and codes related to each other? Is one a subcategory of another?** In keeping with the attention paid elsewhere in this book to the disposition of an individual researcher, engaging effectively in the process of qualitative data analysis is partly a matter of finding what works for you. In the course of running workshops I have come to realize that some individuals are natural 'broad brush' coders whereas others veer towards identifying smaller themes and categories. What matters is not the route they take but that they both get to the same place in the end. It is very important not just to produce a huge number of codes. Computer packages may encourage what Coffey et al. (1996) call a 'coding fetish', simply because it is so easy to create codes. The 'broad brush' coder should break these down into their constituent parts, while the meticulous coder should search for wider concepts and themes under which to group her/his codes. The available computer packages allow you to use up to 9 levels under each broad heading which should be more than sufficient (whether you are carrying out a manual or computer-assisted analysis). Many successful research teams have capitalized on these different orientations and skills as they collaboratively develop coding frames. If you are engaging in the accompanying exercises as part of coursework and have the opportunity for small group work, you will, hopefully, be able to see this in action. Although personal dispositions are likely to surface with regard to your involvement in subsequent projects, you may find that you have to develop new approaches as what works for you on one project may not work on another, due, perhaps to the volume or form of the data generated or as a consequence of time constraints.

- **What sorts of distinctions are made by focus group participants?** Hopefully you may have already been attentive to some of these while generating your data as recommended in Chapters 5 and 6.

Here is part of a provisional coding frame that was produced in the course of one focus group workshop. It shows some broad codes and related sub-categories. Note the inclusion of the two *a priori* codes suggested by questions posed by the focus group topic guide:

PRESSURE
    From the woman
    From society

> **RELATIONSHIP**
> **The Couple**
> *Communication*
> **Fathers and Health Care Professionals**
> *Fathers who are Health Care Professionals*
>
> **ROLE OF FATHERS AT DELIVERIES**
> **Advocacy**
> **Bonding with baby**
> **Sharing the experience with his partner**
> **Supporting his partner**

Trying out your provisional coding frame

Take either the coding frame reproduced above or your own provisional coding frame and have a go at coding the excerpts from focus group transcripts presented below. These focus groups also discussed the issue of fathers' attendance at deliveries and employed the same topic guide presented in the Chapter 6 exercise, together with the two claire Bretecher cartoons which are described in the accompanying scenarios. As you do this, do amend the coding frame to take account of any new codes or sub-categories you identify. When I use this exercise in workshops I often photocopy the provisional coding frame onto a large piece of paper (A3) and encourage participants to scribble on this (with their coloured pens) as they make these changes. You may find it helpful to refer to the thumbnail sketch of participants as you revise your coding frame and begin to ask important questions as to the patterning of perspectives and comments. (This aspect of qualitative data analysis is the focus of the exercise presented in Chapter 10.)

Reviewing your provisional coding frame

It would be very surprising – indeed rather worrying – if you were able to code a whole transcript (or set of excerpts, as in the current exercise) using only the codes produced in your provisional coding frame without the need to develop further codes and/or sub-categories. In reviewing the usefulness of your coding frame and deciding how it should be developed, ask the following questions:

- How useful are the codes?
- Can some codes be broken down further?
- Are different coders referring to the same concepts?
- What sort of language is being used?
- What explanations do the participants advance?

You may wish to photocopy the section from the provision coding frame (presented above) and to amend this as new themes and categories occur to you as you attempt to apportion codes to the segments of text reproduced below.

The transcript excerpts

FOCUS GROUP AM PARTICIPANTS (All men)

Rajan (Moderator): **General/family practitioner with three children**
Joshua: General/family practitioner with children
Tom: Nurse researcher with two children
Barry: Health service manager, no children
Jeremy: General/family practitioner with children

Excerpt A1

Barry:	I've just observed it in theatres, but any time I've observed it in theatres it's caesareans and it's a section. Most of the times, they've tended to faint in the theatre …
Rajan:	Mmmhm …
Barry:	You know, what happened is one out of three fainted … (*inaudible*) I think, they were there – some of those that fainted – they were there because they felt they had to be there. They were frightened of (*inaudible*) They were more scared than the wife was.
Rajan:	Mmmm…
Barry:	I'm not sure it's the thing … that they should be compelled to be there, if they don't feel as though they can be there … and this thing actually shows that if they're there under pressure been forced to go – it's the classical thing …
Jeremy:	I think the problem maybe some of us face is it's maybe difficult to be objective on the top end when one's been familiarized through training with deliveries and situations so, the idea of, you know, being surprised and, you know, just actually keeling over …

Excerpt A2

Rajan:	Do you think it matters that men should be present at deliveries?
Joshua:	I have had the personal experience of working in obstetrics for a long period of time and I've had experience of working in a society where men are not admitted in and, in such a way it's free choice to come in, and, in all honesty, I do not think it matters a great deal. Although I do not have any evidence to back it up.

Jeremy: What – in terms of outcome?

Joshua: In terms of outcome either way – through the child or according to the mother, although some say to the father – some feel more content with having him there, with him being present, at the most important part of that child's life. And, then that's why I say, I don't have evidence either way. But I have also seen fathers taking the father's role properly even when they were not there at the birth of the child, so, either way, I've seen both sides, and, in some situations, it's probably of benefit to the wife if he's there – where the man plays a supportive role. In other situations, it tends not to work too well .. and the man is there and doctors come in and out … and examine her and put their hands all over the place… and it can be quite embarrassing and off-putting.

Barry: Yes, that protective reflex … you feel you ought to protect your wife … Your wife is in pain … and you want to do some protecting … but you can't do anything .. you can't help … and the stress builds up. And it might not be such a good idea for certain men to go into that situation, if they're not prepared for it. They shouldn't be forced to go into it.

Rajan: If I hadn't attended my children's deliveries, regardless of my bonding with them, I think I would have been seen as some kind of a traitor…

Jeremy: … who wasn't playing his part.

Joshua: The pressure is put on you, which is there in a developed society …

Barry: Which is interesting …

Joshua: …where it's accepted that you should be there. Now, if you're liable to opt out now. There's a lot of pressure to face if you want to opt out … if you think you cannot cope with seeing the sight of a lot of blood, or something, so some men want to opt out, but there always has to be somebody who sees this as his place somehow … or for somebody else to be there. … Because society recognizes now that there should be some sort of support network … that the woman understands and that can be comforting to her. If you take that across culture, in some cultures no man will want to be there – no men are even allowed at deliveries – in some cultures.

Barry: In some cultures it would be an intrusion on a woman's privacy to be there, in the first place.

Rajan: Jeremy, were you present at any of your deliveries?

Jeremy: Yes, all of them. I think you've rather underestimated the – sort of – power of a couple's closeness – what they've actually planned to do, and, of course, what they've forgotten is that a lot of deliveries are totally normal and there has been – like what you've been talking about the, eh, coming over from America – that everyone should be there and everything was looking much more technical, wasn't it. …

Barry: Mmmm …

Jeremy: … and I think that would have been more frightening, but I think that nowadays, fathers are involved much more early on – they're taken round the delivery units. They're actually expected to be involved in the pregnancy and, I think that, usually, as a couple, they'd decide that they would both be there, actually .. and I think they do have to talk through the scenarios, and I suppose if things do go wrong, eh, and I imagine in those sort of groups they actually do talk about those sort of feelings and I agree …

Barry:　　I think you are right about that, but I think it depends on whether there's communication there and you might find that in certain sectors of society that they don't communicate …

Jeremy:　　Yes …

Excerpt A3

Rajan:　　I mean, what do you think you gain from being at the delivery?　　}

Talking together

Jeremy:　　I think it's very much a bonding experience and …　　　　　　　}

Rajan:　　What did you gain, do you think, from being at the delivery? I mean bonding is easy to say – it's a nice word – but, what gain do you think you had?

Jeremy:　　Ehm, involvement … investment, ehm … a lot of anxiety, pacing the corridors, as well as being in the room, ehm, I think involvement – yes. And I take your point, you can sort of force yourself and become a doctor, who, you can be more objective, but I think I did find that I wasn't being as objective as I thought I would be.

Rajan:　　It removes the mystique of births, for some, doesn't it, I mean?

Jeremy:　　Yes.

Rajan:　　In those old-fashioned films you'd see the father pacing the corridors and the nurse or somebody bring a baby in – it was, kind of, a mystery. Now it's sort of blood and gore and injections and nether ends and haemorrhoids and, it's not, is it, I mean, … are we taking something for granted?

Jeremy:　　Yes, well, it'll be interesting to see what the all female group feel …

Barry:　　But maybe she doesn't want … her husband to see all that …

Commentary on Focus Group AM excerpts

Although these men acknowledge the **PRESSURE** *on fathers to attend deliveries (deriving both from the* **Women** *involved and from* **Society** *more generally) they do question the need for fathers to be there. They raise the issue of the impact of attending in terms both of the potential squeamishness of some men and the possibility for embarrassment on the part of the women. (Rajan later returns to this latter theme in relation to the loss of mystique/mystery surrounding the event.) This might suggest the addition of a new code (and related sub-codes) which addresses* *the* **IMPACT OF ATTENDING DELIVERIES**, *with the two issues* **Squeamishness** *and* **Embarrassment** *included as sub-categories. Another sub-category under this theme might relate to the impact of attending deliveries which are not straightforward (since the men do refer to caesarean sections) or it might simply be labelled* '**Uncertainty**'. *Alternatively, you might decide to organize these into positive or negative impacts or those which affect men and women separately.*

The men allude to **Bonding** *but go on to question both whether this automatically results from attending a delivery and whether it is possible to bond effectively without having attended a delivery. You might decide to break this down into statements that* **Confirm** *its importance and those which* **Question** *the received wisdom.*

Interestingly, all of these men are health care professionals, although one, Barry, has no children and appears rather horrified at the prospect of fathers attending deliveries. They do also allude briefly to the difference between professional and personal involvement (see Jeremy's comment at the end of Excerpt A1). This would be coded under **Fathers as Health Care Professionals** *(and it is likely that further transcripts would suggest development of further sub-categories relating to specific insights that this dual involvement affords and tensions that it engenders).*

The men in this focus group do not use the word 'advocacy', but how would you code the section in Excerpt A2 where Barry talks about what he calls 'that protective reflex' – is he talking about **Support** *or* **Advocacy** *here? I think I would probably code this under Support, as he goes on to say that 'you can't do anything ... you can't help' and then moves on to talking, again, about the impact on the man of attending a delivery.*

FOCUS GROUP BB PARTICIPANTS
(1 man and 4 women)

<u>**Judy (Moderator):**</u> **Researcher with one child**
Martin: Researcher, no children
Gail: Researcher with one child
Ruby: Nurse researcher, ex-midwife, no children
Caroline: General/family practitioner with two children

Excerpt B1

Ruby: I suppose the only problem arises when ... when it's like your friend [mentioned earlier] – you know, and ... and she doesn't want the husband there – or the partner and.. he wants to be there, you know. She might have chosen her best friend or mother or mother-in-law or somebody, erm ...

Gail: I don't know whether she thought he'd be too squeamish to be there, or whether she ... I don't know. I know she thought it would be very ...

Ruby: But there's also the whole research thing about trauma, isn't there? Erm ... somebody mentioned it earlier, I think, about the sort of sexuality thing ...

Gail: Yes.

Excerpt B2

Judy: … Were you suggesting, Caroline, that you might have chosen not to have the father there?

Caroline: In my situation? No, I would. I would have found it astronomically difficult if he wasn't there, because he's a huge … a huge support to me, you know. He's … he's my best friend – my right-hand man, if you know what I mean? So I would have found it almost impossible ….. but it's a process and that's what it is and to get through it, I think I would have found it very difficult without him being there.

Excerpt B3

Martin: I mean … is there not a tendency that you're .. you're lying there having a baby and you're worried about how your husband or partner is getting on?

Gail: Yes.

Martin: Is he … is he going to be … can he cope? I'm not sure whether that's helpful or not.

Caroline: From personal experience I felt that was, like … er .. I kept asking him if he was OK.

Gail: Yes, I did that – are you OK?

Ruby: But I think the, sort of, fainting business, is .. there's, like, more tales about it, isn't there, than it happens?

Gail: Yes, probably.

Ruby: And there's always, like, the head end and the bottom end business, isn't there. And, you know, if the partner can be kept up at the head end.

Excerpt B4

Ruby: The funniest experience I had was when I was delivering somebody with a vet .. the husband was a vet and erm …

Judy: Did he want to help?

Ruby: Yes – well he was, like, nearly sort of … he was getting me out of the way.

(laughter)

Gail: Oh no!

Ruby: You know, and commenting how it was different .. in what ways it was different and everything, you know. 'What are you doing now?' you know.

Commentary on Focus Group BB excerpts

In the first excerpt (B1) Ruby raises the possibility of the couple disagreeing about the father's attendance. You might, therefore, add a coding category ***'Conflict'*** *under the* **RELATION-SHIP/Couple** *category. Ruby then goes on to allude to the potential of a negative impact for* *the father who attends a delivery – in terms of the specific impact on his sexuality. This suggests the need for a further sub-category 'Negative Impact on Man's Sexuality' under the coding category* **IMPACT OF ATTENDING DELIVERIES**.

Both focus groups so far have alluded to the benefits of a father attending a delivery in terms of sharing the experience with his partner. However, Caroline in excerpt B2 relates this also to the couple's relationship and the expectations of the man as the woman's 'best friend'. This excerpt, then, might be coded under both Support and **RELATIONSHIP/Couple**/*new third-order category of 'Closeness'. Actually, Jeremy in excerpt A2 above also talks about a 'couple's closeness', although he doesn't elaborate. This might, however, retrospectively, be coded under this sub-category.*

Although the male health care professionals in Focus Group AM did not go so far as to cast fathers in the role of obstructive participants, some of their comments do acknowledge that the experience may not be 'all that it's cracked up to be'. The participants in Focus Group BB, however, go further. In excerpt B3, Ruby, who is an ex-midwife, talks about how it is possible to manage fathers in this situation in order to ensure that they do not get in the way of the effective performance of professional tasks. Under **RELATIONSHIP/Fathers and Health Care Professionals** *you might wish to add a third-order category of* **'Fathers as a Liability'** *with 'Strategies for Managing Fathers' as a fourth-order coding category. In excerpt B4, Ruby provides another example of dealing with a 'difficult man', although here she refers simply to his desire to take over and does not provide any suggestions as to how to counter such attempts by fathers.*

FOCUS GROUP CW PARTICIPANTS (All women)

Patsy (Moderator): **Researcher, no children**
Claudia: Health care professional with two children
Cath: Practice nurse, ex-midwife with one child
Ellen: Health care professional with three teenage children
Sophie: Researcher, no children
Marion: Health visitor with two teenage children

Excerpt C1

Patsy: The next kind of area we want to explore in a bit more depth is, really, do fathers serve a useful function in the delivery room?

Marion: They're wonderful for mopping your brow and holding your hand... listening to you swearing.
(*laughter*)

Patsy: Do they provide support?

Ellen: Yes.

Cath: Well, yes, it certainly did in my case.

Marion: Yes, because you've got this stranger, haven't you? Er .. this midwife, who's far more interested in what's happening down below and he's thinking of you as a person, I think.

Claudia: I think that point's about if the midwife is a stranger and you go to a hospital environment … that way of doing it. And it's compassion without involvement, really.

Sophie: What if they faint or just can't handle it?

Marion: They get stepped over.

Cath: (*inaudible*) .. but her husband fainted twice even before she went in for delivery, when she had some of the procedure done – is it amniocentesis they do?

Claudia: Yes.

Cath: And he fainted and she said, 'You're not going to be no use' and he said, 'Oh, I'll come, I'll come' and then that was the thing – he just had to go out, so, you know, she eventually ended up expecting him to be there, but he wasn't, because he just couldn't possibly. It's the whole thing about hospitals.

Ellen: There's that smell in hospitals, yeah …

Excerpt C2

Patsy: Do you think that .. erm .. the fathers – do they have to be an advocate in the delivery room? I mean. Do they get you the best pain relief and things like that? Do you think….

Claudia: It depends on the father, I mean …

Cath: And the noise.

Claudia: Absolutely, yeah, I think that's critical.

Marion: But, yeah, I think that .. er … there's only the woman that can tell you what kind of pain relief she wants.

Cath: Lots of it!

(*laughter*)

Marion: Basically, yeah, I just say you go for as much as you possibly can get.

Ellen: Yes, absolutely.

Claudia: It always amazes me this concept that ….

Marion: Yeah, this concept, you know, of biting on a bullet. For goodness sake!

………

Cath: I can remember very clearly when I was a midwife I delivered a baby at home. It was in a sort of basement tenement flat and, er, this father had said where he wanted to actually deliver the baby, which was exceedingly difficult 'cos it was right in the middle of a double bed and I'm not exactly the tallest person to stretch over to deliver this baby and he said, 'Oh, I just told her that she could have this one at home as well'. And so he was obviously very domineering and he wasn't caring whether she had any pain relief or not, so we can look at the other side as well…

Patsy: So … are you saying, then, that the role of the father – that the function of the father is essentially the support?

Cath: The support.

Patsy: And not really as an advocate?

Cath:	No.
Patsy:	That you don't need an advocate?
Cath:	I think on the whole nowadays you don't need an advocate. That woman did need .. er … to be her own advocate, but she wasn't.
Claudia:	In fact, having her husband there disempowered her …
Sophie:	Yes, that's right.
Claudia:	… from being able to advocate.
Cath:	That's right. She had everybody in. She had all the other children in watching as well. Umm, yeah.
Sophie:	Gosh!

Commentary on Focus Group CW excerpts

It may be that the 'security' of an all-woman group gave the participants in this last group licence to put the woman 'centre stage' and to question the capacity of partners to make judgements about pain relief. This discussion suggests that some men may go too far in pursuing their role as advocate and you might want to consider adding two further sub-categories of **'Positive Aspects'** *and* **'Negative Aspects'** *under* **ROLE OF FATHERS AT DELIVERIES/ Advocacy**. *Interestingly, these women distinguish between Support and Advocacy, suggesting that you would be well-advised to retain these as separate categories, even though some discussions may conflate the two concepts.*

Concluding comments

As suggested above, the composition of the focus groups can affect both the content and tenor of discussions. It is no co-incidence that the most disparaging comments about men's capacity to act as advocates arose in an all-female group, nor that the all-male groups gave rise to more intimate talk about 'feelings' than was evident in mixed-gender groups. Another example is provided in one of the few other all-male focus groups that it was possible to convene:

I've got to say I … I… I'm not sure whether being from a health professional background would make that much difference, in the sense that, er, the seeing a birth is – possibly the shock of birth, no blood and guts issues at all – just going through such a prolonged period of time, seeing somebody who … who you love desperately being in such a … such an amount of pain. (Nick, in all-male Focus Group KM)

Interestingly, expressions of diffidence on the part of men were also confined to the all-male groups, suggesting that this is a topic where both men and women are aware of the potential to offend members of the opposite sex. Ruby's comments in the mixed-gender focus group (AM) are interesting, but the issues she raises are confined to the behaviour of the men in question and how this compromised her ability to carry out her role as midwife. Her comments, therefore, do not challenge the legitimacy of men's involvement and authority as partners. *Although Cath (in Focus Group CW) recounts a story where she had difficulty in performing her professional role as a midwife, both Cath and Marion (a health visitor) do question the appropriateness of the father's role as advocate. This, I hope, demonstrates the importance of using information on group composition as a resource in analysis, since this can go some way towards explaining observed differences in emphasis or perceptions. The exercise at the end of* **Chapter 10** *deals with the identification of such patterns (in relation to a condensed dataset produced through interviews).*

Paying attention to the patterning of responses, however, can also suggest further (second-stage) sampling-strategies. It might, for example, be instructive to convene groups where no one is a health care professional, or to run separate groups with midwives. The men in Focus Group AM talk about the possibility that couples occupying different social class positions may have different patterns of communication and even different expectations of each other. It might, therefore, be interesting to convene further focus groups with men and women of varying ages living in deprived localities.

FURTHER READING

On computer packages

In the late 1990s several useful papers were published which helped qualitative researchers to weigh up the relative merits of the various software packages available. Since then, the novelty of qualitative analysis software has worn off a bit and discussion has moved on to more in-depth discussion of the properties of specific packages. Once you are familiar with a particular package, the best source of information and support is undoubtedly the websites and discussion lists that are a feature of most of the packages on the market. Although now somewhat dated, the following papers are, nevertheless, likely to assist you in making an informed choice as to whether to employ computer-assisted analysis and which package is likely to meet your requirements.

Barry, S.A. (1998) 'Choosing qualitative data analysis software: ATLAS/ti and NUD*IST compared', *Sociological Research Online*, 3(3), <http://www.socresonline.org.uk/socresonline/3/3/4.html>

Buston, K. (1997) 'NUD*IST in action: Its use and its usefulness in a study of chronic illness in young people', *Sociological Research Online*, 2(2), <http://www.socresonline.org.uk/socresonline/2/3/6.html>

Coffey, A., Holbrook, B. and Atkinson, P. (1996) 'Qualitative data analysis: Technologies and representations', *Sociological Research Online*, 1(1),<http://www.socresonline.org.uk/socresonline/1/1/4.htm>

Fielding, N. (1996) 'Qualitative data analysis with a computer: Recent developments', *Social Research Update*,1,<http://www.soc.surrey.ac.uk/sru/SRU1.html>

Kelle, U. (1997) 'Theory building in qualitative research and computer programs for the management of textual data', *Sociological Research Online*, 2(2), <http://www.socresonline.org.uk/socresonline/2/2/1.htm>

Stanley, L. and Temple, B. (1995) 'Doing the business: Using qualitative software packages in the analysis of qualitative datasets', in R.G. Burgess (ed.) *Computing and Qualitative Research*, Greenwich, CT: JAI Press.

A more recent reference is:

Kelle, U. (2004) 'Computer-assisted qualitative data analysis', in C. Seale, G. Gobo, J.F. Gubrium and D. Silverman (eds) *Qualitative Research Practice*, London: Sage, pp. 473–489.

On analysis

For detailed advice on using qualitative analysis software see also:

Lewins, A. and Silver, C. (2007) *Using Software in Qualitative Research*, London: Sage.

Barbour, R.S. and members of the Worlds Primary Care Research Network (WoReN) (2000) 'Acquiring qualitative skills for primary care research: Review and reflections on a three-stage workshop. Part 2: Analyzing interview data', *Family Practice*, 17(1): 83–89.

Of further interest

You may also find it useful (in seeking to contextualize the data excerpts presented above and in thinking about developing new coding categories and/or carrying out second-stage sampling) to read a book chapter that draws both on observational work in labour wards and on interviews with first-time parents:

Barbour, R.S. (1990) 'Fathers: The emergence of a new consumer group', in J. Garcia, R. Kilpatrick and M. Richards (eds) *The Politics of Maternity Care*, Oxford: Clarendon Press, pp. 202–216.

10
INTERROGATING YOUR DATA – IDENTIFYING PATTERNS

AIMS

- This chapter provides instruction on how to go about identifying patterns in your data – through the continuous revision of coding frames and re-coding of transcripts and through a process involving simple counting.
- It demonstrates how to assemble and employ 'grids' in order to identify and portray patterns.
- It provides an opportunity to actively engage in using the 'constant comparative method' to learn about how to transform disparate comments into a coherent argument.
- It encourages the reader to capitalize on the analytic potential afforded by reflexivity (understanding how you as a researcher affect both the data generated and the way in which this is interpreted).
- It also provides hints on how to harness the differing skills and knowledge of team members.

INTRODUCTION

Crucially, this aspect of qualitative data analysis involves an active process on the part of the researcher, who is encouraged to 'worry away' at the data. In keeping with the iterative process that underpins the qualitative research endeavour, this also involves refining your provisional coding frame. This is an aspect of analysis that tends not to be described in full, being something that the researcher picks up along the way. This chapter, however, seeks to illuminate the process through discussing one team supervision meeting and its contribution towards refining a coding frame and suggesting fruitful avenues for further analysis and, ultimately, explanation. Thorough analysis involves categories being subjected to 'interrogation'. So, too, is the data – both in order to highlight exceptions, contradictions or disconfirming excerpts (which may lead to revision of the coding frame or individual categories) and to identify the patterns in the data (with respect to what is saying what and in which context). The recommended approach which provides access to such patterning (and provides the starting point for 'theorizing') utilizes counting (as distinct from quantification, which strives for explanation solely in terms of frequencies and associations). Silverman (1993) stresses the value of 'simple counting' in avoiding anecdotalism. He makes the point that systematic attention to who is saying what and in what context may also remove nagging doubts about the accuracy of researchers' interpretations of the data, thus strengthening the rigour of the work. The chapter discusses uses and limitations of the often cited 'framework analysis' of Ritchie and Spencer (1994), with emphasis being put on the need to provide an explanation and, in particular, to use contradictions and exceptions to analytic advantage. The reader will then have the opportunity to engage in just this sort of exercise in relation to the condensed sub-fertility dataset.

REFINING YOUR PROVISION CODING FRAME

As you code successive transcripts, you are likely to want to make further revisions to your coding frame (as, hopefully, became evident as you engaged in the exercise at the end of the previous chapter). Sometimes issues don't 'jump out' at you until someone says something particularly vehemently or articulately. However, this does not mean that it isn't present in earlier transcripts. Once sensitized, you may be surprised to find how many other instances you can find. Some researchers invoke the concept of 'saturation' to denote that point at which they consider they have exhausted their data and the potential to develop new categories. However, as with the use of this concept to refer to exhausting sampling strategies, I fear that this could make the researcher a hostage to fortune.

Even if a pure conversation analysis (CA) approach is not being followed, awareness of the sorts of things routinely attended to in producing a CA transcript can provide useful suggestions as to what to look out for, for example the use of 'we' denoting inclusiveness and the use of 'they' to achieve distance and sometimes also disapproval.

The context in which something is said may also have a bearing on how you interpret it. Particularly if you are using more than one source of data (for example any combination of observational fieldwork, interviews and focus groups), you may distinguish between whether a comment was made in private or in front of others. Becker et al. (1961) advocated using the following three criteria:

1. Whether the statement or action was volunteered by the respondent or directed by questioning by the researcher or, *in the case of focus groups, whether it was suggested by another participant.*

2. Whether the statement or action occurred in public or in private; in the company of other respondents or in the company of the researcher alone. *Here, you should consider the composition of the group and the extent to which this is likely to have influenced what was said. You may have supplementary written material to draw on here or interview data to provide material for comparison.*

3. The number of negative cases where the respondent either denies the legitimacy of a perspective or acts in a manner contrary to the ideas contained in the perspective. Focus groups afford an opportunity to interrogate contradictions from the point of view of their potential for signalling the development of ideas during the session. This can be in terms of shifts in individuals' views or for understanding what is occurring in the course of the group discussion. (adapted from Becker et al., 1961: 39–44, *my italics*)

THE CONSTANT COMPARATIVE METHOD

The 'constant comparative method' lies at the root of all qualitative data analysis and does exactly what it says, relying on constantly comparing and contrasting. It involves looking systematically at who is saying what and in what context. Although it was mentioned as part of the original formulation of 'grounded theory', it is not invoked with anything like the same frequency as is the broader term. One reason for this may be that it involves a painstaking and somewhat unglamorous process. However, it is absolutely essential in producing rigorous analyses. It relies on identifying patterning in your data and this means that you need to do some counting. This stops short of making statistical inferences. However, if you are going to claim that something was an issue for all your interviews, you should ensure that this claim is firmly based. Similarly, you will want to establish whether certain perspectives arise in all focus groups and, if not, what might the reasons be for this not being addressed in the others? You should also take pains to make sure that you are not simply counting lots of comments from one individual, who may be the only person to raise an issue, but that there is evidence that this is a shared perspective. Ritchie and Spencer (1994), whose approach has come to be known as 'framework analysis', provide some useful hints on how to carry out a systematic analysis, using grids to establish what the patterns look like. Figure 10.1 is an example using the same topic of fathers' attendance at deliveries.

Examining the occurrence of particular perspectives within the groups can be instructive. Once you have carried out this process, of course, this simply gives rise to another set of questions:

- How might you explain exceptions?
- How might exceptions highlight general principles?
- What patterns emerge?
- How might you begin to explain these patterns?

Focus group	Fathers as a liability	Men feeling deskilled	The need to act as an advocate	The difficulty of opting out
All women			C; E; S; G	
All men		C; B	C; B; R; T; W	F; N; T
Male doctors	J	J; P; D; O; M	P; O; M	
Midwives	R; B; C; J	C		
Men and women			H; S; D; A	

NB: The letters are used to refer to individual focus group participants.

FIGURE 10.1   SYSTEMATIC ANALYSIS USING GRIDS

For example, it might be helpful to know that, of the seven male doctors in one of the groups, five were fathers and each of these five men talked at some point about feeling deskilled. Thus, it is important to worry away at your data in order to identify all the patterns that may be relevant and seek to develop a possible explanation for these.

A further helpful question would be:

- What explanations are advanced by your respondents?

Although it is important not to take these at face value, they may nevertheless provide valuable leads in making sense of the patterning you identify.

While our research respondents and participants can alert us to the existence of helpful conceptual models or lenses through which to interpret our data, we also need to remain alert to the seduction of ready-made theoretical frames or concepts and their capacity to hide as much as they can potentially reveal. Staller (2003) recounts her experience of returning to an environment of a juvenile police unit (that was familiar to her through previous contact when working in a crisis centre for runaway/homeless teenagers). She became intrigued by the analytic possibilities of the term 'skullduggery' that was used by a key informant to sum up police work and the changes that had taken place since Staller's previous engagement with himself and colleagues:

> For me, stumbling into an environment that had been altered unexpectedly from what I had known, I needed to come to terms with the deep-seated nature skulduggery played in constructing Sgt. T.'s day-to-day world. It provides a persuasive world view as well as a method of organizing activities … for Sgt. T. it meant living in, and with, a world where 'nothing is as it appears'. Sgt. T.'s skulduggery provided me with an interpretive lens for making sense of his world. I came to believe that police operate, to a large measure, in territory where appearances, perceptions and realities shift ground as easily as patterns in a kaleidoscope… (Staller, 2003: 552)

However, Staller came to the conclusion that 'skullduggery' was not so helpful as an analytical tool for the researchers, since it did not readily accommodate diversity and was therefore not a helpful device for interrogating her data.

INTERPRETATIVE PHENOMENOLOGICAL ANALYSIS

Psychologists engaging in qualitative research have developed an approach named 'interpretative phenomenological analysis' (IPA). This involves what Smith and Osborn (2003: 51) describe as combining 'an empathetic hermeneutics with a questioning hermeneutics', which emphasizes 'sense-making by both participant and researcher' (2003: 52). They explain:

> IPA is concerned with trying to understand what it is like, from the point of view of the participants, to take their side. At the same time, a detailed IPA analysis can also involve asking critical questions of the texts from participants, such as the following: What is the person trying to achieve here? (Smith and Osborn, 2003: 51)

IPA favours semi-structured interviews as the main method for generating data and focuses on meanings throughout the process of analysis. Smith and Osborn (2003) are at pains to point out that they do not see IPA as a prescriptive methodology. Indeed, their description of looking for themes, connecting themes (including looking at clustering of themes), continuing the analysis with other cases and their view of writing-up as yet another part of the process of analysis is remarkably similar to the approaches advocated in the current textbook – and by many other qualitative researchers, none of whom have specifically labelled this 'interpretative phenomenological analysis'. In summary, there is much to recommend the advice dispensed by Smith and Osborn (2003): it is not how you label an approach that is important, but how you demonstrate rigour and the incremental building up of your explanation through systematic interrogation of your data.

IMMERSION AND CRYSTALLIZATION

Judith Okely (1994) reminds us of the creative aspects involved in qualitative data analysis:

> Data analysis is not only a cerebral activity – it involves the whole person. No matter how systematic and stringent the analysis strategy employed, important insights and discoveries may be made by chance, or in situations or contexts seemingly removed from the daily and detailed work of coding and analysis. It is important to recognize the place of creativity and intuition in all stages of research. It is equally important to make such 'creative' discoveries explicit in the final analysis. (Okely, 1994: 21)

Retracing our theoretical 'trails' and making these explicit and transparent is something that presents a very real challenge. However, part of the answer, as so often with qualitative research, lies in the prosaic rather than the esoteric. I am referring here to the invaluable role of the fieldwork diary. If you routinely use this to record your thoughts – and, like the aids employed by some smoking cessation approaches, the context in which these ideas occurred to you – then this will be an enormous help. It may also encourage you to revisit some of these sources which can lead to further insights.

Additional insights can always be obtained from revisiting data you have generated earlier – either in the course of the current project or even in relation to work carried out some years previously. Indeed, this is why anthropologists would traditionally carry out a substantial period of intense fieldwork and return to this over and over again throughout the remainder of their academic lives. When you revisit your own data, even after a short absence, you may find that you have become sensitized to new issues. This is even more likely after a longer period of time has elapsed. Mauthner et al. (1998) reflect on their experience of re-analyzing data that they had generated themselves some years previously on separate projects. Mauthner comments that, although she developed many of the same codes, the fact that she had since become a mother herself led her to look at some of the comments from mothers of young children through a slightly altered lens. Sometimes, then, we may be able to derive new insights simply from continually revisiting our data. We can also benefit from enlisting the help of others. Reason and Marshall (1987: 124) highlight the value of interacting with 'friends willing to be enemies in order to reveal the blind spots and unarticulated assumptions inherent in any inquiry'.

It is also important not to be seduced by the appeal of concentrating on one's data without seeking to put this into a wider context. Glaser and Strauss (1967: 254) recommend that 'the researcher regard all statements about events pertaining to the area under study as being data. This means that the statements and writings of colleagues are data as much as those of laymen'.

CAPITALIZING ON THE ANALYTIC POTENTIAL OF TEAMS

There has, of late, been some debate about the role of multiple coders and the potential for strengthening the rigour of qualitative research. Inter-rater reliability has long been recognized in quantitative research as potentially strengthening validity and researchers have carried out further tests in order to establish that coding categories are being utilized consistently. Such exercises provide reassurance that the data has been analyzed systematically and that research practice has been held up to scrutiny: 'In a sense, an inter-rater reliability exercise can be understood as a test of the potential readership of a research report, to examine the degree to which this is likely to convey shared meanings consistently.' (Seale, 1999: 154).

While inter-rater reliability – or an appropriate variant – might be appropriate in terms of providing such reassurance for the internal consistency of qualitative analysis categories, parallel procedures are difficult to operationalize with regard to qualitative research – partly due to the cumbersomeness of the data involved and the time commitment required on the part of team members. Congruence of coding categories, however, is only part of the story and perhaps the least illuminating of the checks that can be carried out, using the research team as a resource. As Seale (1999: 155) points out, research team meetings provide 'further opportunities for fallibilistic research practice' in that they can be harnessed in order to check the robustness of codes and the assignment of comments to specific categories and to guard against individual, idiosyncratic or highly subjective interpretations creeping into the analysis.

There are, however, other reasons for the reluctance exhibited in some quarters with respect to engaging in these types of exercise. There has, at times, been a tendency towards preciousness among qualitative researchers – reflected in the assertion that only the person who has generated the data can analyze it. Although the individual who has generated the data has unrivalled insights and access to contextual information, the challenge, once the project moves to an intensive analysis phase, is likely to become how to capitalize on such knowledge to inform the analysis. This is because, in reality, it is often a junior person who generates the data, while the 'principal investigator' will carry out much of the analysis. This situation may arise because of tight deadlines and limited funding, where the contract research assistant may well have moved to another post before the bulk of analysis is carried out. Thus, some of the deeply held views about qualitative research and tenets regarding how analysis is carried out are actually at variance with common research practice.

Armstrong et al. (1997) invited six experienced researchers from different disciplines to independently code the same focus group transcript. As the coders were given very little information about the context of the project, this was a somewhat artificial exercise. Nevertheless the results were interesting in that they demonstrated general agreement between the coders with regard to the main categories identified. Alongside such overlaps, however, the exercise highlighted some differences in labelling and terminology used. How individuals 'package' data excerpts is likely to reflect their differing disciplinary bodies of knowledge and the corresponding theoretical frameworks which they habitually apply. The situation in most research teams is likely to be somewhat different from that involved in this exercise, in that the principal investigator, although not necessarily involved in the 'hands-on' data generation, is likely to have taken a lead in writing the proposal and thus would be conversant with or even immersed in the background and aims of the study.

Although it can provide some reassurance to know that independent coders have identified the same or similar themes in a set of transcripts, the distinctive feature of qualitative research is its capacity to illuminate through interrogating patterns in the data and by paying particular attention to exceptions. Qualitative researchers who confine the use of comparisons between team members' coding to identifying confirmatory instances or similarities are missing what are perhaps the most important possibilities afforded by the team setting: namely using tensions creatively and analytically. Such instances generally highlight situations where you, as the researcher, have 'got at' something of importance and the challenge is to tease out as far as possible why these different interpretations might be occurring. It's curious that, as academics, we talk a lot about the social construction of meaning and often employ group methods to generate data, while not capitalizing on the full potential of the team for the process of analysis.

Like so much that eventually finds its way into qualitative methods textbooks, this simply reflects what often happens anyway – particularly in the course of supervision. Students frequently bring to supervision sessions excerpts or even whole transcripts which have presented challenges for coding. As supervisor, I generally like to see some examples of how the student is developing a coding frame and applying this to the 'raw' data, in order to ensure that s/he is fully capitalizing on potentially illuminating distinctions and tensions, that is maximizing the analytic potential and not relying solely on codes suggested by the interview schedule or topic guide (*a priori* codes).

An illustrative example is provided by a supervision session carried out in the course of a piece of research into professionals' experiences and views of Advance Directives (or Living Wills) (Thompson et al., 2003a, 2003b).

USING THE TEAM TO DEVELOP AND REFINE A CODING FRAME AND TO ADVANCE TENTATIVE EXPLANATIONS

At this meeting Trevor Thompson (TT – Principal Investigator/GP and Higher Professional Training Fellow), myself (RB – supervisor/medical sociologist) and Lisa Schwartz (LS – critical reader/philosopher/ethicist) fed back our initial thoughts on developing a provisional coding frame. TT had chosen one focus group and one interview transcript for this exercise. The focus group had been chosen because it featured considerable disagreement between participants, and the interview had been chosen because it had been carried out with community psychiatric nurses who had experience of working with the elderly with psychiatric problems and who had detailed knowledge of dementia.

Prior to this meeting, TT and the two team members who had not actively generated the data (RB and LS) had each independently marked up both transcripts, without, at this stage, using any pre-defined codes.

Like the researchers who took part in the exercise carried out by Armstrong et al. (1997), we had also packaged some of the data according to different labels, reflecting our separate disciplinary backgrounds. TT, as an experienced GP, was particularly interested in the factors that were likely to give rise to adherence to Advance Directives (ADs). Drawing on his preliminary coding of all of the focus group and interview transcripts, he speculated that there were five components involved in individuals' willingness to implement ADs:

- Whether they felt the individual making the AD had been coerced.
- Whether they understood what it was they were signing ('informedness').

- The irreversibility or otherwise of the condition.
- Judgements about what constitutes a reasonable quality of life with dementia.
- Changing perspectives of living will makers.

RB had also used a coding category which reflected the last of these issues, although she had called this 'anticipatory preferences' and TT had used 'update issues'.

RB had also highlighted the 'subjective meanings of quality of life' and this led on to discussion as to the difficulty of making decisions in the light of changing priorities and the challenges posed by lucid period even after dementia has been diagnosed. RB had also coded excerpts that related to who was the most appropriate person to make such decisions. This led on to a consideration of ideas expressed in the transcripts as to what constituted 'knowing' a patient, and whether this reflected differing professional roles or the quality of the relationship. LS referred to a distinction in the ethics literature between the snapshot view provided through acute admissions, for example, and the 'longue mettrage' whereby professionals such as GPs have ongoing contact with patients and get to 'know' them over many years. RB wondered whether this might reflect professional rivalries and possibly also different orientations towards patients.

RB had been intrigued by the different ways in which focus group participants, in particular, talked about the families involved – sometimes invoking the fact that they had talked with them as justification for re-interpreting the content of an AD, and at other times talking about the patient's views versus the family's views and presenting families as an obstacle to be negotiated in making decisions about appropriate treatment. LS commented that she had been particularly struck by the suspicion, distrust and antagonism expressed towards families. She also reflected that in virtually all discussions of advocacy, to which she personally has been party, there is always someone who wants to be an advocate, saying that they know what someone wants and that this is identical to what's best for the patient. This led to a discussion about the intersection of the personal and the professional and how some of the research participants could be seen to invoke both in their responses to this contentious issue. TT commented: 'I've heard a relatively inexperienced junior geriatrician saying, "The family would want a person to live as long as possible, surely?" On the one hand, she was speaking as a doctor, but in saying "Anyone would want someone to live longer", she was talking from personal experience. In fact, she was probably talking from lack of personal experience too.'

REFLECTIONS ON THE VALUE OF TEAM EXERCISES AND THE IMPLICATIONS FOR CODING QUALITATIVE DATA

Reassuringly, the team exercise reported above displayed considerable congruence in terms of our interpretation of strips of interaction and individual comments. Where categories were derived 'in vivo' (Barbour et al., 2000; Kelle, 1997), utilizing respondents' own terms, the three collaborators had often selected the same words or phrases (for example 'Playing God'). All three had used the coding category 'the subjective meaning of Quality of life'. The codes 'Discussing with the family' and 'Engaging with the family' were sufficiently similar to be included in this congruent category and were used by the three collaborators to code the same sections of transcripts.

However, a closer inspection of the whole transcripts, in relation to these common codes, established that individual coders had missed some instances, although, in retrospect, we agreed that the code in question was relevant to a specific section of a transcript. This underlines the importance of being systematic in applying previously developed coding categories, even in the face of what may seem to be the much more exciting task of identifying new codes.

The exercise also highlighted the danger of succumbing to the temptation to fix meanings and categories too early in the process of analysis. The supervisory session discussion had started with TT's focus on trying to tease out factors that lead to different decisions. He had identified one focus group participant as being located at the paternalistic end of the spectrum, as compared to one other participant, who was situated right at the other end of the spectrum, in terms of respecting the patient's autonomy. Being mindful, however, of the dangers of assigning people too neatly to such categories, RB commented that several people could also be seen to move about between positions. This relates to earlier comments in Chapter 6 with regard to the impossibility of measuring individuals' views.

Thus, apparently definitive positions may also be overstated – or even 'artefactual' – in that they may arise because focus group participants and interviewees may feel they *have* to express an opinion. While we hear more frequently about the potentially problematic 'consensus effect' of focus groups, the opposite effect may also come into play. The only safeguard against taking such comments at face value is to systematically examine the transcripts for disconfirming or contradictory statements.

The full potential of such exercises, however, is in relation to the ongoing refinement of the coding frame and the process of theorization (which is revisited, together with some further observations on the supervision meeting discussed here, in Chapter 11).

Ultimately, however, one person (in the above example, TT, whose MSc project this was) is required to take responsibility for sorting out these competing views, deciding on the coding categories to be employed and which to concentrate upon in the analysis and writing-up of the project. Regardless of the final decision on these matters, engaging in this process of comparing interpretations, discussing alternatives and refining the coding frame serves to provide reassurances for the reader that analysis has been systematic and rigorous:

> If exercises like this are carried out by qualitative researchers, and research reports contain accounts of coding schemes with illustrative examples of typical instances coded under each heading, readers are more likely to be persuaded that care has been taken to analyze data in ways that are, at least, logically consistent. This aspect of internal reliability is not, of course, a guarantee of truth or validity. It does, however, help to guard against the errors associated with sole researchers who, free from the checks and balances imposed by the need to demonstrate consistency to others, present readers with categories poorly connected with field observations. (Seale, 1999: 155–156)

HINTS ON IDENTIFYING PATTERNS

- You should constantly re-visit your transcripts and think about revising your coding frame as you are alerted to new distinctions or categories.
- Ask yourself who is saying what?
- Why might similarities and differences occur? Is this related to characteristics of individuals, the different settings, or even the different context in which data has been generated (i.e. through observational fieldwork, interviews, or focus groups)?
- Are there stark differences between respondents or groups or is there a continuum of views/perspective?
- What distinctions do respondents make? Might these be helpful avenues to pursue in terms of identifying patterns?
- What surprises you as a researcher? Does this provide any useful insights?
- Do research team members have differing interpretations and responses? Might this provide useful insights?

FURTHER READING

Barbour, R.S. and members of the Wolds Primary Care Research Network (WoReN) (2000) 'Acquiring qualitative skills for primary care research: review and reflections on a three-stage workshop. Part 2: Analyzing interview data', *Family Practice*, 17(1): 83–89.

Ritchie, J. and Spencer, L. (1994) 'Qualitative data analysis for applied policy research', in A. Bryman and R.G. Burgess (eds) *Analyzing Qualitative Data*, London: Sage, pp. 173–194.

EXERCISE

This exercise is about identifying and seeking to begin to explain patterns in the data. I have provided a table (Table 10.1) which gives demographic details for each of the 12 couples whose interview data excerpts have been used for this exercise. (NB. This was a longitudinal study which started out with 24 couples, but for the purposes of the exercise – as distinct from the analysis carried out on the real project – this has been condensed.) When I use this 'data' in a workshop, I usually advise people to put the table with demographic details to one side to act as a thumbnail sketch, as they will return to this repeatedly as a resource as they seek to identify and make sense of the patterning of the data excerpts provided. You may find that it is more helpful to photocopy the demographic details sheet and, indeed, the data excerpts.

Each couple has been given a unique identifier and the woman is referred to as 'F' and the man as 'M' throughout. Of course, there are many other details that might potentially help you in interpreting the data excerpts and, in the course of a face-to-face workshop, I do often provide some additional information – for example, regarding the nature of the couple's fertility problems. However, the information provided here should be sufficient to enable you to engage in the exercise without diverting you to a fascinating but perhaps confusing set of many potential avenues of interpretation and 'theorizing'. Note that, as the codes are 'in vivo' rather than 'a priori' ones – apart, of course, from the demographic information, which was routinely collected – there are not necessarily examples from each of the couples included under any one heading. This is because the exercise reflects the situation in a real-life project, where the absence of comment on a topic can sometimes tell you almost as much as a comment that relates directly to a particular view or concept. In making sense of the data excerpts you should therefore be asking (either of yourself, or your 'team-mates', if you elect to do this as a group exercise) the following questions:

• Who is saying what?
• Why might this be a particular issue/not a particular issue for them?

Suggestions on how to use this exercise
In a workshop I would normally dip into and out of the small group discussions, helping them to pose other relevant questions, which lead on to the next set of excerpts in the pack. In order to reproduce this format as closely as is possible in a textbook exercise, I would urge you to cover up the commentary at the end of each set of coded excerpts and look at this only when you feel that you've exhausted your discussion on the meaning of the patterning of the excerpts you've looked at. Hopefully, the commentary will simply reiterate the questions that you've already started to ask. If you are working in a group, it will be interesting to see how different members may react differently to some of the quotes and this can be used as a resource in your analysis. Do keep your notes on this exercise, as the exercise at the end of Chapter 12 invites you to use this as the basis for doing a piece of writing.

Data excerpts 1: Concerns about the woman's age

All of the following women expressed concern about their age and their wish to conceive as soon as possible:

PFD23	WBY36	LHMR67
BIH32	HHH64	DF85
LGR32		

Table 10.1   Demographic details

Couple's identifier	F's age M's age	Marital status	Length of relationship	Time trying to conceive	Existing children
HSW17	F – 20 yrs M – 31 yrs	Married	3 years	3 years	M had 3 in previous relationship
YCL20	F – 27 yrs M – 30 yrs	Cohabiting	5 years	3.5 years	F already has daughter who lives with them
PFD23	F – 30 yrs M – 37 yrs	Married	13 years	4.5 years	None
BIH32	F – 29 yrs M – 27 yrs	Cohabiting	2 years	2 years + 5 years in previous relationship (for F)	None
HH32	F – 29 yrs M – 30 yrs	Cohabiting	4 years	2 years	None
LGR32	F – 28 yrs M – 30 yrs	Married	12 years	5 years	None
WBY36	F – 34 yrs M – 39 yrs	Married	10 years	4 years	None
FNFN63	F – 33 yrs M – 39 yrs	Cohabiting	3 years	2 years	None
HHH64	F – 30 yrs M – 32 yrs	Married	2 years	2 years	None
LHMR67	F – 32 yrs M – 25 yrs	Cohabiting	4 years	4 years + 5 years in previous relationship (for F)	F had early miscarriage
DF85	F – 30 yrs M – 33 yrs	Married	8 years	2.5 years	None
MH85	F – 28 yrs M – 48 yrs	Cohabiting	4 years	2 years	None

One other woman emphasized that she wanted to conceive as soon as possible, but did not cite her age:

HSW17

Negative cases/exceptions

I'm still young enough. I'm quite relaxed.   *(HH32; F)*

I don't feel, like some people do, that the clock's ticking, sort of thing … but I think I'm quite selfish because I don't want babies when I'm 40 …   *(YCL20; F)*

Lots of my friends had babies when they were in their 20s, but age has never bothered me.   *(FHFN63; F)*

Commentary

- What might explain the different 'takes' on the importance of the woman's age and the urgency with which she wants to conceive?
- What difference do the following things make?

  - The length of time they've been together
  - Whether or not they have children from a previous relationship (and which partner has these children)
  - How long they've been together and how long they've been trying to conceive?
  - Is this just about the **woman's** age? (See the excerpts below)

Data excerpts 2

Comments on the age of the man/time running out
They said at the clinic – and my GP said too – that there are some women where they just can't find any reason for it – who just can't conceive and she said what sometimes happens is that just before menopause, when your hormones change and stuff a lot of women fall pregnant. It seems ages away. I don't want to wait that long and poor M will be in his 60s… late 50s.   *(MH85; F)*

I don't feel this biological imperative as much as F does.   *(HSW17; M)*

> F: … We would look at paying for this (IVF) and maybe that would be a bit quicker.
> M: Yes, because I'm 40 this year, so I'm getting on a bit, you know.
> F: Yeah, M's 40.
> M: So I'm 40 this year and you don't want to leave it too long, do you? You have to go for it, because you don't know how long …   *(WBY36; F&M)*

I would prefer to pay and get on with it because, as I say, with me coming up to 40 this year and F 34, I feel that 18 months down the road I'll be that much older and, say, there's a year on top of that – I'll be in my mid 40s and it gets harder and harder, doesn't it? And you [to wife] you'll be into your later 30s. So that's one of the reasons we want to get on and do it …   *(WBY36; M)*

Commentary

- Is this just about age *per se*?
- Or is it about what age means in relationship to ideas about when it's most appropriate to have children? (See next page)

Data excerpts 3: Ideas about the appropriate age to have babies

I don't feel, like some people do, that the clock's ticking, sort of thing … but I think I'm quite selfish because I don't want babies when I'm 40 …   *(YCL20; F)*

It could maybe be another 5 years – that would really worry me – I don't want to be a really old mum.   *(BIH32; F)*

I keep thinking I wanted one before I'm 30.   *(BIH32; F)*

(There's a 2 year waiting list for IVF) Ooh, I'll be too old to be a mum. I'll be too old to appreciate it.   *(LHMR67; F)*

If we don't have a family what am I going to do for the next 30 to 40 years?   *(DF85; F)*

Commentary

In workshops this last quote is usually viewed as being particularly poignant, but also gives rise to the most discussion, as it tends to highlight the difference between the centrality of the role as mother for this woman as compared to workshop participants, who are usually also involved in pursuing a research career as an equally (or even more) important other identity.

These quotes all refer to how having a baby fits into the couples' lives.

- Where do they get their ideas from about the 'right time to have babies'?
- What about their peer group? (See next page)

Data excerpts 4: Getting left behind

F: I was quite disappointed really, because all my friends, of course, you know, sort of a few years ago – they all started having their babies then, you see. So I thought, 'Why isn't this happening to me?' …. I felt very disappointed …

(*They move on to talk about other things. Later the husband returns to this theme:*)

M: …. You feel a bit left out when other people (*goes on to talk about a friend whose partner was pregnant when he met him and who have since had a second baby*). The older you get the further you seem to get left out, well in a way …   *(PFD23; F&M)*

You just seem to get more and more disheartened, you know. You hear so many people are pregnant and you think … 'We've still failed' …   *(LGR32; F)*

Everybody's pregnant – we're standing still.   *(MH85; F)*

My sister's just had her third – and she's only 26!   *(BIH32; F)*

M: All our friends are going away together with their kids, aren't they? Couples and kids – so everyone's going away with kids, except us.

F: I don't know why, but I just seem to get more pressurised now, really, like I was round the other night at my friend's and she's expecting a baby and it's all arranged for next year – like, six of them and their children to go away, and I said, 'Oh, we won't be included in that, because we don't have any children' and it's really quite sad, isn't it?   *(BIH32; F&M)*

M: We've got five sets of friends who're pregnant at the moment.

F: There's been a massive baby boom. It's a total nightmare!   *(BIH32; F&M)*

I think a lot of the problem is, as I say, we like to think that we're doing quite well in our lives and worked hard – got a nice house and everything else – and people expect your life to be going on quite normally. And we start seeing other couples having kids – people expect you to be having kids as well. So, obviously, we've taken a lot of stick over the last four years, haven't we?   *(WBY36; M)*

Commentary

These couples talk a lot about having planned for having children and some talk about having decided to delay pregnancy and childrearing until they feel they are financially secure. They have the house, the garden, the secure job etc., but what is still missing is the baby.

• Do they regret this at all? (See below)

Data excerpts 5: Lost opportunities

I've been married before, you see, and I didn't want one then. But as soon as I met him I wanted one. Sad aren't we … ?   *(HHH64; F)*

When we first got married we were so careful – don't want to get pregnant now. We wanted to be able to save up plenty of money so that when we did start a family we would have a secure home and everything and then you think, 'Well, we've got the money – where's the baby?' you know. Well, I've said this to M before and it may be a negative thing to say, but, you know, we just sort of married and we've been married for eight and a half years now and, you think … I feel annoyed that we waited so long before we actually started trying. I mean, the only reason we did leave it so long is what I've just said, so we could spend some quality time together before a family came along and that we could have sufficient money to be able to give a child or children a good home and then I keep kicking myself no, thinking, 'Well, why did we leave it so long?' you know, 'We could have managed even if we hadn't much money. Maybe if we'd started two or three years earlier we would have a baby by now …   *(DF85; F; second Interview)*

You know, I think it's just typical of me – to presume, you know, 'Well I want to do this and that's when I'll have babies' and then you can't. All those years spent taking precautions …   *(WBY36; F)*

Commentary

Some of the couples do talk about regrets about having delayed pregnancy, assuming all the time that they were in control of their own fertility. Now they realize, with a shock, that this may be out of their control.

- What is the emotional impact on them of being 'left behind' and having their hopes frustrated?
- How does this affect their wider relationships – with friends and family? (This issue is further explored in the exercise at the end of Chapter 11, which involves theorizing around the concept of 'Biographical Disruption'.)

Concluding commentary

Hopefully, this exercise will have shown how you can start with what seems a pretty routine category – age and the importance of the woman's age and declining fertility – in explaining couples' perceptions and experiences. However, through comparing and contrasting the comments from couples with differing demographic details, you will, hopefully, have 'unpicked' the significance of age. It's not just about the woman's chronological age. It's also about the man's age and their capacity to parent as a couple. Although the problems may be medical in origin (at least for some of the couples) sub-fertility is experienced *socially*.

11
THEORIZING IN QUALITATIVE DATA ANALYSIS

AIMS

- This chapter shows the reader how to use qualitative datasets to interrogate theoretical frameworks.
- It shows how to move beyond the merely descriptive use of theory to critically engage with theory and to revise or expand frameworks.
- Hints are provided on gaining analytical purchase through considering exceptions, opposites, synonyms and parallels.
- It shows readers how to draw on the available literature as a resource for constant comparison.

INTRODUCTION

This chapter will examine the role of theory in developing accounts of qualitative research. Again, an important distinction is made between merely utilizing theories to describe processes observed in data and using data to interrogate theoretical frameworks. Readers are encouraged to treat theoretical frameworks and, indeed, their own notes from reading the relevant literature in a manner akin to data, using a similar coding frame to retrieve relevant sections and to identify and interrogate any discrepancies, omissions or contradictions. This means using the constant comparative method to greatest advantage.

Some attention will be paid to the disciplinary and personal backgrounds of researchers and how this impacts on their interpretation of data. The focus on disciplinary backgrounds relates to some of the discussion in Chapters 7 and 8 on mixing methods and engaging in action research. However, within-discipline preferences can also impact on the way in which data is interpreted. Again, these different approaches are regarded as a resource to be capitalized upon rather than as rigid temples which dictate how the process of analysis should proceed. The different possibilities afforded by utilizing some aspects of distinctive approaches to analysis will be examined, such as the potential of paying attention to silences, turn-taking, structure of comments and use of language, which characterizes conversation or discourse analysis. Frequently, however, it is as an individual with a specific biography or characteristics that one responds during analysis to a respondent's comment rather than as a researcher *per se*. We all use parts of ourselves in analysis. Often what alerts us to 'interesting use of language' – something that jars or jumps out at the researcher – is our own personal reaction. This chapter will also discuss reflexivity as a resource in analysis and will provide examples drawn from the author's experience of working as a member of interdisciplinary teams. This section will retrace the unfolding refinement of coding frames to illustrate how researchers can gain analytic purchase in making sense of their data.

USE OF THEORY

Theory may be invoked in several different guises. Research can, for example, be designed to test specific theories. This is relatively unusual in qualitative research, however, possibly because so much research in this genre is exploratory in nature, with relevant theoretical frameworks only suggesting themselves once we are in the business of attempting to shed light on the data we have generated. Theory is also evident, though, in the form of the epistemological underpinnings of studies and the way in which methodological approaches are justified and brought into being. That this is so often implicit rather than explicit is what gives rise to the agonizing of many novice researchers – particularly PhD students (as discussed in Chapter 1). Part of their reluctance to 'nail their colours to the mast', however, stems from the fear that research that claims to have a theoretical foundation risks being judged more harshly – perhaps being seen as having grandiose aspirations. Research that purports to provide theoretical insights does tend to attract considerable hostility – particularly from the growing constituency of practitioner-researchers (see further discussion in Chapter 13). In our attempts to render the familiar strange, we often seem to touch a raw nerve. 'There is, then, a danger that, to "insiders" our analyses are seen as "common-sensical", reproducing – although usually also commenting upon – their "taken-for-granted" (Schutz, 1972) views'. The case is further weakened by some versions of 'theorizing' which confine themselves to assigning descriptive labels. Here, researchers can appear to be offering insights similar to those provided by John Cleese, in the guise of paleobiologist Ann Elk, in an often re-televised sketch, where, with considerable gravitas, 'she' expounds her 'theory' that 'all dinosaurs are thin at one end, much, much fatter in the middle, and thin again at the other end'. (Barbour, 1998b: 186)

We have already looked at 'grounded theory' and the pitfalls associated with the unimaginative use of this approach, as well as its many advantages. Janice Morse (2003) has highlighted the potential for what she calls 'theoretical congestion', which, she argues, arises when researchers rely exclusively on their own data to develop theory and neglect to locate their findings within the wider context of existing work, failing to identify instructive parallels or interrogate any differences between their own findings and those of other studies. This means that each research project can, in effect, 'reinvent the wheel' or, in many cases, simply reiterate yet another version of what is not essentially a particularly exciting theory in the first place. Morse illustrates her argument with reference to the large body of work on the experience of chronic illness, where many studies have developed a staged model to explain the process of accommodation to illness, each coining its own terms and labels, but not advancing theoretical debate in the process. Theory may also be employed in a purely descriptive way to organize data. I am always rather suspicious of any qualitative report or paper where the data are purported to fit neatly into any theoretical framework. Experience suggests that real life – and systematic and thorough qualitative data analysis – is much more complex.

Although in this case referring to a review of 37 qualitative papers, Pound et al. (2005) show how they built on and modified a model developed by Dowell and Hudson (1997) to take account of the insights offered by other papers on the same topic of lay experiences of medicine taking. They explain:

> Dowell and Hudson (1997) authors of one of the studies in the synthesis, had previously developed a model of medicine taking that was similar in many ways, but which was unable to 'hold' or account for all the findings from the studies in our synthesis. Our model proved to be an invaluable organizational aid during the synthesis process. We then brought together the reciprocal translations by synthesizing them. This involved reading and rereading each one [referring to the original papers where necessary] and analyzing and interpreting the data thematically, the themes corresponding to the headings given in the synthesis findings … [to produce] what Noblit and Hare (1988) describe as a 'line of argument synthesis'. At this stage a reconceptualization of the findings is possible, which is an attempt to produce a concept or concepts that explain all the data if possible [or, in the case of analysis of empirical data, all the data coded under a specific theme or heading] in a fresh way. (Pound et al., 2005: 135)

This is what we should be aiming for in our analysis of our own data, for, as is argued in this chapter, the distinction between the findings of our own studies and those of others is a permeable one – at least in terms of using both sources to refine our explanations. (This is why the topic of meta-analysis is not discussed separately in the present volume, since the principles are the same.) This chapter argues that it is possible – with a little more effort and meticulous attention to patterning and the important exceptions and 'grey' areas in between typologies – to use both data and notes from reading and rereading the relevant literature to interrogate and refine theoretical frameworks. The exercise accompanying this chapter aims to provide hands-on experience of using data excerpts in exactly this way to interrogate the theoretical framework of 'biographical disruption' (Bury, 1982) and the insights provided by subsequent papers that have investigated the usefulness of this concept.

USING PATTERNING TO INTERROGATE A THEORETICAL FRAMEWORK

What often alerts us to the potential of existing theoretical frameworks are the puzzles thrown up by our data, as we attempt to code them into meaningful chunks and are faced with myriad distinctions, qualifications, and contradictions. While these may, at first sight, seem to threaten attempts to utilize theory, it is these very 'messy' or grey areas, which defy neat assignment to particular categories or concepts in our emerging explanatory frameworks, that hold the key to moving beyond descriptive outputs to achieve analytically sophisticated accounts.

An example is provided by my attempts to make sense of my observations about the ways social work students used humour as they negotiated the demands of their new role. Having read around the topic of humour and its many functions, I came across Goffman's 'Frame Analysis' (1974), which suggested a potentially fruitful avenue for further exploration of my data. Having read Goffman's text, it became apparent from closer inspection that some strips of activity that I had previously coded under the general heading of 'humour' actually involved the 'guying' (or playfully exaggerated playing out) of a (pretend) exchange between a social worker and a client. Goffman's concept of 'make believe keying' thus afforded a promising category.

The argument that 'make believe keyings' allowed students to both express and deflect anxiety was strengthened by being able to demonstrate patterning in this data, where such instances were found to occur with greater frequency at the start of the course and in the immediate run-up to the six-month placement between the first and second year of the course. A systematic examination of fieldnotes and interview transcripts (affording access to public and private accounts) also identified a relationship between humorous and serious deployment of social work terms, suggesting that joking may lay the groundwork for the internalization of new roles and professional identities:

Other patterns revealed by an analysis of the data point to a possible link between joking and the adoption of serious 'cross-framing' behaviour. I became aware that those very students who [publicly] ridiculed social work jargon … utilized such vocabulary in private without inhibition or humorous intent. The public mockery/ private adherence dichotomy became evident when fieldnotes and interview scripts were compared. … That joking allowed students the opportunity of 'having it both ways' – disclaiming seriousness whilst actually gaining practice in using new concepts – is further supported by the finding that serious usage of this jargon outlived the humorous usage and was fairly evenly distributed over the last three interviews in the series. Serious usage was also seen to involve students who had not been observed initiating or taking part in keyings, suggesting that they may nevertheless have derived some benefit from keying activities of their colleagues. (Barbour, 1985: 522)

The notion of 'taken-for-granted cross-framings' extended Goffman's original categorizations, but allowed me to investigate the possible functions of this activity in terms of facilitating a shift to a new professional identity. A strip of interaction was classified as an 'unacknowledged' or 'taken-for-granted cross-framing' if:

1   The incident or comment involved was similar to one which, at another time, had been used as the butt of a student joke (whether or not the same student was involved), *or*
2   The incident or comment was similar to one singled out by a student as an instance of a self-reported cross-framing (whether or not the same student was involved), *or*
3   This similarity was neither at the time nor retrospectively acknowledged by the students involved, either verbally or by the use of cues. (Barbour, 1985: 522–523)

Students did sometimes disagree about the significance or appropriateness of such behaviour and it was often their comments that alerted me to shifts in perceptions.

It is, however, very difficult to provide reliable instructions about how to identify potential theoretical leads. One of the most convincing attempts is provided by C. Wright Mills, who talks about the research process in relation to sociological work but applies, in essence, to the process of engaging analytically with data. He advises:

An attitude of playfulness towards the phrases and words with which various issues are defined often loosens up the imagination. … Often you get the best insights by considering extremes – by thinking of the opposite of that which you are directly concerned. …. [by] deliberately inverting your sense of proportion … (C. Wright Mills, 1959: 212, 213 and 215)

A thesaurus can be an extremely valuable tool in seeking to gain analytic purchase. Not only does this provide synonyms and opposites, but it can also suggest other distinctions and gradations and can often help in labelling for codes and sub-categories. It is, hard, however, as Howard Becker (1998: 9) acknowledges, to build such activities into research timetables:

> None of the tricks of thinking in this book have a 'proper place' in the timetable for building such a contraption (i.e. a theoretically informed explanation). Use them when it looks like they might move your work along – at the beginning, in the middle, or toward the end of your research.

Certainly, multidisciplinary teams can be helpful in providing us with a richer vocabulary and alternative sets of concepts. However, as Barry et al. (1999) point out, open discussion at multidisciplinary team meetings takes courage, as we bring to the research endeavour not only our paradigmatic and disciplinary histories and predispositions, but also our personal biographies. I would argue that we can only begin to explore the full potential of integrating quantitative and qualitative data analysis when we are able to use team tensions as a resource in the analysis. Barry et al. (1999) provide one of the few accounts of attempting to do just this, through members of the research team making explicit their own value stances and sharing personal information with each other.

   However, the example of our own supervision session, which was discussed in the previous chapter, gives a flavour of the sorts of discussion likely to be involved. Importantly, it also underlines the varying slants that people are likely to have in terms of interpreting snatches of transcripts in the light of their own disciplinary backgrounds and customary ways of thinking. While TT (the GP) was interested in understanding the factors that gave rise to differing perceptions and perhaps behaviour, LS (the philosopher/ethicist) was able to provide illumination and allow us to critically interrogate data excerpts with reference to separate and potentially contradictory notions of 'autonomy' which stemmed from different philosophical traditions. This was, ultimately, helpful in alerting us to and guiding us through the philosophical implications and potential tensions and dilemmas that professionals were likely to encounter in espousing conflicting principles. As the medical sociologist on the group, I interpreted many of the comments relating to autonomy in the light of the existing literature in the sociology of the professions. Hopefully, if you are engaging in the exercises as part of a course, you may already have seen the value and power of such comparative exchanges.

   Of course, in the context of a real project, one person usually has to decide what the main focus of the analysis will be. (This does not preclude other members of the team from taking the lead in writing up papers with a different focus commensurate with their own disciplinary interest.)

You may also derive serendipitous insights from your wider reading, or from attending conference presentations on unrelated topics, which may, nevertheless, yield potentially useful theoretical concepts that you can employ in making sense of your own data. Many valuable theoretical leads stem from advice provided by knowledgeable and well-read colleagues, who may recommend a particular paper or textbook – in many instances precisely because a particular parallel strikes them on seeing data generated in an entirely different context. It is, therefore, always likely to be worthwhile to take time out to present your ongoing work, even though your analyses remain far from polished. The best advice, however, is probably to read continuously and widely and to reread theoretical papers and books that have previously caught your own attention and that of your disciplinary community. On considering the comments made by the couples in the sub-fertility study, I was struck by the sense of disjuncture and uncertainty that they conveyed. This led me, in turn, to revisit Mike Bury's (1982) classic paper on 'biographical disruption', which has been utilized by many qualitative researchers studying the experience of individuals with a variety of chronic illnesses. This is the theoretical framework that I have chosen for the exercise below. Although many such studies have merely utilized this concept descriptively to order the data generated, I have come across a few studies which have used empirical research to interrogate the idea of 'biographical disruption', and have thus advanced the debate and served to refine and extend this useful concept. It is important to note here that such papers were identified by reading around the substantive topic area of sub-fertility.

HINTS ON USING THEORY

- Don't worry if you don't know at the outset which theoretical frameworks will be most relevant in making sense of your data.
- Do ensure that you attend seminars and conference papers on other substantive topic areas which may provide instructive parallels and may suggest new theoretical directions.
- Don't expect one theory to be able to explain all of your data.
- Don't attempt to fit your data into existing theoretical frameworks. Instead pay particular attention to those data excerpts or issues that don't quite fit or that contradict theoretical propositions. The constant comparative method is what allows you to engage systematically in doing this.
- Do use your own data to explore ways in which theoretical frameworks might be revised or expanded.

FURTHER READING

Becker, H.S. (1998) *The Tricks of the Trade*, Chicago: University of Chicago Press (especially Chapters 2 and 4).

Pound, P., Britten, N., Morgan, M., Yardley, L., Pope, C., Daker-White, G. and Campbell, R. (2005) 'Resisting medicines: A synthesis of qualitative studies of medicine taking', *Social Science and Medicine*, 61: 133–155.

Wright Mills, C. (1959) *The Sociological Imagination*, London: Penguin.

EXERCISE: INTERROGATING DATA AND REFINING A THEORETICAL FRAMEWORK
THEORETICAL FRAMEWORK OF 'BIOGRAPHICAL DISRUPTION'

Bury, M. (1982) 'Chronic illness as biographical disruption', *Sociology of Health and Illness*, 4(2): 167–182.

The key components of Bury's theory can be summarized as follows:

Illness, and especially chronic illness, is precisely that kind of experience where the structures of everyday life and the forms of knowledge which underpin them are disrupted. (1982: 169)

This disruption involves:

• taken-for-granted assumptions and behaviours
• explanatory systems – leading to a fundamental rethinking of the person's biography and self-concept.

Responses may involve mobilization of resources (1982: 175)

I have also provided some summaries of the relevant papers. The comments and findings I have chosen to highlight are, of course, highly selective and dependent on my own reading of the papers. If you decide to read any of these papers in full, you may well pull out different issues – my reading, after all, is only one among many possible interpretations. Here, I would also point out the potential for employing a package such as N-Vivo to code your notes from your reading of the literature – just as you would do with your transcripts. (The notes reproduced here have been coded using the package ATLAS-ti.) You may find these codes helpful as you organize your thoughts on the papers you have read to reflect the ideas explored in your data. You may also find that having read some of the papers you are encouraged to revisit transcripts and re-code these utilizing new themes or subcategories to which your reading has sensitized you. I have employed a rough coding scheme for the notes I have taken from these papers, highlighting the issues that are also raised by the accompanying excerpts from a condensed set of transcripts derived from the same real-life study as those used in the exercise at the end of Chapter 10. You may recognize some of the quotes and, in this, the exercise mirrors the real-world process of qualitative data analysis, as we ponder and reponder the same utterances and explore their multiple potential meanings.

Suggestions on how to use this exercise

In workshops I sometimes suggest that individual small-group members each read a different summary. Of course, if you're doing this exercise in conjunction with a taught course – or even engaging in it alone – you will have the opportunity to read these (and possibly other papers on this popular theme) in full. Even if you only use the excerpts and opt to divide these among your small working group, it may be helpful to swap these over. You are likely to show them to each other in any case, as you work through this exercise.

Conclusion

Hopefully, this exercise will have provided a flavour of what is involved in the iterative process whereby you can extract relevant ideas from the available literature and use these to revisit your data, refine your coding frame and develop new codes. As well as allowing you to see data extracts in a new light, such an exercise also allows you to engage with the arguments presented via theoretical frameworks and to see where these describe what is going on in your data and – even more importantly – where your own data may suggest that a qualification or amendment to the original propositions is required. The papers summarized in Figure 11.1 demonstrate the relevance of the concept of 'biographical disruption' for understanding the experiences of individuals dealing with a range of chronic conditions. However, they also question some of the ideas that underpin 'biographical disruption'.

In terms of the large literature on chronic illness, however, these papers are somewhat unusual. In the years following the publication of Bury's influential paper, the eagerness with which subsequent grateful researchers have seized upon the concept of 'biographical disruption' and the limits of their largely descriptive usage have, perhaps, overemphasized the universality of this experience.

The Literature Notes and Codes:

01
02
03 **PAPER 1:**
04 Faircloth, Christopher A., Boylstein, Craig, Rittman, Maude, Young, Mary Ellen & Gubrium,
Jaber (2004) 'Sudden illness and biographical flow in narratives of stroke recovery', *Sociology of Health & Illness*, 26(2); pp.242-261.
05
06 (p.244) Not all physiological changes resulting from a particular chronic condition have the same impact on people's lives. The lives of people who have a stroke are not inevitably disrupted. …. While some find their lives disrupted by the stroke, others may 'bracket off' the impact of the stroke, maintaining a sense of a coherent pre- and post-stroke self.
07
08 (p.252) …rather than the stroke being a source of biographical disruption it is simply expressed as one event in an ongoing life.   ⟶ FEATURES: not a universal experience
09
10 (p.256) We have suggested that instead of disrupting a biography, an illness such as stroke can be integrated with various social contingencies in constructing a biography that continues to flow across time and space. …. The ill 'are theoreticians of both illness and medicine', but are actively working towards maintaining a certain level of quality of life.   ⟶ STRATEGIES: not just passive
11
12 (pp.258-9) Treating all survivor experiences as universal may gloss over some important aspects of the survival experience.   ⟶ FEATURES: not a universal experience
13
14
15 **PAPER 2:**
16 Asbring, Pia (2001) 'Chronic illness - a disruption in life: identity-transformation among women with chronic fatigue syndrome and fibromyalgia', *Journal of Advanced Nursing*, 34(3).
17
18 A transformation of identity was described in various ways in the interviews. … The consequences of a biographical disruption for identity does not …. have to be unequivocal: it can be expressed either as a partial transformation of identity - i.e. a somewhat changed identity, or as   ⟶ FEATURES: different experiences?   TENSIONS: questions 'neatness' of transformation

two completely discrepant identities.

19

20 The disruption may vary in significance and bring with it various consequences for different people. Some may, depending on the symptom profile, maintain more of the activities important to their identity than others. The interview responses showed, therefore, that biographical disruptions were partial rather than total. (Some, for example, managed to keep working.)

21

22 Biographical disruptions were not viewed as entirely negative by the interviewees. The illness experience may also have brought with it positive changes in identity, because of new insights with regard to the previous life and life in general. Paradoxically the dilemmas to be faced, for some, also became positive experience.

23

24

25 **PAPER 3:**

26 Mathieson, Cynthia M. & Stam, Henderikus, J. (1995) 'Renegotiating identity: cancer narratives', *Sociology of Health & Illness*; 17(3); pp.283-306.

27

28 (p.288) Self-narratives are part of an open-ended process, with continuous transformations, which provide a meaning to daily interactions. As such, these narratives are social constructions; they emerge from social interchange. No single narrative is ever final but part of the negotiation of ongoing, intersecting and multiple influence. These constructions of narrative order are essential in providing one's life with meaning and a sense of direction for the future.

29

30 (p.293-4) ... personal identity (has been described) as a 'feeling of fit' that develops among the individual's past, present, and the meanings available for interpreting such experiences. .... We used this terminology 'disrupted feelings of fit' to characterise early signals of threats to identity. In the early stages of a cancer diagnosis, participants were beginning to identify the discrepancies between their former health lives and their lives revised by illness. ... Some discrepancies arose from disruptions to daily routines caused by medical intervention .... Participants (also) alluded to disruptions of relationships with friends ... and the bodily disruption involved (in treatment)

31

STRATEGIES: seeing in a positive light

STRATEGIES: negotiated narratives

FEATURES: impact on relationships
FEATURES: threat to identity

32   (p.299) Individuals engage in biographical work over the life span as a stable requirement of identity; events of one's life must be articulated in a coherent story. … it seems that a diagnosis of cancer challenges older self-narratives and motivates the search for newer narratives that incorporate the meaning of illness. The cancer patient must ultimately decide how the events of illness fit in among the other event of her life. This inevitably entails revisions of future plans..   ❖ FEATURES: challenge to existing narratives

33

34   (p.300) Here then are the major biography-altering facts of cancer: altered relationships, a curtailed sense of agency, and a changed vision of the future.   ❖ STRATEGIES: re-constructing the future

35

36

37

38   **PAPER 4:**

39   Exley, Catherine & Letherby, Gayle (2001) 'Managing a disrupted lifecourse: issues of identity and emotion work', *Health*, 5(1); pp.112-132.

40

41   (p.112) (Both) 'infertility' and/or 'involuntary childlessness' and terminal illness have a disruptive effect on daily lives and future expectations.   ❖ FEATURES: threat to future plans

42

43   (p.114) Social identity theory suggests that identity rests on the process of social comparison, whereby in order to evaluate their own opinions and abilities individuals compare themselves with similar others in the course of social encounters … We would suggest that terminally ill people and those who are 'infertile'/'involuntarily childless' may perceive themselves as a 'stranger' in social encounters with others, and further their status as terminally ill or 'infertile'/'involuntarily childless' affects their relationship with others and their sense of self.   ❖ FEATURES: comparison with others   ❖ FEATURES: impact on relationships

44

45   (p.115) In addition, as we will argue, from our respondents' accounts, it is possible to suggest that such disruption can have positive as well as negative effects on self-identity, but achieving such positive effects often involves hard work. 'emotion work' (involves) regulating and managing others' feelings.   ❖ STRATEGIES: emotion, work

46

47   (p.125) …respondents are managing strong emotions such as jealousy and grief and struggle with concerns about how to make themselves and/or others feel better.

48

49 (p.124) ...complex processes are at work here, respondents wanted others to recognise the disruption they were experiencing, yet did not want to be excluded from discussions focussing on expected lifecourse progress and events. Thus, whereas they wanted their 'strangerhood' to be acknowledged, they did not want to be treated like 'outsiders'.

50

51 (p.129) Emotion work, for the respondents in our research, was a means of reaffirming their identities as people who were still part of the mainstream groups, not just individuals who were terminally ill or 'infertile' and/or 'involuntarily childless'. Thus, there is a link between emotion work and lifecourse disruption.

52

53

54 **PAPER 5:**

55 Hallowell, Nina & Lawton, Julia (2002) 'Negotiating present and future selves: managing the risk of hereditary ovarian cancer by prophylactic surgery', *Health*, 6(4); pp.423-443.

56

57 (p.428) Control - or loss of control - was the major theme that underpinned all of the women'' accounts. On the one hand, women talked about oophorectomy as providing them with a means to regain control over their bodies, as enabling them to manage their risk of cancer and thereby to ensure the survival of self in the future. On the other, they described prophylactic surgery as precipitating a loss of bodily control, as potentially undermining their self-identity in various ways. .... as far as these women are concerned, choosing surgery requires them to balance the contradictory effects of oophorectomy on their present and future selfhood.

58

59 (p.431) The women involved in this study repeatedly talked about the ability to reproduce as being central to 'being a woman'. Thus, insofar as losing one's ovaries results in a loss of control over one's fertility, it was described as compromising one's femininity.

60

61 (p.438) ....as this article has demonstrated, in reality the management of ovarian cancer by prophylactic surgery requires careful consideration of the costs and benefits for present and future self-identity.

62

FEATURES: getting left behind
FEATURES: impact on relationships

STRATEGIES: emotion, work

FEATURES: loss of control & choice
FEATURES: threat to identity

63
64
65 **PAPER 6:**
66 Williams, Simon J. (2000) 'Chronic illness and biographical disruption or biographical disruption as chronic illness? Reflections on a core concept', *Sociology of Health & Illness*, 22(1); pp.40–67.
67
68 (p.41) Does a focus on 'disruption' mask as much as it reveals? Can equal weight be accorded both to chronic illness' role in the creation of biographical disruption and biographical disruption's role in the creation of chronic illness? Finally … are these process confined to chronic illness?
69
70 (paraphrased) Is re-negotiation of identities/biographical disruption a feature only of responses to chronic illness or is it more pervasive in relation to dealing with 'normal crises' - and therefore useful for understanding a wider range of experiences and situations?
71
72 (p.57) Confronted with a pluralization of life-style options and choices about everything from the food we eat to the clothes we wear, the occupations we pursue, to the sexual identities we adopt, the management of our bodies and our emotional selves becomes a continual process of biographical revisions and reversals, successes and failures.

TENSIONS: questions direction of influence

FEATURES: loss of control & choice
STRATEGIES: reconstruction (ongoing)

FIG 11.1 P1: THE LITERATURE NOTES AND CODES. DOC

NB: I have not listed the accompanying papers chronologically, but have, instead, ordered them in a way that aids the developing argument and associated refinement of the various theoretical concepts invoked by the over-arching theme of 'biographical disruption'. You may wish to read the notes (and, indeed the data excerpts) while covering up the accompanying coding framework, allowing you to compare notes later.

EXCERPTS ALL CODED UNDER THE BROAD THEME OF 'BIOGRAPHICAL DISRUPTION'

001

002
003

004 You can either get on with your life in the sense you're not going to have a baby – 'Let's just get on and take life as it comes'. Or you've (to partner) got to plan for a career break and we start planning to empty out the spare room and that sort of thing. You can't do it either, so we want to know what's going to happen.

❀ FEATURES: 'in limbo'
❀ FEATURES: threat to future plans

005 (YCL20; Man)

006

007 You know, I think it's just typical of me - to presume, you know, 'Well, I want to do this and that's when I'll have babies' and then you can't. All those years spent taking precautions ....

❀ STRATEGIES: looking back/castigating a past self

008 (WBY36; Woman)

009
010

011 Interviewer: Did they ask you if you wanted artificial donor insemination?
012 Woman: Not – not interested. I think it's too much of a grey area. We both feel that, really. At first I did ... I was sort of thinking in my mind, 'Well, Jack's sort of denying me the right to have a child, though, with a donor, but then I can see it form his point of view that, well, you know, it might go on for years and years and then something can spark it and he might turn round and say, 'That child isn't mine' – because really it wouldn't be, would it? Biologically it wouldn't and then you might as well adopt ...

❀ STRATEGIES: anticipating problems
❀ STRATEGIES: constructing future narrative
❀ TENSIONS: individual or couple?

013 (HHH64; Woman)

016 If we don't have a family what am I going to do for the next 30 to 40 years?
017 (DF85; Woman)

❀ FEATURES: threat to future plans
❀ FEATURES: threat to identity

020 Man: I can't see the point in worrying.
021 Woman: I don't think he understands what I'm going through, because
022 it's **me** that's the problem.
023 (ESC86 - Couple)

❀ TENSIONS: individual or couple?

026 I'm guilty until proven innocent and she's innocent until proven guilty
027 (YCL20; Man)

❀ TENSIONS: individual or couple?

030 I feel a failure (in tears). I've let Martin down.
031 (LHMR67; Woman)

❀ TENSIONS: individual or couple?

034 We were saying that the only way we could actually have taken control
035 was to decide **not** to do this (embark on ICSI) ... but then the fear is
036 then you would be left with the worry of 'What if ...?'
037 (PWH34; Man)

❀ STRATEGIES: taking control
❀ TENSIONS: between taking control & anticipating

040   We would do IVF – we've talked about this long and hard. If we don't, I think, down the line in 10 …20 years' time, we'd say, 'Well, what if we'd tried IVF?'

041   (VL061; Woman)

042

043

044   Last time I went 7 weeks and we were both convinced. I spend my life waiting …

045   (TCL60; Woman)

046

047

048   Woman: I have said that I don't want to get married or anything, as

049   it wouldn't be fair on him. Because I know that Dave really does want children and (to partner) you really are quite paternal, aren't you? And I think it would devastate him if he knew that he couldn't have his own. I'd probably up and leave him (laughs)…

050   Man: I'd say that, if the worst came to the worst, and we couldn't

051   have kids I'd still marry her – know what I mean? I wouldn't, like, get rid of her because she couldn't have kids.

052   Woman: I might just go anyway (laughs).

053   (BIH32; Couple)

054

055

056

057   If we've had a bad day, I say, 'The easiest thing would be for us to split up and him - if he wants a child – to go and have one with someone else'. I **do** mean it some days.

058   (VL061; Woman)

✿ STRATEGIES: taking control

✿ TENSIONS: between taking control & anticipating

✿ FEATURES: 'in limbo'

✿ TENSIONS: individual or couple?

✿ TENSIONS: individual or couple?

061 A friend has had 3 (IVF) attempts. Somewhere along the line you've got to put
a full stop to this and say, 'This can't go on forever',

062
063 (DF85; Man)
064

✿ STRATEGIES: taking control: calling a halt

065 We'll adopt. We know of other couples who have gone on for further treatment
and IVF. There's a girl at work who's had 4 IVF attempts. I'd maybe try it once …

066 (HH32; Woman)
067
068

✿ STRATEGIES: taking control: calling a halt

069 Woman: I was quite disappointed really, because all my friends, of course, you
know, sort of a few years ago – they all started
070 having their babies then, you see. So I thought, 'Why isn't
071 this happening to me?' I felt very disappointed.
072 Man: .... You feel a bit left out when other people have kids. One
073 of my friends, his partner was pregnant when I met him and
074 they've gone on to have a second baby. The older you get the further
you seem to get left out - well, in a way …

075 (PFD23; Couple)
076
077

✿ FEATURES: getting left behind

078 You just seem to get more and more disheartened, you know. You hear so many
people are pregnant and you think, 'We've still failed' ….

✿ FEATURES: comparison with others
✿ FEATURES: getting left behind

079
080
081 (LGR32; Woman)

082 My sister's just had her third - and she's only 26!
083 (BIH32; Woman)

♣ FEATURES: comparison with others
♣ FEATURES: getting left behind

084
085
086 I've been married before, you see, and I didn't want one then. But as soon as I met him I wanted one. (To partner) Sad aren't we?
087 (HHH64; Woman)

♣ TENSIONS: crisis or shifting priorities?

088
089 I think a lot of the problem is, as I say, we like to think that we're doing quite well in our lives and working hard – got a nice house and everything else – and people expect your life to be going on quite normally. And we - start seeing other couples having kids – people expect you to be having kids as well. So, obviously, (to partner) we've taken a lot of stick over the last 4 years, haven't we?

♣ FEATURES: comparison with others
♣ FEATURES: forced emotion work?
♣ FEATURES: getting left behind

090 (WBY36; Man)
091
092
093 When we first got married we were so careful - don't want to get pregnant now. We wanted to be able to save up plenty of money so that when we did start a family we would have a secure home and everything and then you think, 'Well, we've got the money- where's the baby?' you know. Well, I've said this to Steve before and it may be a negative thing to say, but, you know, we just sort of married and we've been married for eight and a half years now and you think … I feel annoyed that we waited so long before

♣ STRATEGIES: reconstructing the past/ castigating

we actually started trying. I mean, the only reason we did leave it so long
is what I've just said, so we could spend some quality time together before
a family came along and that we could have sufficient money to be able to
give a child or children a good home and then I keep kicking myself, you
know, thinking, 'Why did we leave it so long?' you know, 'We could have
managed it even if we hadn't much money'. Maybe if we'd started
2 or 3 years earlier we would have a baby by now ...

094 (DF85; Woman)
095

✿ STRATEGIES: reconstructing the past/ castigating

096 You know, I think it's just typical of me - to presume, you know, 'Well,
I want to do this and that' when I'll have babies' and then you can't. All
those years spent taking precautions ...

097 (WBY36; Woman)
098

✿ FEATURES: comparison with others
✿ FEATURES: getting left behind n
✿ STRATEGIES: emotion, work/ limits

099 I mean, we got invited to the christening (of her brother's baby), didn't we?
And we really didn't want to go, but we knew we had no choice. We couldn't
turn round and say, 'Well, I'm sorry, but we can't come'. We had to go ...
ehm ... and both of us said – when we knew the christening was coming
up – 'We don't want them to ask us to be godparents' ...ehm ... and they didn't.
They asked her sister instead and another couple who had nothing to do with
the family - they're not related or anything – and I sat feeling really jealous
that they hadn't asked us. They can't win! But it (the christening)
was quite an ordeal really (to partner) wasn't it?

100 (DF85; Woman)
101

✿ FEATURES: comparison with others
✿ FEATURES: getting left behind
✿ FEATURES: others doing 'emotion work'

102 Man: You feel a bit left out. I met a friend during a course, didn't I?
(to his partner) And, at that time, his girlfriend was already pregnant.
He's since become a very good friend, hasn't he? (to his partner)

103 Woman: Yes.

105 Man: And, em, and also it seems she's had another one.

108 Woman: I think the thing is, they aren't married, like, you know ... and what made it
                worse, really was that this baby was born and he was only 5 months old
                when his girlfriend got pregnant with the second one, so that sort of ...

109
110 Man: In fact, he was very reluctant to tell us – he had us guessing for quite a while.
111 (PFD23; Couple)

FIG 11.2 EXCERPTS ALL CODED UNDER THE BROAD THEME OF 'BIOGRAPHICAL DISRUPTION'

NB: When I use these data excerpts in workshops I usually photocopy them and literally cut them up. You may find it helpful to do this and to use large pieces of paper (on the large table recommended!) in order to play around with grouping and re-grouping them under different themes, categories and sub-categories as you develop and refine these. Again, you may initially choose to cover up the coding categories I have assigned to these excerpts and may be interested in trying out your own independent coding exercise.

Several of the papers reviewed here point out that individual experiences may differ significantly – even to the extent that some people may not report the dramatic discontinuity and loss of identity and meaning commonly identified in other studies. In addition, despite reporting some of the features associated with 'biographical disruption', the impact of chronic illness and the 'biographical work' in which people engage need not always be negative: there may be some positive aspects.

The Exley and Letherby (2001) paper is of particular interest as it reflects on data generated by two independent studies on very different topics. However, this serves to emphasize the salience of 'emotion work' as a strategy for dealing with and possibly minimizing the impact (of terminal cancer and sub-fertility, respectively) on relationships. The data excerpts presented in this exercise testify to the involvement of the couples in seeking to put such strategies into operation. A few of the excerpts indicate that it is not only the couples who are engaging in such 'emotion work', but friends and family 'tip-toe' around their feelings of vulnerability. Indeed, one of the excerpts raises the possibility that couples may, at times, be forced by others to engage in 'emotion work'. However, a couple of the excerpts suggest that the couples are also engaged in 'emotion work' with each other, as sub-fertility raises important and uncomfortable questions about the viability of their joint future. This highlights another aspect of this dataset which challenges the inherently individual/biographical emphasis of Bury's notion of 'biographical disruption'. The couples interviewed for this study are wrestling not just with the implications of sub-fertility for their personal biographies, but with the implications for their biography as a couple. Sub-fertility is a condition that frequently affects only one person in each couple and, thus, even if fertility treatment fails, childlessness is not a fate that need necessarily befall both – unless, that is, they remain together as a unit.

Williams' (2000) paper poses some challenging questions, suggesting that 'biographical disruption' may be even more significant for the individuals involved than is their chronic condition. He also points out 'biographical disruption' may be more pervasive than is suggested by its confinement to studying chronic illness. He suggests that 'biographical disruption' may be a feature of responses to a wide range of 'normal crises' and that, therefore, it may help to illuminate other transitions and situations that impact on identity and self-image. Sub-fertility (which does not usually have a clinical cause) presents an interesting potential 'case study' of the relevance of 'biographical disruption' in the more general context of 'coupledom' and child-bearing. This dataset, therefore, allows us to study the impact of 'biographical disruption' without having to contend with the onset and physical repercussions of chronic illness, which makes it more difficult to speculate meaningfully about the direction of causality. The frequency and the poignancy with which the couples in this study invoked the tensions and challenges involved in the 'biographical disruption' associated with their experience of sub-fertility certainly indicate that sub-fertility is important as a social rather than clinical phenomenon – precisely because it disrupts their biography as individuals and as a couple. It is not sub-fertility *per se* that is seen as the problem, but rather the way in which it compromises futures, pasts and present relationships and identities.

12
PRESENTING AND WRITING UP QUALITATIVE RESEARCH

AIMS

- This chapter equips the reader to rise constructively to the challenges involved in writing-up qualitative research.
- It provides guidance on the ordering of material and on providing an 'audit trail' that demonstrates a thorough approach to analysis.
- It shows how to contextualize a piece of qualitative research by acknowledging its limitations but also by considering the transferability of findings.
- Hints are provided with regard to using the process of writing to further interrogate data.
- Finally, it offers detailed advice with regard to getting published and formulating a publications plan.

INTRODUCTION

Notwithstanding the importance of modified grounded theory approaches, potential papers also play an important role in determining the direction in which analysis proceeds. Different coding levels can be utilized on writing the very different papers required – a report to the funding body, an overview 'findings' paper, a more in-depth paper on a few selected themes, or a much more theoretical piece which does not rely to any great extent on reproducing data excerpts. There are many challenges involved in publishing qualitative research: the pressure to produce summary papers, the constraints of word limits, and the difficulty of telling succinctly the complicated story of how the research project evolved.

The dangers of succumbing to formulaic 'checklist'-type accounts are discussed and a middle ground is advocated, whereby careful attention is paid to the appropriateness for the specific research project and rationale for techniques such as purposive sampling, multiple coding, triangulation and respondent validation. Researchers are strongly advised simply to tell the story of the project and explain the research design decisions made rather than inserting references to the listed techniques after the event, by way of a belated claim to rigour.

It is argued that it is a good idea to develop a publications strategy for each project, which lists potential journals to which papers might be submitted, takes account of the different audiences that might be addressed, and which plans the sequence in which papers should appear. Some examples are provided from past projects.

THE CHALLENGES OF WRITING UP QUALITATIVE RESEARCH

There are many challenges involved in presenting and publishing qualitative research. The standard journal format of introduction/background, methods, sample, results, discussion, and conclusions/recommendations does not leave much room for manoeuvre. Particularly taxing is the distinction, between results and discussion, especially given the iterative nature of the qualitative analysis process. However, it is sometimes possible to challenge this. I have on occasion used the heading of 'Findings' to combine the two, and sometimes this is successful.

Word limits often present another challenge, although this varies considerably from journal to journal. It can be hard to describe a complex study design and methodology, particularly given the absence of available templates. Telling the 'story' of the project is often the only way to explain the gradual refining of the focus and development of the analysis, including the role of reflexivity. It can be useful to reference methodological papers to support your choices of methods and approach to analysis – if you can find any that are appropriate. It is important not to fall into the trap of employing formulaic appeals to 'purposive sampling', 'grounded theory' and the like, however, as this can merely obfuscate, especially if you are invoking these terms after the event, rather than as an accurate description of what you actually did. Some qualitative researchers despair at the word limits of journals such as the *British Medical Journal*, but this can provide good discipline in forming your argument and cutting down on extraneous material. Another way to address this is to tailor a set of papers to different journals. Journals such as the *BMJ* are ideal places to publish an overview paper, which is generally similar to a final report to funding bodies. A further difficulty is presented in terms of selecting quotes to illustrate your argument. Qualitative researchers delight in swapping horror stories along the lines of: 'And do you know what they said? They said to remove all my quotes!' However, nowadays journals are a bit more accommodating and it is often possible to include quotes in a (limited) number of tables which do not count towards the final calculations of word length. Some journals, such as the *BMJ*, also have a facility whereby it is possible to lodge additional material, but I am not altogether convinced that this resource is used very much by readers.

When you come to producing theoretical papers, however, word limits are likely to present much less of a problem: first, because of the more generous work allowance of the discipline-specific journals that you are likely to be targeting; but, secondly, because theoretical papers (unlike the 'overview papers' discussed above) do not need to use large amounts of data to pursue their argument. What is essential, however, is that you can demonstrate that your argument has been systematically built up through thorough interrogation of distinctions, qualifications and patterning in your data (as outlined in Chapter 11).

Academic life abounds with reference to the period of writing-up as though it were a discrete phase, signalling the culmination of a piece of work. However, apart from generic student guides, there is little advice that is relevant to presenting qualitative research findings:

> Sociological (and indeed, other disciplines') methods texts … deal … with what soci-
> ologists contend happens when research is carried out, and not with how sociologists
> go about the process of translating 'the research' – a multi-faceted experience in
> time – into writing. This latter experience is rarely written about in a standard research
> account, but is instead systematically stripped from it. (Aldridge, 1993: 54–55)

ORDERING OF MATERIAL

In advising students about writing-up I often make a distinction between what are 'helpful notes to yourself' and headings that are meaningful in terms of developing your argument or separating and categorizing material. Notes to yourself facilitate recall of specific sections or examples you may wish to include. These do not necessarily produce a sound rationale for sub-headings which set out your argument or trace the 'thread' through your explanations.

Jan Morris, the acclaimed travel writer, has chosen to provide us with intriguing sub-headings, surely designed originally as aide-mémoire for the writer (suggesting that she may have acquired this skill, as do ethnographers, through producing shortened key points so that they can write up at their leisure). Chapter 17 of her book, for example, begins with: '*Summer – exiles – Freud – Anastasia – going native – varied refugees – meeting a Nazi – "and me!"*' (Morris, 2006: 137). The meaning of these is not immediately apparent and retaining these is perhaps an example of Morris's playful sub-commentary on the craft of writing that underpins her entire book.

PRESENTING YOUR FINDINGS

As well as summarizing your main findings, the main challenge in presenting your qualitative research findings is to provide reassurance that you've been systematic. This is where your grids (see Chapter 11) stand you in good stead. However, it is important not to over-burden the reader with lots of numbers. Again you need to have counted, but you need not reproduce all of these 'aide-mémoirs'. All that is required is reassurance that you have engaged in some sort of counting exercise. I like to use the analogy of geometric proofs – at least as this was taught when I was a school child. We were always advised not to erase our rough working, but rather to draw a line through this and leave it to one side so that the examiner could check this and perhaps award us extra marks for getting the process right even if our answers were wrong. It is in a sim-ilar spirit that you should try to indicate that you have checked the grounds for making claims about the popularity of particular perspectives or accounts. You can do this by using phrases such as 'all except one', 'only two', or 'virtually all', 'most' or 'a few'. Of course you should be able to substantiate such claims further (sometimes by going on to describe characteristics involved in exceptions and furnishing a potential explanation) and should certainly not use these phrases strategically or dishonestly.

It is also important to acknowledge any exceptions and to incorporate these in your analysis, where space allows. If space is particularly tight you can sometimes just acknowledge that you are outlining broad patterns, but that there were some individ-uals or situations that did not quite fit. Perhaps here you might be able to reference another paper in press or in preparation. Likewise, it is advisable to avoid invoking 'overly neat' fits with typologies – unless you issue a similar 'disclaimer'.

TRANSFERABILITY

In making a case for the transferability of the theoretical framework I had presented, drawing on my empirical study of professional socialization for social work training, I sought to contextualize what some might label an 'intrinsic case study' (Yin, 1994) of one social work course by implicitly comparing it with training for and the prac-tice of other professions. This involved me in theorizing as to which aspects of professions increase the likelihood of training making 'transsituational' demands of recruits. Social work is a highly visible profession, broad in its scope in terms of types of intervention and client groups involved, which does not require the use of props or specialized equipment. Most members of the general public, including students' friends and family, will have preconceived notions as to what it involves and are likely to have ideas about its merits. It has a professional lore which specifies the personal qualities necessary for practitioners and course requirements include the capacity for personal change or development, which was echoed in students' stated aspirations for the course. However, unlike recruits to Catholic seminaries, social work students were not required to undergo their training in isolation from the outside world. This pro-vided more opportunities for the interaction between personal and professional worlds and identities, and hence, I argued, was more likely to provide opportunities for 'transsituational' demands to arise.

I concluded my paper on 'transsituational' demands as follows:

> 'It is possible to conceive of occupations as forming a continuum with regard to the likelihood of their making 'transsituational' demands on the recruit. At one end of the continuum would be social work, the people-processing occupation par excellence. ... Located somewhere in the middle would be such professions as medicine and law which, although dealing with people, have less capacity for transsituational application, due both to the need for some props and their greater reliance on technical expertise. ... At the other extreme ... would be highly technical occupations [such as architecture or engineering, which stress] selection criteria other than ... personality.
>
> In the absence of any comparable studies of professional socialization as involving the negotiation of 'transsituational' demands, the observations made here are necessarily tentative and speculative in nature. ... However, I would argue that the categories of frame-work activity outlined in this paper ... can be used to study empirically the internalization of the beliefs associated with any occupational role, or indeed, any role which is assumed in adult life and which involves a crucial transition in the life cycle of the individual. (Barbour, 1985: 529–530)

THE CRAFT OF WRITING

There is surprisingly little explicit guidance about writing, apart from general 'how to' manuals aimed at a generic student audience. Writing up qualitative research, however, involves more than acquiring presentational skills in order simply to report on the achievements of their project.

> Students are trained to observe, listen, question and participate. Yet they are trained to conceptualize writing as 'writing up' the research rather than as a method of discovery. Almost unthinkingly, qualitative research training validates the mechanistic model of writing, even though that model shuts down the creativity and sensibilities of the individual researcher. (Richardson, 1994: 517)

However, the relationship between the apparently mechanistic and the creative is a complex one. In supervision sessions one student was wrestling with the structure of her thesis and how to write up her findings. She complained that she was 'going round in circles'. This is a common experience and was not a weakness of this student. Rather, it reflects the iterative process involved in analysis, which continues even as we 'write up'. Indeed, some of the most valuable insights may occur at this stage: 'Writing is also a way of "knowing" – a method of discovery and analysis. By writing in different ways, we discover new aspects of our topic and our relationship to it. Form and content are inseparable.' (Richardson, 1994: 516). The student in question had produced a first draft of a findings chapter which looked at the experiences of male partners of women with breast cancer. In order to build on the existing body of literature – and because it made obvious sense given the topic – this initial analysis had focused on examining the men's experiences at various points throughout the clinical trajectory of illness and treatment. The design of the study, which relied on recruiting men whose partners were at different stages in this trajectory, had importantly established that the intervals between the identified and most commonly studied stages were sometimes highly significant and problematic for the male partners, since these periods were often characterized by uncertainty and anxiety. However, through the accounts of the men, there were tantalizing little details about their individual situations and relationships with their wives and I wondered if these might make equally useful headings under which to organize and interrogate the data. Taking breast cancer as the constant backdrop had de-emphasized the importance of the couple's relationship as the other enduring feature of the experiences that were being recounted, and perhaps this merited further exploration. While some couples had apparently led very separate lives, pursuing different activities independently of each other, and some had domestic arrangements that were organized along very traditional gendered lines, others portrayed themselves as 'each other's best friends'. Focusing on these aspects of couples' lives and relationships, the student then went about systematically interrogating the similarities and differences in the men's accounts of the impact of breast cancer. As she wrote, she found that new ideas and possible explanations occurred to her, underlining the potential of writing as an activity to facilitate discovery. The finished thesis (Harrow, 2006) contains a chapter on the social context and has sub-headings that relate to work and employment, roles and relationships, and ages and stages (in terms of whether couples had dependent children or grandchildren, and such like). This afforded her a new arena in which to pursue comparative analysis and provided a much richer and more theoretically informed account, drawing on and interrogating theoretical frameworks, such as that afforded by family systems theory.

Trustworthiness and authenticity

> It is, by and large, the ethnographer's direct personal contact with others that is honoured by readers as providing a particularly sound basis for reliable knowledge. (van Maanen, 1995: 3)

Seale (1999) has alluded to the many and varied rhetorical textual devices used by qualitative researchers to substantiate and render persuasive the claims they are making. Academic researchers certainly do not have a monopoly on good writing, and some of us may struggle, particularly those without an arts faculty background. Indeed, much can be learned from perusing exemplary writing produced by writers in parallel genres, which nevertheless share some of the hallmarks of our own writing 'trade'. The task of the travel writer has similarities with that of the ethnographer and, in so far as it draws also on 'informal interview' with 'respondents', also provides inspiration with regard to how to utilize such insights in our own accounts. Rather than being simply a catalogue of sights and sounds – both exotic and mundane – permeated by a sprinkling of relevant history, the consummate travel writer may display a healthy scepticism alongside remarkable attention to detail and can provide an illuminating reflexive commentary, which helps us as readers to process and mediate the text. The following selected excerpts serve to illustrate the skills of the travel writer, whose craft is really quite similar to that of the ethnographer.

> It is 5 May, the day of the Roof-Race. As the horse-race is to Siena, as the bull-running is to Pamplona, as Derby Day is to the English, or even perhaps Bastille Day to the French, so the day of the Roof-Race, is to the people of Hav. ... The goblet is still presented ... at the finishing line, and the winner remains one of the heroes of Hav for the rest of his life – several old men have been admiringly pointed out to me in the streets as Roof-Race winners of long ago. The race is so demanding that nobody over the age of twenty-five has ever run it – no woman at all yet – and only once in recorded history has it been won by the same runner twice ... (Morris, 2006: 71–72)

> It is not known for sure how this fascinating institution began, though there are plenty of plausible theories. ... The most familiar account of the race's origins is this. During a rising against the Ottoman Turks, soon after their occupation of Hav, a messenger was sent clandestinely from Cyprus to make contact with the patriotic leader Gamal Abdul Hussein, who was operating from a secret headquarters in the Medina. The messenger landed safely on the waterfront at midnight, but found every entrance to the Old City blocked, and every street patrolled by Turkish soldiers ... he was spotted by Turkish sentries and a hue and cry was raised; but ... without a second thought he leapt up on to the ramparts of the Medina, and began running helter-skelter over the rooftops towards the mosque. Up clambered the soldiers after him, scores of them, and there began a wild chase among the chimney-pots and wind-towers; but desperately leaping over alleyways, slithering down gutters, swarming over eaves and balustrades, the messenger found his way through an upper window of Gamal's house, presented his message, and died, there and then, as Hav legendary heroes must, of a cracked but indomitable heart.
>
> Such is the popular version, the one that used to get into the guide-books. ... Magda has another version altogether. ... Most Havians, though, seem to accept the story of the messenger; and in my view, if it wasn't true in the first place, so many centuries of belief have made it true now. (Morris, 2006: 71–73)

These excerpts come from the book *Last Letters from Hav*, published in 1985, before the occurrence – we are told by the author of the subsequent *Hav* (Morris, 2006) – of the cataclysm of 1985 (known nowadays as the Intervention) and which fundamentally changed the city and made its name familiar throughout the world. Morris did not, however, provide precise details as to Hav's location and this omission plunged the world of travel writing and her wider readership into endless and invigorating speculation as to its true identity. In the Epilogue to *Hav,* which comprises *Last Letters from Hav* and the sequel *Hav of the Myrmidons*, Morris (2006) recounts being accosted in the Map Room of the Royal Geographical Society by a reader eager to have her point out the exact whereabouts of Hav. Morris then reveals, 'Only one single correspondent, an octogenarian lady in Iowa, saw my little book as an allegory'. That the above accounts – and Hav itself – are fictional only serves to reinforce the points I wish to make about the production of persuasive and convincing writing. Writing is not just a matter of recording one's experiences and producing illustrative snippets or quotes, it is itself an active pursuit that can transform diverse observations and insights into a compelling argument or explanation.

> In preparing for any telling or writing, and in imagining the perspective of his specific audience, the researcher is apt to see his data in new ways: finding new analytic possibilities, or implications he has never before sensed. This process of late discovery is full of surprises, sometimes even major ones, which lead to serious reflection on what one has 'really' discovered. Thus, it is not simply a matter of the researcher writing down what is in his notes or in his head; writing or telling as activities exhibit their own properties which provide conditions for discovery. (Schatzman and Strauss, 1973: 132)

SOME ADVICE ON PUBLISHING

With the advent of the Research Assessment Exercise in the UK context and the increasing competitiveness of academic life everywhere, publishing is essential for a successful research career. There are many challenges involved, some of which adhere to publishing in general and some of which arise particularly in relation to publishing qualitative papers. Although qualitative researchers often complain about what they perceive as an unsympathetic publishing environment, some of the difficulties encountered may stem from a lack of understanding of the imperatives of the publishing industry and the processes involved rather than being a feature of writing up qualitative research *per se*.

Qualitative researchers frequently bemoan the lack of availability of templates that allow for concise accounts of the process involved in carrying out their studies, sometimes looking wistfully to the purported usefulness of descriptions that characterize quantitative research, such as 'double-blind randomized control trial'. Certainly, given the lively debate with respect to virtually all aspects of the qualitative research endeavour, it is difficult to find non-contentious ways of describing our approaches. However, it is possible to cite relevant methodological papers in terms of justifying our approaches. If such papers do not exist, there is always the possibility of publishing them yourself. If you are able to publish this in advance of submitting your 'findings' papers (see discussion below on the sequencing of publications), then this can be very helpful.

Sometimes we indulge in telling each other horror stories about the lack of understanding of journal reviewers or editors, assuming that their antipathy towards our papers stems from our qualitative focus. There may be many other reasons, however, for papers being rejected. One of the most common is the failure to familiarize oneself with the style and content of the journal involved and the audience for this publication. It is also useful to read journal editorials – new editors may wish to take a journal in a new direction and editorials may signal a willingness to consider papers that might previously have been deemed unsuitable for that journal. It is important to remember that the published papers you read are generally not the author/s' 'first stab' at writing. Papers may have gone through several versions before being accepted for the journal.

Perhaps because they are daunted by the quality of the published papers they read, many novice writers tend to delay submitting their papers to journals until they feel they have honed them to an acceptable standard. While it is advisable to consult the journal in question and to attempt to produce a coherent and well-argued account, it is impossible to 'second guess' reviewers' comments. Do give them an opportunity to provide constructive criticism. Most reviewers are incredibly generous with their time and suggestions, and are able to provide ideas for restructuring your paper or developing your argument that would never occur to you, however many revisions you produce prior to submission. Most reviewers do provide constructive suggestions and a good editor will weed out any disparaging remarks that are best not passed on to authors. Do take reviewers' comments seriously: you need not make each and every one of the recommended changes, but it is helpful (not least for the editor/s) if you send an accompanying letter with your re-submitted paper, showing where you have made changes and providing a rationale for omitting to take others 'on board'.

Rejection always stings, but it is as well to be prepared for this – do remember that you don't know how many journals have been approached or versions produced by others before they succeed in getting an article published. A paper that is rejected by one journal may very well be highly suitable for the readership of another journal – and good reviewers or editors will often provide suggestions along these lines.

Getting involved as a reviewer yourself is enormously helpful in terms of exposing you to the craft of writing – and, crucially, re-writing. Journal editors are always on the lookout for new reviewers and this is a very good way of ensuring that you are at the cutting-edge of ongoing debates in your field. Although some journals use blind reviewing, whereby neither the reviewer nor the author is provided with each others' identities, others do reveal the identity of authors and some are experimenting with opt-in systems whereby reviewers can choose to identify themselves. It can sometimes be off-putting for relatively junior reviewers (as sometimes happens) to be confronted with papers written by senior figures in their discipline and, in this instance, they are probably well advised not to reveal their own identity. Where reviewers do provide contact details, this can sometimes herald the beginning of long and fruitful collaborations, and it can be helpful at least to make contact in order to clarify their suggestions, such as asking for references to relevant published work that you may have overlooked in your initial version of your paper.

FORMULATING A PUBLICATION PLAN

Although quality remains as important as quantity, we are all under increasing pressure to maximize our publications. It is, therefore, helpful to produce a publication plan, which allows you to think a bit more strategically. Qualitative research, mercifully, is not subject to the 'positive publication bias' noted with regard to quantitative studies. Since there are generally no clearly formulated hypotheses to test, so, too, there are unlikely to be any nasty surprises and it should be possible to capitalize on the publication potential of unanswered questions or puzzling findings.

A further advantage of developing a publication plan well in advance of writing up your research is that it allows you to address that ever-contentious issue of formulating a publications strategy and allocating authorship. An example is provided by Barry et al. (1999), who capitalized on the insights provided by a multidisciplinary team in terms of the focus on separate papers and team members' knowledge of a variety of journals. Although some of your findings may appear unremarkable when looked at through the lens of your own discipline or sub-discipline, they may be considered novel in another field; one of the aims of publishing is, after all, to convey our message to a wider audience.

It is useful to identify the different types of paper you could write – review papers, overview findings papers, articles on specific theoretical issues or phases of the study. However, see the discussion (in Chapter 7) about the potential limitations of publishing quantitative and qualitative findings in different journals. It is well worth keeping an eye on relevant journals to see whether any appear to be amenable to publishing papers that seek to integrate quantitative and qualitative findings rather than advocating a more purist approach. Don't be discouraged, however, if this does not seem to happen – you might just be the person to publish that ground-breaking article!

With reference to producing 'findings' papers, a useful strategy is to try to match coding categories or level of analysis with potential papers. Don't forget that you can reconfigure your coding schemes to facilitate this process. Think of coding categories as you would a pack of cards – sometimes you may want to sort by aces; other times you may want to pull out all the hearts. As would have become apparent as you engaged with the exercises in Chapters 9 and 10, some data excerpts can be coded with reference to several codes, and these codes themselves can be grouped under several different thematic headings – depending on what you are writing. Make sure, however, that you don't discard any provisional analysis and always keep copies of all versions of your coding frame.

Don't rule out revisiting your data for further papers. Qualitative research – particularly if it addresses theoretical issues – is unlikely to have a 'sell-by date'. Whereas quantitative researchers live in fear of someone beating them to the finishing line in terms of discoveries, this is much less of an issue for those of us engaged in qualitative research.

Think also about turning difficulties to your advantage. For example, problems with gaining access or recruitment, or obtaining ethical approval can provide an opportunity for a paper, provided of course that you can rise above your own poignant story to make points of more general relevance.

Giving conference papers can be an invaluable aid to developing your analyses and theoretical explanations. Many conferences also have associated journals and potential reviewers are likely to be in the audience at your oral presentations. Therefore, feedback in this context can be especially helpful.

Think also about turning difficulties to your advantage. For example, problems with gaining access to recruitment, or obtaining ethical approval (McDonach et al., in press) can provide an opportunity for a paper or a methodological paper before your findings papers are due to appear, you can provide brief details in subsequent papers and refer to these published sources. Importantly, this allows you to conserve space for discussing your findings, since these are already helpfully contextualized by reference to your own earlier papers. In making such plans it helps to think about the lag-time of various journals. Annual General Meetings held at conferences with associated journals can often provide valuable up-to-date information on average turnaround times and acceptance rates for their associated journals, and can be invaluable in formulating your own publication plan.

An example is provided by my own experience of publishing – and, indeed, failing to publish – from a study of the impact of HIV/AIDS on professionals. This shows also the role of serendipity and academic networks as well as the potential to write different sorts of paper for a range of audiences.

AN EXAMPLE OF PUBLICATIONS FROM ONE STUDY: THE DEMANDS OF HIV/AIDS FOR PROFESSIONALS

Two publications arose from presenting papers at the 'social Aspects of AIDS Conferences', held in London in 1991 and 1993, respectively (with a relatively short lag-time between presentation and publication). Their 'soundbite-type' titles reflect their provenance as conference papers:

Barbour, R.S. (1993) ' "I don't sleep with my patients – do you sleep with yours?": Dealing with staff tensions and conflicts in AIDS-related work', in P. Aggleton, P. Davies and G. Hart (eds) *AIDS: Facing the Second Decade*, London: Falmer.

Barbour, R.S. (1994) 'A telling tale: AIDS workers and confidentiality', in P. Aggleton, P. Davies and G. Hart (eds) *AIDS: Foundations for the Future*, London: Taylor & Francis, Chapter 11 (pp. 147–158).

(Continued)

This second chapter was the result of substantial revision and I am particularly grateful to Graham Hart for his editorial suggestions.

Although I had hoped to publish a review paper to which I could refer in subsequent 'findings' papers, this did not turn out according to plan. The 'review' paper from this study, in the event, was published after these two 'findings' chapters – or at least, too late to reference it in either. This was due to a combination of circumstances. I had produced an MRC discussion paper based on a review of literature carried out near the start of the project:

Barbour, R.S. (1991) 'The impact of HIV/AIDS on front-line workers: A review of the literature', *MRC Medical Sociology Unit Working Paper No. 28*.

However, the dearth of qualitative studies on this topic meant that the review – and a version submitted to a journal and rejected by it – was largely descriptive. Only the subsequent publication of several key papers allowed the discussion to 'move up a gear' and led to a reworked review paper which was then published in another journal:

Barbour, R.S. (1994) 'The impact of working with people with AIDS: A review of the literature', *Social Science and Medicine,* 39(2): 221–232.

Although this was a qualitative study, it involved interviews with 153 people (and covered all professionals in specialist AIDS posts in the four cities involved – with the exception of two settings which withheld consent). This meant that I was also able to publish an overview findings paper that treated the data in a 'quantitative' manner:

Barbour, R.S. (1995) 'The implications of HIV/AIDS for a range of workers in the Scottish context', *AIDS Care,* 7(4): 521–525.

Around half of my interviewees were nurses and I therefore opted to submit a paper that dealt exclusively with the challenges for this group to a nursing journal:

Barbour, R.S. (1995) 'Responding to a challenge: Nursing care and AIDS', *International Journal of Nursing Studies,* 32(3): 213–223.

I did not publish any methodological papers from this study – perhaps because I was initially uncertain as to the advisability of using (or owning up to using) a pragmatic combination of re-coding into an SPSS-amenable format in order to identify patterning for further interrogation using more conventional qualitative methods. However, I am now more confident about such an approach and have subsequently referred to it in this volume (see Chapter 10). An interesting development, however, was a paper that emerged as a product of a support group for female researchers working in the HIV/AIDS field, which reflected on some of our experiences in the field:

Green, G., Barbour, R.S., Barnard, M. and Kitzinger, J. (1993) 'Who wears the trousers? Sexual harassment in research settings', *Women's Studies International Forum,* 16 (6): 627–637.

There were two further 'spin-offs' from this study. Familiarity with the HIV/AIDS literature allowed me to focus on this for a chapter in a textbook:

Barbour, R.S. (1993) 'HIV/AIDS and medical sociology in the nineties', Chapter 4 in M. Haralambos (ed.) *Developments in Sociology*, Ormskirk: Causeway, Chapter 4 (pp. 79–95).

The other 'spin-off' involved an edited collection, which arose from discussions with my co-editor at successive conferences, where we found ourselves presenting papers from separate studies, but visiting some of the same themes and dilemmas. This led us to believe that other researchers in the AIDS field might be similarly exercised by the same issues concerning the social production of knowledge in this burgeoning research field. We subsequently persuaded other anthropologists and sociologists to write about their own experiences in the following book:

Barbour, R.S. and Huby, G. (eds) (1998) *Meddling with Mythology: AIDS and the Social Construction of Knowledge*, London: Routledge.

Some of these papers were planned, while others arose as a result of collaborations, giving conference presentations and networking.

HINTS ON PUBLISHING

- Identify journals to which you might submit and familiarize yourself with their style and focus.
- Identify the different types of paper you could write – review papers, overview findings papers, papers on specific issues or phases of the study.
- Use your successive coding frames in order to help plan papers to provide overviews as well as more in-depth examinations of specific issues or theoretical frameworks.
- Make sure you reference relevant debates, especially those that have appeared in the journal to which you are submitting.
- Identify potential papers and journals and be prepared for rejection by having alternatives in mind. (Bear in mind the different audiences and focus of journals)
- Perhaps, though, the best advice of all is to read, read, and read.

FURTHER READING

You may wish to read a fuller account of how the full dataset from the sub-fertility study was subsequently revisited to interrogate the theoretical framework of 'biographical disruption':

Aldridge (1993) 'The textual disembodiment of knowledge in research account writing', *Sociology*, 27(1): 53–66.

Barbour, R.S. (2007, submitted) 'Sub-fertility and "biographical disruption": An empirical exploration of the usefulness of a theoretical framework', *Sociological Research Online*.

Loseke, D.R. and Cahill, S.E. (2004) 'Publishing qualitative manuscripts: lessons learned', in C. Seale (eds) *Qualitative Research Practice*, London: Sage, pp. 576–591.

Richardson, L. (1994) 'Writing: a method of inquiry', in N.K. Denzin and Y.S. Lincoln (eds) *Handbook of Qualitative Research*, London: Sage, pp. 516–529.

EXERCISE

I suggest that you return to the exercises you carried out at the end of Chapters 10 and 11 and that you write up an account of the process of analysis you followed and the insights that they provided into couples' experiences of sub-fertility. There is no right or wrong way of doing this, but the challenge is to make transparent the process you engaged in, while providing reassurance that you've been systematic and thorough. Once you've carried out this exercise, you might be interested to read selected excerpts from the final project report produced for this real life-study (see below).

A LONGITUDINAL STUDY OF OUTCOMES IN A SAMPLE OF SUB-FERTILE COUPLES ATTENDING A FERTILITY CLINIC: EXCERPTS

Introduction

This study sought to chart over a 12-month period the experiences of a sample of heterosexual couples referred to one fertility clinic, regardless of treatment options pursued. The intention was to explore the range of alternative options presented to couples and to document couples' decision-making processes as these unfolded.

Excerpt 1 – (Limitations)

It is important to bear in mind, however, that this study concerns a clinic population and may, thus, by definition, have excluded couples who have resolved their fertility problems without recourse to fertility treatment. This could, in theory, cover a number of options: ranging from those who have pursued investigations but have decided not to embark on treatment; those who have taken a more fatalistic approach, continuing to try to conceive naturally; those who have decided to adopt; or those who have resigned themselves to remaining childless. Future research into the experiences of a wider range of couples confronting fertility problems could provide valuable insights by further contextualizing the decision-making processes engaged in by the couples in the present study.

Excerpt 2 – (Age and perceptions of sub-fertility – issues identified in the exercise at the end of Chapter 10)

As might have been expected, age – especially the age of the women trying to conceive – was an important factor in couples' perceptions of the urgency of their fertility problems. Women over or nearing 30 years of age tended to express more concern than did younger women with regard to the potential for 'running out of time' and most were aware, even at their first interview, of the age cut-off for NHS treatment. However, this was not true for all of the women in this position. Although many of her friends had produced children while in their 20s, one 33-year-old woman told the interviewer: 'Age has never bothered me' (*FHFN63: F; first interview*)

As regards women under 30 years of age, the picture was more complex, with some expressing concerns about running out of time while others viewed their relatively young age as a cause for optimism. One 27-year-old woman stressed repeatedly throughout her interview that she did not feel that the 'clock was ticking' (*YCL20*) and another woman just under 30 years of age commented: 'I'm still young enough. I'm quite relaxed.' (*HH32: F; second interview; aged 29 years*)

Ideas as to what constituted 'having left things too late' varied from couple to couple and drew on notions about the optimum age for having babies: 'It could maybe be another 5 years – that would really worry me – I don't want to be a really old mum'. (*BIH32: F; first interview; aged 29 years*)

Excerpt 3 – (Contextualizing comments about Age)

However, differences in couples' responses were not entirely explained by differences in age of the women concerned: several other factors appeared to influence their perceptions – most importantly relationships with members of their peer group and the extent to which their friends, and sometimes former partners, were currently involved in childbearing and childrearing.

The husband (aged 31 years) of the youngest woman in the study (aged 20 years) explained: 'I don't feel this biological clock imperative as much as F' (*HSW17: M; first interview*). However, this couple's differing perceptions were not related only to gender – the husband already had three children from a previous relationship. This highlights the significance which the birth of a baby can have with regard to consolidating new partnerships and moving on from previous relationships.

While reproduction is a very private matter, non-production of babies is highly visible, as couples' lives are played out against the backdrop of friendship and family networks. With the exception of the one couple mentioned above (where most of the woman's friends had had babies several years earlier), all of the couples whose peer group were currently involved in childbearing and childrearing expressed concerns about 'getting left behind' as their friends moved in to parenthood.

Excerpt 4 – (Contextualizing experiences and perceptions – the couple rather than the individual as the unit and implications for the concept of 'biographical disruption' – see further discussion in the exercise at the end of Chapter 11)

Only one of the couples alluded to the age of the man. With the man aged 48 years and the woman aged 28, this couple had the biggest age gap between them and the man was also the oldest person in the sample. In recounting her latest round of visits to the clinic and her GP, the woman of this couple considered the implications for her husband of a delay in her conceiving:

They said at the clinic – and my GP said too – that there are some women where they just can't find any reason for it – who just can't conceive and she said what sometimes happens is that just before menopause, when your hormones change and stuff, a lot of women fall pregnant. It seems ages away. I don't want to wait that long and poor M will be in his 60s … late 50s! (*MH85: F; third interview*)

(NB: Sub-headings in parenthesis have been added for the purposes of this discussion: different sub-headings were used in the original report.)

13
NEW CHALLENGES AND PERENNIAL DILEMMAS

AIMS

- This Chapter examines critically both the possibilities and challenges involved in recent developments, including the potential of the internet and the resource of archived qualitative data.
- It will highlight, in particular, some of the ethical issues involved, arguing that these throw into sharp focus considerations that we should be aware of throughout our qualitative research practice.
- It is argued that such new challenges also serve to highlight perennial dilemmas for qualitative researchers, as we take a critical perspective with regard to issues of power and representation.
- Participatory research approached, in particular, should lead us to ask some – perhaps uncomfortable, but necessary – questions about our mandate to research and the uses to which our findings are put.
- Finally, readers are urged to remain mindful of the policy, political and funding climate in which our research is carried out and how this shapes our responses. Again, it is essential that we maintain a critical perspective.

INTRODUCTION

This chapter examines both the opportunities and challenges afforded by recent developments, such as the internet and secondary analysis of qualitative data. While both raise exciting new possibilities, they also introduce perennial dilemmas in relation to the role and positioning of the researcher. Issues of power are discussed, with particular reference to participatory approaches and our 'mandate to research' and interpret. The chapter also examines the dilemmas involved in the dissemination of qualitative research and the use to which our research is put.

QUALITATIVE RESEARCHING ONLINE

One of the most interesting of recent developments, in terms of new opportunities it affords for qualitative research has been the appearance of the World Wide Web. 'Harvesting' existing online data certainly can afford economies of time and effort, while still allowing the researcher to embed her/his analysis in wider socio-political issues (for example Stubbs, 1999). The immediacy of the internet and its enormous popularity make for myriad research possibilities. As well as affording access to individuals and groups world-wide, the internet can also afford researchers the opportunity to study groups where physical fieldwork contact might put them in some danger. For example, Geistenfeld, Grant and Chiang (2003) used the internet to study extremist groups. Moreover, using online resources allows for a variety of research approaches, ranging from cyber-ethnography (ward, 1999), which studies online communications in their own right (Hine, 2006), to 'real-time interviewing' (Chen and Hinton, 1999). Notably, it is a flexible resource which allows for different levels of researcher engagement and input. Bloor et al. (2001) point out that whereas 'real-time' discussions can be very rapid and difficult to follow, asynchronous exchanges which unfold over time may be easier to process. However, the choice will depend, as always, on the research question being posed and the types of data that researchers wish to generate.

In relation to carrying out 'virtual focus groups' online, Bloor et al. (2001) highlight the advantages of the internet in terms of its immediacy and capacity to overcome the constraints associated with geographical distance. For example, Kenny's (2005) experience showed that the internet was invaluable in accessing widely dispersed nurses working throughout Australia. In particular, harvesting of online discussions can be especially economical in terms of recruitment, travel and transcribing (as these are already transcribed).

Qualitative researchers, however, may be concerned as to whether online data is likely to be as comprehensive and as amenable to addressing their disciplinary and theoretical interests as is data generated by more conventional methods. An instructive comparison is provided by Campbell et al. (2001), who carried out both online and face-to-face focus groups on patients' perspectives on risks and colon cancer. They conclude that, while some individuals were reluctant to share sensitive information in face-to-face focus groups, others were clearly inhibited by the need to type responses in online groups, thus leading to shortened contributions, which may have omitted material of potential interest to the researchers. Schneider et al. (2002) also compared online focus groups and face-to-face discussions – in a study of users' views of a number of health-related websites – and observed that contributions to the online discussion were shorter and more succinct. They conclude that face-to-face and online discussions may fulfil different roles, depending on the relative importance to the research study in question of elaborated or short responses.

The harvesting of existing online data may recommend itself as a particularly attractive option for researchers who are worried about the impact of the researcher on the data. Campbell et al. (2001) point out that online encounters are less likely to be influenced by respondents' attributions in terms of gender or even age of the moderator, although, of course, the language and style of communication that we use as researchers are likely to provide important clues. Again, this could be an advantage in certain contexts, where differences between researcher and researched are likely to impede access or willingness to share experiences.

However, for those who see the role of the researcher in co-constructing data as an invaluable resource, the concern may be, instead, the lack of opportunity for the researcher to engage actively with respondents. Although online discussions may afford less scope for the researcher to mediate interactions, this may not be an unavoidable property of the medium and it may simply be that qualitative researchers need to develop new skills in this area (Stewart and Williams, 2005).

Regan (2003), for example, highlights the importance of preparation in ensuring that a virtual environment is conducive to discussing sensitive topics. Online research is still in its infancy and it may take some time to build up a stock of knowledge and techniques. However, this is evidence of a willingness to share advice and expertise. O'Connor and Madge (2001) share the software conferencing technique they developed, and Chen and Hinton (1999) also provide details of their technique for carrying out computer-mediated interviewing.

The use of naturally occurring online discussions as data also raises important issues concerning anonymity (Bloor et al., 2001). Stewart and Williams (2005) point out that some web-boards require discussants to complete a registration process and, hence have the potential for quotes to be attributed to individuals. They also highlight the complications concerning data storage and anonymizing, since the original data is automatically available to all discussants. This means, in turn, that individuals can, at least in theory, be identified by others through deductive disclosure.

Again, the issue of context raises its head, as some commentators point out that researchers utilizing online data have less opportunity to request relevant background information that can be crucial in terms of interpreting their data (Bloor et al., 2001: 78). This is not necessarily an insurmountable problem, but the researcher would have to weigh up carefully the benefits of requesting additional information against the danger of inhibiting spontaneous discussion.

Concerns have also been expressed with regard to the authenticity or 'trustworthiness' of online data, given the propensity of the internet to foster fantasy and role-playing: 'How is it possible to defend data in a field where anonymity and pseudonymity are the norm and where participants may choose to exploit the virtuality of the medium to experiment with presentation of the self?' (Mann and Stewart, 2000: 208). Interestingly, these are much the same concerns as have been aired more generally with reference to the qualitative research endeavour – regardless of whether this involves observational fieldwork, interviews or focus group discussions. Fantasy and role-playing notwithstanding, discussion fora involve real people and the line between the make-believe and reality can be blurred. For example, the recent conviction of three UK paedophiles who used the internet to plan the abduction and rape of two young sisters underlines that, in the eyes of the law, the internet can be a powerful medium for turning fantasy into actuality (Carter in *Guardian*, 6 February, 2007). For the purposes of most qualitative research, however, we are not in the business of eliciting 'the truth' and the internet may therefore be a valuable resource that affords us unparalleled access to the 'virtual' but fascinating world of identity formation and expression.

Researchers vary in terms of their enthusiasm for online methods. Some commentators, such as Chen and Hinton (1999), advocate using this approach alongside more traditional methods, since they consider that there may be important constraints in terms of both the samples and the data yielded using the internet. Certainly, Campbell et al. (2001) noted that the online participants in their study tended to be younger and to be more highly qualified than were those they recruited using the more traditional route of employing an earlier survey as a sampling pool. However, as the internet becomes acceptable and accessible to a wider range of people, such concerns may diminish in importance. It may, for example, prove an invaluable resource in accessing those who are unable or who may be unwilling to attend face-to-face sessions. Already it would appear that the internet is no longer the preserve of the young and trendy, although it may take longer for online discussion groups to attain such popularity among other sectors of society. Bloor et al. (2001) also urge caution in terms of forsaking more traditional face-to-face focus groups in favour of their online variant, advocating instead that we view them as simply another approach to add to our qualitative tool box.

SECONDARY ANALYSIS OF QUALITATIVE DATA

The ESRC Qualitative Data Archive was established in the early 1990s, and this funding Council now requires all researchers to whom they award grants to lodge their data, unless they can provide a detailed argument as to why this should not happen. However, despite the considerable resources and enthusiasm directed at this project, this archived qualitative data resource is still not widely utilized (Corti and Thompson, 2004). One of the barriers (identified by Corti herself (2000)) to archiving data, and also to its use for secondary analysis, is the unwillingness among the qualitative research community to see data as having an independent existence. While this may be partly accurate, I do wonder, however, whether the sort of curiosity that compels us to ask questions that can be addressed through qualitative methods also stems from a compulsion to get out into the field and generate one's own data? I have suggested elsewhere (Barbour, 2003) that qualitative researchers may be 'congenitally indisposed' to utilizing pre-existing datasets.

There are, undeniably, many exciting possibilities opened up by access to archived data. It can certainly have historical significance and the argument that it can potentially illuminate the process of social change may seem persuasive. However, even this ambition is not as straightforward as it might first appear. As Blaxter (2004) points out, studies may reflect a historically specific understanding of social problems or phenomena which reflect social trends (while purporting to study these) and this, in turn, can define research frameworks. Gillies and Edwards (2005) warn that utilization of qualitative datasets generated in the past:

> requires far more than a simple historical comparison of data. The focus of … studies shifts over time, limiting the contextual commensurability between different historically and culturally specific data sets and generating numerous conceptual and methodological questions. … Relevant themes and accounts are likely to be embedded within a range of topic areas that were previously ascendant.

All research projects are, to some extent, a product of their place and time. The definitions employed unquestioningly at a previous point in time may seriously limit sampling coverage and selection of research settings and thus hamper meaningful comparative analysis. This is because other criteria and dimensions (for example social class, gender or sexual orientation) may have subsequently assumed centre stage as potentially important characteristics for their use in the systematic interrogation of datasets on a specific topic. Moreover, some topics or themes may not be visited or evidenced in previous datasets, which begs the question as to what to make of such silences or gaps. Again, this is an issue that is not exclusive to secondary analysis of qualitative data, but is one that is thrown into particularly sharp focus in discussions about the value and rigour of attempts at re-analysis.

We have seen (in Chapter 3) that it is not always possible to specify at the outset exactly what the focus of a qualitative research project will be, which causes difficulties in ensuring that we obtain informed consent from our respondents. This is also an issue for secondary analysis (Heaton, 2004) as even the original researchers may have little inkling of the likely focus of re-interpretation of data and the use to which their study will ultimately be put by future researchers. Such concerns about confidentiality may lead researchers to 'neutralize' their data to an extent where it lacks the context necessary to interpret it effectively. Researchers may also seek to protect the identity of respondents by falsifying inessential details, but these may assume importance with re-analysis and a fresh focus (Parry and Mauthner, 2004). As Parry and Mauthner (2004: 147) conclude:

> Respondents' attitudes towards the research and their willingness to co-operate may be adversely affected by knowledge that the data will be accessible at some later date to (unknown) others. Furthermore, even where respondents are informed about archiving, guarantees which are originally extended to them will not necessarily be obtained once control over the dataset is relinquished. This begs the question

of whether research respondents can grasp the full implications of data archiving, when researchers still struggle to do so.

Changing fashions and political stances (such as the current preoccupation with 'political correctness') may expose respondents' comments and use of terminology in a bad light. Spoken words remain frozen in an earlier time and place, where usages now considered invidious had yet to acquire their current meaning or political charge (Bornat, 2005). This risk, however, is not confined to secondary analysis of data: we all write for posterity (whether or not we choose to archive our data) and a rereading of the original published papers and quotes can also expose our respondents in this way. This is, nevertheless, an important consideration when re-analyzing datasets that include prominent individuals who may be identifiable, as was the case with Bornat's (2005) re-analysis of Margot Jeffrey's interview study of pioneers of geriatric medicine.

There are also practical challenges involved in carrying out secondary analysis of archived data. Bornat (2005) has commented on the constraints imposed by storage and access arrangements with regard to the transcripts of the above dataset held in the British Museum. As we have seen in Chapter 9 (where decisions about transcription are discussed), the form of the data can also limit re-analysis possibilities. Van den Berg (2005 para. 11) reminds us that how data are 'constructed as analyzable … [is] deeply entwined' with methodological and theoretical assumptions and procedures. There is always a danger that data have been 'selected/produced that fit in well with pre-existing theoretical expectations'. Van den Berg here reports on the experience of carrying out secondary analysis of a set of interviews conducted in New Zealand in the 1980s by Margaret Wetherell on the topic of racism and race relations. The re-analysis was carried out by several discourse analysts, using a variety of approaches in this broad field. Notably, this required the re-transcription of the interviews in order to render them amenable to discourse analysis (see discussion in Chapters 1 and 9 on producing CA transcripts). This may not be possible where only paper copies or text files of transcripts are available, but the new digital technology available may allow more scope for future re-transcription of data. This, in turn, however, raises important questions about ensuring confidentiality – particularly if video recordings are involved.

Perhaps the most common objection to archiving and secondary analysis of qualitative data is the assertion that only the original researcher possesses the requisite background knowledge to render the data amenable to meaningful analysis that is cognizant of context. However, this may not stand up to scrutiny. Although the original researcher has access to specific 'cultural, discursive and linguistic resources' (van den Berg, 2005), it may be possible to provide sufficient background material in order to contextualize the data for a researcher who is approaching it afresh. This would appear to be the rationale behind the recently adopted practice of journals, such as the *British Medical Journal,* which now have a facility that allows for the posting of supplementary contextual material. It remains unclear, however, how this 'pseudo-publication' affects the potential of authors to re-use such material in further papers.

The ESRC Qualitative Data Archive has also sought to address this by including contextual information and there is also the option, in some cases, of establishing contact with the original researchers (see, for example, Blaxter's (2007) commentary on Libby Bishop's re-analysis of her dataset). Other commentators, however, would not see the absence of context as necessarily constituting a problem. Schlegloff (1997), for example, contends that the text itself defines which elements should be considered relevant in guiding our interpretations and analyses, and we have recently seen a similar debate being played out with reference to the controversy surrounding the use of a psychoanalytic framework to analyze qualitative data (see below). Van den Berg (2005) offers excellent advice: 'To avoid the risk of endless regress, the researcher should adhere to the principle of parsimony. This principle implies the recognition that complete contextualization is unattainable and the contextualization is always limited.' He goes on to argue that the extent to which the context is important depends on the research goal, the type of data involved and the amount and content of the supplementary information available.

Mason (2007) also questions whether 'unique epistemological privilege can be accorded to the (original) researchers' reflexive practices'. Secondary analysis is, in any case, already standard practice in many studies where the principal grant-holder is likely to be involved in analyzing data generated by a research assistant. We have also looked in Chapters 10 and 11 at the potential of insights provided by members of a multidisciplinary research team, who may interpret data in different ways that help us to interrogate and refine our coding categories and emergent explanatory frameworks. Secondary analysis, then, might also yield similar fresh interpretations that can advance our understanding of the original dataset and its role in addressing disciplinary or theoretical concerns. Bishop (2007) argues that secondary analysis can identify new themes which may not have been explored or coded in the original dataset. This is, however, a lot of retrospective analysis in 'regular' qualitative research, as researchers are sensitized to new issues.

There is one area where secondary analysts may be at a disadvantage: as Bishop (2007) concedes, it is not possible when dealing with archived data to add questions to an interview schedule as new topics emerge, and one is therefore subject to the constraints of the dataset. This assumes, though, that original researchers are able to recognize all potential avenues of enquiry and the questions that one wishes they had posed may well be those that have assumed new importance over the ensuing years and which did not attract researchers' interest at the time of the study. Rather than treating this as an unfortunate shortcoming of secondary analysis, however, this can be recast as a resource, provided that sufficient attention is paid to what Moore (2007) calls 'the reflexivity of the current (i.e. secondary analysis) project'. Moreover, the fact that initial analysis of an archived dataset did not focus on particular issues may speak volumes about their importance, if these can be shown, on re-examination, to feature in the data, despite being overlooked by the original researchers. As van den Berg (2005) reminds us, our focus on context can deflect attention away from the extent to which 'the empirical has a momentum of its own'.

Importantly, archiving qualitative data involves, for the original researchers, relinquishing of control (Parry and Mauthner, 2004: 142), and this lies behind many of the objections and reservations about the practice of secondary analysis. Although many of the debates around secondary analysis concern the implications for protecting the confidentiality of respondents, issues of researcher confidentiality and anonymity rarely surface (Parry and Mauthner, 2004: 145). Re-analysis of our data inevitably opens us, and our research practices, to scrutiny. Although there is considerable scope for the original researchers to embargo the use of their data until a specific period of time has elapsed, and there is also some provision for dialogue between original and secondary researchers, the concept of lodging data in an archive is based on the principle of open access to future researchers. Behind many of the concerns raised with regard to archiving, confidentiality and rigour of re-analyses lies a crucial but generally unstated question. This is not whether secondary analysis is possible or desirable, but rather '*Who* would we be happy to have re-analyze our data?' This again raises – albeit in a somewhat different context – the issue of the mandate to research, which is discussed in more depth later in this chapter.

The introduction of qualitative data archiving has changed forever the backdrop against which we carry out our research. It may be no bad thing that researchers now operate in a context where they know their practices, judgements and decisions may later be subjected to detailed scrutiny, since this can serve to encourage us all to pursue rigour and transparency. However, keeping a weather eye open for the potential of retrospective criticism can also have a negative impact on how we do our research. It may, for instance, adversely affect our capacity to achieve empathy and rapport through revealing sometimes uncomfortable details of our own situations and behaviours (Parry and Mauthner, 2004: 145). While we may be perfectly happy to share these with 'consenting respondents' in the intimacy afforded by one-to-one interviews, we may not wish to share such revelations with the whole academic world. Some disciplines and sub-disciplines, of course, may be kinder than others with regard to whether they view such information as 'fair game' in the making and breaking of reputations, which is, whether we like it or not, part and parcel of the wider academic arena in which we all operate. This brings us back to the discussion in Chapter 1 about the capacity of different disciplines to put their own stamp on the practice of qualitative research. Some of the reluctance to embrace the idea of archiving and secondary analysis of qualitative data may have its roots in the underlying assumptions of social scientists, who, like classical anthropologists, may see data as their personal property to be revisited later as a reward for their persistence in generating this in the first place. This may be in marked contrast to oral historians, who, according to Parry and Mauthner (2004), view their data as a communal resource. Social scientists traditionally have not had this perspective.

It would be a pity if secondary analysis of qualitative data were dismissed out of hand, as it undoubtedly opens up many interesting possibilities. However, it is important that we do not allow debates about the re-use of specific datasets to overshadow discussion as to how to realize the full potential of secondary analysis. Rather than focusing on an individual study, or even seeking to use separate studies in the aggregative manner that characterizes quantitative meta-analysis, a comparative approach, which is sympathetic to the main thrust of qualitative research endeavours, is likely to yield dividends (Barbour and Barbour, 2003). Such an approach moves the focus away from re-scrutiny and re-mining of existing data to produce a definitive overview of findings, to emphasize, instead, the implications of secondary analysis for interrogating and developing theory. It may be here that secondary analysis can make its most significant contribution, mirroring the way in which we already integrate and re-examine findings – if not data – from other studies through the constant comparative method (as we have seen in the exercise in Chapter 11). This version of secondary analysis would concentrate less on re-analyzing a whole dataset and may involve gleaning only very small amounts of relevant data from several studies, thus allowing researchers to capitalize on material which, although present in the original transcripts, may have been overlooked due to the relatively few mentions involved. This is not a problem if the aim is to interrogate theoretical frameworks rather than to rework previous analyses. (As we saw in Chapter 11, when the aim is to refine theory, it is not necessary to utilize all the data available and theoretical papers may draw on a relatively small number of instances of a particular phenomenon, although it is likely to involve a thorough investigation of patterning and variants.) Importantly, this also underlines the potential for combining a fresh theoretical focus with the generating of new empirical data. Indeed, one of the most successful attempts at qualitative 'meta-analysis' (Campbell et al., 2003) involved exactly this *prospective* rather than retrospective approach (Barbour and Barbour, 2003).

In conclusion, it looks as though the debate about secondary analysis is likely to run for some time to come and it remains to be seen whether the qualitative research community will whole-heartedly embrace this new possibility. What is certain, however, is that its full potential can only be realized if we qualitative researchers have the courage to question our deeply held convictions and to strive to be imaginative in our approaches to employing secondary analysis in the context of a wider range of studies and research topics. The future of secondary analysis will also be determined to a large extent by the funding climate and wider political agenda. One factor which may militate against greater reliance on existing datasets is the current emphasis on participatory approaches, although these are not without their own challenges – whether these are practical, political or ethical.

PARTICIPATORY APPROACHES AND ISSUES OF POWER

Although never far from the surface in any qualitative research project, the dilemmas raised throughout this book can be exacerbated by particular versions that privilege certain aspects of the researcher's role and position. If we engage with our respondents with the principal aim of refining our theoretical and disciplinary knowledge, then we may encounter additional dilemmas. When researching *in situ*, however, it can be difficult to maintain a stance of 'dispassionate expert' – even assuming that this was considered desirable in the first place. Particularly difficult issues regarding responsibilities are raised for practitioners engaged in research who are frequently torn between concern for clients or patients and professional loyalties.

For some researchers, the method can become the vehicle for resolving such problems. Some commentators, such as Johnson (1996), have argued that qualitative methods – in his case focus groups – can themselves be emancipatory. Some research projects can be deemed to have transformed personal troubles into public issues (Wright Mills, 1959) through engaging participants in discussing and 'problematizing' their situation. A good example would be the work of Pini (2002) with farm women in the Australian sugar industry, which, with its overtly feminist stance, harks back to the idea of 'consciousness raising' that was a central tenet of that movement. Such successes notwithstanding, it is necessary to subject to critical scrutiny claims about the inherently emancipatory capacity of qualitative methods such as focus groups. As Bloor et al. (2001: 15) remind us, 'focus groups are not the authentic voice of the people' and their capacity to effect change – political or personal – depends ultimately on the context in which such methods are employed. Research does not take place in a vacuum and key to the impact of participatory methods is the position of the researcher or research team *vis-à-vis* policy-makers or decision-makers, who can influence and sanction political, organizational or professional change.

Another key component of action research approaches is the emphasis placed on the co-production of knowledge, but, this too requires further explanation. The 'epistemology' of action research (i.e. what it views as constituting knowledge) is outlined by Reason (2000) as emphasizing or 'privileging' valid and relevant practical knowledge, which is developed or produced through planned action, and which is useful in the everyday context of people's lives. Knowledge is viewed as reflecting a range of 'ways of knowing' – 'experiential', 'practical' and 'presentational' (according to Heron, cited by Ladkin, 2004: 538). These mirror the varying emphases of the activities that could be loosely grouped together as action research, that is individual reflective approaches (practitioner-focused); collective approaches (including some varieties of professional and organizational development); and more theoretical approaches which aim to understand patterns and build models (Waterman et al., 2001). Eikeland (2006: 45) in a similar vein, advocates making a distinction between what she calls 'communities of practice' (which might well encompass the 'reflective practitioners' excluded from the definitions provided by commentators such as McMahon 1999) and 'communities of inquiry', but such approaches need not be mutually exclusive. Action research projects may generate and draw on different types of knowledge at different stages in the action research cycle, or may produce these various types of knowledge at the same time.

However, the potential of such knowledge to effect the desired change rather depends on how the action researcher or action research team views the properties of knowledge and how it can and should be used in the social context of organizations, educational, or health and social care settings (the 'stage' for action research projects). In other words, it depends on the answers to 'ontological' questions about how this social world works and how it can best be studied and influenced.

Some would argue, perhaps, that 'knowledge *is* power'. Certainly, withholding of information can be a vital tactic in terms of oppressing individuals and groups and pursuing a 'hidden agenda'. However, knowledge can be a double-edged sword, as Hilsen (2006: 29) reminds us:

> Research practices can be liberating and increase people's capacity to influence their own environments and implement solutions to their own, experienced problems, or it can confirm stereotypes and constricting images of people, and so render people less able to change their environments.

Knowledge of problems experienced without an understanding of *how* social and organizational structures, procedures and models produce such inequities and inconsistencies is unlikely to form a useful basis for initiating change. Commenting here on politically-motivated research Seale (1999: 10) argues:

> it is a mistake to assume that oppressed groups have the best insights into the sources of their oppression (although they can explain some of its consequences), which the uncritical advocacy of ... standpoint epistemology can assume. If this were the case, oppression might not be so common.

Hilsen (2006: 31) reminds us that, since, action research is essentially 'reformist', it needs to address questions of power. She is talking, here, in the context of her own action research work, which seeks to reduce age discrimination and promote more democratic practices in a large Norwegian workplace with an ageing workforce:

> The ethical demand of action research is about the power relationships inherent in the social sciences. Because the social sciences can make a difference in people's lives, power and responsibility are unavoidable issues. ... Thus, I argue that our ability as researchers to affect people's lives is the basis for our responsibility to act in the best interest of all. Action research's commitment to promote social justice makes it even more of an ethical demand to take responsibility for the social consequences of the research and make it explicit both in our practice and our communications about that practice...
>
> Organizational development through broad participation implies an attack on aspects of bureaucracy and centralized control and decision-making in the organization. When local situations and centralized control cause conflicts, such situations can be used as effective cases for confrontation and clarification of the organizational commitment to change ... and this is the responsibility of researchers committed to social justice and democratization of work life. (Hilsen, 2006: 33)

This, then, is a far cry from the disinterested scientist of other paradigms, as it moves the researcher to centre stage as a passionate advocate of change and the entitlement of specific individuals within the organization that is the setting for the action research project. This appeals to the notion of third-person engagement (as outlined by Heron, cited by Ladkin, 2004). Such approaches implicitly – but crucially – draw on a wider body of knowledge and theoretical frameworks both in making sense of data and in formulating recommendations for change. Hilsen contrasts her own more confrontational approach with that of other commentators who favour 'tempered radicalism' and position themselves as working *with* the system with the aim of achieving change *within* it. This echoes the earlier debates within social work and community work, with respect to the potential for radical action, by employees of statutory agencies, who, despite their political convictions and alignment with clients, are nevertheless still subject to bureaucratic, organizational and legal structures and constraints. Interestingly, the following heart-felt comment mirrors the preoccupation with the possibility of self-destruction of the social workers I studied in the late 1970s and even hints at their thesis of 'the deserting social worker' (as discussed in Chapter 1):

> The challenges of action researchers … clearly approximate the common challenges of social reformers and revolutionaries at all times: By what means can we achieve change and promote our goals, without self-destruction, destroying the realization of our goals through the application of our means, through our own practice? (Eikeland, 2006: 44)

In this same paper, Eikeland also reflects the suspicion with which many action researchers appear to view the academic endeavour and the role of theory:

> … action research, as practised, is often simultaneously pulled in opposite directions, both towards standards set by externally based academic research, and towards internal indigenous standards, creating ethical dilemmas. But action research can hardly let go of the indigenous standards without losing its soul and becom(ing) mainstream research. (Eikeland, 2006: 40)

Despite the laudable political efforts of many action researchers to position themselves alongside those who are disenfranchised or oppressed, power differentials in the field (i.e. in relationships between researchers and participants – or 'co-researchers' as some commentators would style them) can seriously impair the capacity of action research to effect change.

In many respects, pieces of work, such as the one summarized above and Meg Bond's description of her own action research while acting as manager of the unit in question, appear similar to management projects. Lilford et al. (2003) have argued:

> In view of its emphasis on the production and evaluation of change, it seems most appropriate to conceive of action research as a form of managerial intervention containing research rather than a form of research *per se*, its primary features being

those of an iterative cycle of research and action, participation of the researched and flexibility in its approach. … Both Total Quality Management (TQM) and action research are based on a cycle consisting of identifying problems, analyzing their cause and selecting and testing solutions. (Lilford, Warren and Braunholtz, 2003: 101)

Many of the debates surrounding action research – and, indeed, other forms of qualitative research – appear to owe more to concerns about territoriality and claims to ownership of different approaches than to a desire to advance research methods, and many opportunities to learn from the methods of those working within other disciplinary frameworks are therefore likely to be missed. One of the challenges facing action researchers – and qualitative researchers in general – is how to adopt and adapt the approaches of overlapping but separate research traditions to enhance one's own practice without diluting its potential. This might well include embracing some of the insights of management approaches while developing a more critical management study framework, as recently suggested by Learmonth (2003).

The emphasis within some variants of action research on making all involved into combined 'practitioners-researchers-researched' (Lee, 2001) may have the unfortunate consequence of homogenizing expertise and impeding helpful cross-fertilization (which is an important advantage of multidisciplinary teams).

Although many action research texts position this approach as a 'bottom-up' rather than 'top-down' endeavour, such a distinction frequently breaks down in practice. Perhaps truly 'bottom-up' research is a contradiction in terms, since, if those at the receiving end of inequality or injustice had the resources and skills necessary to mount such initiatives, then the project would, by definition, be unnecessary. Many action researchers present themselves as championing the interests of the underprivileged, and acting as their advocates. However, they also need to acknowledge and subject to critical scrutiny the sources of their own influence, professional membership, loyalties and responsibilities, and the potential to become caught up in complex political, professional and organizational dialogues and agendas. As Hart and Bond (1995: 8) observe:

> …action research which is initiated by senior people to promote change at grass roots level is fraught with potential difficulties. Our analysis would suggest that this often involves a clash both of values and of methodological approach, such that top-down goals and bottom-up initiatives come into conflict, despite what might appear as a convergence of interests around a particular problem.

THE MANDATE TO RESEARCH, INTERPRET AND REPORT

Action research has been promoted by some researchers as an alternative to other approaches which are often criticized for treating research respondents as 'the other'.

Sociologists and anthropologists have also wrestled with the implications of power relations for the research encounter and have sought to address this – sometimes by emphasizing the commonalities of researcher and respondents. Oakley (1981) argued that, in the case of women interviewing other women, not only did power differentials cease to shape the research encounter, but that this could generate 'better' or 'fuller' data by virtue of the researcher being able to draw both interactionally and analytically on a shared social position. Stanley and Wise (1993), again commenting on researching women from a feministic perspective, talk about the experience of knowing as an 'epistemological privilege'. This they define as emanating from access to a priori knowledge of informants' subjective realities.

Shah (2006) also talks of her insights into a world shared by her respondents as an 'ontological privilege', emphasizing the potential to use empathy in the research encounter. However, she also acknowledges the complexities involved, commenting: 'nevertheless, as a British Indian professional disabled woman in her early 30s, only part of my life history resembled that of each informant' (Shah, 2006: 211). We cannot always anticipate how we and our claims to shared identities will be received by those whose worlds we wish to research through the lens of our self-conferred identities. Chiu and Knight (1999) comment that some of their focus group participants did not process the information that Chiu was Chinese and so did not accord her the 'insider' status that she had assumed would be a feature of her engagement with them.

Hurd and McIntyre (1996) also point out that there can be a 'seduction in sameness', whereby the researcher shares too many of the group's taken-for-granted assumptions and is, therefore, unable to expose these to critical scrutiny. Whereas this might provide impeccable credentials in terms of challenges as to the right to research particular groups, it may not be a profitable position in terms of affording the ability to 'stand back' from issues that can make such a valuable contribution in analysis. This is not to say that the qualitative researcher should strive for that illusive concept of 'objectivity'; rather that it is hard to question other people's 'taken-for-granted' assumptions if we ourselves are party to these.

One of the perennial difficulties in anticipating analysis of qualitative data is that we often do not know, in advance, precisely what our focus will be. Among other things, this makes it difficult to provide detailed accounts in our research proposals (see Chapter 2) and ethics applications (see Chapter 3). Several anthropologists and ethnographers (for example Brettell, 1993) have written about the guilt that is often a feature of the process of analysis, as we come to look critically at the accounts provided by our study participants, looking for inconsistencies and the functions that stories fulfil, or providing our own version of what people are 'really' saying. I am sure that many researchers have experienced unease similar to that I encountered when faced with stories told to me by HIV/AIDS workers. In the course of talking with workers about the demands of their jobs, I was repeatedly told how resourceful and imaginative many clients were, as they negotiated a social world very different from those inhabited by the average social worker, nurse or doctor. Such tales emphasized the reluctant admiration that workers held for people living in very stressful and demanding situations. However, I was told virtually identical stories by different workers (see the fuller discussion in Chapter 5), which posed a dilemma for me in writing up the research.

Perhaps it is this potential for discomfort that leads so many qualitative researchers to settle for providing a descriptive rather than analytical account. I am, however, always slightly suspicious of claims that researchers 'want to protect the integrity of what respondents told them', as this can so easily let the researcher 'off the hook' in terms of meeting what I consider to be an important obligation: that of furnishing an overview by putting individuals' accounts into the broader context. Such an approach also, conveniently, avoids the need to systematically and laboriously interrogate the data (as described in Chapter 10).

There are unavoidable tensions between the agendas of researcher and respondents (as noted by Mazeland and ten Have, 1996), since, by definition, they are involved in the project of the research for different reasons. Respondents are telling us their individual stories, and even in the context of focus group research, participants may see the group context as affording the opportunity to share their stories with like-minded people – perhaps deriving some cathartic benefit along the way, or even viewing the group as a vehicle for initiating a politicized response (whether or not the researcher or research team view the project as involving action research). However, this does not guarantee that respondents will be happy with the way in which researchers use the data that they have co-produced. All of these issues are raised with particular poignancy when it comes to considering secondary analysis of qualitative data.

Chapter 4 emphasizes that the fieldworker is constantly engaged in negotiating and renegotiating access and the topic of research findings is likely to arise long before the final report is available. Many researchers have had the experience of sharing their findings only to be met by comments such as 'It didn't tell us anything we didn't know before'. In so far as qualitative research attempts to provide an insider's view, then such comments should perhaps be received as praise – albeit back-handed praise – rather than as implied criticism Qualitative research does not usually yield earth-shattering conclusions/findings and may thus be seen as wanting, at least in the eyes of a public who tend to celebrate a view of science and research as hopefully producing revelatory or even salacious findings (as commented upon by Davis, as long ago as 1971):

> All interesting theories constitute an attack on the taken-for-granted world of their audience. … If it does not challenge but merely confirms one of their taken for granted beliefs, they [the audience] will respond to it by rejecting its value while affirming its truth. (Davis, 1971: 311)

Qualitative research is unlikely to produce 'sound bites' of the order of 'Twenty per cent of social workers are cross-dressers' (i.e. the research equivalent of 'Freddy Starr ate my hamster'). Instead, it focuses on and 'problematizes' the 'mundane' or 'taken for granted'. As Wittgenstein observed, 'The aspects of things that are most important for us are hidden because of their simplicity and familiarity' (cited by Silverman, 1993: 145).

However, qualitative research findings can give participants a sense of where their own views and experiences fit with those of others in similar situations and can, in some contexts, provide a powerful tool for arguing their collective but anonymized case. It is for this reason that qualitative approaches have proved so popular in studies which aspire to being participatory or even action research projects (see Chapter 8). Perhaps we should be less apologetic about qualitative research's tendency to raise uncomfortable questions and more upbeat about its capacity to illuminate. We could also be more explicit about our role in providing an overview and perhaps should be less precious with respect to checking our interpretations with individual respondents, as respondent validation frequently serves more as a means of protecting the researcher than as a way of ensuring the well-being of research participants.

While, as researchers, we usually have some choice over which aspects of our findings to report and to which audiences, our published work is in the pubic domain and therefore open to full scrutiny. Some of our participants, of course, are more likely than others to read what we write (Brettell, 1993). Talking particularly with reference to carrying out research in other cultures, Ryen (2004) points out that anonymity is not always prized and that some research participants may see it as discourteous if researchers do not give them a named acknowledgment in their reports. This issue can also arise when we carry out research on elites, such as the Irish academics studied by Sheehan (1993).

Researcher discomfort is likely to be even greater when we utilize data to explore disciplinary or theoretical issues, rather than treating respondents' accounts as interesting in their own right (Barbour, 1998b; Strathern, 1987). This could be viewed as a 'top-down' (Frosh and Emerson, 2005) approach at variance with the currently more popular – and more politically correct – 'bottom-up' approach. Strathern (1987: 289) argues: '…using people's experiences to make statements about matters of anthropological (or, indeed, sociological or psychological) interest in the end subordinates them to the uses of the discipline'.

Several researchers (for example Frosh et al., 2003; Wetherell, 2003) have recently advocated the use of the psychoanalytic framework for interpreting qualitative data. Frosh and Emerson (2005: 308) argue that this can afford valuable insights into 'the conscious and unconscious "reasons" behind a specific individual's investment in any rhetorical or discursive position'. Other commentators – (for example, Day Sclater in Andrews et al. 2004) are critical of such approaches, as they are seen to breech the content given by respondents. I suspect that one's stance regarding the acceptability of the psychoanalytic framework in making sense of qualitative data depends on one's personal view of psychoanalysis. Such issues are particularly pertinent with regard to the mandate to interpret archived data, since our own theoretical and disciplinary focus changes with the passage of time.

The debate also raises the important question as to how one views the purpose of the research endeavour. Although I do not personally possess any psychoanalytic skills, the above statement from Frosh and Emerson does not strike me as being at variance with how I view the purpose and process of qualitative data analysis. So is the issue, rather, that of whether the end justifies the means? Frosh and Emerson (2005: 308) go on to argue that psychoanalytic theory, when applied to data analysis, can provide such insights while still stopping short of 'having recourse to assumptions concerning the stability of self-hood or the separate sphere of the "personal"'. Another key difference is that the researcher – unlike the therapist – is not engaged in the process of sharing such insights with the individual respondent face to face, as in therapeutic consultations where the two work together to effect change. Even if such psychoanalytically informed observations do find their way into presentations or published reports to which research respondents have access, these are unlikely to be attributable to a specific individual – at least if ethical undertaking to provide anonymity have been observed.

In an ideal world it might be desirable that we put our prior theoretical knowledge to one side, but, as critics of purist approaches to grounded theory (see Chapter 9) have pointed out, this is not a realistic goal. What is not mentioned in this ongoing debate about the use of psychoanalytic theory is the question of whether it is *ever* possible to put to one side 'what you know'. I would, for example, find it very difficult to discount or 'switch off' my sociological knowledge when interpreting any data extract. Indeed, personal and disciplinary identities are so closely bound up (by virtue of our professional socialization from a relatively early age and for long periods of time) that this is probably impossible. If we accept this premise, then to argue that using a psychoanalytic framework is never permissible is not so different from saying that individuals trained in psychoanalysis should never be involved in doing qualitative research – and I suspect that most of us would baulk at such a bald proclamation. Perhaps, again, the best advice is simply to be as transparent as possible about your own disciplinary standpoint and the theoretical frameworks on which you are drawing, and to be explicit about the purpose to which you are employing these, ensuring that you do not become diverted from the research focus of the particular project. This would afford researchers the opportunity to use knowledge and skills that are derived from other sources in interpreting data, but emphasizes the importance of being reflexive throughout the process of analysis.

We should try, therefore, to subject to critical examination our own theoretical assumptions in the same way as we would treat the explanatory frameworks of our respondents' assumptions. The question then becomes 'How?' I would suggest that it is here that the full potential of the multidisciplinary team becomes apparent. (This is discussed in Chapter 10 in relation to interpreting and interrogating data and developing coding categories and coding frames.) Interestingly, Frosh and Emerson also allude to this in reflecting on the implications of their dialogue about psychoanalytic and discursive analytic interpretations, which forms the content of their paper. They conclude that this debate 'serves … to raise questions of difference as possibilities for collaboration (if not corroboration)' (Frosh and Emerson, 2005: 323).

In some projects, however, feeding back preliminary findings to respondents can go some way towards guarding against getting carried away by the power of our favoured explanations. Frosh and Emerson (2005) suggest doing this in the context of the research interview and this 'summarizing' or 'checking out' is sometimes a feature of focus group discussions. I would also argue that even *thinking* about feeding back to respondents can be helpful in highlighting some of the unwarranted assumptions we might be making in our analyses, by engaging us in 'playing devil's advocate' (as is suggested in Chapter 11).

However, the issue of 'respondent validation' is neither as straightforward nor as quintessentially egalitarian and inclusive as it may at first glance appear. As Bloor (1997) highlights, this may not even be all that helpful in research terms, as discussion is likely to focus on broad agreement or minor details rather than on major interpretative issues. Some researchers undertake to share transcripts with respondents, but there are several ethical considerations to take into account. Although interviewees may have freely shared their upsetting experiences with the researcher, it can cause them renewed distress to read these accounts as a stark text devoid of all the attendant empathetic gestures that we so pride ourselves on, as qualitative researchers, enabling us to elicit our data. Williamson (2000) provides an unusually reflective account of her experiences of sharing transcripts with women who had experienced domestic violence, and concludes that she would never again employ this strategy without considerable forethought.

CONCLUSION

A backward glance reveals that qualitative research has been influenced by passing fashions and enthusiasms. It has always been at the forefront in studying new forms of interaction and has, for example, been quick to explore the possibilities afforded by the advent of the internet, while studying the form of such communications within their wider cultural and political context, as well as drawing on their content as data.

Although qualitative research, particularly where it problematizes and questions the 'taken for granted', has the potential to be subversive, there is also considerable potential for co-option, and this has become ever more evident as a growing number of disciplines and professional groups have come to embrace qualitative research and to seek to apply it to questions of their own choosing. A surprise for those of us who have been involved in qualitative research for a long time is the enthusiasm with which the medical professional has come to accept qualitative approaches. More recently this has led to calls to incorporate into the evidence base the knowledge derived through qualitative research. While this suggests that qualitative research may finally have come of age, it brings a new set of challenges. Foremost among these is the issue of evaluating qualitative research and the potential for secondary analysis of qualitative data. As has been argued throughout this volume, this involves more than a cursory manipulation of templates designed for evaluating and synthesizing quantitative research.

It is important, however, not to forget the powerful influence of wider funding and the political climate on the development and practice of qualitative research. I suspect, for instance, that increasingly rigorous and time-consuming ethical procedures (see Chapter 3) are one of the drivers for the renewed vigour with which some members of the qualitative research community are currently pursuing the possibilities afforded by the internet and secondary analysis.

In examining critically the implications of such new endeavours, however, the issues that surface reflect the same perennial issues that have always accompanied qualitative research – albeit perhaps with a slightly different slant. These are issues concerning confidentiality, consent, ethics, relationships between researcher and researched, ownership and power, the mandate to research and interpret, and the importance of reflexivity and context.

We carry out our research against a constantly evolving backdrop and one of the most important changes in recent years has been the widening of membership of the qualitative research community. Now that many practitioners and clinicians are themselves active in designing and conducting qualitative research, we find ourselves negotiating a new set of relationships and engaging in new debates. The time has long since passed when qualitative research was the preserve of a few consenting academics intent on pursuing their own disciplinary interests. Indeed, we now frequently find ourselves having to defend the place of theory in our analyses. Action research, in particular, has been born of disenchantment with traditional research methods – both quantitative and qualitative. Nurse researchers appear to have found this particularly persuasive and have sought to develop participatory approaches with patients as they seek to translate findings into policy and practice.

We are also required to be responsive to policy-makers' priorities, which are translated into funding opportunities. Many health services researchers find themselves doing sociologically- or psychologically-relevant research virtually by stealth – largely because of short timescales. In some environments the idea of knowledge for its own sake has become a short-hand derisory term applied to theoretically driven research and many funding streams privilege the production of knowledge that is directly relevant to practice. I would like to see a future where there is room for us all. To my mind there is danger in insisting that fundable projects must achieve both clinical relevance and theoretical sophistication. This is a tall order and difficult to ensure from the outset, but it is also likely that research will be impoverished as we wrestle with this requirement, inevitably, perhaps, settling for less ambitious and more straightforward topics.

There is, of course, considerable potential in multidisciplinary teams to address both issues and perhaps disciplinary and professional imperatives, but there is a danger that theoretical concerns are down-played. Crucially, it depends upon who is leading the project, but funding – particularly of multidisciplinary projects in the arena of health – is often focused on relevance to the NHS. Perhaps the requirement to make links between research findings and, say, clinical practice need not always be demanded of the original researcher or research team, but might be regarded as the responsibility of practitioners and those who train other clinicians. If teaching is informed by research, then such links can be made by the reader, which is probably a fitting outcome for qualitative research which would probably not insist on one 'true' reading of findings, since these are likely to be influenced by context. There is, then, more than one route through which research can be rendered relevant to the evidence base.

Working at the interface between theory and practice and between different disciplines is uncomfortable and challenging, but can – because of these tensions – be a spur to enhancing the rigour and transparency of our research practice. Such collaborations can result in many added benefits. Several commentators have bemoaned the lack of theory in much published health services research or action research. Some such projects, however, never get as far as appearing in academic peer-reviewed journals, since many written accounts of small locality-specific research projects contribute instead to the 'grey literature' of local authority or health authority archives, where they are not readily accessible to other researchers addressing similar issues. This can lead to unfortunate and wasteful duplication of effort. While the findings of small-scale research projects may have limited application in other contexts, they could, nevertheless, contribute incrementally to what action researchers themselves refer to as 'practical knowledge'. Rather than foreswearing academic writing endeavours, action researchers and those who see themselves as carrying out activities more akin to 'audits' could gain further benefits and access wider audiences by developing additional writing skills and exploring other outlets for their work. This could perhaps be achieved through collaboration with researchers better versed in the craft of academic writing and who may be able to identify a wider range of possible journals. The internet also affords many possibilities for making action research knowledge, in particular, more readily available and accessible to a variety of audiences.

However, I would question whether participatory approaches and disciplinary or theoretically-driven research endeavours are, in fact, necessarily mutually exclusive. Many action research texts appear somewhat defensive when arguing for the distinctiveness of action research and the need to apply a new set of criteria in evaluating it. Such arguments may, in effect, do action research a disservice by over-emphasizing such differences at the expense of similarities with other research. 'Good action research' can, and frequently does, contribute to the development of theory and 'bad academic qualitative research' may take refuge in extolling the virtues of a participatory approach.

Wiles et al. (2006), however, note a growing, and perhaps disturbing, trend for participatory research to be equated with the ethic of good research practice. They conclude: 'While this is appropriate for certain types of emancipatory and evaluative approaches, it does pose risks for researchers seeking to extend disciplinary knowledge or to adopt critical approaches to their "subject matter"' (Wiles et al., 2006: 294).

Although she is, here, speaking about action research, Ladkin's comments serve as a useful reminder of our responsibilities towards respondents and the need to consider the potential impact of our engagement with them as well as the products of our research:

> Working collaboratively does not mean that there is no initiating, holding or leadership function required. It does call for a style of enacting that function that

is sensitive to the emergent quality of inquiry, along with an ability to articulate perceptions of what is happening and openness to other interpretations of those perceptions. It also calls for a sensitivity to the political implications and processes involved. (Ladkin, 2004: 543)

I think that it may be time to reinstate the expertise of the researcher and to acknowledge the value of providing an overview and explanation – even one that addresses specific theoretical issues – rather than settling for mere description or championing of particular groups. This volume is intended as a spur to maximizing the rigour, and hence relevance, of qualitative research. It is only through honing our skills that we can interrogate and respond creatively to the many challenges – both exciting and worrying – that face us.

HINTS ON FACING CHALLENGES AND DILEMMAS

- Be aware that the new possibilities afforded by the internet and secondary analysis also raise several of the perennial dilemmas that characterize the qualitative research endeavour.
- You need to be mindful of the different agendas of the various stakeholders in the research enterprise and give attention to these as you prepare your materials for dissemination and publication.
- You need to give some thought, at the outset of the project, to your role and position as researcher and to formulate some guidelines with regard to how you will respond to particular issues that might arise. (You may need to seek advice in this respect, or to include project consultants with specialist knowledge.)
- Remember that funding opportunities, fresh topics and new collaborations may all have implications for your role and your research practice.
- Maintain a critical perspective at all times.

FURTHER READING

Barbour, R.S. (1998) 'Engagement, presentation and representation in research practice', in R.S. Barbour and G. Huby (eds) *Meddling with Mythology: AIDS and the Social Construction of Knowledge*, London: Routledge, pp. 183–200.

Bloor, M. (1997) 'Techniques of validation in qualitative research: A critical commentary', in G. Miller and R. Dingwall (eds) *Context and Method in Qualitative Research*, London: Sage, pp. 37–50.

Brettell, C.B. (ed.) (1993) *When They Read What We Write: The Politics of Ethnography*, Westport, CT/London: Bergin and Garvey.

EXERCISE

You might like to re-read the paper/s you selected for the 'critical appraisal'-type exercise at the end of Chapter 1 and consider the following:

- How would your new review differ from your original?
- What supplementary questions (if any) might you add to the list presented in Chapter 1?

GLOSSARY

Action research   Research carried out in an organizational or work (e.g. nursing education) setting (often done by practitioners) with the express aim of effecting change.

Analytic induction   This is a process in analyzing qualitative data which concentrates on exceptions and uses these to refine and rework emergent explanations to take account of both these 'disconfirming' instances and other relevant data.

A priori codes   These are categories assigned to data excerpts which derive from the researcher's preconceived ideas as to what is likely to be important (and which may reflect questions included in an interview schedule of focus group topic guide).

Case study   This relates to study design and to sampling, either of individuals or settings, in order to allow study of specific identified characteristics and their impact on the phenomenon being researched. Such studies can involve one setting or multiple settings selected to enhance the possibility of making comparisons.

Coding   This refers to an attempt to 'package' data excerpts under broad headings and sub-categories in a way that allows subsequent retrieval for the purposes of comparison.

Coding frame   This relates to a scheme for organizing data. It details broad headings and sub-categories and makes explicit the linkages between these.

Constant comparative method   This relates to the process involved in constantly comparing and contrasting coded data excerpts or findings from other studies in order to identify and attempt to explain the patterns that emerge.

Conversation analysis   This is a particular approach to generating and analyzing qualitative data that relies on detailed transcription of spoken exchanges utilizing an agreed set of conventions. It is concerned with illuminating how speakers accomplish a variety of tasks through speech.

Critical incident technique   This derives from the aeronautical industry and the study of near misses of aircraft. It is closely related to the principles of analytic induction as it too relies on using the unusual in order to explicate the routine. It can refer either to the selection of 'cases' or to using exceptions identified in a dataset.

Diaries   This involves asking respondents to keep a record of their activities and experiences for research purposes. It can involve using highly structured or unstructured templates and can also be used to stimulate discussion at subsequent interviews when used within the context of a longitudinal study.

Discourse analysis   This involves the detailed study of talk and focuses particularly on the use of language and its role in constituting social and psychological life.

Documentary analysis   This relates to the analysis of pre-existing documents and is often carried out as part of a mixed methods approach utilizing data generated through other methods. It can involve a variety of document types, including medical records, internet discussions, newspaper reports or policy documents.

Enhanced case records   This relates to the practice of requesting additional information of professionals as an adjunct to collecting data in the course of routine organizational tasks.

Epistemology   This means our theories of knowledge, how we come to know the world and our ideas about the nature of evidence and knowledge.

Ethnography   This most often relates to research involving observational fieldwork, but is occasionally used to refer to carrying out interview studies where the researcher has privileged access to a setting which allows data to be interpreted taking such additional information into account.

Ethnomethodology   This refers to work which aims to explain how individuals build a stable social order both in specific interactional encounters and in society more generally.

Focus group discussions   This is a method for generating data through encouraging discussion between participants. Groups can either be convened for research purposes or can consist of pre-existing groups (e.g. work teams).

Grounded theory   This is an approach to analyzing qualitative data that argues that it is possible, through interrogating, comparing and contrasting pieces of data, to build up theoretical accounts.

Indexing   This refers to the initial stages of coding, where the researcher begins by assigning broad headings in order to divide the data into the main themes (to be explored in greater detail later in the process).

Interpretative phenomenological analysis   This is an approach developed by psychologists. It refers to the dual aim of seeking to understand respondents' meanings, while also subjecting these to more critical/theoretical scrutiny. It is compatible with most versions of qualitative data analysis.

Interpretive interactionism   This term was coined by Norman Denzin, who attempted to carry out a synthesis of several separate but closely related approaches to qualitative research (including symbolic interactionism, phenomenology, ethnography and some strands of feminist research).

In vivo **codes**   This refers to codes (assigned to data excerpts by the researcher) that derive from concepts or even vocabulary invoked by research participants.

Macro   This is a term that relates to the broader social or political structures within which we carry out our research.

Methodology   This refers to discussions about the assumptions that underpin different approaches to doing research and their implications for conducting research and developing theory.

Methods   This refers to the specific practical measures and tools employed to access or generate data – generally, but not necessarily (see document analysis), through different forms of interaction.

Micro   This relates to the small-scale settings in which we study interpersonal interactions (e.g. the small group, the family, the professional consultation or the couple).

Observational fieldwork   This is an approach to generating data that relies on observing naturally occurring activities (whether these are routine or in some way exceptional). It has been the method most often employed by anthropologists.

Ontology   This means our views about what constitutes the social world and how we can go about studying it.

Phenomenology   This is the study of the meanings conferred by individuals and groups, particularly those that relate to common-sense or taken-for granted understandings and accounts.

Reification   This refers to the distortion inherent in according greater emphasis and less questioning to a concept or set of assumptions than would be called for in a more critical examination.

Saturation   This can refer either to sampling or the development of coding categories. In both cases it refers to the (possibly illusory) stage whereby the researcher has explored all possible avenues (to ensure coverage in sampling and comprehensiveness in terms of making sense of data).

Semi-structured interviews   This is a well-established method for eliciting individuals' perspectives and accounts and involves the researcher in asking a set of questions.

However, these are not always asked in the same order and there is room for the interviewee to raise additional issues that are salient for her/him. The researcher can also add questions to the schedule in response to comments by current or previous interviewees.

Social constructionism   This approach is based on the idea that people construct reality and their understandings through the process of interaction, but, unlike phenomenology, it is possible for such an approach to take account also of structural factors that influence this process. These can be articulated and studied through thoughtful sampling.

Sub-categories   This relates to 'second-order' codes, that is further divisions used to allocate additional labels to data excerpts, but retaining links with the broader categories or themes used to organize data through using a coding frame. Up to eight levels of subdivision, in terms of developing further coding categories, are allowed with most computer software packages for the analysis of qualitative data and should be more than enough for most analyses.

Symbolic interactionism   This approach purports that individuals' actions and meanings are conferred and enacted through the process of interacting with each other.

Themes   These are the broad codes assigned to the main issues arising in data (and are usually justified in terms of the frequency with which they occur). These are then used in order to organize data, with reference also to related sub-categories.

REFERENCES

Aldridge, J. (1993) 'The texual disembodiment of knowledge in research account writing', *Sociology*, 27(1): 53–66.

Alford, R. (1996) 'Towards a theory of data and method: Beyond positivism and postmodernism', Plenary presented at the Fourth International Sociological Association Social Science Methodology Conference, University of Essex, Colchester, UK.

Anderson, N. (1992) 'Work group innovation: A state of the art review', in D.M. Hosking and N. Anderson (eds) *Organizational Change and Innovation: Psychological Perspectives and Practices in Europe*, London: Routledge, pp. 149–160.

Andrews, M., Day Sclater, S., Squire, C. and Tamboukou, M. (2004) 'Narrative research', in C. Seale, G. Gobo, J.F. Gubrium and D. Silverman (eds) *Qualitative Research Practice*, London: Sage, pp. 109–124.

Angell, E. (2006) 'Research ethics committees: What troubles them and how consistent is their decision-making?', paper presented at *British Sociological Association Annual Medical Sociology Conference*, Edinburgh, September.

Anthony, R. (2005) 'Consistency of ethics review', *Forum Qualitative Sozialforschung/Forum Qualitative Social Research* [online journal], 6(1), Art. 5, available at: http://www.qualitative-research.net/fqs-texte1/05/05-1-5-e.htm [Date of access, 11/01/2006].

Armstrong, D. (1983) *The Political Anatomy of the Body: Medical Knowledge in Britain in the Twentieth Century*, Cambridge: Cambridge University Press.

Armstrong, D., Gosling, A., Weinman, J. and Marteau, T. (1997) 'The place of inter-rater reliability in qualitative research: An empirical study', *Sociology*, 51: 597–606.

Askham, J. and Barbour, R.S. (1996) 'The negotiated role of the midwife in Scotland', in S. Robinson and A.M. Thomson (eds) *Midwives, Research and Childbirth* (Vol. 4), London: Chapman and Hall, pp. 33–59.

Atkinson, P.A. (1997) 'Narrative turn or blind alley?', *Qualitative Health Research*, 7(3): 325–344.

Atkinson, P.A. (2004) 'Performance and rehearsal: The ethnographer at the opera', in C. Seale, G. Gobo, J.F. Gubrium and D. Silverman (eds) *Qualitative Research Practice*, London: Sage, pp. 94–106.

Atkinson, P.A. and Silverman, D. (1997) 'Kundera's *Immortality*: The interview society and the invention of the self', *Qualitative Inquiry*, 3(3): 304–325.

Banks, M. (2007) *Using Visual Data in Qualitative Research*, (Book 5 of the Sage Qualitative Research Kit), London: Sage.

Barbour, R.S. (1983) 'Negotiating transsituational demands: A study of professional socialization for social work', unpublished PhD thesis, University of Aberdeen.

Barbour, R.S. (1984) 'Social work education: A training in pessimism or parable?', *Social Work Education*, 4(1): 21–28.

Barbour, R.S. (1985) 'Dealing with the transsituational demands of professional socialization', *Sociological Review*, 33(3): 495–531.

Barbour, R.S. (1990) 'Fathers: The emergence of a new consumer group', in J. Garcia, R. Kilpatrick and M. Richards (eds) *The Politics of Maternity Care*, Oxford: Clarendon Press, pp. 202–216.

Barbour, R.S. (1993) ' "I don't sleep with my patients – do you sleep with yours?": Dealing with staff tensions and conflicts in AIDS-related work', in P. Aggleton, P. Davies and G. Hart (eds) *AIDS: Facing the Second Decade*, London: Falmer, pp. 159–168.

Barbour, R.S. (1995) 'The implications of HIV/AIDS for a range of workers in the Scottish context', *AIDS Care*, 7(4): 521–525.

Barbour, R.S. (1998a) 'Mixing qualitative methods: Quality assurance or qualitative quagmire?', *Qualitative Health Research*, 8: 352–361.

Barbour, R.S. (1998b) 'Engagement, presentation and representation in research practice', in R.S. Barbour and G. Huby (eds) *Meddling with Mythology: AIDS and the Social Construction of Knowledge*, London: Routledge, pp. 183–200.

Barbour, R.S. (1999a) 'Are focus groups an appropriate tool for analyzing organizational change?', in R.S. Barbour and J. Kitzinger (eds) *Developing Focus Group Research: Politics, Theory and Practice*. London: Sage, pp. 113–126.

Barbour, R.S. (1999b) 'The case for combining qualitative and quantitative approaches in health services research', *Journal of Health Services Research and Policy*, 4(1): 39–43.

Barbour, R.S. and Huby, G. (eds) (1998) *Meddling with Mythology: AIDS and the Social Construction of Knowledge*, London: Routledge.

Barbour, R.S. and Kitzinger, J. (eds) (1999) *Developing Focus Group Research: Politics, Theory and Practice*, London: Sage.

Barbour, R.S., Featherstone, V.A. and members of the Wolds Primary Care Research Network (WoReN) (2000) 'Acquiring qualitative skills for primary care research: review and reflections on a three-stage workshop. Part 1: Using interviews to generate data', *Family Practice*, 17(1): 76–82.

Barbour, R.S. and members of the Wolds Primary Care Research Network (WoReN) (2000) 'Acquiring qualitative skills for primary care research: review and reflections on a three-stage workshop. Part 2: Analyzing interview data', *Family Practice*, 17(1): 83–89.

Barbour, R.S. (2001) 'Checklists for improving the rigour of qualitative research: A case of the tail wagging the dog?', *British Medical Journal*, 322: 1115–1117.

Barbour, R.S. (2003) 'The newfound credibility of qualitative research? Tales of technical essentialism and co-option', *Qualitative Health Research,* 13(7): 1019–1027.

Barbour, R.S. (2007) *Doing Focus Groups*, London: Sage (Book 5 of *The Qualitative Research Kit*).

Barbour, R.S. and Barbour, M. (2003) 'Evaluating and synthesizing qualitative research: The need to develop a distinctive approach', *Journal of Evaluation in Clinical Practice*, 9(2): 179–186.

Barbour, R.S., Bryce, G., Connelly, G., Furnivall, J., Lewins, A., Lockhart, E., Phin, L., Stallard, A., van Beinum, M. and Wilson, P. (2006) *Only Connect: Addressing the Emotional Needs of Scotland's Children and Young People: A Report on the SNAP Child and Adolescent Mental Health Phase Two Survey*, Edinburgh/Glasgow: Health Scotland.

Barbour, R.S., Stanley, N., Penhale, B. and Holden, S. (2002) 'Assessing risk: Professional perspectives on work involving mental health and child care services', *Journal of Interprofessional Care*, 16(4): 323–333.

Barnard, M. (2005) 'Discomforting research: Colliding moralities and looking for "truth" in a study of parental drug problems', *Sociology of Health and Illness*, 27(1): 1–19.

Barry, S., Britten, N., Barber, N., Bradley, C. and Stevenson, F. (1999) 'Using reflexivity to optimize teamwork in qualitative research', *Qualitative Health Research*, 9(1): 26–44.

Becker, H.S. (1967) 'Whose side are we on?', *Social Problems*, 14: 239–247.

Becker, H.S. (1998) *The Tricks of the Trade*, Chicago: University of Chicago Press.

Becker, H.S. and Geer, B. (1957) 'Participant observation and interviewing: A comparison', *Human Organization*, 26: 28–34.

Becker, H.S. et al. (1961) *Boys in White*, Chicago: University of Chicago Press.

Belam, J., Harris, G., Kernick, D., Kline, F., Lindley, K., McWatt, J., Mitchell, A. and Reinhold, D. (2005) 'A qualitative study of migraine involving patient researchers', *British Journal of General Practice*, 55: 87–93.

van den Berg, H. (2005) 'Reanalyzing qualitative interviews from different angles: The risk of decontextualization and other problems of sharing qualitative data' [48 paragraphs], *Forum Qualitative Sozialforschung/Forum Qualitative Social Research* [on line journal], 6(1), Art. 30. Available at: http://www.qualitative-research.net/fqs-texte/1-05/05-1-30-e.htm [Date of access, 11/26/2006].

Berger, P. and Luckmann, T. (1966) *The Social Construction of Reality*, London: Penguin.

Bishop, L. (2007,) 'A reflexive account of reusing qualitative data: Beyond primary/secondary dualism', *Sociological Research Online*, 12(3) http://www.socresonline.org.uk/12/3/bishop.html

Black, E. and Smith, P. (1999) 'Princess Diana's meanings for women: Results of a focus group study', *Journal of Sociology*, 35(3): 263–278.

Blaxter, M. (2004) 'Understanding health inequalities: From transmitted deprivation to social capital', *International Journal of Social Research Methodology, Theory and Practice*, 7(1): 55–59.

Blaxter, M. (2007) 'Commentary', *Sociological Research Online*, 12(3) http://www. socresonline. org.uk/12/3/blaxter.html

Bloor, M. (1991) 'A minor offices: The variable and socially constructed character of death certification in a Scottish city', *Journal of Health and Social Behaviour*, 32(3): 273–287.

Bloor, M. (1995) *The Sociology of HIV Transmission*, London: Sage.

Bloor, M. (1997) 'Techniques of validation in qualitative research: A critical commentary', in G. Miller and R. Dingwall (eds) *Context and Method in Qualitative Research*. London: Sage, pp. 37–50.

Bloor, M., Frankland, J., Thomas, M. and Robson, K. (2001) *Focus Groups in Social Research*. London: Sage.

Blumer, H. (1969) *Symbolic Interactionism: Perspective and Method*, Englewood Cliffs, NJ: Prentice-Hall.

Bornat, J. (2005) 'Recycling the evidence: Different approaches to the reanalysis of gerontological data'. [37 paragraphs], *Forum Qualitative Sozialforschung/Forum Qualitative Social Research* [online journal], 6(1), Art. 42. Available at: http://www.qualitative-research.net/fqs-texte/1-05/05 -1-42-e.htm [Date of access, 11/26/2006].

Borochowitz, D.Y. (2005) 'Teaching a qualitative research seminar on sensitive issues: an autoethnography', *Qualitative Social Work*, 4(3): 347–362.

Bourne, J. (1998) 'Reseachers experience emotions too', in R.S. Barbour and G. Huby (eds) *Meddling with Mythology: AIDS and the Social Construction of Knowledge*, London: Routledge, pp. 90–103.

Bowen, E.S. (1967) *Return to Laughter*, New York: Anchor.

Brennan, M. (2006) 'Sociological eye on condolence books', *Network*, (Newsletter of the British Sociological Association), 94: 24.

Bretecher, C. (1985) *Mothers* (translated from the French by Angela Mason and Pat Fogarty), London: Methuen.

Brettell, C.B. (1993) 'Introduction: Fieldwork, text and audience', in C.B. Bretell (ed.) *When They Read What We Write: The Politics of Ethnography*, Westport, CT/London: Bergin and Garvey.

Bridges, J., Meyer, J., Glynn, M., Bentley, J. and Reeves, S. (2003) 'Interprofessional care co-ordinators: The benefits and tensions associated with a new role in UK acute health care', *International Journal of Nursing Studies*, 40: 599–607.

British Sociological Association (2002) *Statement of Ethical Practice for the British Sociological Association*, Durham: British Sociological Association. Available at: http://www.britsoc.co.uk/index.php?link_id=14&area=item1

Brown, S. (2003) 'The health beliefs of men: With special reference to coronary heart disease', Unpublished PhD thesis, University of Hull.

Burman, M.J., Batchelor, S. and Brown, J.A. (2001) 'Researching girls and violence', *British Journal of Criminology*, 41: 443–459.

Bury, M. (1982) 'Chronic illness as biographical disruption', *Sociology of Health and Illness*, 4(2): 167–182.

Butterfield, L.D., Borgen, W.A., Amundson, N.E. and Maglio, A.-S.T. (2005) 'Fifty years of the critical incident technique: 1954–2004 and beyond', *Qualitative Research*, 5(4): 475–497.

Callaghan, G. (2005) 'Accessing habitus: Relating structure and agency through focus group research', *Sociological Research Online*, 10(3), http://www.socresonline.org.uk/10/3/callaghan.html

Cameron, A., Lloyd, L., Kent, N. and Anderson, P. (2004) 'Researching end of life in old age: Ethical challenges', in M. Smyth and E. Williamson (eds) *Researchers and Their 'Subjects': Ethics, Power, Knowledge and Consent*, Bristol: Policy Press, pp. 105–117.

Campbell, M.K., Meier, A., Carr, C., Enga, Z., James, A.S., Reedy, J. and Zheng, B. (2001) 'Health behaviour changes after colon cancer: A comparison of findings from face-to-face and on-line focus groups', *Family and Community Health*, 24(3): 88–103.

Campbell, R., Pound, P., Pope, C., Britten, N., Pill, R., Morgan, M. and Donovan, J. (2003) 'Evaluating meta-ethnography: a synthesis of qualitative research on lay experiences of diabetes and diabetes care', *Social Science and Medicine*, 56: 671–684.

Carr, W. and Kemmis, S. (1986) *Becoming Critical: Education, Knowledge and Action Research*, London: The Falmer Press.

Carter, H. (2007) 'Paedophiles jailed for hatching plot on internet to rape two teenage sisters', *Guardian*, 6 Feb, http://www.guardian.co.uk/crime/article/0,,2006752,00.html [Date of access, 18/04/07].

Casarett, D. and Karalawish, J. (2000) 'Are special ethical guidelines needed for palliative care research?', *Journal of Pain and Symptom Management*, 20(2): 130–139.

Casey, C. and Edgerton, R.B. (eds) (2005) *A Companion to Psychological Anthropology: Modernity and Psycho-cultural Change,* Oxford: Blackwell Publishing.

Cawley, M.R. (2004) 'The psychosocial aspects of obesity: A quantitative and qualitative study', Unpublished PhD thesis, University of Glasgow.

Chapple, A. and Rogers, A. (1998) 'Explicit guidelines for qualitative research: A step in the right direction, a defence of the "soft" option, or a form of sociological imperialism?', *Family Practice*, 15(6): 556–561.

Chen, P. and Hinton, S.M. (1999) 'Realtime interviewing using the World Wide Web', *Sociological Research Online*, 4(3), http://www.socresonline.org.uk/socresonline/4/3/chen.html

Chiu, L.F. (2003) 'Transformational potential of focus group practice in participatory action research', *Action Research*, 1(2): 165–183.

Chiu, L.F. and Knight, D. (1999) 'How useful are focus groups for obtaining the views of minority groups?', in R.S. Barbour and J. Kitzinger (eds) *Developing Focus Group Research: Politics, Theory and Practice*. London: Sage, pp. 99–112.

Clark, A.M., Barbour, R.S. and McIntyre, P.D. (2004) 'Promoting participation in cardiac rehabilitation: An exploration of patients' choices and experiences in relation to attendance', *Journal of Advanced Nursing*, 47(1): 5–14.

Clifford, J. and Marcus, G. (eds) (1986) *Writing Culture: The Poetics and Politics of Ethnography*, Berkeley: University of California Press.

Coffey, A., Holbrook, B. and Atkinson, P. (1996) 'Qualitative data analysis: Technologies and respresentations', *Sociological Research Online*, 1(1), http://www.socresonline.org.uk/1/1/4.html

Cohen, S. and Taylor, L. (1977) 'Talking about prison blues', in C. Bell and H. Newby (eds) *Doing Sociological Research*, London: Allen & Unwin, pp. 67–86.

Collins, P. (1998) 'Negotiating selves: Reflections on "unstructured" interviewing', *Sociological Research Online*, 3(3), http://www.socresonline.org.uk/socresonline/3/3/2.html

Coomber, R. (2002) 'Signing your life away? Why research ethics committees (REC) shouldn't always require written confirmation that participants in research have been informed of the aims of a study and their rights – the case of criminal populations', *Sociological Research Online*, 7(1), http://www.socresonline.uk/socresonline/7/1/coomber.htm

Corrigan, O. (2003) 'Empty ethics: The problem with informed consent', *Sociology of Health and Illness*, 25(7): 768–792.

Corti, L. (2000) 'Progress and problems of preserving and providing access to qualitative data for social research: The international picture of an emerging culture' [58 paragraphs], *Forum Qualitative Sozialforschung/Forum Qualitative Social Research* [online journal], 1(3), Art. 2. Available at: http://www.qualitative-research.net/fqs-texte/3-00/3-00corti-e.htm [Date of access, 11/26/2006].

Corti, L. and Thompson, P. (2004) 'Secondary analysis of archived data', in C. Seale, G. Gobo, J.F. Gubrium and D. Silverman (eds) *Qualitative Research Practice*, London: Sage, pp. 327–343.

Crabtree, B.F., Yanoshik, M.K., Miller, M.L. and O'Connor, P.J. (1993) 'Selecting individual or group interviews', in D.L. Morgan (ed.) *Successful Focus Groups: Advancing the State of the Art*, Newbury, CA: Sage, pp. 137–149.

Crombie, I.K. with Davies, H.T.O. (1996) *Research in Health Care: Design, Conduct and Interpretation of Health Services Research*, Chichester: John Wiley & Sons.

Crossley, M.L. (2002) ' "Could you please pass one of those health leaflets along?" Exploring health, morality and resistance through focus groups', *Social Science and Medicine*, 55(8): 1471–1483.

Crow, G. (2002) *Social Solidarities: Theories, Identities and Social Change*, Buckinghamshire: Open University Press.

Davis, M.S. (1971) ' "That's interesting!" Towards a phenomenology of sociology and a sociology of phenomenology', *Philosophy of the Social Sciences*, 1: 309–344.

Dean, J.P., Eichorn, R.L. and Dean, L.R. (1967) 'Fruitful informants for intensive interviewing', in J.T. Dolby (ed.) *An Introduction to Social Research*, 2nd edition, New York: Appleton-Century Crofts.

Delamont, S. (2004) 'Ethnography and participant observation', in C. Seale, G. Gobo, J.F. Gubrium and D. Silverman (eds) *Qualitative Research Practice*, London: Sage, pp. 217–229.

Denzin, N.K. (1989) *Interpretive Biography*, London: Sage.

Dingwall, R. (1977) *The Social Organization of Health Visiting*, London: Croom Helm.

Dingwall, R. (1992) ' "Don't mind him: He's from Barcelona!", Qualitative methods in health studies', in J. Daly, I. McDonald and E. Willis (eds) *Researching Health Care*, London: Tavistock/Routledge, pp. 161–175.

Dingwall, R. (1997) 'Accounts, interviews and observations', in G. Miller and R. Dingwall (eds) *Context and Method in Qualitative Research*, London: Sage, pp. 51–65.

Dingwall, R. (2006) 'Confronting the anti-democrats: The unethical nature of ethical regulation in social science', Plenary presented at the British Sociological Associations' Annual Medical Sociology Conference, Edinburgh, 14 September.

Doig, B. (2004) 'Working backwards: The road less travelled in quantitative methodology', in B. Somekh and C. Lewin (eds) *Research Methods in the Social Sciences*, London: Sage, pp. 269–273.

Dolan, B. (1999) 'The impact of local research committees on the development of nursing knowledge', *Journal of Advanced Nursing*, 30: 1009–1010.

Dowell, J. and Hudson, H. (1997) 'A qualitative study of medicine-taking behaviour in primary care', *Family Practice*, 14(5): 369–375.

Drew, P. (2003) 'Conversation analysis', in J.A. Smith (ed.), *Qualitative Psychology: A Practical Guide to Research Methods*, London, Sage.

Eikeland, O. (2006) 'Condescending ethics and action research: Extended review article', *Action Research*, 4(1): 37–47.

Elliott, H. (1997) 'The use of diaries in sociological research on health experiences', *Sociological Research Online*, 2(2), http://www.socresonline.org.uk/socresonline/2/2/7.html

Ellis, C. (1995) *Final Negotiations: A Story of Love, Loss and Chronic Illness*, Philadelphia, PA: Temple University Press.

Exley, C. and Letherby, G. (2001) 'Managing a disrupted lifecourse: Issues of identity and emotion work', *Health*, 5(1): 112–132.

Fairhurst, K. and Huby, G. (1998) 'From trial data to practical knowledge: Qualitative study of how general practitioners have accessed and used evidence about statin drugs in their management of hypercholesterolaemia', *British Medical Journal*, 317: 1130–1134.

Fardy, H.J. and Jeffs, D. (1994) 'Focus groups: A method for developing consensus guidelines in general practice', *Family Practice*, 11(3): 325–329.

Farquhar, C. with Das, R. (1999) 'Are focus groups suitable for "sensitive" topics?', in R.S. Barbour and J. Kitzinger (eds) *Developing Focus Group Research: Politics, Theory and Practice*, London: Sage, pp. 47–63.

Fenton, S. and Charsley, K. (2000) 'Epidemiology and sociology as incommensurate games: Accounts from the study of health and ethnicity', *Health*, 4(4): 403–425.

Fine, G.A. (1993) 'Ten lies of ethnography: Moral dilemmas in field research', *Journal of Contemporary Ethnography*, 22(3): 267–294.

Foster, C. (1998) 'Of tales, myth, metaphor and metonym', in R.S. Barbour and G. Huby (eds) *Meddling with Mythology: AIDS and the Social Construction of Knowledge*, London: Routledge, pp. 146–161.

Fowler, B. (2005) 'Collective memory and forgetting: Components for a study of obituaries', *Theory, Culture and Society*, 22(6): 53–72.

Frankland, J. and Bloor, M. (1999) 'Some issues arising in the systematic analysis of focus group materials', in R.S. Barbour and J. Kitzinger (eds) *Developing Focus Group Research: Politics, Theory and Practice*, London: Sage, pp. 144–155.

Freire, P. (1972) *The Pedagogy of the Oppressed*, Harmondsworth: Penguin.

Frosh, S. and Emerson, P.D. (2005) 'Interpretation and over-interpretation: Disputing the meaning of texts', *Qualitative Research*, 5(3): 307–324.

Frosh, S., Phoenix, A. and Pattman, R. (2003) 'Taking a stand: Using psychoanalysis to explore the positioning of subjects in discourse', *British Journal of Psychology*, 42: 39–53.

Garfinkel, H. (1967) *Studies in Ethnomethodology*, Englewood Cliffs, NJ: Prentice-Hall.

Geertz, C. (1973) *The Interpretation of Cultures*, New York: Basic Books.

Geistenfeld, P.B., Grant, D.R. and Chiang, C-P. (2003) 'Hate online: a content analysis of extremist internet sites', *Analyses of Social Issues and Public Policy*, 3(1): 29–44.

Gergen, K.J. (1973) 'Social psychology as history', *Journal of Personality and Social Psychology*, 26: 309–320.

Gillies, V. and Edwards, R. (2005) 'Secondary analysis in exploring family and social change: Addressing the issue of context' [30 paragraphs], *Forum Qualitative Sozialforschung/Forum Qualitative Social Research* [online journal], 6(1), Art. 44. Available at: http://www.qualitative-research.net/fqs-texte/1-05/05-1-44-e.htm [Date of access: 11/26/2006].

Glaser, B. and Strauss, A. (1967) *The Discovery of Grounded Theory*, Chicago: Aldine.

Goffman, E. (1974) *Frame Analysis*, Harmondsworth: Penguin.

Goode, E. (1999) 'The ethics of deception in social research: A case study', in A. Bryman and R.G. Burgess (eds) *Qualitative Research* (Vol. 4), London: Sage, pp. 412–432.

Goode, J. (2006) 'Research identities: reflections of a contract researcher', *Sociological Research Online* 11(2) http://www.socresonline.org.uk/11/2/goode.html

Goodwin, D., Pope, C., Mort, M. and Smith, A. (2003) 'Ethics and ethnography: An experiential account', *Qualitative Health Research*, 13(4): 567–577.

Graham, H. (1993) *When Life's a Drag: Women, Smoking and Disadvantage*, London: HMSO.

Green, G., Barbour, R.S., Barnard, M. and Kitzinger, J. (1993) 'Who wears the trousers? Sexual harassment in research settings', *Women's Studies International Forum*, 16(6): 627–637.

Green, J. and Thorogood, N. (2004) *Qualitative Methods for Health Research*, London: Sage.

Greene, J.C., Kreider, H. and Mayer, E. (2004) 'Combining qualitative and quantitative methods in social enquiry', in B. Somekh and C. Lewin (eds) *Research Methods in the Social Sciences*, London: Sage, pp. 274–281.

Greenhalgh, T. (1998) *How To Read a Paper*, London: BMJ Books.

Greenwood, J. (1994) 'Action research: a few details, a caution and something new', *Journal of Advanced Nursing*, 20(1): 13–18.

Grenz, S. (2005) 'Intersections of sex and power in research on prostitution: A female researcher interviewing male heterosexual clients', *Signs*, 39(4): 2091–2113.

Guillemin, M. (2006) 'Human research ethics review and practice in Australia', paper presented at *British Sociological Association's Annual Medical Sociology Conference,* Edinburgh, September.

Guthrie, E. and Barbour, R.S. (2002) 'Patients' views and experiences of obesity management in one general practice', final project report submitted to Scottish Chief Scientist's Office.

Hammersley, M. (2004) 'Teaching qualitative method: Craft, profession or bricolage?', in C. Seale, G. Gobo, J.F. Gubrium and D. Silverman (eds) *Qualitative Research Practice*, London: Sage, pp. 549–560.

Hammersley, M. and Atkinson, P. (1995) *Ethnography: Principles in Practice* (2nd edition), London: Routledge.

Hampshire, A., Blair, M., Crown, N., Avery, A. and Williams, I. (1999) 'Action research: A useful method of promoting change in primary care?', *Family Practice*, 16(3): 305–311.

Harding, G. and Gantley, M. (1998) 'Qualitative methods: Beyond the cookbook', *Family Practice*, 15: 76–79.

Harding, J. (2006) 'Questioning the subject in biographical interviewings', *Sociological Research Online* 11(3) http://www.socresonline.org.uk/11/3/harding.html

Harrow, A. (2006) 'Betwixt and between: The experience of male partners of women with breast cancer', Unpublished PhD thesis, University of Dundee.

Hart, E. and Bond, M. (1995) *Action Research for Health and Social Care: A Guide to Practice*, Buckingham: Open University Press.

ten Have, P. (2004) 'Ethnomethodology', in C. Seale, G. Gobo, J.F. Gubrium and D. Silverman (eds) *Qualitative Research Practice*, London: Sage, pp. 151–164.

Heaton, J. (2004) *Reworking Qualitative Data*, London: Sage.

Hepburn, A. and Potter, J. (2004) 'Discourse analytic practice', in C. Seale, G. Gobo, J.F. Gubrium and D. Silverman (eds) *Qualitative Research Practice*, London: Sage, pp. 180–196.

Hilsen, A.I. (2006) 'And they shall be known by their deeds: Ethics and politics in action research', *Action Research*, 4(1): 23–36.

Hine, C. (2004) 'Social research methods and the internet: a thematic review', *Sociological Research Online* 9(2) http://www.socresonline.org.uk/9/2/hine.html

Hodgkin, K. and Radstone, S. (eds) (2003) *Contested Pasts: The Politics of Memory*, London/New York: Routledge.

Hughes, E.C. (1958) *Men and their Work*, London: Collier-Macmillan.

Humphreys, L. (1970) *Tearoom Trade*, Chicago: Aldine.

Humphreys, L. (1975) *Tearoom Trade*, Chicago: Aldine (enlarged edition).

Hunt, S.A. and Benford, R.D. (1997) 'Dramaturgy and methodology', in G. Miller and R. Dingwall (eds) *Context and Method in Qualitative Research*, London: Sage, pp. 106–118.

Hurd, T.L. and McIntyre, A. (1996) 'The seduction of sameness: Similarity and representing the other', in S. Wilkinson and C. Kitzinger (eds) *Representing the Other*, London: Sage, pp. 78–82.

Hussey, S., Hoddinott, P., Dowell, J., Wilson, P. and Barbour, R.S. (2004) 'The sickness certification system in the UK: A qualitative study of the views of general practitioners in Scotland', *British Medical Journal*, 328: 88–92.

Johnson, A. (1996) ' "It's good to talk": The focus group and the sociological imagination', *The Sociological Review*, 44(3): 517–538.

Kelle, U. (1997) 'Theory building in qualitative research and computer programs for the management of textual data', *Sociological Research Online*, 2, http://www.socresonline.org.uk/ 2/2/1.html

Kelle, U. (2001) 'Social explanations between micro and macro and the integration of qualitative and quantitative methods [43 paragraphs], *Forum Qualitative Sozialforschung/Forum Qualitative Social Research* [online journal], 2(1). Available at http://www.qualitative-research.net/fqs/fqs-eng.htm [Date of access, 11/01/2006].

Kemmis, S. and McTaggert, R. (1988) *The Action Research Planner*, Victoria, Australia: Deakin University Press.

Kennedy, A. (2002) *Living with a Secret: An Action Research Report on Women and Service Providers' Views of the Termination of Pregnancy Services – Glasgow*, Glasgow: Family Planning Association Scotland.

Kenny, A.J. (2005) 'Interaction in cyberspace: An online focus group', *Journal of Advanced Nursing*, 49(4): 414–422.

Kitzinger, J. and Barbour, R.S. (1999) 'Introduction: The challenge and promise of focus groups', in R.S. Barbour and J. Kitzinger (eds) *Developing Focus Group Research: Politics, Theory and Practice*, London: Sage, pp. 1–20.

Kitzinger, J., Green, J. and Coupland, V. (1990) 'Labour relations: Midwives and doctors on the labour ward', in J. Garcia, R. Kilpatrick and M. Richards (eds) *The Politics of Maternity Care*, Oxford: Clarendon Press, pp. 149–162.

Kleinman, S. and Fine, G.A. (1979) 'Rhetorics and action in moral organizations: Social control of Little Leaguers and ministry students', *Urban Life*, 8(3): 275–294.

Kroll, T., Barbour, R.S. and Harris, J. (2007, in press) 'Using focus groups in disability research', *Qualitative Health Research*.

Kuzel, A.J. (1992) 'Sampling in qualitative inquiry', in B.F. Crabtree and W.I. Miller (eds) *Doing Qualitative Research*, Newbury Park, CA: Sage, pp. 31–44.

Ladkin, D. (2004) 'Action research', in C. Seale, G. Gobo, J.F. Gubrium and D. Silverman (eds) *Qualitative Research Practice*, London: Sage, pp. 536–548.

Learmonth, M. (2003) 'Making health services management research critical: A review and a suggestion', *Sociology of Health and Illness*, 25(1): 93–119.

Lee, D. (1997) 'Interviewing men: Vulnerabilities and dilemmas', *Women's Studies International Forum*, 20(4): 553–564.

Lee, S.S. (2001) 'A root out of a dry ground: resolving the researcher/researched dilemma', in J. Zeni (ed.) *Ethical Issues in Practitioner Research*, New York: Teachers College Press, pp. 61–71.

Lilford, R., Warren, R. and Braunholtz, D. (2003) 'Action research: A way of researching or a way of managing?', *Journal of Health Services Research and Policy*, 8(2): 100–104.

Loseke, D.R. and Cahill, S.E. (2004) 'Publishing qualitative manuscripts: lessons learned', in C. Seale, G. Gobo, J.F. Gubrium and D. Silverman (eds) *Qualitative Research Practice*, London: Sage, pp. 576–591.

van Maanen, J. (1995) *Representation in Ethnography*, Thousand Oaks, CA: Sage.

MacDougall, C. and Fudge, E. (2001) 'Planning and recruiting the sample for focus groups and in-depth interviews', *Qualitative Health Research*, 11(1): 117–125.

MacGregor, T.E., Rodger, S., Cumming, A.L. and Leschied, A.W. (2006) 'The needs of foster parents: a qualitative study of motivation, support and retention', *Qualitative Social Work*, 5 (3): 351–368.

Mann, C. and Stewart, F. (2000) *Internet Communication and Qualitative Research: A Handbook for Researching Online*, London: Sage.

Marshall, C. and Rossman, G.B. (1995) *Designing Qualitative Research* (2nd edition), London: Sage.

Mason, J. (1996) *Qualitative Researching*, London: Sage.

Mason, J. (2006) 'Mixing methods in a qualitatively driven way', *Qualitative Research*, 6(1): 9–25.

Mason, J. (2007, in press) *Sociological Research Online*, 12(3) http://www.socresonline.org.uk/ 12/3/Mason.html

Masson, J. (2004) 'The legal context', in S. Fraser, V. Lewis, S. Ding, M. Lellet and C. Robinson (eds) *Doing Research with Children and Young People*, London: Sage: pp. 43–58.

Mauthner, N.S., Parry, O. and Backett-Milburn, K. (1998) 'The data are out there, or are they? Implications for archiving and revisiting qualitative data', *Sociology*, 32(4): 733–745.

Mays, N. and Pope, C. (1995) 'Rigour and qualitative research', *British Medical Journal*, 311: 109–112.

Mazeland, H. and ten Have, P. (1996) 'Essential tensions in (semi-) open research interviews', in I. Maso and F. Wester (eds) *The Deliberate Dialogue: Qualitative Perspectives on the Interview*, Brussels: VUB University Press. (Online version 1998: http://www.pscw.uva.no/emca/ET.htm)

McDonach, E., Barbour, R.S. and Williams, B. (in press) 'Reflections on applying for NHS ethical approval and governance in a climate of rapid change: Prioritising process over principles?', *International Journal of Research Methodology*.

McKeganey, N., Barnard, M. and Leyland, A. (1992) 'Female prostitution and HIV infection in Glasgow', *British Medical Journal*, 305: 801–804.

McKeganey, N.P. and Boddy, F.A. (1988) 'General practitioners and opiate abusing patients', *Journal of the Royal College of General Practitioners*, 38: 73–75.

McMahon, T. (1999) 'Is reflective practice synonymous with action research?', *Educational Action Research*, 7(1): 163–169.

McTaggert, R., Henry, H. and Johnson, E. (1997) 'Traces of participatory action research: Reciprocity among educators', *Educational Action Research*, 5: 123–140.

Melia, K.M. (1997) 'Producing "plausible stories": Interviewing student nurses', in G. Miller and R. Dingwall (eds) *Context and Method in Qualitative Research*, London: Sage, pp. 26–36.

Merry, S.E. (1990) *Getting Justice and Getting Even*, Chicago: University of Chicago Press.

Meyer, J.E. (1993a) 'New paradigm research in practice: The trials and tribulations of action research', *Journal of Advanced Nursing*, 18: 166–172.

Meyer, J.E. (1993b) 'Lay participation in care: A challenge for multi-disciplinary teamwork', *Journal of Interprofessional Care*, 7: 57–66.

Meyer, J.E. (1993c) 'Lay participation in care: Threat to the status quo', in J. Wilson-Barnett and J. Macleod Clark (eds) *Research in Health Promotion and Nursing*, London: Macmillan, pp. 86–100.

Meyer, J. (2000) 'Using qualitative methods in health related action research', *British Medical Journal*, 320: 178–181.

Meyer, J. and Batehup, L. (1997) 'Action research in health care practice: Nature, present concerns and future possibilities', *Nursing Times Research*, 2(3): 175–184.

Michell, L. (1999) 'Combining focus groups and interviews: Telling it like it is; telling how it feels', in R.S. Barbour and J. Kitzinger (eds) *Developing Focus Group Research: Politics, Theory and Practice*, London: Sage, pp. 36–46.

Milgram, S. (1963) 'Behavioral study of obedience', *Journal of Abnormal and Social Psychology*, 67: 371–378.

Miller, G. (1997a) 'Introduction: Context and method in qualitative research', in G. Miller and R. Dingwall (eds) *Context and Method in Qualitative Research*, London: Sage, pp. 1–11.

Miller, G. (1997b) 'Contextualising texts: Studying organizational texts', in G. Miller and R. Dingwall (eds) *Context and Method in Qualitative Research*, London: Sage, pp. 77–91.

Miller, G. (1997c) 'Toward ethnographies of institutional discourse: Proposal and suggestions', in G. Miller and R. Dingwall (eds) *Context and Method in Qualitative Research*, London: Sage, pp. 155–171.

Miller, R.L. (2000) *Researching Life Stories and Family Histories*, London: Sage.

Milne, C. (2005) 'Overseeing research: Ethics and the Institutional Review board [33 paragraphs], *Forum Qualitative Sozialforschung/Forum Qualitative Social Research* [online journal], 6(1), Art. 41. Available at: http://www.qualitative-research.net/fqs-texte1/05/05-1-4-e.htm [Date of access, 11/01/2006].

Mischler, E. (1986) *Research Interviewing: Context and Narrative*, Cambridge, MA: Harvard University Press.

Monaghan, L. (1999) 'Creating the "perfect body"', *Body and Society*, 5(2–3): 267–290.

Monaghan, L. (2001) 'Looking good, feeling good: The embodied pleasure of vibrant physicality', *Sociology of Health and Illness*, 23(3): 330–356.

Moore, N. (2007 in press) '(Re)using qualitative data?', *Sociological Research Online*, 12(3) http://www.socresonline.org.uk/12/3/Moore.html

Moran-Ellis, J., Alexander, V.D., Cronin, A., Dickinson, M., Fielding, J., Sleney, J. and Thomas, H. (2006) 'Triangulation and integration: Processes, claims and implications', *Qualitative Research*, 6(1): 45–59.

Morgan, D.L. (1988) *Focus Groups as Qualitative Research*, Thousand Oaks, CA: Sage.

Morris, J. (2006) *Hav*, London: Faber & Faber.

Morse, J.M. (2000) 'Theoretical congestion', *Qualitative Health Research*, 10(6): 715–716.

Morse, J.M. (2004) 'Preparing and evaluating qualitative research proposals', in C. Seale, G. Gobo, J.F. Gubrium and D. Silverman (eds) *Qualitative Research Practice*, London: Sage, pp. 493–503.

Munday, J. (2006) 'Identity in focus: The use of focus groups to study the construction of collective identity', *Sociology*, 40(1): 89–105.

Munhall, P. (1988) 'Ethical considerations in qualitative research', *Western Journal of Nursing Research*, 10(2): 150–162.

Murphy, B., Cockburn, J. and Murphy, M. (1992) 'Focus groups in health research', *Health Promotion Journal of Australia*, 2: 37–40.

Myers, G. and Macnaghten, P. (1999) 'Can focus groups be analyzed as talk?', in R.S. Barbour and J. Kitzinger (eds) *Developing Focus Group Research: Politics, Theory and Practice*, London: Sage, pp. 173–185.

Nelson, S. (2004) 'Research with psychiatric patients: Knowing their own minds?', in M. Smyth and E. Williamson (eds) *Researchers and Their 'Subjects': Ethics, Power, Knowledge and Consent*, Bristol: Policy Press, pp. 91–103.

Noblit, G.W. and Hare, R.D. (1988) *Meta-Ethnography: Synthesizing Qualitative Studies*, London: Sage.

Oakley, A. (1981) 'Interviewing women: A contradiction in terms?', in H. Roberts (ed.) *Doing Feminist Research*, London: Routledge, pp. 30–61.

O'Connor, H. and Madge, C. (2001) 'Cybere-mothers: Online synchronous interviewing using conferencing software', *Sociological Research Online*, 5(4), http://www.socresonline.org.uk/socresonline/5/4/o'connor.html

O'Kane, C. (2000) 'The development of participatory techniques', in P. Christensen and A. James (eds) *Research with Children: Perspectives and Practices*, London: Falmer Press, pp. 136–159.

Okely, J. (1994) 'Thinking through fieldwork', in A. Bryman and R.G. Burgess (eds) *Analyzing Qualitative Data*, London: Sage, pp. 18–34.

Olesen, V.L. and Whittaker, E.W. (1967) 'Role making in participant observation: Processes in the researcher–actor relationship', *Human Organization*, 26: 273–281.

Olesen, V.L. and Whittaker, E.W. (1968) *The Silent Dialogue*, San Francisco: Jossey-Bass.

Ong, B.N. (1993) *The Practice of Health Services Research*, London: Chapman and Hall.

Ong, B.N. (1996) *Rapid Appraisal and Health Policy*, London: Chapman and Hall.

Owen, S. (2001) 'The practical, methodological and ethical dilemmas of conducting focus groups with vulnerable clients', *Journal of Advanced Nursing*, 36(5): 652–658.

Padilla, R.V. (1993) 'Using dialogical research methods in group interviews', in D.L. Morgan (ed.) *Successful Focus Groups: Advancing the State of the Art*, London: Sage, pp. 153–166.

Parker, I. (1992) *Discourse Dynamics: Critical Analysis for Social and Individual Psychology*, London: Routledge.

Parry, O. and Mauthner, N. (2004) 'Whose data are they anyway? Practical, legal and ethical issues in archiving qualitative research data', *Sociology*, 38(1): 139–152.

Peräkylä, A. (2004) 'Conversation analysis', in C. Seale, G. Gobo, J.F. Gubrium and D. Silverman (eds) *Qualitative Research Practice*, London: Sage, pp. 165–179.

Pink, S. (2004) 'Visual methods', in C. Seale, G. Gobo, J.F. Gubrium and D. Silverman (eds) *Qualitative Research Practice*, London: Sage, pp. 391–406.

Pini, B. (2002) 'Focus groups, feminist research and farm women's opportunities for empowerment in rural social research', *Journal of Rural Studies*, 18(3): 339–351.

Platt, J. (1992) 'The case method in sociology', *Current Sociology* 40(1): 17–48.

Plummer, K. (1995) *Telling Sexual Stories: Power, Change and Social Worlds*, London: Routledge.

Poland, B. and Pederson, A. (1998) 'Reading between the lines: Interpreting silences in qualitative research', *Qualitative Inquiry*, 4(2): 293–312.

Popay, J., Williams, G. and Rogers, A. (1998) 'Rationale and standards for the systematic review of qualitative literature in health services research', *Qualitative Health Research*, 8: 341–351.

Pope, C. (1991) 'Trouble in store: Some thoughts on the management of waiting lists', *Sociology of Health and Illness*, 13: 193–212.

Pope, C. and Mays, N. (eds) (1995) *Qualitative Research in Health Care* (2nd edition). London: BMJ Books.

Pound, P., Britten, N., Morgan, M., Yardley, L., Pope, C., Daker-White, G. and Campbell, R. (2005) 'Resisting medicines: A synthesis of qualitative studies of medicine taking', *Social Science and Medicine*, 61: 133–155.

Powney, J. (1988) 'Structured eavesdropping', *Research Intelligence (Journal of the British Educational Research Foundation)*, 28: 10–12.

Prior, L. (2003) *Using Documents in Social Research*, London: Sage.

Prior, L. (2004) 'Documents', in C. Seale, G. Gobo, J.F. Gubrium and D. Silverman (eds) *Qualitative Research Practice*, London: Sage, pp. 375–390.

Puchta, C. and Potter, J. (2004) *Focus Group Practice*, London: Sage.

Punch, M. (1994) 'Politics and ethics in qualitative research', in N.K. Denzin and Y.S. Lincoln (eds) *Handbook of Qualitative Research*, Thousand Oaks, CA: Sage, pp. 833–897.

Rapley, T. (2001) 'The art(fulness) of open-ended interviewing: Some considerations on analysing interviews', *Qualitative Research*, 1(3): 303–323.

Rapley, T. (2004) 'Interviews', in C. Seale, G. Gobo, J.F. Gubrium and D. Silverman (eds) *Qualitative Research Practice*, London: Sage, pp. 15–33.

Reason, P. (ed.) (1988) *Human Enquiry in Action: Developments in New Paradigm Research*, London: Sage.

Reason, P. (1994) 'Three approaches to participatory inquiry', in N.K. Denzin and Y.S. Lincoln (eds) *Handbook of Qualitative Research*, Thousand Oaks, CA: Sage, pp. 324–339.

Reason, P. and Bradbury, H. (eds) (2001) *Handbook of Action Research: Participative Inquiry and Practice*, London: Sage.

Reason, P. and Marshall, J. (1987) 'Research as personal process', in D. Boud and V. Griffen (eds) *Appreciating Adult Learning*, London: Kogan Page, pp. 112–126.

Reason, P. and McArdle, K. (2004) 'Brief notes on the theory and practice of action research', in S. Becker and A. Bryman (eds) *Understanding Research Methods for Social Policy and Practice: Themes, methods and Approaches*, Bristol: Policy, pp. 114–122.

Reeves, S., Meyer, J., Glynn, M. and Bridges, J. (1999) 'Coordination of interprofessional health care teams in a general and emergency medical directorate', *Advancing Clinical Nursing*, 3: 49–59.

Regan, S. (2003) 'The use of teleconferencing focus groups with families involved in organ donation: dealing with sensitive issues', in J. Lindsay and D. Turcotte (eds) *Crossing Boundaries and Developing Alliances through Groupwork*, New York: Haworth Press, pp. 115–131.

Reinharz, S. (1979) *On Becoming a Social Scientist*, San Francisco: Josey-Bass.

Richardson, L. (1994) 'Writing: A method of inquiry', in N.K. Denzin and Y.S. Lincoln (eds) *Handbook of Qualitative Research*, Thousand Oaks, CA: Sage, pp. 516–529.

Riessman, C.K. (1993) *Narrative Analysis*, Newbury Park, CA: Sage.

Riessman, C.K. (1994) 'Subjectivity matters: The positioned investigator', in C.K. Riessman (ed.) *Qualitative Studies in Social Work Research*, London: Sage, pp. 133–138.

Ritchie, J. and Spencer, L. (1994) 'Qualitative data analysis for applied policy research', in A. Bryman and R.G. Burgess (eds) *Analyzing Qualitative Data*, London: Routledge, pp. 173–194.

Rosaldo, R. (1983) 'Grief and a headhunter's rage: On the cultural force of emotions', in E. Bruner (ed.) *Text – Play and Story: The Construction and Reconstruction of Self and Society*, Washington, DC: Proceedings of the American Ethnological Society, pp. 178–195.

Rosaldo, R. (1989) *Culture and Truth: The Remaking of Social Analysis*, London: Routledge.

Rosenhan, D.L. (1973) 'On being sane in insane places', *Science*, 179: 250–258.

Rosenthal, G. (2004) 'Biographical research', in C. Seale, G. Gobo, J.F. Gubrium and D. Silverman (eds) *Qualitative Research Practice*, London: Sage, pp. 48–64.

Rubin, H.J. and Rubin, I.S. (1995) *Qualitative Interviewing: The Art of Hearing Data*, Thousand Oaks, CA: Sage.

Ryen, A. (2004) 'Ethical issues', in C. Seale, G. Gobo, J.F. Gubrium and D. Silverman (eds) *Qualitative Research Practice*, London: Sage, pp. 230–247.

Sacks, H. (1972) 'An initial investigation of the usability of conversational data for doing sociology', in D. Sudnow (ed.) *Studies in Social Interaction*, New York: The Free Press, pp., 31–74.

Saunders. T. (2004) 'Controllable Laughter: Managing sex work through humour', *Sociology*, 38(2): 273–291.

Schatzman, L. and Strauss, A. (1973) *Field Research: Strategies for a Natural Sociology*, Englewood Cliffs, NJ: Prentice-Hall.

Schegloff, E.A. (1997) 'Whose text? Whose context?', *Discourse and Society*, 8: 165–187.

Schneider, S.J., Kerwin, J., Frechtling, J. and Vivari, B.A. (2002) 'Characteristics of the discussion in online and face to face focus groups', *Social Science Computer Review*, 29(1): 31–42.

Schulz, K.F. (1995) 'Subverting randomization in controlled trials', *Journal of the American Medical Association*, 274: 1456–1458.

Schutz, A. (1972) *The Phenomenology of the Social World*, London: Heinemann.

Schwartz, M.S. and Schwartz, C.G. (1955) 'Problems in participant observation', *American Journal of Sociology*, 60: 343–353.

Scott, S. (1984) 'The personable and the powerful; gender and status in sociological research', in C. Bell and H. Roberts (eds) *Social Researching: Politics, Problems, Practice*, London: Routledge and Kegan Paul, pp. 165–178.

Scraton, P. (2004) 'Speaking truth to power: Experiencing critical research', in M. Smyth and E. Williamson (eds) *Researchers and Their 'Subjects': Ethics, Power, Knowledge and Consent*, Bristol: Policy Press, pp. 175–194.

Seale, C. (1998) 'Qualitative interviewing', in C. Seale (ed.) *Researching Society and Culture*, London: Sage, pp. 202–216.

Seale, C. (1999) *The Quality of Qualitative Research*, London: Sage.

Seale, C. (2001a) 'Sporting cancer: Struggle between language in news reports of people with cancer', *Sociology of Health and Illness*, 23(3): 308–329.

Seale, C. (2001b) 'Cancer in the news: Religion, fate and justice in news stories about people with cancer', *Health*, 5(4): 425–440.

Seymour, J., Bellamy, G., Gott, M., Ahmedzai, S.H. and Clark, D. (2002) 'Using focus groups to explore older people's attitudes to end-of-life care', *Ageing and Society*, 22(4): 517–526.

Shah, S. (2006) 'Sharing the world: The researcher and the researched', *Qualitative Research*, 6(2): 207–220.

Sheehan, E.A. (1993) 'The student of culture and the ethnography of Irish intellectuals', in C.B. Bretell (ed.) *When They Read What We Write: The Politics of Ethnography*, Westport, CT/London: Bergin and Garvey.

Shweder, R.A. (1990) 'Cutural psychology – What is it?' in J.W. Stigler, R.A. Shweder and G. Herdt (eds) *Cultural Psychology: Essays on Comparative Human Development*, Cambridge: Cambridge University Press, pp. 1–45.

Silverman, D. (1993) *Interpreting Qualitative Data: Methods of Analyzing Talk, Text and Interaction*, London: Sage.

Sim, J. (1998) 'Collecting and analyzing qualitative data: Issues raised by the focus group', *Journal of Advanced Nursing*, 28(2): 345–352.

Small, N. (1998) 'The story as gift: researching AIDS in the welfare marketplace', in R.S. Barbour and G. Huby (eds) *Meddling with Mythology: AIDS and the Social Construction of Knowledge*, London: Routledge, pp. 127–145.

Smith, J.A. (ed.) (2003) *Qualitative Psychology: A Practical Guide to Research Methods*, London: Sage.

Smith, J.A. and Osborn, M. (2003) 'Interpretative phenomenological analysis', in J.A. Smith (ed.) *Qualitative Psychology: A Practical Guide to Research Methods*, London: Sage, pp. 51–80.

Somekh, B. (1994) 'Inhabiting each other's castles: towards knowledge and mutual growth through collaboration', *Educational Action Research*, 2(3): 357–381.

Sparks, R., Girling, E. and Smith, M.V. (2002) 'Lessons from history: Pasts, presents and future of punishment in children's talk', *Children and Society*, 16: 116–130.

Stake, R.E. (1995) *The Art of Case Study Research*, London: Sage.

Staller, K.M. (2003) 'Working the scam: Policing urban street youth in a new world context', *Qualitative Inquiry*, 8(5): 550–574.

Stanley, L. and Wise, S. (1993) *Breaking Out Again: Feminist Ontology and Epistemology*, London: Routledge.

Stanley, N., Penhale, B., Riordan, D., Barbour, R.S. and Holden, S. (2003) *Child Protection and Mental Health Services*, Bristol: Policy Press.

Stewart, K. and Williams, M. (2005) 'Researching online populations: The use of online focus groups for social research', *Qualitative Research*, 5(4): 395–416.

Stimson, G. and Webb, B. (1978) 'The face-to-face interaction and after the consultation', in D. Tuckett and J.M. Kaufert (eds) *Basic Readings in Medical Sociology*, London: Tavistock, pp. 144–152.

Stokoe, E.H. and Smithson, J. (2001) 'Making gender relevant: Conversation analysis and gender categories in interaction', *Discourse and Society*, 12(2): 217–244.

Strathern, M. (1987) 'An awkward relationship: The case of feminism and anthropology', *SIGNS: Journal of Women in Culture and Society*, 12(2): 276–292.

Strickland, C.J. (1999) 'Conducting focus groups cross-culturally: Experiences with Pacific Northwest Indian people', *Public Health Nursing*, 16(3): 190–197.

Stubbs, S. (1999) 'Virtual diaspora: imagining Croatia online', *Sociological Research Online* 4(2), http://www.socresonline.org.uk/4/2/stubbs.html.

Suoninen, E. and Jokinen, A. (2005) 'Persuasion in social work interviewing', *Qualitative Social Work*, 4(4): 469–487.

Tarleton, B., Williams, V., Palmer, N. and Gramlich, T. (2004) '"An equal relationship?", People with learning difficulties getting involved in research', in M. Smyth and E. Williamson (eds) *Researchers and Their 'Subjects': Ethics, Power, Knowledge and Consent*, Bristol: Policy Press, pp. 73–88.

Thomas, H. (2004) 'From patient to person: Identifying a sociology of Recovery', paper presented at American Sociological Association Annual Conference, San Francisco, August 2004.

Thompson, W.I. and Thomas, D. (1929) *The Child in America*, New York: Alfred Knopf.

Thompson, T., Barbour, R.S. and Schwartz, L. (2003a) 'Advance directives in critical care decision making: A vignette study', *British Medical Journal*, 327: 1011–1015.

Thompson, T., Barbour, R.S. and Schwartz, L. (2003b) 'Health professionals' views on advance directives – a qualitative interdisciplinary study', *Palliative Medicine*, 17: 403–409.

Thorne, S. (1998) 'Ethical and representational issues in qualitative secondary analysis', *Qualitative Health Research*, 8(4): 547–554.

Tinker, A. and Coomber, V. (2004) *University Research Ethics Committees: Their Role, Remit and Conduct*, London: King's College.

Traulsen, J.M., Almarsdóttir, A.B. and Björnsdóttir, I. (2004) 'Interviewing the moderator: An ancillary method to focus groups', *Qualitative Health Research*, 14(5): 714–725.

Trow, M. (1957) 'Comment on participant observation and interviewing: A comparison', *Human Organization*, 16: 33–35.

Truss, L. (2005) *Eats Shoots and Leaves: The Zero Tolerance Approach to Punctuation*, London: Profile Books.

Tully, J., Ninis, N., Booy, R. and Viner, R. (2000). 'The New System of Review by Multi-Centre Research Ethic Committees: Prospective Study.' *British Medical Journal*, 320: 1179–1182.

Umaña-Taylor, A.J. and Bámaca, M.Y. (2004) 'Conducting focus groups with Latino populations: Lessons from the field', *Family Relations*, 53(3): 261–272.

Vickers, M.H. (2003) 'Researchers as storytellers: Writing on the edge – and without a safety net', *Qualitative Inquiry*, 8(5): 608–621.

Vidich, A.J. (1955) 'Participant observation and the collection and interpretation of data', *American Journal of Sociology*, 60: 354–360.

Virdee, S., Kyriakides, C. and Modood, T. (2006) 'Codes of cultural belonging: racialized national identities in a multi-ethnic Scottish neighbourhood', *Sociological Research Online* 11(4), http://www.socresonline.org.uk/11/4/virdee.html

Wallis, R. (1977) 'The moral career of a research project', in C. Bell and H. Newby (eds) *Doing Sociological Research*, London: Allen and Unwin, pp. 149–169.

ward, k.j. (1999) 'The cyber-ethnographic (re)construction of two feminist on-line communities', *Sociological Research Online*, 4(1), http://www.socresonline.org.uk/socresonline/4/1/ward.html

Waterman, H., Tillen, D., Dickson, R. and de Konig, K. (2001) 'Action Research: A Systematic Review and Guidance for Assessment', *Health Technology Assessment*, 5(23).

Waterton, C. and Wynne, B. (1999) 'Can focus groups access community views?', in R.S. Barbour and J. Kitzinger (eds) *Developing Focus Group Research: Politics, Theory and Practice*, London: Sage, pp. 127–143.

Wax, M.L. (1980) 'Paradoxes of "consent" to the practice of fieldwork', *Social Problems*, 27: 272–283.

Wetherell, C. (2003) 'Paranoia, ambivalence and discursive practices: Concepts of position and positioning in psychoanalysis and discursive psychology', in R. Harré and F. Moghaddam (eds) *The Self and Others: Positioning Individuals and Groups in Personal, Political and Cultural Contexts*, New York: Praeger/Greenwood Publishers, pp. 99–121.

Whyte, W.F. (ed.) (1991) *Participatory Action Research*, New York: Sage.

Wiles, R., Charles, V., Crow, G. and Heath, S. (2006) 'Researching researchers: Lessons for research ethics', *Qualitative Research*, 6(3): 283–299.

Wiles, R., Crow, G., Charles, V. and Health, S. (2006) 'Informed consent and the research process: Following rules or striking balances?', *Sociological Research Online*, 11(4), http://www.socresonline.org.uk/11/4/wiles.html

Wilkinson, S. (1999) 'How useful are focus groups in feminist research?', in R.S. Barbour and J. Kitzinger (eds) *Developing Focus Group Research: Politics, Theory and Practice*, London: Sage, pp. 64–78.

Wilkinson, S. (2003) 'Focus groups', in J.A. Smith (ed.) *Qualitative Psychology: A Practical Guide to Research Methods*, Thousand Oaks, CA: Sage, pp. 184–204.

Williams, S.J. (2000) 'Chronic illness and biographical disruption or biographical disruption as chronic illness? Reflections on a core concept', *Sociology of Health and Illness*, 22(1): 40–67.

Williamson, E. (2000) 'Caught in contradictions: Conducting feminist action-oriented research within an evaluated research programme', in J. Radford, M. Friedberg and L. Harne (eds) *Women, Violence and Strategies for Action: Feminist Research, Policy and Practice*, Buckingham: Open University Press, pp. 136–148.

Willig, C. (2003) 'Discourse analysis', in J.A. Smith (ed.) *Qualitative Psychology: A Practical Guide to Research Methods*, London: Sage, pp. 159–183.

Wolfinger, N.H. (2002) 'On writing fieldnotes: Collection strategies and background expectancies', *Qualitative Research*, 2(1): 85–95.

Wright, S., Waters, R., Nicholls, V. and members of the Strategies for Living Project (2004) 'Ethical considerations in service-user-led research: Strategies for Living Project', in M. Smyth and E. Williamson (eds) *Researchers and Their 'Subjects': Ethics, Power, Knowledge and Consent*, Bristol: Policy Press, pp. 19–34.

Wright Mills, C. (1959) *The Sociological Imagination*, London: Penguin.

Yin, R. (1994) *Case Study Research: Design and Methods*, (2nd edition), Newbury Park, CA: Sage.

INDEX